Popular Ghosts

Popular Ghosts

The Haunted Spaces of Everyday Culture

edited by
María del Pilar Blanco
and Esther Peeren

continuum

The Continuum International Publishing Group Inc
80 Maiden Lane, New York, NY 10038

The Continuum International Publishing Group Ltd
The Tower Building, 11 York Road, London SE1 7NX

www.continuumbooks.com

Library of Congress Cataloging-in-Publication Data
Popular ghosts: the haunted spaces of everyday culture / edited by María del Pilar Blanco and Esther Peeren.
    p. cm.
Includes bibliographical references and index.
ISBN-13: 978-1-4411-6369-1 (hardcover : alk. paper)
ISBN-10: 1-4411-6369-7 (hardcover : alk. paper)
ISBN-13: 978-1-4411-6401-8 (pbk. : alk. paper)
ISBN-10: 1-4411-6401-4 (pbk. : alk. paper) 1. Ghosts. 2. Haunting. 3. Popular Culture. 4. Everyday Life. I. Blanco, María del Pilar. II. Peeren, Esther. III. Title.

BF1461.P67 2010
133.1--dc22

                            2009028514

Typeset by Free Range Book Design & Production
Printed in the United States of America

Contents

Introduction

María del Pilar Blanco and Esther Peeren

> ... every period has its ghosts (and we have ours), its own experience,
> its own medium, and its proper hauntological media.[1]

> Well, what do you know? The place is haunted.[2]

It seems that ghosts are everywhere these days. Whether in rock songs, Internet news feeds, or museum exhibits, we appear to have entered an era that has reintroduced the vocabulary of ghosts and haunting into everyday life. The drafting of this introduction happened to coincide with the appearance of the inaugural issue of a British magazine called *Ghost Voices: The Magazine of All Things Haunted*. The discovery of such a publication on the shelves of a popular newsagent in northern England represents an unabashedly paramount moment in the history of the topic we set out to explore in this collection. When ghosts, and the search for ghosts, reach such a level of popularity *qua* normality, or – better put – when the word "ghosts" is seen alongside magazine covers featuring topics as far ranging as politics, brides, horse riding, and fashion, we can assume that a very important recognition has been established. This recognition is that ghosts, which, along with fantastic stories, the Argentine author Adolfo Bioy Casares rightly referred to as "old as time itself," have entered, and are indeed part of, the popular realm.[3]

If ghosts are old, they are certainly not tired. While *Ghost Voices* features articles on what we could call "good, old-fashioned haunting" (haunted houses, mediums, and so on), we can also speak of new etymologies and epistemologies of haunting that are endemic to our global times. In April 2009, for example, the FBI caught a ring of Puerto Rican and Dominican identity thieves who had managed to infiltrate public schools to steal copious amounts of children's personal information (including social security numbers and dates of birth) to produce false immigration documents for Dominicans trying to enter the U.S. Identity theft is our contemporary crime of "ghosting" others to unblock global passages that would otherwise remain unsurpassable. The idea that one person from a specific nationality can become the operative "ghost" of another (in this case a Puerto Rican child) in order to gain access to a new way of life independent of the "real" identity holder, offers a fascinating prospect of a fluctuating world map where haunting can become a thing of, and for, the living.

As the ways of becoming a ghost have become so varied, the first thing we must establish is what we understand by that term. What *are* ghosts? For "ghost," the *Oxford English Dictionary* lists a plethora of definitions, the most common of which – the ghost as "the soul of a deceased person, spoken of as appearing in a visible form, or otherwise manifesting its presence, to the living" – dates back to Chaucer. This definition has become prevalent as the non-figurative sense of the word, which in this case does not entail a statement about the ontological status of such beings (for a consideration of their cultural function, it is largely immaterial whether ghosts do or do not exist). In a figurative capacity, "ghost" has acquired many technical meanings as well: in optics, biology, metallurgy, mathematics, theater, and, most prominently, in visual media like cinema, photography, and television, where it refers to the appearance (through various causes) of an unintended, secondary image. Generally, the ghostly can be said to refer to that which is present yet insubstantial (the spirit rather than the body), secondary rather than primary (a faint copy, a trace, a ghost writer), and potentially unreal or deceptive (a spurious radar signal). The axiological quality of the ghost varies: while etymologically the word can be traced to the pre-Teutonic *ghoizdo*, meaning "fury, anger," the *OED* lists both "a good spirit, an angel" and "an evil spirit" as obsolete meanings and its description of the ghost as the return of the dead refrains from assigning a particular purpose or emotion either to the apparition or to the one who witnesses it.

In this collection, we discuss both non-figurative ghosts – those manifestations, in some form or another, of the returning dead, and other ghostly beings or images emanating from realms beyond what is considered the "real" – and figurative ghosts, including marginalized citizens, invisible terror threats, the illusionary presences of computer-generated imagery (CGI), and the intangible, spectral nature of modern media, ostensibly unmoored from distinct locations in time and space. We believe these two types of ghosts do not represent totally distinct cultural phenomena, but constantly feed into each other, so that the increasing ghostliness *of* new media influences the representation of ghosts *in* media – think of the use of the video-tape in Hideo Nakata's film *The Ring* (1998) – and vice versa, as when, for example, the metaphorical ghostliness of media is negotiated by materializing it in supernatural sightings, like the early 1960s phenomenon of the TV ghost.[4] Similarly, the recent use of the ghost or specter as a designation for social outcasts (illegal immigrants, *desaparecidos*, the homeless, prisoners)[5] can be seen to impact on the current portrayal of many non-figurative ghosts as impotent and ineffectual victims rather than powerful aggressors. This tendency governs the filmic portrayals of haunting in Alejandro Amenábar's *The Others* (2001) and M. Night Shyamalan's *The Sixth Sense* (1999), where the ghosts remain unaware of their own deceased status, and in television series like *Medium* and *Ghost Whisperer*, where the dead can only resolve their problems with the help of the living. Such moments of cross-fertilization indicate that non-figurative and figurative ghosts haunt each other, and should therefore be considered in tandem, in this case through a *conceptual* approach to the ghost. As

Mieke Bal notes, "[e]ven those concepts that are tenuously established, suspended between questioning and certainty, hovering between ordinary word and theoretical tool, constitute the backbone of the interdisciplinary study of culture – primarily because of their potential *intersubjectivity*. Not because they mean the same thing for everyone, but because they don't."[6] The ghost, which itself hovers between different realms and meanings, might be seen as an exemplary cultural concept that we will unpack in a deliberately intersubjective and interdisciplinary manner, tracing its travels (Bal speaks of *traveling concepts*) in time and space through various media and theoretical paradigms.

Jacques Derrida, whose *Specters of Marx* (1994) perhaps makes him the most indelible recent theorist of haunting, has argued that each age has its own ghosts. Upon describing the (limited) possibility of demarcating the historical, philosophical, and social "singularity" of haunting, however, he pushes for a near immediate reinsertion of such explorations into what he calls a "much larger spectrological sequence."[7] This is in part due to Derrida's insistence on haunting as a temporal, rather than spatial, phenomenon, where the ghost is not tied down to an idea of physical location. *Popular Ghosts* seeks to redress the balance by situating ghostly appearances in time *and* space, in line with Roger Luckhurst's critique of the *spectral turn* in cultural criticism as "symptomatically blind to its generative loci."[8] The way the hauntological machine of what Luckhurst calls the "London Gothic" (the locus of his critique) comprises divergent visions of haunting, some popular and some aligned with a certain cabalism among the writers and readers of the city's haunted topography – a "just between you and me" relationship between "visionary" and complicit reader (532) – is obscured in "the generalized economy of haunting" (534). This economy, of which Derrida is the main representative, forgets about the specificity of ghosts, the fact that they appear in specific moments, and specific locations, and also forgets that ghosts are "*symptoms*, points of rupture that insist their singular tale be retold and their wrongs acknowledged" (542).

Where Luckhurst describes the London Gothic and Julian Wolfreys has noted a "London-effect" of haunting in his *Writing London*, whereby aspects of everyday life in this city gain increasing subterranean and haunted meanings,[9] we seek to open pathways to an understanding and critique of a *global effect* of haunting, not to argue that all ghosts are now the same, but to establish a more rigorously comparative approach. Rather than privileging only Western, urban, high-literary examples of the ways in which our everyday lives have taken a turn toward the spectral, the essays compiled in *Popular Ghosts* expand discussions about ghosts and haunting to different geographies, as well as diverse fields of popular knowledge and communication. We are interested in seeing what the different ghosts of our era look, sound, and feel like, as well as what functions they have in our cultural imagination, without losing sight of the ongoing revisions and revitalizations of previous spectral turns.[10] Our understanding of the contemporary – the realm in which we emphatically place the idea of the ghost – engages with multiple manifestations of haunting in the present, but also asks how we can look at certain cultural moments in the past to shed light on our current theorizations of the ghostliness of globalized everyday life and its popular cultural products.

In accordance with the ubiquitous high-street presence of the newsagent selling the *Ghost Voices* magazine, the popular is taken up here in its most straightforward meaning of "widely favored" or "well-liked" and divested of the more pejorative connotations Raymond Williams outlines in *Keywords*.[11] Although various contributions will refer to the ineluctable link between the popular and consumerism, this volume does not subscribe to Theodor Adorno and Max Horkheimer's acerbic critique of the culture industry as an insidiously oppressive system that turns audiences into passive, mindless zombies.[12] No matter how ingrained consumerism is as a validated, prescribed, and subjectifying activity within the global capitalist system, it nevertheless presupposes active choices: magazine titles, for example, not only create markets, but also reflect existing interests. On the other hand, we also do not align ourselves with certain strands of cultural studies that view popular culture as exclusively "the culture of working people, the labouring classes and the poor,"[13] or as inherently subversive.[14] Rather, the popular, precisely by virtue of concerning that which is appreciated by many (often across gender, class, ethnic, race, and even national borders), is considered as a dynamic realm of contestation between various cultural forces in which hegemony *and* resistance, conformity *and* subversion, may be produced. The popular realm includes both so-called "high" and "low" culture, since we believe that this distinction has become untenable now that both forms are seen to constantly inflect – or should we say "haunt" – each other: high art museums, for example, relentlessly popularize and proliferate their priceless, unique artworks by putting them on anything from postcards and posters to mugs, pencils, and fridge magnets, while graffiti moves effortlessly from street corners to swish galleries. Significantly, the ghost itself points to a collapse of the "high" culture/"low" culture distinction, since its ongoing association with superstition, folklore, and the genre of the Gothic marks it as a distinctly low-brow figure even when it appears in the work of established, high-brow authors such as Henry James, Thomas Hardy, Samuel Beckett, or Elfriede Jelinek.[15]

The haunted spaces of popular culture – and popular culture as itself a ghostly space in the sense that, despite the many volumes seeking to define or exemplify it, remains an elusive, contested concept with blurry boundaries – may seem like an obvious topic, but despite the fact that the ghost's most common appearance at the present time is as a figure of popular culture entertainment in (horror) films, television series, popular fiction, and even country music, this space of the ghost remains remarkably under-theorized. We ask what happens to current theorizations of the ghost and to the spectral turn when they enter into dialogue with the contemporary popular cultural realm, where the ghost certainly does not roam unproblematically, but poses new questions and opens up new avenues of research.

One of these new avenues of research and a returning topic in this volume concerns the changed relationship between the ghost and the everyday, which comes to the fore when we have another look at the *Ghost Voices* magazine and its three American counterparts: *Ghost! For the Ghost Hunting Enthusiast*, *Haunted Times*, and *Beyond Investigation*.[16] All four magazines were started in the first decade of the twenty-first century and each refers to a preoccupation with ghostly phenomena as a legitimate and, crucially, everyday affair. The people running these magazines and the audiences they target are not, like the Victorians involved in the Society for Psychical Research, professional scientists or members of an intellectual elite bent on proving the existence of ghosts beyond any doubt. Although the appeal to scientific objectivity has not been fully relinquished, these present-day magazines mainly seek to register the ghostly as a force within the everyday. Rather than looking to determine the precise nature of haunting or its ethical and moral implications, they aim to perpetuate a sense of wonder, a titillating uncertainty. The ghost has become a possibility to be entertained and a figure that entertains. Of course, providing entertainment was always part of the ghost's assigned social function – for example, in Gothic novels, phantasmagoria, and séances – but the question of their objective existence tended to dominate in earlier periods. Whereas most visitors to séances in the nineteenth and early twentieth century hoped to establish contact with their dearly departed, present-day ghost hunters seek out the ghostly in general, approaching it more like a coin collector looking to build a collection or as an extreme sport than as a quest for personal, scientific, or social enlightenment.

This volume posits the everyday as no longer strictly opposed to the supernatural realm of the ghost or simply disturbed by it on specific occasions, but as fundamentally intertwined with the ghostly. Rather than being confined to cultural margins and fringe genres, ghosts now appear as part of the mainstream, invading the everyday realm and, in doing so, providing a cultural commentary on its increasingly spectral construction. Ghosts are no longer just perceived as mysterious, otherworldly manifestations that need be put to rest *elsewhere* to restore order, but are seen to reveal something of the enigma of everyday life, the way it can no longer be taken as straightforward but "presents us with a recalcitrant object that does not give up its secrets too readily."[17] The everyday is like a ghost – secretive, ungraspable, yet with an acutely felt presence – and is itself beset by ghosts. Michel de Certeau famously posited that "haunted spaces are the only ones people can live in"[18] and the "Ghosts in the City" chapter in the second volume of *The Practice of Everyday Life* draws attention to the way the modern city is haunted by its pasts; taking the form of old buildings, trees, furniture, photographs, and other "wild objects," a population of spirits "spreads out its ramifications, penetrating the entire network of our everyday life ... this population traverses time, survives the wearing away of human existences, and articulates a space."[19] A different connection between the everyday and the ghost is established when, in his introduction to *The Everyday Life Reader*, Ben Highmore writes: "everyday life is haunted by implicit 'others,' who supposedly live outside the ordinary, the everyday" (1). Whether the everyday is haunted by what is outside it or by what used to be part of it, it is insistently represented as a haunted/haunting structure, where what you see is never quite what you get.

We want to suggest that the everyday is ghostly not only in the rather general manners charted by de Certeau and Highmore, but also in more concrete, historically specific ways. The everyday, we argue, has become more spectralized in recent times because of various social and technological developments: its association with repetitive, unchanging routines (tasks that are never done for the first time and will always need to be done again) links the everyday to ghostly entropy; the space and time of the everyday have become disjointed, simultaneously contracting and expanding under the influence of complex and often contradictory processes of globalization, (trans)nationalism, and localization; the ghost has become an increasingly appropriate metaphor for the way marginal populations – like the Dominicans seeking access to the U.S. – haunt the everyday, living on the edge of visibility and inspiring a curious mix of fear and indifference; and the everyday exhibits an ever-growing reliance on spectral technologies like the Internet, mobile telephony, and digitalized media.[20] In addition, the inherent spectrality of money, central to Marx's theory of capital, has re-emerged with startling visibility in the exploitative structures of global capitalism and its creation of "spectral labor,"[21] as well as in the current global economic crisis (which, incidentally, is seeing the return of the ghost town as an everyday phenomenon). And since 9/11, the everyday has been haunted by the specter of the "War on Terror," which itself features an unprecedented degree of spectrality, waged as it is against mysterious, unlocalizable, and endlessly mediated enemies, in an indeterminate space (everywhere yet nowhere), and within an infinite timeframe (the threat never abates but promises eternal regenerations).

Conversely, the ghostly has become everyday as the effort to live *with* ghosts (in accordance with Derrida's famed injunction) has superseded the traditional tendency to exorcise ghosts and lay them to rest. This is apparent in the new notion of ghost hunting as an only slightly-out-of-the-ordinary hobby (no more peculiar than trainspotting or metal-detecting) that aims to contact ghosts without imposing a specific agenda. The increasing normalcy of the ghost also manifests in the way many ghosts in current fiction, film, and television are portrayed in an exceedingly mundane manner, as part of the everyday and as having everyday concerns. Whereas it used to be common to find ghosts trying to drag the living out of the everyday into a world of horrors on "the other side," what contemporary ghosts want more than anything, it seems, is to be normal.[22] Consequently, one of the prevailing fears in relation to the contemporary ghost is not that it might terrify us, but that we might not notice or recognize it at all. A related, even more disturbing fear, which is charted in various contributions to this volume, is that ghosts may have their own everyday, in which they forge relations independently of their ties to the living they left behind. Thus, it is not just that we might not notice them, but that they might not care whether we do or not, that they might not want to speak to us at all.

The idea that the ghost no longer transcends the everyday or utterly disjoints it is what has allowed it to be reduced to a collectable curiosity. This brings us to the increasing commercialization of the ghost, which appears to be a side-effect of its having made itself comfortable in the everyday. In this regard it is worth mentioning the recent popularity of the ghost in modern design, a realm that defiantly straddles high and low culture ("exclusive" products for the masses often sold in the stores of prestigious art institutions) and explicitly caters to the everyday. The online MoMA (Museum of Modern Art) store features Yee-Ling Wan's Ghost Clock (2005) and Jon Russell's Ghost Candelabra (2004),[23] while Philippe Starck designed the Louis Ghost chair (2002), in the style of the Louis XV period but made out of clear transparent polycarbonate. In 2008 Dutch design firm Design Drift exhibited its own Ghost chair at the Salone del Mobile Milan. This chair is made of Plexiglas with ghost-like forms, created with laser technology, floating inside. The designers describe it as "a futuristic concept of a chair, three dimensionally captured within the boundaries of reality. It gives you a bit of a dramatic feeling: unbelievable, high-tech, but beautiful."[24] Although the ghost is still associated with the "unbelievable" and with a sense of futurity, the way it is "captured within the boundaries of reality" signals its domestication. The possibility of comfortably sitting on a ghost proclaims its new status as a familiar, everyday object whose unsettling effects are sublimated in the aesthetic. Additionally, the ghost that floats inside the chair can be customized, pointing again to its nature as a commodity that is thoroughly reproducible, controllable and, above all, *useful*. The ghost, therefore, is no longer primarily a source for possible knowledge of the afterlife, but has been brought down to earth, while the question of whether ghosts exist has been subsumed under the possibility of commercial viability. The notion that ghosts sell is similarly highlighted by the aforementioned magazines, by the way the many recent television series focused on ghost hunting have spawned a cottage-industry that markets ghost-hunting equipment to amateur groups, and by the proliferation of haunting tourism.

However, it is not enough to signal the contemporary association of the ghost with the popular, the everyday, and the commodity; this nexus needs to be theorized across disciplines and media in order to become meaningful. Before we can do this it is necessary to take stock of the theorization of the ghost to date. Located in the ambivalent realm between life and death, ghosts have always inspired cultural fascination as well as theoretical, philosophical, and theological consideration, but until recently such consideration was either focused on the ontological question of whether they exist or it used the ghost as a metaphor to address another, more important quandary (as in Gilbert Ryle's critique of the Cartesian mind–body split in terms of the ghost in the machine).[25] The ghost has also often been used *within* established disciplines or fields to elucidate a particular concept or problem. Thus, in psychoanalysis, the ghost, in some form or another, has been crucial to Freud's uncanny,[26] Lacan's discussion of desire,[27] and Abraham and Torok's theory of intergenerational trauma.[28] In literary studies, it is integral to the Gothic, as a primary genre characteristic. It was, however, with Derrida's *Specters of Marx* that the ghost not only acquired a deconstructive dimension, but emerged as a methodology in and of itself. Derrida's extrapolation of the disjointing function of the ghost in *Hamlet* to ontology, history, and the wider social realm, as well as his association of the specter with absolute alterity, notions of inheritance, hospitality, and the messianic, have proved immensely popular and productive.[29] However, whereas Derrida's *hauntology* ultimately plays upon much the same aspects of deferred meaning and absence-presence as other, earlier figures of deconstruction like the trace and the hymen, thus subsuming it to a wider theoretical framework, this volume aims to put the ghost center stage.

If Derrida incites us to learn to live *with* the ghost, we go beyond this by exploring *how we live with it already*, using concrete examples of ghostly appearances and haunting scenarios. In the contributions to this volume, the ghost or specter is traced through many objects and disciplines, yet each contributor takes care to delineate the way they are using the concept and how they are supplementing or specifying its meanings and uses. As Bal notes, "[w]hile groping to define, provisionally and partly, what a particular concept may *mean*, we gain insight into what it can *do*. It is in the groping that the valuable work lies" (11). What is vital, however, is that in this groping the ghost is not reduced to a superficial rhetorical figure, as in a number of recent works that refer to the ghost or specter in their titles without including a sustained discussion of its conceptual implications.[30]

We also position ourselves in a particular way in relation to Gothic studies, which has been remarkably successful in appropriating the ghost and turning it into a generic marker. Not only does the ghost participate in many other literary genres (for example, the fantastic and magical realism), but its appearance on the cultural scene far precedes the emergence of the Gothic genre in the eighteenth century and is only one (non-obligatory) element of its "aesthetic based on pleasurable fear."[31] This volume therefore insists that by no means all ghosts are Gothic and that each haunting should be read on its own terms, according to its specific characteristics and functions. Those authors that do take up the Gothic here show it in a new light, by returning to its underilluminated beginnings and/or showing how the Gothic has been transformed by contemporary culture and its intersections with other literary and social paradigms. In this way, they move beyond the generic coherence posited by Sedgwick to emphasize the dynamism of the concept. Significantly, this dynamism has itself been thought through the ghost: Catherine Spooner, in *Contemporary Gothic*, suggests that the Gothic genre has no true origin; rather, it has "throughout its history taken the form of a series of revivals" that can be reconfigured as "returns from the dead."[32] And Fred Botting follows his account of *Dracula*'s murder of the traditional Gothic with a vision of "spectral returns."[33] The fact that the ghost can be used to conceptualize the history of Gothic is a powerful indicator of its excessive relation to this genre; an excessiveness that is also brought out by the *Routledge Companion to Gothic*, where almost all the chapter titles contain the word "Gothic," with the exception of those in the section "Gothic concepts," which deal with "Hauntings," "The Uncanny," and "Abjection and Grotesque."[34] Precisely because haunting is a *concept* with the ability to travel, the Gothic genre proves unable to contain it.[35] Conversely, as Luckhurst points out in his discussion of the contemporary London Gothic, "the generalized structure of haunting" that characterizes the spectral turn cannot fully explicate the "specific topography" of this version of Gothic (528). The two concepts, therefore, are far from equivalents – while they do frequently impinge on each other, each also has its own (after)life to live and *Popular Ghosts* seeks to disentangle the specter from reifying generic affiliations.

Such reification, Luckhurst points out, threatens the Gothic itself, with the London Gothic revival (comprising the work of, among others, Iain Sinclair and Peter Ackroyd) exhibiting a "fascination with its own generic past" tending to "self-referential involution" (530). This implies that the Gothic, which in a surge of scholarship from the past two decades has come to encompass so many aspects of life, narrative, and aesthetics, has been tied to the idea of genre to the point of becoming generic. Genre, as a tool for reading, is predicated on generalization and always runs into the danger (or tedium) of producing allegorical and conventional(izing) readings of an everyday life that is so often messy and non-linear – such moments of life call not for another genre, but for specific readings through concepts like the ghost and specter that do not seek to put everything into the same mold.

By turning to the everyday, this volume seeks to give new territories to the ghost, outside of the Gothic and distinct from the Derridean spectral turn. We also challenge perceptions of what the everyday entails, by making it clear that the everyday covers both the domestic and the public sphere (the house and the street), as well as more phantasmatic transnational structures like globalized capitalism and terrorism. While this volume's commitment to interdisciplinary and intermedial research and its focus on the everyday in contemporary culture causes it to distance itself from the Gothic as the privileged framework for thinking the ghost, it does take from Gothic studies – with its varieties of dark landscapes and haunted houses – its concentration on the spatial dimension of haunting.

Even though the contributions consciously look to broaden the spaces inf(l)ected by the spectral from the traditional trope of the haunted house, a spatial emphasis is auspicious in the face of recent theorizations of the ghost that have analyzed it in terms more temporal than spatial, perhaps as a prolongation of Derrida's decision in *Specters of Marx* to flesh out Hamlet's famous haunted observation, "the time is out of joint." Alongside the current poststructuralist emphasis on the ghost as a figure of relentless repetition and temporal disturbance, psychoanalytic critics have also stressed the temporal dimension of the ghost by aligning their apparitions with theories of the reactivation of trauma and the return of the repressed (two examples are Avery Gordon's hugely influential *Ghostly Matters* and Renée Bergland's *National Uncanny*, which deals with the pervasiveness of Native American hauntings in U.S. literature). While this scholarship has helped us understand the ghost in its irrevocable connection with the realms of memory, history, and the workings of language, we have yet to consolidate the methods used to define the ghost in order to discuss it in spatial terms, as a physical occupation of everyday sites that emphasizes the materiality of the ghost and defines its agency as grounded in a particular locale – in a disturbance of space as much as of time. In many ways reiterating Luckhurst's preoccupation with specifying and historicizing the spectral turn, Judith Richardson claims, in her excellent *Possessions*, that a consideration of haunting in terms of its temporal *and* spatial architecture is imperative: "Always the subject of tremendous popular interest, hauntings demand deeper investigation because of what they reveal about how senses of the past and of place are apprehended and created."[36]

Popular Ghosts is devoted to an explicit identification of our contemporary senses of place. Following Raymond Williams's groundbreaking work in *The Country and the City*, it is now a critical commonplace that our interactions with space are no longer discreetly regional, or neatly separable as either urban or rural. As Williams noted, our understanding of this separation becomes increasingly global, and ceases to comply with singular national, economic, or cultural identifications.[37] The spaces of the contemporary are not only best understood in terms of global socioeconomic interactions (which can also reflect the reactive centrifugality of resurgent nationalism and localism), but now need to be increasingly apprehended according to different levels of virtuality, given our ever-expanding use of media to communicate with neighbors, as well as members of the transnational communities we forge with increasing facility in the online spaces we inhabit. If by "everyday" we understand the ways that subjects go about their daily routines, then we need to understand these quotidian movements in terms of an interaction with intermedial, culturally hybrid spaces where we exist as ourselves and as ghosts of ourselves and others. Haunted spaces are therefore not simply describable as Gothic spaces, or informed by the languages of necromancy and melancholia, but as actual living spaces that need to be explored in terms of their present singularity. Moreover, given the cultural spectral turn that we now recognize, we increasingly engage in backward- and forward-looking interactions with our spaces, as part of a wider understanding of space as profoundly historical, already inhabited, but nevertheless living.

The essays in *Popular Ghosts* are arranged into five sections, representing distinct but related perspectives on the contemporary nexus of haunting, popular culture, and the everyday. Given the collection's preoccupation with addressing the diversity of theoretical avenues via which to approach haunting, the first section, entitled "Genealogies of the Ghost," engages in a consideration of how *the space of theory itself* has come to be haunted – in philosophy, by Derrida, and behind him, Marx; in literature, by figures like Thomas Hardy and Samuel Beckett; and in the social realm, by the Victorian scientification of the paranormal. The essays here compiled also explore how a theory of haunting and its applicability to contemporary texts is necessarily an engagement with philosophical tenets we hold dear as modern subjects, particularly skepticism. In this way, the section on genealogies presents new considerations of the continuities between the ghosts that haunt the beginning of a long twentieth century and our current period. Looking at spaces as diverse as Hardy's Christminster in *Jude the Obscure*, the illuminated theatrical stage in the works of Beckett, and the mausoleums that house the embalmed corpses of Mao Zedong and V. I. Lenin, Julian Wolfreys, Martin Harries, and Peter Hitchcock each note the increasing need to understand ghosts and haunting in diverse, rather than theoretically monological ways. While Wolfreys looks to Heidegger's idea of the uncanny to revise Freud's theory, Harries returns to McLuhan's conception of media as extensions of the self, while Hitchcock's essay combines cyborg theory with what he calls "uncanny Marxism" to think about the afterlives of socialist revolutions. Colin Davis and Justin Sausman, finally, reflect on our condition as modern subjects exploring our contemporary philosophical and scientific preoccupation with certainty and belief, and the ways in which this anxiety is translated in contemporary cinematic and literary ghost stories.

Specifically, Wolfreys looks to Thomas Hardy as not only a figure that has received a great deal of attention in recent academic explorations of haunting in literature, but also one that might shed light on how to write contemporary being, and what it means to be modern. Through Hardy and Heidegger, he offers an analysis of the eruptions of the supernatural and paranormal as an alternative alethic mode, a condition of dwelling in the world as both a subject and an other, what Hardy himself calls, in *Jude*, "self-specter." Harries explores the intersections of ghosts, technology, and theater, in an analysis of haunted modernity and what he calls "slow" popular culture. Arguing that Beckett's incorporation of technology into his work reflects the uneven arrival of advancement into the landscapes of the twentieth century, Harries looks at the haunted characters in the playwright's oeuvre as reflections of a permanence of ideas of enchantment within modern existence. Hitchcock studies the work of the Mausoleum Group, in charge of preserving the embalmed bodies of Mao and Lenin, as well as the film *Goodbye Lenin* (Becker, 2003), in order to ask whether the present (popular) cultural moment asks for a new hauntology, one that preserves a material dimension and reconfigures repetition in terms of likeness. Sausman's essay explores the genealogical and historical (dis)connection between the fascination with ghosts and spiritism in the nineteenth-century *fin de siècle* and depictions of mediums in contemporary fiction, specifically Victoria Glendinning's novel *Electricity* (1995). Finally, Davis's analysis of Alejandro Amenábar's film *The Others* (2001) points to the affective and intellectual conundrum of skepticism we face in our explorations of haunting as an event that makes its appearance in the spaces of the popular. Given that the ghost says much about how we relate to others, as well as the spaces we inhabit, Davis argues that popular cultural artifacts dealing with ghosts and haunting – especially film and fiction – become a medium for the negotiation of skepticism and lived spaces.

The second section, "Spectral Politics of the Contemporary," contains essays that theorize the connection between the ghost, contemporary politics, and the space(s) of the everyday. The changing spaces of everyday culture, in the current environment of globalization, transnationalism, postmodernism, and the postcolonial, require new theoretical appraisals, within which the ghost can serve as a productive conceptual tool. As an apposite approach to a variety of political, economical, and ethical problems, care needs to be taken not to turn the ghost into an abstract, universal figure or catch-all, as Derrida's hauntology risks doing. A more careful spectral turn teases out the differences between various ghostly phenomena, bearing witness to their status as concrete, culturally specific, and historically and socially situated events. The essays in the section explore how the ghost can be used to reflect on the situation of marginalized citizens and the position of socialism in post-partition India, the aftermath of 9/11 and the War on Terror, the African postcolony, and contemporary practices of population administration, surveillance, and imprisonment. Caroline Herbert's "National Hauntings" studies the representation of Bombay/Mumbai as a city caught between a socialist past and a predatory capitalist future-present in the Hindi films *Shree 420* (1955) and *Deewar* (1975). Following Arjun Appadurai's recent designation of Mumbai as a dramatic scene of spectral citizenship, she argues that the figure of the ghost offers a paradoxical embodiment of the material and discursive failures of the socialist secular nation-state. In her essay about the spectral legacies of the twin towers, Georgiana Banita presents another hauntology related to an equally specific locale and political situation: post-9/11 New York. Her discussion of 9/11 as a post-event whose haunting quality is compounded by its relentless mediation in popular culture brings into consideration the ungraspable nature of contemporary spaces of terror, which refuse to stay separate from the everyday, as well as the complexities of mourning absent, invisible victims. The boundary between the everyday and the ghostly is central to Esther Peeren's contribution. The way the ghosts in the work of Nigerian authors Amos Tutuola and Ben Okri are not banished to a separate realm but participate in daily life is seen to change the nature of haunting and to necessitate modifications to Western theories of the ghost and of the everyday. The Cameroonian political theorist Achille Mbembe's notion of ghostly terror is read together with Tutuola and Okri to present an alternative model capable of accommodating both the ghostly everyday and everyday ghosts. Michael Cuntz also explores what happens when ghosts appear as part of the everyday, only in a Western context. He uses the idea of "the mixed zone" to theorize the spatio-temporal actualization of the meeting between the living and those returned from the dead in Jean Echenoz's novel *Au piano* (2003) and Robin Campillo's film *Les revenants* (2004), showing how the portrayal of this mixed zone is overdetermined by contemporary disciplinary practices of containment, categorization, medicalization, and surveillance. The issue of containment is further explored by Benjamin D'Harlingue in relation to U.S. haunted prison tourism, which constitutes an eerie and potentially uncomfortable literalization of the social death suffered by prisoners under the penal gaze and renders visible the exclusions upon which citizenship is founded, in particular in terms of race.

"Chasing Ghosts in(to) the Twenty-first Century" further underlines *Popular Ghosts*'s dual focus on the contemporary and the popular. Starting from the notions, explored by Colin Davis, that a historical shift has occurred in the representation of ghosts and their intermediaries and that nowadays ghosts are related more to skepticism than to belief, the essays in this section explore the different ways in which twenty-first-century popular culture (specifically television) re-envisions the conjuring, chasing, and contacting of ghosts, and the living's communication with them. What emerges from the three essays taken together is that questions focused on the ghosts themselves (Do they exist? How may we contact them?), which dominated the resurgence of spectral inquiry in the Victorian age, have been replaced with queries about how ghosts affect those they haunt and how they lead us to interrogate various categories that govern our everyday lives, such as reality, authenticity, and knowledge. In the spectral contemporary these questions aspire to a self-consciously sensationalist exploration of our enjoyment of the terror and uncertainty provoked by ghostly appearances or their simulacra. Karen Williams explores the ostensibly oxymoronic phenomenon of supernatural reality TV, focusing on the subgenre of youth paranormal shows. *MTV's Fear*, as Williams explains, combines a documentary aesthetic with the tropes and affects of the horror genre, thus demonstrating a particular contradiction: a claim to scientific purpose coupled with sensational spectacle that relies more on suggestion and emotional response than on scientific rigor. Meanwhile, the more conventional *Paranormal State* represents an interventionist model of investigating possible hauntings, where ghosts become symbolic of everyday traumas that have to be overcome in accordance with the individualistic dictates of neoliberalism, but where haunting also produces a vision of paranormal citizenship. The investigation into the nexus of the documentary and the paranormal is continued by Alissa Burger, who examines the popular SciFi Channel series *Ghost Hunters* and the model of simulated participation it creates for its viewers through its narrative structure, its self-reflexive evocation of skepticism, and its combined use of televisual and ghost-hunting technology. Moving from reality TV to television fiction, Catherine Spooner considers haunting as a subject of academic interest in the British television series *Sea of Souls*, where academic skepticism towards the supernatural is linked to questions concerning the nature of knowledge and academia's relevance to contemporary culture.

In "Other Ghostly Spheres" haunted space is reconfigured by pointing to the necessary evolution of traditional tropes like that of the haunted house and the emergence of new sites of haunting specific to contemporary culture, its new technologies, and its changed social and political landscape. The first three essays revisit the genre of the Gothic and its claustrophobic conception of haunted space in order to explore how this has been reconfigured. Looking at Georg Klein's "Our Beloved Dead: A Spiritual Attempt" and Elfriede Jelinek's *The Children of the Dead*, Arno Meteling traces the Gothic nexus of static memory and location to the ancient practice of mnemonics and its "theater of memory." He argues that the contemporary or neo-Gothic, under the influence of new media, frees ghosts from spatial confinement and displaces them to mobile non-places, namely the mediated world of the afterlife in Klein and the living-dead nation in Jelinek. In "Haunted Habitability," Christine Wilson explores the changing perspectives on North American haunted house narratives through the lens of Henri Lefebvre's theory of space and in relation to the rise of environmentalism and ecocriticism. She argues that the haunted house is frequently represented as a wilderness which inhabitants either seek to "tame" through various gendered modes of domestication or resign themselves to by forming what ecocriticism calls a "place attachment." The section's widening and deepening of the theoretical frame of Gothic studies is taken further by Bruno Lessard, who explains the negative reception of Jan de Bont's 1999 "remake" of *The Haunting* by arguing that the affect generated by the Gothic has to be reassessed in light of the transformations generated by the age of biopolitics and the development of digital media, specifically CGI. Starting with Hardt and Negri's notion of "affect-value," Lessard uncovers historical antecedents for this type of affect in Wilhelm Worringer's work on Gothic architecture and argues that de Bont's film does not fail to produce the Gothic but pushes its principles to their logical, monstrous conclusion. Alla Gadassik continues the focus on new technologies, moving beyond discussing the Gothic and CGI's function in bringing the ghost to (nonorganic) life to explore the way animation is itself, to an ever greater degree, a ghostly technique that threatens to erase or spectralize the bodily presence of the animator. Closing the section, Pamela Thurschwell examines adolescence as a ghostly, liminal stage between childhood and adulthood. As portrayed in Daniel Clowes's graphic novel *Ghost World* (and its 2001 film adaptation), late twentieth-century adolescents are seen to reside in "out of joint" temporalities and locations. Haunting and haunted by the commodified wasteland of postmodern culture, there appears to be no escape, except into Jameson's apolitical "libidinal historicism." Thurschwell, however, proposes temporal drag and magical realism as alternative exits, which might provide more livable elsewheres or, in the terms of this section, other, more productive ghostly spheres.

"Ambient Ghosts," the final section of the volume, explores the different atmospheres of haunting in a variety of popular media, ranging from alternative country music and paranormal Polaroid photography, to television soundtracks and tattoo art. While spectrality, as Hitchcock points out, has so often been studied according to its immateriality, the chapters in this section propose readings of how ghosts are in fact embodied in accordance with the human sensorium. Focusing on the paranormal "thoughtographs" of Chicago bellhop Ted Serios, María del Pilar Blanco's essay links the renewed interest in ghost photography and the death of Polaroid technology to questions about how we have come to understand the everyday. Serios's thoughtographs constitute what Blanco calls an "everyday paranormal" that begs renewed explorations of everyday life theory, aesthetics, and ideas of perception. Anthony Hutchison reveals the haunted side of alternative country music songs, which describe even the most modernized landscapes as necessarily haunted topographies. Deploying a critique of psychogeography and Greil Marcus's work on North American music and his identification of an "old weird America," Hutchison looks at contemporary alt-country music in terms of what is effectively a "new weird America." Isabella van Elferen's contribution on the haunting soundscapes of David Lynch's 1990s TV series *Twin Peaks* comments on the show's transgressive qualities, where language, dream, reality, music, and image contain an irreversible and disturbing non-referentiality as well as an intermedial emptiness. Finally, Sean Somers's essay explores the inscription of spectrality on the living body in the work of contemporary Japanese tattoo artist Horiyoshi III. His work involves a melding of skin and spirit which reunites the spiritual and the physical realms, allowing the ghostly to be channeled through the living body.

Each speaking for different ghostly realms, the essays in *Popular Ghosts* produce an eclectic map of the ways in which the global everyday continues to incorporate haunting into its operative functions and creative representations. Taking the popular to mean that which attempts to encompass the varied tastes, movements, and fascinations of subjects in the various societies here represented, each chapter reflects on the importance of incorporating, questioning, and renewing the languages of haunting in(to) the world of the living to explore the historicity of being and location, the nature of community, and the ways in which we can continue existing *with* ghosts.

NOTES

1   Jacques Derrida, *Specters of Marx: The State of the Debt, the Work of Mourning, & the New International*, trans. Peggy Kamuf (New York and London: Routledge, 1994), 193, n21.

2 .   Joan Crawford in *Humoresque* (dir. Jean Negulesco, 1946).

3   Jorge Luis Borges, Adolfo Bioy Casares, Silvina Ocampo, *Antología de la literatura fantástica* (Buenos Aires: Editorial Sudamericana, 1998), 5.

4   See Jeffrey Sconce, *Haunted Media: Electronic Presence from Telegraphy to Television* (Durham: Duke University Press, 2007), 124–127.

5   See Derrida, *Specters of Marx*; Avery Gordon, *Ghostly Matters: Haunting and the Sociological Imagination* (Minneapolis and London: University of Minnesota Press, 2008);

Arjun Appadurai, "Spectral Housing and Urban Cleansing: Notes on Millenial Mumbai," *Public Culture* 12, no. 3 (2000): 627–651; and, in the cultural realm, Nick Broomfield's 2006 film *Ghosts*, which deals with illegal Chinese immigrant workers in the UK.

6   Mieke Bal, *Travelling Concepts in the Humanities: A Rough Guide* (Toronto: University of Toronto Press, 2002), 11, emphasis in original.

7   Derrida, *Specters of Marx*, 193, n21.

8   Roger Luckhurst, "The Contemporary London Gothic and the Limits of the 'Spectral Turn'," *Textual Practice* 16, no. 3 (2002): 528.

9   Julian Wolfreys, *Writing London: The Trace of the Urban Text from Blake to Dickens* (Basingstoke: Palgrave, 1998), 8.

10   See Terry Castle, *The Female Thermometer: Eighteenth-Century Culture and the Invention of the Uncanny* (Oxford: Oxford University Press, 1995); Julian Wolfreys, *Victorian Hauntings: Spectrality, Gothic, the Uncanny and Literature* (London: Palgrave Macmillan, 2001); Alex Owen, *The Darkened Room: Women, Power, and Spiritualism in Late Victorian England* (London: Virago, 1989); Roger Luckhurst, *The Invention of Telepathy, 1870–1901* (Oxford: Oxford University Press, 2002); Marina Warner, *Phantasmagoria: Spirit Visions, Metaphors, and Media into the Twenty-first Century* (Oxford: Oxford University Press, 2006).

11   Raymond Williams, *Keywords: A Vocabulary of Culture and Society* (London: Fontana Press, 1988), 236.

12   Max Horkheimer and Theodor Adorno, "The Culture Industry: Enlightenment as Mass Deception," in *Media and Cultural Studies: KeyWorks*, ed. Meenakshi Gigi Durham and Douglas M. Kellner (Oxford: Blackwell, 2001), 71–101.

13   Stuart Hall, "Notes on Deconstructing 'the Popular'," in *Cultural Theory and Popular Culture: A Reader*, ed. John Storey (London: Prentice Hall, 1998), 442.

14   See, for example, John Fiske, *Understanding Popular Culture* (London and New York: Routledge, 1992).

15   On the Gothic as an essentially popular genre, see Eugenia C. Delamotte, "Introduction: The Genre, the Canon, and the Myth," in *Perils of the Night: A Feminist Study of Nineteenth-Century Gothic* (Oxford: Oxford University Press, 1990), 3–28.

16   See, respectively, www.ghostmag.com, www.hauntedtimes.com, and www.beyondinvestigation.com.

17   Ben Highmore, ed., *The Everyday Life Reader* (London and New York: Routledge, 2002), 1.

18   Michel de Certeau, *The Practice of Everyday Life*, trans. Steven Rendall (Berkeley: University of California Press, 1988), 108.

19   Michel de Certeau, Luce Giard and Pierre Mayol, *The Practice of Everyday Life. Volume 2: Living & Cooking*, trans. Timothy J. Tomasik (Minneapolis: University of Minnesota Press, 1998), 135–136. This book also features an interview with Madame Marguerite, a 77-year-old woman who assigns spiritualism an important role in her account of everyday life in the old Croix-Rousse neighborhood of Lyon (122–125).

20   See, for example, Jacques Derrida and Bernard Stiegler, *Echographies of Television*, trans. Jennifer Bajorek (Cambridge, UK: Polity Press, 2006); Geoffrey Batchen, "Spectres of Cyberspace," in *The Visual Culture Reader. Second Edition*, ed. Nicholas Mirzoeff (London and New York: Routledge, 2005), 237–242.

21   See Jean and John Comaroff, "Alien-Nation: Zombies, Immigrants, and Millenial Capitalism," *South Atlantic Quarterly* 10, no. 4 (2002): 779–805.

22   This tendency is exemplified by the 2009 BBC television series *Being Human*, about a ghost, a vampire, and a werewolf sharing a house in Bristol, desperate to fit into regular society and suppress their supernatural powers.

23 www.momastore.org.

24 www.dezeen.com/2008/04/20/ghost-chair-collection-by-design-drift/.

25 Gilbert Ryle, *The Concept of Mind* (Chicago: University of Chicago Press, 1984).

26 Freud designates the ghost as "this example, perhaps the most striking of all, of something uncanny." Sigmund Freud, "The Uncanny," in *Writings on Art and Literature* (Stanford: Stanford University Press, 1997), 218.

27 Lacan uses the ghost to figure the ungraspable and unquantifiable nature of all desire and all objects of desire, especially the phallus: "One cannot strike the phallus, because the phallus, even the real phallus, is a *ghost* ... the body is bound up [*engagé*] in this matter of the phallus – and how – but the phallus, on the contrary, is bound to nothing: it always slips through your fingers." Jacques Lacan, "Desire and the Interpretation of Desire in *Hamlet*," *Yale French Studies* 55/56 (1977): 50–52.

28 For Abraham and Torok, the "crypt" designates the haunting result of processing a trauma by incorporating it as a foreign body in the self. "Phantom" indicates the even more ungraspable situation in which a crypt that originated in *someone else's* trauma is inherited (usually from a previous generation) and produces symptoms. See Nicholas Abraham and Maria Torok, *The Shell and the Kernel: Renewals of Psychoanalysis. Volume I* (Chicago: University of Chicago Press, 1994) and Colin Davis's "*État Présent*: Hauntology, Spectres and Phantoms," *French Studies* 59, no. 3 (2005): 373–379, which presents a cogent comparison between Abraham and Torok's theory and Derrida's hauntology.

29 For sympathetic and critical Derrida-inspired discussions, see Jodey Castricano, *Cryptomimesis: The Gothic and Jacques Derrida's Ghost Writing* (Montreal: McGill-Queen's University Press, 2003); Colin Davis, *Haunted Subjects: Deconstruction, Psychoanalysis and the Return of the Dead* (Basingstoke: Palgrave Macmillan, 2007); Peter Buse and Andrew Stott, eds, *Ghosts: Deconstruction, Psychoanalysis, History* (Basingstoke: Palgrave Macmillan, 1999); Peter Hitchcock, "( ) of Ghosts," in *Oscillate Wildly: Space, Body, and Spirit of Millennial Materialism* (Minneapolis: University of Minnesota Press, 1999); Nicholas Royle, *The Uncanny: An Introduction* (Manchester: Manchester University Press, 2002).

30 See, for example, Brian Ladd, *The Ghosts of Berlin: Confronting German History in the Urban Landscape* (Chicago: University of Chicago Press, 1998); Gilberto Perez, *The Material Ghost: Films and their Medium* (Baltimore: The Johns Hopkins University Press, 2000); Ulrich Baer, *Spectral Evidence: The Photography of Trauma* (Cambridge, MA: The MIT Press, 2005).

31 Eve Kosofsky Sedgwick, *The Coherence of Gothic Conventions* (London and New York: Routledge, 1986), 11.

32 Catherine Spooner, *Contemporary Gothic* (London: Reaktion Books, 2006), 10, 11.

33 Fred Botting, *Gothic* (London: Routledge, 1996), 180.

34 Catherine Spooner and Emma McEvoy, eds, *The Routledge Companion to Gothic* (London and New York: Routledge, 2007). The only other chapter title that does not contain the word "Gothic" is "Contemporary Horror Cinema" in the "Gothic Media" section, where again another *concept* – horror – is in play.

35 The "Hauntings" chapter further confirms this by a gradual generic shift from the Gothic to ghost stories. Andrew Smith, "Hauntings," in *Routledge Companion to Gothic*, 147–154.

36 Judith Richardson, *Possessions: The History and Uses of Haunting in the Hudson Valley* (Cambridge, MA: Harvard University Press, 2003), 3.

37 See Raymond Williams, *The Country and the City* (Oxford: Oxford University Press, 1973).

Part One

Genealogies of the Ghost

Chapter 1

Ghosts: Of Ourselves or, Drifting with Hardy, Heidegger, James, and Woolf

Julian Wolfreys

...'tis not to married couples but to single sleepers that a ghost shows himself when 'a do come. One has been seen lately, too. A very strange one.[1]

I thought you were the ghost of yourself.[2]

We shall go away, a very long distance, hundreds of miles from these parts, and such as this can never happen again, and no ghost of the past reach there.[3]

I

As my three epigraphs indicate, the idea of the ghost has a certain frequency, if not a currency, for Thomas Hardy. I shall come back to Hardy as "ghost-writer" of modernity shortly, but it is necessary to recognize Hardy's significance regarding the idea of the ghost. He is our first example because he remains the writer of spectrality *par excellence*, whose writing more than any other shifts, or makes possible, the reorientation of thought apropos haunting, the phantom or phantasm, the apparition, the revenant, and the ghost in relation to questions of subjectivity and historicity, as well as to the relation between writing and the past. This can be read in a consideration of the epigraphs. A briefly adumbrated reading of the spectral trope in these citations opens for us a mobile, provisional epistemology of haunting as it is received in the last decades of the nineteenth century. In retrospect, and perhaps more significantly, it might also be said that Hardy reveals that which could not have been anticipated in the thinking of haunting.

The first epigraph admits a spectral convention framed folklorically as a narrative of received, shared wisdom. The second resonates differently, suggesting the experience of the uncanny, an apprehension – a *frisson*, the touch of which announces the countersignature of phenomenological reception – of the self as other, the self received as the doppelgänger, the living as dead. The ghost thus arrives before it arrives, it "returns" unexpectedly as the anticipation of a future, from that future, as that which is to come. The last epigraph's "ghost," mere metaphor as it seems, admits to a number of modern conceits: on the one hand, it appears to suggest psychological burden, that which is written on subjectivity and the subject's psyche. On the other hand, it bespeaks a certain historical psychic weight, wherein memory and history, the personal and broader cultural or material events, might coincide. It remarks a desire for a different place for the subject, as if place itself were – perhaps fetishistically – haunted. It also intimates that a ghost cannot leave its given place, whilst, perhaps naively, expressing the hope that if a ghost is a thing of the past, it also remains outside memory and conscience, *not really* inscribed within the subject. And of course, finally, for now, this last epigraph, in its phrasing – *ghost of the past* – determines haunting as a matter of structural figuration, whilst signaling that, in the words of Jacques Derrida, the "age already in the *past* is in fact constituted in every respect as a *text* … [as] such the age conserves the values of legibility and the efficacy of a model and thus disturbs the time (tense) of the line or the line of time."[4]

This is not to deny the past, of course. Only the most perverse misreading or avoidance of reading would assume such a thing. Instead, it is to acknowledge that the past *as such* can never be present in the present, and that to acknowledge this is to acknowledge also that what we name the past exceeds any mere present moment by virtue of its being legible, by leaving legible traces and inscriptions, the very persistence and revenance of which disturb both structure and history, as Derrida's chiasmus gives us to comprehend. That chiasmus places the absolute separation of text and context, word and world, under erasure. In this crossing through, an unsuturable fissure opens, and the ghost of modernity appears. Its apparition causes us to comprehend how being is written. More than this, however, being, in being apprehended as what Derrida terms "*l'être écrit*" (31), the being written/the written being, is written as being haunted: subject to the traces of historicity, and to those disquieting eruptions that remain all too legible, one's being – if it can be expressed thus – is never on time with itself, its presence and its present always already disturbed by the ghost of itself, and also the ghosts of all its others. Any ontology of being is therefore always already ruined from the start. The house of being is a haunted locus, and Tess's naïve desire to escape the ghost of the past fails in its tragic comprehension to appreciate the extent to which the ghost remains with us, as that which we cannot admit determines who we are. Tess's desire cannot comprehend how, if the past is a ghost, then so too is that which is to come, and that the future, irreducible to a program by which we can anticipate our "future anterior," is the apparition of "ce monde à venir et … ce qui en lui aura fait trembler …" – "that world to come … and that which will have made [or caused it to] shake" (14; translation my own).

II

The question of the unexpected arrival that catches one unawares, so that one's response cannot be calculated or anticipated, is central to the thought of the other's haunting of the subject, whether that other arrives from the past or a certain future. In this scenario, the subject's unpreparedness defines the modern condition. Apropos the subject's awaiting the other, it is arguable that "ambiguity and incompletion are indeed written into the very fabric of our collective existence rather than just the works of intellectuals."[5] The ghost is thus not only, no longer, a thing of the past; it is no longer containable, on the one hand, to a realm of investigation and research, or on the other, to popular narratives and genres, communities of oral transmission, or folkloric traditions – if it ever was. What we name "ghost" acknowledges no boundaries, other than to mark their porosity, as is well known.

If Hardy – of whom there is more to be said – signals the modernity of the apparition, he is not the only writer to do so. In an appreciation of the modernity of Henry James's writing, Virginia Woolf observes, in a well-known and frequently quoted passage on what might be registered as the epochal shift from the Gothic to the psychoanalytic, that

Henry James's ghosts have nothing in common with the violent old ghosts – the blood-stained sea captains, the white horses, the headless ladies of dark lanes and windy commons. They have their origin within us. They are present whenever the significant overflows our powers of expressing it; whenever the ordinary appears ringed by the strange.[6]

Marked as it is with a tacit, and almost imperceptible, admission of the uncanny, Woolf's reading of James has the effect of dating – if such a thing is possible – the interiorization or incorporation of the ghostly and spectral. Consigning the "origin" (finding, or at the very least, inventing, the return of a phantasm always already at work, but hitherto unavailable to apprehension of such disquieting forces) to an otherwise inexpressible significance "within us," Woolf acknowledges James as a writer whose work moves across, or through, a boundary, on one side of which lie narratives about the ghostly, and on the other, manifestations of "ghostly narrative," to borrow a fine and significant distinction drawn by Nicholas Royle.[7] What Woolf admits into the discourse and experience of the ghostly is, most obviously, a psychological dimension, one which, in writers of the nineteenth century, was, if not "explained," then at least narrated through tales of mediumship, uncanny foresight, visions, and so forth. What marks James's writing, or, perhaps better said, the difference by which James's text remarks itself as being haunted, is that explanation is inevitably found wanting, as James's ghostly narratives do not so much close as remain open to the undecidable, the possibility of the impossible, and the experience of the other.

This is entirely appropriate to any hauntological event, for, to recall the words of Derrida, "[g]hosts always pass quickly, with the infinite speed of a furtive apparition, in an instant without duration, presence without present of a present, which, coming back, only *haunts*."[8] What Derrida's appreciation of the spectral – as the phenomenal flickering of the trace of the other – shares with Woolf, after a certain fashion, and differently, with James, is the apprehension of the unexpected related, on the one hand, to eruption or overflow and, on the other hand, to duration or frequency. Derrida continues:

> The ghost, *le re-venant*, the survivor, appears only by means of figure or fiction, but its appearance is not nothing, nor is it mere semblance. And this "synthesis of the phantom" enables us to recognize in the figure of the phantom the working of … the transcendental imagination … whose temporalizing schemes … are indeed "fantastic" – are, in Kant's phrase, those of an *art hidden* in the depths of the soul … the art of memory and … the memory of art. (64)

Irreducible to mere representation, that which is approximated as a quasi-ontological quasi-being, the ghost, is nevertheless *only possible* through a tropic, fictional *coming-to-pass*. Inasmuch as it can be said to take its passage, its significance is only ever perceived, if at all, belatedly, as Woolf's affirmation of "the significant" that overflows. What comes to overflow only becomes available as "the significant" after the event of its having come to pass, and having retreated in its becoming, leaving behind the trait that one attempts to read as the signature of "significant." This phenomenon, that which discloses itself in coming to light and so shedding light in those places where we have no direct expression for the experience, is both the art of memory and the memory of art, to reiterate Derrida's words. To conjure the ghost of Hegel, art, it has to be said, therefore, "is a thing of the past" (64).

If that which survives beyond any mere existence returns through a phantasmic and phantastic revenant temporal scheme, whether through the memory of art or the art of memory, then this is to admit, in the most ghostly terms, that memory and art stage the phantoms of history in a performative projection of the trace of historicity. Yet, it is just this opening to historicity's ghostly remnant, its rem(a)inder, which is not acknowledged in Woolf's psychoanalytic and phenomenological appreciation of Jamesian modernity. The ghostly trace of historicity must then be acknowledged as the supplement to that which is already supplementary, the haunting opening of modernity's narratives. To become modern one must open oneself to those manifestations of what Derrida describes as "a past which has never been present and will never allow itself to be reanimated in the interiority of consciousness" (65). This admission takes place, if it occurs at all, "through writing, the sign, *tekhnē*, with that thinking memory, that memory without memory" (65), which narrative has the possibility of enabling. Thinking this, we are opening the thinking of narrative as a form of *tekhnē*, a *mnemotechnic* to be precise, "whose movement" and operation as an exteriorized, archived, and prosthetic survival of memory without memory, marks it as a phantom machine – both a ghostly mechanism constructed out of nothing other than writing, the sign, and so forth, and also a machinic medium the purpose of which is to conjure and project its singular-collective of phantasmagorical traces – "whose movement carries an essential affirmation, a kind of engagement beyond negativity … which is mourning itself" (65).

Arguably – and this is to make a claim that I cannot hope to support here – such mourning does not concern James; or, at least, it cannot, is not to be admitted. Similarly with Woolf's reading. So "modern" is the Jamesian interiorization of the specter in those characters that Woolf takes to be figures of analogy with "us," whose powers of expression have momentarily failed, allowing the upsurge of the phantom, that it is, in effect and in fact, dated, past its sell-by date. James's is an old-fashioned, even a quaintly anachronistic modernity, a modernity in which is written the anticipation of a modern*ism*, the very coming of which would always already have dated it with the trace of an historical moment, the tragedy of which is that it is without the fortune to have become anachronistic, or to have been countersigned by a necessary affirmative anachrony making it other than its times. James's "modern" ghostly narrative becomes dated precisely because it gives no access to what Derrida calls "the immemorial or unrememberable, with an archive that no interiorizing memory can take into itself" (67), by which a text might announce an "affirmative ... an amnesic fidelity" with the "dead being that will never itself return, never again be there, present to answer to or to share" (66), what amounts to a faith, keeping faith with a past that can never be present. To open in a proper fashion to that which memory cannot take into itself, and so risk everything on the invention of a historicity at once *more* and *less* modern, we have to turn back to Thomas Hardy.

III

Hardy's interest in haunting addresses a concern for which we have to take account: what it means to have a world. As Derrida reminds us, apropos Heidegger, the human has a world, while, problematically, seemingly paradoxically, and admitting to a "logical contradiction," the animal "does and does not have a world."[9] As Derrida is quick to point out, the fault, or let us call it limit, to thought and to be thought is not with the ontology of the animal, animality, and so forth; it is with the thinking of "world," specifically the concept of world rather than its material counterpart. The question thus becomes one of *spirit*, for this, and "Heidegger insists on this, is the name of that without which there is no world" (51). To have a world and not have a world according to the apprehension of a spirit to which one nevertheless has no access is, I would argue, that which presents Hardy's characters – and the narrator of certain of his poems – with their own abject being-in-the-world. They are marked as human animals through a poverty of spirit and perception. Oddly, uncannily, the Hardy "being" or, if you will, a Hardyesque expression and therefore an anticipation of *Dasein*, anticipating phenomenologically the Heideggerian project of determining the Being of beings according to thrownness, en-worlding, en-owning, temporality, care, and death, is somewhere between the fully human and the animal. Becoming-human, and therefore reminded of his or her materiality, his or her belonging materially as a mortal to the earth and shut out from spirit, the Hardy being perceives that which he or she can never become.

Hardy's characters are haunted by the specter of a humanity to which they will never have full access because, on the one hand, they are excluded from a future and the becoming-culture of modern England, which can never be theirs, whilst they are also expelled, compelled to wander and drift, and so are haunted also by the traces of a past that informs their being but, again, remains unavailable to them. Hardyean subjectivity is thus placed as the axial locus naked before a world to-come, and incapable of understanding those traces of the past by which it is haunted. The most poignant figures for this are of course Tess and Jude: the former stooping in a field picking vegetables, and seen from some god-like vantage point by a narrative eye that compares her with an insect on the landscape; the latter standing on the Ickeneild Way looking towards Christminster (Oxford), but neither fully able to enter that spiritual life (as is figured cruelly by his inability to grasp Greek), nor to turn back to a rural community or spirit which, historically, he has outgrown. Thus, Tess, Jude, and other Hardy figures are haunted by the impossibility of their temporal condition, an impossibility remarked through their perception *and* their lack of access. In this, they lack spirit. More than animals, they are less than human. They become the figures of a spectral liminality, the product of a modernity that marginalizes historically and materially, and leaves them without access to future or past. In having been sacrificed in this manner, they thus become phantasms of modernity itself.

Hardy's novels are notably free of "literal" ghosts, even as particular human beings have their being put under erasure, crossed out but maintained as a material reminder of the possibility of one's becoming anachronistic and surviving only to haunt where one both is and is not, leaving in the wake of this crossing-out or crossing through, only a "benumbedness,"[10] a condition which closes one off whilst simultaneously leaving closure open, remarking an access through which the figure cannot go. It is this hovering on the threshold that marks Hardy's characters in their spectrality, announcing that spectral condition, a *becoming-spectral*, as a modern symptom of being anachronic, belated. The ghost in Hardy, or rather, say, the phenomenon of becoming-spectral, is thus tied to an existence that is neither of a world touched by spirit (and so not fully alive), nor of one in which one's death is absolute, unconditional, without doubt. Hardy's characters exist as mere poor beings that hover, as if they were dead.

Where the term *ghost* does appear in Hardy's text, it is, for the most part, as metaphor or simile – at least on the surface. Objects and characters assume momentarily the guise of the ghostly for others. There is superstitious speculation on the reasons for ghostly visitations, as we have seen in the first of the three epigraphs. But across fourteen novels, there is not one ghost *as such.* It might be thought, therefore, that to write of Hardy's ghosts as if there were ghosts in the text of Hardy, is a little odd, not to say perverse. Certainly, ghosts, phantoms, and other modes of apparitioning take place in the poetry, and there are ghostly effects, unexplained phenomena, and uncanny occasions to be found in various short stories, of which more below. However, regarding the novels, it is this very absence which might give us pause, and, from that, a place to begin again in drifting. What can be said is that, at a certain point towards the close of his novel-writing career, with the publication of *Jude the Obscure* and the revised version of *The Well-Beloved,* a small, almost imperceptible change in the work of the spectral trope is to be read. Here are two examples of ghostly disturbance from Hardy's two final novels:

Knowing not a human being here, Jude began to be impressed with the isolation of his own personality, as with a *self-spectre*, the sensation being that of one who walked but could not make himself seen or heard. He drew his breath pensively, and, seeming thus almost *his own ghost*, gave his thoughts to the other *ghostly presences* with which the nooks were *haunted*.[11]

The evening and night winds here were, to Pierston's mind, *charged with a something* that did not burden them elsewhere. They brought it up from that sinister Bay to the west, whose movement she and he were hearing now. *It was a presence – an imaginary shape or essence* from the human multitude lying below: those who had gone down in vessels of war, East Indiamen, barges, brigs, and ships of the Armada – select people, common, and debased, whose interests and hopes had been as wide asunder as the poles, but who had rolled each other to oneness on that restless sea-bed. *There could almost be felt the brush of their huge composite ghost as it ran a shapeless figure over the isle, shrieking for some good god who would disunite it again.*[12]

Arguably, neither passage takes part in the conventions of the ghost story. Something quite singular, possibly novel, is at work here; certainly Hardy invents the phenomena of ghosting in a disturbing manner. The passages are disquieting precisely because they touch on the experience of being haunted, as if the reader were to find him- or herself in the place of the narratives' subjects, Jude Fawley and Jocelyn Pierston.

Taking each in turn, if we observe the opening of the chapter from which comes Jude's uncanny sense of self and the place in which he finds himself, we will find the aura of the spectral already at work. In the opening sentence of the first chapter of Part II, "At Christminster," it is remarked that "he appeared gliding steadily onward through a dusky landscape" (77) on his way to Hardy's fictional rendering of Oxford. The time of day, that liminal and crepuscular instant of transition, a "between times" as it were, is given somewhat indistinctly, in being "dusky." The image is hardly made any more solid by Jude's appearance of gliding. There is something ethereal, barely of the material world about this initial representation, even though Hardy does attempt to ameliorate the phantasmic perception in the next paragraph but one, in which the author seeks to make Jude more materially there through detailed representation. Yet, in commenting on his being a stone mason, Jude's hair and beard are shown as having the traces of stone-dust still upon them, at least implicitly. If such "whitening" does not make Jude ghostly exactly, it has the odd effect of making him appear older than he is. From this, the reader is informed of a photograph belonging to Jude's aunt, which despite his asking for it, his aunt had refused to give, the consequence of which being that "it haunted him" (78). Arriving in Christminster in the evening, and exploring the streets, Jude "saw nothing of real city in the suburbs" (78). Anything he perceives which is not in "harmony" with the medieval college buildings, his eyes do not see. Following the tolling of a bell, "fewer and fewer people were visible, and still he serpentined among the shadows," maintaining that barely physical motion, with which he had been introduced to the reader at the start of the chapter (77). And thus he finds himself in "obscure alleys, apparently never trodden now by the foot of man, and whose very existence seemed to be forgotten, [in which] there would jut into the path porticoes, oriels, doorways of enriched and florid middle-age design, their extinct air being accentuated by the rottenness of the stones. It seemed impossible that modern thought could house itself in such decrepit and superseded chambers" (79). And so it is, we arrive, with Jude, at that experience of being a "self-spectre," his "own ghost," surrounded by the haunted material of college buildings. Much here has to do with Jude's own perception, of course.

It is Jude's openness to the phenomenological impression of place that Hardy registers so carefully throughout the opening paragraphs of the chapter. What is significant, however, is that the registration takes place in the narrative, and so is turned in parabasis toward the reader. The writing takes up the spectral trope, in order to assume its own haunting force and to pass beyond the merely constative or descriptive, objective act, to enter into a performative dimension, doing in words what it seeks to convey concerning Jude's own psychic faculties. We are witness to a phenomenology of the spectral here, if not an ontology. Indeed, that the spectral manifestation is implicitly of a phenomenological kind suggests that the ontological cannot be determined as agreed conceptual frame. Fiction thus becomes haunted by the work of thought and perception, turned simultaneously towards representation of another's state of mind on the one hand, and, on the other, towards the very interiority of the reader's imaginative projection.

Regarding the passage from *The Well-Beloved*, Hardy again, typically, presents the reader with a perception on perception, particularly turned towards that which is at the limits of, or just beyond, representation, visibility, and articulation. Borne on the wind, there is a *something* that appears indistinctly to Jocelyn's mind. This spectral manifestation takes on the condition of imaginary presence, shape, or essence. Hardy's language pursues the chase of Pierston's psyche, which moves not after the form as such, but after a term appropriate to giving shape to the trace of the specter, as that which belongs in turn to all the dead who appear to make themselves felt through the unnerving touch of a "huge composite ghost." Yet, this is still unavailable to any direct representation, for we read of the specter, indirectly revealed as a shapeless figure, a flow of energy or force desirous of being dismembered. Like Jude, Jocelyn is confronted with the phantasmic apparition that he can barely comprehend. In each singular event, the spectral touches as intimately as it announces exclusion from fully human apprehension. Both men experience the traversal of their internal worlds, behind which is the revelation of being that lets itself be known to perception. Being and meaning are aligned, though with this distinction: both Pierston and Fawley gain momentary access to a perception of being that can never be theirs, as if, in their material exclusion, they are shown to be not fully human. In this poverty, they are perceived as somewhat ghostly witnesses to humanity's historicity through a fracturing of being. And this fracture – through which perception of the spectral other arrives – announces the secret of modernity's arrival, for the fracture of being is also, and at the same moment, the fracture of the present and of pure presence in which phantasms "hover like anxious shades."[13] As in the entirety of another Hardy novel, *A Laodicean*, the two scenes – two events – from *Jude the Obscure* and *The Well-*

Beloved bracket the present with shades of the past and the future, leaving the subject to assume responsibility "as it faces the singular" manifestation of the other.[14]

IV

The spectral and ghostly thus admits to a relation, without relation, of past with future, wherein consciousness, "seeing the phantom of being-in-itself vanish before it" and encountering also to itself the "disappearance of an essence that exists only for it, for it qua specific consciousness," gives place to a truth "which is both in-itself and for consciousness."[15] The specter of modernity thus enables the momentary "reconciliation of the history of thought with thought itself."[16] Such reconciliation is scant comfort, however, for reconciliation is the place where the spectral announces itself to consciousness, only as consciousness, subjectivity, or being apprehend themselves in relation to being other. Thought is always this affirmation of the other within the self, whereby the self is revealed to itself as an other.

What Hardy makes clear, then, is that there is an inescapable uncanniness by which the modern subject is caused to suffer, through the self-reflection of thought that dwells on the relation between thought and being, and the revelation to being's consciousness that the self is at the axis of past and future, with the responsibility to decide on the meaning of being in the face of the undecidable. With this consideration of the uncanniness of being in mind, we should turn to Heidegger.

On a number of occasions, Martin Heidegger had recourse to think the uncanny. Reflection on the uncanny appears in lectures, seminars, and texts from the 1920s to the 1960s, not least in particular passages of *Being and Time* and in the work immediately preceding – and in some senses rehearsing – Heidegger's most famous interrogation of the question of Being, *History of the Concept of Time: Prolegomena.*[17] Elsewhere, the uncanny surfaces as a topic for rigorous meditation in correlation with the thinking of Being in lectures dedicated to the texts of Parmenides and Hölderlin.[18] In every case, however, regardless of the local orientation of Heidegger's theses, the uncanny is woven into the philosophical mediation of the question of Being, the Being of beings, and the question of home, the homely, unhomeliness, the hearth, and, of course, the question of what it means to dwell, the latter topic broached in some of Heidegger's most significant essays produced in the post-war years ("Building, Dwelling, Thinking," "... Poetically, Man Dwells ..."), after the alleged "turn" (*die Kehre*).[19] Though Heidegger uses terms such as homely, unhomely, or hearth, and does not refer to "dwelling" in the earlier works (with the obvious exception of certain somewhat rapid sketches in *Being and Time*, particularly H61–63, where Heidegger gathers "dwelling" together with "looking-at" and "perception," apropos what one might term provisionally the un-homely technicity of being), it is nevertheless the case that the thinking and questioning of being *qua* dwelling arises directly out of Heidegger's readings in Parmenides and Hölderlin amongst others.

Those already familiar with such discussions will know that, though Heidegger's uncanny touches on aspects of that topic which overlap with Freudian thinking, the philosopher's consideration has more profound, even radical implications apropos the nature of what we take to be uncanny. Sharing with Freud an insistence on semantic and etymological considerations, Heidegger departs from the psychoanalyst by rejecting the uncanny as "impression" or "effect" that arises in particular situations. In doing so, the philosopher perceives the uncanny as being of the essence of being itself, of the Being of beings, as he would put it. In such a fundamental and, again, radical reorientation, Heidegger steps beyond all the impasses and aporia up against which Freud repeatedly finds himself in his famous essay of 1919, without resolving or doing away with the essential uncanniness of the experience of undecidability. In this, the uncanny appears as both radically interior to being and yet also of the world and thus the trace, however undecidable or unreadable, of being's materiality, its historicity. And it is precisely because Heidegger privileges the uncanny in its many manifestations, its "manifold" essence, that he is able to overcome the psychologistic limit imposed on what is, for him, of the most crucial importance. While for Freud, the problem of the uncanny is that it cannot be determined, for Heidegger, undecidability is of the essence and so not a problem to be resolved or reconciled. If James had been merely modernist in relation to a Hardyean modernity of subjectivity and being, then, in a different fashion, the same relation between Freud and Heidegger may also be posited.

Given certain commentaries on Heidegger, though, which do not stress this word, *unheimlich*, is it wrong or even a little perverse to give such significance to the uncanny – the unhomely to be more precise and to follow Heidegger's own distinction, on which he insists in order to move the thinker away from the misperception of mere effect? Take the following commentary by David Farrell Krell: "Heidegger's thought," Krell insists correctly, "circles about a double theme: the meaning of Being and the propriative event (*Ereignis*) of disclosure." Krell continues:

> *Sein* and *aletheia* remain the key words, *Sein* meaning coming to presence, and *aletheia* the disclosedness or unconcealment implied in such presence … [However] Coming to presence suggests an absence before and after itself, so that withdrawal and departure must always be thought together with *Sein* as presencing; disclosedness or unconcealment suggests a surrounding obscurity. The propriative event is always simultaneously expropriative.[20]

Sein and *aletheia*: Being and modalities of truth's disclosure or unveiling. Heidegger's keywords announce the ghost, although its force is never nominated as such. That motion of coming to pass, of retreat, of absence and obscurity from which the disclosedness emerges and into which it retreats: these are the very motions of the spectral, all the more uncanny for being so forcefully announced and yet never named. As an introduction to the thinking of Heideggerian being, Krell's commentary strikes at the very heart of what motivates Heidegger, and situates in its own terms both the thinking of temporality – withdrawal and departure – *and* spatiality – the place, as well as the event, of disclosedness and that "surrounding obscurity" without which we cannot begin to appreciate the *topos* of being as the place of a certain experience of haunting; and which in turn lends to the Heideggerian notion of *Dasein* its historicity and groundedness (without which there would be the risk of a retrenchment back into just another mode of German idealism). It is this very temporal placedness, this being-in-the-world, the material self-consciousness that comes to one as a complex relation, at the nexus of which is the thinking being, which makes possible the thinking of dwelling in the lectures of 1951 already mentioned.

Yet, such a way of thinking would not be possible without earlier investigations on Heidegger's part into Parmenides. Parmenidean reasoning holds that it is impossible to think what does not exist. Even if, like Hardy's characters, I imagine something which has never been seen "in person," because I can visualize that "something" it exists. True enough, its existence is of a different order than, say, a chair or table. Nevertheless, its non-existence in the world as I inhabit it is not, for Parmenides, a true non-existence; for were this "it" not to exist, I could not have thought it. It is this which the following fragment encapsulates: χρὴ τὸ λέγειν τε νοεῖν τ᾽ ἐὸν ἔμμεναι ... ("It needs must be that what can be thought and spoken of is {Saying [i.e., the letting show itself] and [the thus occurring] perceiving are necessary ... [to take up]}").[21] The logic here develops from the fundamental understanding on Parmenides's part concerning the inextricable interrelatedness of thinking and being, and so discloses to us the Heideggerian thinking of the *unheimlich*. There is no thinking without being, and there is no being save for thinking: τὸ γὰρ αὐτὸ νοεῖν ἐστίν τε καί εἶναι. ("The same is thinking and being/For it is the same thing that can be thought and that can be {'perceptual mean-ing and being are the same'}").[22]

In an early essay from 1912, "The Problem of Reality in Modern Philosophy," Heidegger expresses a similar notion: "All being [*Sein*]," he argues, "is being-conscious [*Bewußt-Sein*]. The concept of consciousness includes both the conscious subject and the object of consciousness, but these two moments are only separable by abstraction. The result of this is the inextricable concatenation of thought and being."[23] In 1928, in the lecture course published as the volume *The Metaphysical Foundations of Logic*, Heidegger takes up Parmenides's claim on the correlation between thinking and being. Doing so in order to counter misreadings of idealism in Parmenides, Heidegger observes how "[t]here were attempts in the nineteenth century to claim [Parmenides's] statement for ... 'the first glimmerings of idealism,' as if Parmenides had held that the subject is what first posits beings as beings, or as if ... objects order themselves according to our knowledge."[24] In a comparison between the nineteenth-century misreading of Parmenides and a similar misperception of Kant, Heidegger continues, accepting that a kernel of truth exists in the misreading, inasmuch as – and here he acknowledges the statement made in my first epigraph – "being is related to the subject" (142). However, in turning to the semantic play in the Greek, Heidegger argues that there "is no causal ontic dependency" and that "interpretations of Parmenides's thought as 'realism' are equally untenable" (142). In order to clarify the error, Heidegger states categorically that: "The point is not whether the subject posits beings or whether it, as knowing subject, directs itself towards beings, but the point is rather the way in which the human being as such understands anything like being at all" (142–143). Failing to perceive this, one fails to grasp what is at stake with, as Heidegger has it, "sufficient radicality" (143). The "basic problem," as the philosopher sees it, is not at all a problem of epistemology (143). Such interpretations remain within traditions of thought that do not fully perceive that which constitutes the disclosedness of Being to beings.

At Freiburg, in the summer of 1942, Heidegger presented his final major lecture course on Friedrich Hölderlin.[25] In these lectures, the philosopher devoted considerable attention to the human being as the "uncanniest of the uncanny" (51ff.) and, as a consequence, proposed the uncanny as the "ground of human beings" (68ff.), as this in turn relates to the home and the homely, and so to the question of the relation of one's being in relation to dwelling. In those lectures, Heidegger addresses uncanniness as it pertains to looking. Looking is not merely the gaze, the act or ability of a human to see, and so to know, the world, as sight gives to the human the representation of that world. Looking distinguishes humans from other merely existing animals because looking gives access to "the Being of beings." Looking, remarks Heidegger, "shows [that] Being itself is not something human but belongs to the essence of Being itself as belonging to appearance in the unconcealed."[26]

Yet, what is perhaps most uncanny about the look is that it cannot give us to comprehend the truth of being. Jude looks along the road; Pierston looks over the bay; each has disclosed to them the haunting experience of being unable to access the truth of Being. Being's spectral disclosedness retreats in the moment that I perceive its having returned. We have no access to the essence of truth, Heidegger tells us, because "we neither comprehend the essence of truth nor do we comprehend ourselves, and we do not know who we ourselves are" (162). It is, however, "good to know this ignorance," Heidegger continues, and this at least is what we read in Hardy's tragic figures: being's historicity, its haunted modernity, is revealed but this no more gives them to know themselves than it gives them access to truth. The "truth" of haunting perceived by Woolf, and read in James, is merely one revelation of a certain historical experience. For Hardy's figures, what haunts – even though they do not fully comprehend it – is, to recall Heidegger, that the "being and non-being" of "historical people" and "European culture" remains "undecided, unquestioned, and even forgotten" (162). Thus it is that Hardy's characters remain haunted, trapped epochally in the experience of the unhomely which no psychoanalysis can resolve. As with Jude on the road, or Jocelyn on the cliff, humans remain on the verge, at the limit, always homeless and always drifting. Without the "truth of Being, beings are never steadfast" (162), but remain haunted by an apperception of "the destination toward which" one is always "underway, namely the home" of the truth that Heidegger, after Parmenides, names the Goddess, who is nominated in the very idea of *Aletheia* (162–163). The home "also directs the course of the thinker's genuine experience," but, conversely, brings back that sense of being haunted in being *unheimlich*, without home, "from which all history begins" (162). Hardy's language thus expresses that which remains inaccessible to his own characters, albeit that their experience gives access to the disclosure of Being; but, in a different way, it confesses that which remains unknowable also to James or Woolf; Hardy's language articulates and affirms "the essence of history, and history, because it is the sending of Being and because Being only comes to light unexpectedly, is appropriated always in the unexpectedness of the primordiality of the beginning" (163).

V

Do we know where we're going? Is this idea, that one knows where one is headed, true, strictly speaking, or ever? Of course there is always death, we are all beings toward death; and in this anticipatory retrospect, in our "future anterior," we are vouchsafed the most uncanny of "dwellings," an inescapable authenticity in the negation of being as its ownmost inevitability. I can imagine myself no longer the "myself," when I am no longer even a body without organs, merely a without. Yet, it is important to acknowledge that in knowing where we are going, nothing in fact could be less certain. For while death is that which is inescapable, that which is the future therefore, and one of the few events to which one can, properly speaking, give the name "future" as opposed to speaking of that which is to come (that which may one day arrive but which cannot be anticipated or programmed), nevertheless, I cannot experience what I call "my death." The authenticity of futurity is always already haunted therefore by its own inauthenticity, except in the fiction of the *als ob*, the as if; it is haunted by the impossibility of knowing ahead of time, ahead of the absence of all time, all world, and therefore, all consciousness of dwelling. It is haunted by the impossibility of knowing either ahead of time, in time, or on time. When death arrives, it does so in a manner where time is not, and can never be the issue at stake. Ultimate anachrony, all time gone. Dwell on this: untimely death. If what haunts authenticity is inauthenticity, that from which the former cannot escape, then the felicity of a performance is always troubled, spooked we might say, by the very possibility, the *eigenartigkeit*, the strangeness and singularity of infelicity, the *Heimlich, Heimisch* as *unheimlich, unheimlisch.* Heidegger apprehends as much in those movements that he traces of the uncanny, the *unheimlich*, as the self flees the self in the face of being's ownmost authenticity.

So there you have it, suspended for a moment and all time, in no time, a solitary figure, his back towards you, as if he were about to walk away, stepping off in mediation through the forest, on no discernible path. We cannot get away from Heidegger, even though he appears to want to get away from us. Think of that well-known photograph, in which the philosopher is caught, walking away, his cane held behind his back, thumbs aligned along its uppermost surface, his hat not a little reminiscent of Buster Keaton. No path, just the leaves, the trees, and a vanishing point into which he will become as nothing. A future forestalled, home deferred indefinitely, whereby a locale comes into existence, only by virtue of what lies ahead, but *in which* he will never witness himself, or be capable of retreating from; therein is a space and becoming suspended, an image as the impossible time, representing the inauthenticity of being in the oncoming face of the authenticity of a line of flight, mapping the unmappable becoming of *Dasein*. Thus in the photo, within representation, we attain a glimpse of what we do not see, indirectly we have made known to us, in temporal suspension, "the boundary [as] that from which something *begins its essential unfolding.*"[27] The silence here in the woods may well be deafening, as, despite himself, Heidegger gets off the beaten path; but a performative deterritorialization of the recuperative ontology of *Dasein* initiates itself, lying in wait.

Heidegger walks without path, in the experience of that which cannot be interpreted *as such*. In this gesture, which many attribute to bad writing, obfuscation, a terrorist obscurantism, and so forth, he institutes the becoming of what, invisibly, is already underway, on the way, without a map of the way: that is to say an "inceptual thinking in the other beginning," which "en-thinks the truth of be-ing."[28] This necessary gesture, a leap of sorts, will nonetheless fall into the machinic; this is always its risk, thereby forcing an "opening of the still undecided decision unto the grounding of this truth," even and especially when authenticity always retreats before inauthenticity, the felicitous recuperated in the infelicitous, resulting in "the failure to enact the grounding ... [as] the necessary destiny of the first beginning" (55). *Destiny. First. Enact. Grounding.* The transcendentalism of a teleological onto-technics manifests itself in these words, in their reliance on performativity, originarity, and eschatological assumption. But where does dwelling remain? Dwelling is always *alethic*, a movement, a becoming which is also, and simultaneously, an unbecoming, haunted by its own ineluctability, and as that which might arrive, which remains to come, but which remains undecidable, and all the more ghostly and haunting for that; in becoming other than myself, as the limit of myself, across that limit, *there* remains on the way to death. This, at least, is what is perceived in our thinking of the ghost – the specter of the other. Neither immaterial nor material, there, a *there* irreducible to any here, a past or future irreducible to any present or presence, haunting takes place; but always at borders, between all those "ones" and "others" – alive and dead, present and absent, there and not there, visible and invisible – the pairings of which serve to map out, in a kind of spectro-tropo-topology, the spaces in-between. If there is apparitioning, the apperceived motion of revenance, taking place is "its" condition in its disclosedness, and giving place in its having come to pass, the experience of that which, though no being as such, touches me most intimately.

NOTES

1   Thomas Hardy, *Return of the Native* (London: Penguin Classics, 1999), 30.
2   Hardy, *Return of the Native*, 374.
3   Thomas Hardy, *Tess of the D'Urbervilles* (London: Penguin Classics, 2003), 208.
4   Jacques Derrida, *Of Grammatology*, trans. Gayatri Chakravorty Spivak (Baltimore: Johns Hopkins University Press, 1967), lxxxix–xc. Spivak's translation includes "tense" in parentheses, following the first reference to time, in order to distinguish between the two uses of *temps* in Derrida's text. Derrida's chiasmus relies in part on that which is legible, and so comprehensible, between the two uses as a "writing effect" not available through voice. To have given the translation as "the age [or epoch] ... thus disturbs the tense of the line and the line of time," would have lost the disruptive graphic motion that Derrida inscribes in the iterable term *temps*, and thus render invisible that which haunts the French original. Another point to make here concerns Derrida's use of "époque." Generally, Spivak's translation favours "age." While both "age" and "epoch" can be used, commonly, to refer to periods of time, epoch also, and in contradistinction to the common use, signifies in its Greek

roots the suspension or stoppage of time. Derrida's preference here arguably has this double sense in mind, especially as the notion of epoch in its other sense would serve, presumably, in the "demand that reading should free itself, at least in its axis, from the classical categories of history" (lxxxix).

5   Maurice Merleau-Ponty, *The World of Perception*, trans. Oliver Davis (London: Routledge, 2008), 81.

6   Virginia Woolf, "Henry James's Ghost Stories," in *The Essays of Virginia Woolf: 1919–1924*, Vol. 3, ed. Andrew McNeillie (New York: Harcourt Brace Jovanovich, 1988), 324.

7   Nicholas Royle, "Clipping," *Forum: The University of Edinburgh Postgraduate Journal of Culture and the Arts* 7 (Autumn 2008): 1.

8   Jacques Derrida, *Memoires for Paul de Man* (New York: Columbia University Press, 1989), 64.

9   Jacques Derrida, *Of Spirit: Heidegger and the Question* (Chicago: University of Chicago Press, 1991), 51.

10   Ibid., 54.

11   Thomas Hardy, *Jude the Obscure* (London: Penguin, 1998), 75, emphasis added.

12   Thomas Hardy, *The Pursuit of the Well-Beloved and the Well Beloved* (London: Penguin, 1997), 186, emphasis added.

13   David Appelbaum, *Jacques Derrida's Ghost: A Conjuration* (Albany: SUNY Press, 2009), 48.

14   Ibid.

15   Jean Hyppolite, *Genesis and Structure of Hegel's "Phenomenology of Spirit"* (Evanston: Northwestern University Press, 1974), 228.

16   Ibid.

17   Martin Heidegger, *Being and Time*, trans. Joan Stambaugh (1927; repr. Albany: SUNY Press, 1996); Martin Heidegger, *Being and Time*, trans. John Macquarrie and Edward Robinson (1927; repr. New York: Harper & Row, 1962); Martin Heidegger, *History of the Concept of Time: Prolegomena*, trans. Theodore Kisiel (1927; repr. Bloomington: Indiana University Press, 1985).

18   Martin Heidegger, *Parmenides*, trans. André Schuwer and Richard Rojcewicz (1942–43; repr. Bloomington: Indiana University Press, 1992); Martin Heidegger, *Hölderlin's Hymn "The Ister,"* trans. William McNeill and Julia Davis (1942; repr. Bloomington: Indiana University Press, 1996).

19   Martin Heidegger, *Four Seminars*, trans. Andrew Mitchell and François Raffoul (1966, 1968, 1969, 1973; repr. Bloomington: Indiana University Press, 2003).

20   David Farrell Krell, "General Introduction: The Thinking of Being," in *Martin Heidegger: Basic Writings from Being and Time (1927) to The Task of Thinking (1964)*, ed. David Farrell Krell (London: Routledge, 1993), 32.

21   Parmenides, "Fragment VI, 1," in *The First Philosophers of Greece*, ed. and trans. Arthur Fairbanks (London: Kegan Paul, Trench, Trubner, 1898), 91.

22   Parmenides, "Fragment I, 3," in *The First Philosophers of Greece*, 91.

23   Martin Heidegger, "The Problem of Reality in Modern Philosophy," in *Supplements: From the Earliest Essays to Being and Time and Beyond*, ed. John van Buren, trans. Phillip J. Bossert (1912; repr. Albany: SUNY Press, 2002), 42.

24   Martin Heidegger, *The Metaphysical Foundations of Logic*, trans. Michael Heim (1928; repr. Bloomington: Indiana University Press, 1984), 142.

25   Heidegger, *Hölderlin's Hymn*, ix.

26   Heidegger, *Parmenides*, 104.

27   Martin Heidegger, "Building Dwelling Thinking," in *Martin Heidegger: Basic Writings*, 356.

28   Martin Heidegger, *Mindfulness*, trans. Parvis Emad and Thomas Kalary (London: Athlone Press, 2006), 55.

Chapter 2

Beckett's Ghost Light

Martin Harries[1]

For Neni Panourgiá

In the middle of the twentieth century, millions went back in time. That period saw the end of the old regime in places modernization reached only by mid-century; it also thrust many into predicaments that reversed the momentum of that same modernization. If, as Eric Hobsbawm has stressed, writing of that century now over, the "most dramatic and far-reaching social change of the second half of this century, and the one which cuts us off for ever from the world of the past, is the death of the peasantry," large-scale dislocations early in that period also produced, on a massive scale, new peasants.[2] Refugees across Europe and across the world found themselves living in terrible versions of the worlds they had lost. In Roussillon, the French village where he had fled for safety from the Nazi occupation of Paris, Samuel Beckett and his partner became gleaners: "although the fields were a sea of mud following the potato harvest, he and Suzanne were allowed to search in the ground, picking and keeping whatever had been overlooked by the farmworkers."[3] Beckett was hardly alone in this experience of total war's production of historical regression, and his experience was far from the worst. But readers have largely not noticed that the spectral bodies of Beckett's plays occupy landscapes shaped by the everyday experience of such historical dislocation. It would be ingenious but wrongheaded to claim Beckett for popular culture.[4] And yet Beckett's postwar work is structured around historical experiences that required neither atavism nor mysterious collective memory for people to recall.

War's simultaneous acceleration and reversal of the trajectories of modernization emphasized the fragility of whatever comforts modernization provided. Criticism of Beckett has largely treated his work as implausibly ahistorical or, equally implausibly, as directly linked to particular historical incidents. Beckett's ghosts wave us to a more removed but no less historical ground. These are not ghosts of this or that event, but ghosts of the *longue durée*, and Beckett registered what it felt like to live and die in that duration. Beckett was interested, for instance, in the history of light, what electricity meant, and what it meant not to have it.

The Dead Voices, Once Again

Is this about ghosts?

ESTRAGON	In the meantime let us try and converse calmly, since we are incapable of keeping silent.
VLADIMIR	You're right, we're inexhaustible.
ESTRAGON	It's so we won't have to think.
VLADIMIR	We have that excuse.
ESTRAGON	It's so we won't hear.
VLADIMIR	We have our reasons.
ESTRAGON	All the dead voices.
VLADIMIR	They make a noise like wings.
ESTRAGON	Like leaves.
VLADIMIR	Like sand.
ESTRAGON	Like leaves.
	[*Silence.*]
VLADIMIR	They all speak at once.
ESTRAGON	Each one to itself.
	[*Silence.*]
VLADIMIR	Rather they whisper.
ESTRAGON	They rustle.
VLADIMIR	They murmur.
ESTRAGON	They rustle.
	[*Silence.*]
VLADIMIR	What do they say?
ESTRAGON	They talk about their lives.
VLADIMIR	To have lived is not enough for them.
ESTRAGON	They have to talk about it.
VLADIMIR	To be dead is not enough for them.
ESTRAGON	It is not sufficient.
	[*Silence.*]
VLADIMIR	They make a noise like feathers.
ESTRAGON	Like leaves.
VLADIMIR	Like ashes.
ESTRAGON	Like leaves.
	[*Long silence.*]
VLADIMIR	Say something![5]

The lyricism often detected in this passage stems from something quite different from the irrepressible expressive urge often held to be the lyric's source.[6] This exchange represents, instead, a willed and willful production of speech designed to drown out "All the dead voices." It is with some desperation that Vladimir finally implores Estragon to say something, as though that long silence were silent for the audience only, and, for Vladimir and Estragon, crowded with the voices they are trying not to hear. As Joseph Roach writes, "The poetic and dramatic tension of 'All the dead voices,' then, arises from the onomatopoeic reproduction of echoes that only the characters can hear in a landscape hollowed by loss and forgetfulness."[7] And yet even that onomatopoeic quality, rustling and whispering, is disturbed by their different accounts of what these voices sound like. Vladimir's variety (wings, sand, feathers, ashes) is the counterpoint to Estragon's sameness: for Estragon, the voices insistently "rustle"; they always sound like leaves. And if it is true that this landscape is "hollowed by loss and forgetfulness," it is also the case, here, that for Estragon and Vladimir, that landscape is not yet hollow or forgettable enough. Roach writes that the landscape of *Godot* is "haunted": "From Ibsen on, modern drama has been troubled by ghosts. Their ubiquity stems in part from the fact that they conveniently represent the past that is dead but refuses final interment" (85–86). The history of modern drama's stage ghosts remains to be written, though, alongside Roach's provocation, recent books by Marvin Carlson and Alice Rayner have opened up crucial questions.[8] Here I limit myself to Beckett's engagement with ghosts and things that resemble ghosts. That distinction, between ghosts and things that resemble them, strikes me as important. One of the striking qualities of the passage about "dead voices" is its rigorous resistance to the word "ghost" itself. And in this resistance the passage is consistent with Beckett's reluctance to use the word "ghost" exactly where it would seem most to belong; Ruby Cohn has made a similar point.[9] *Are* "dead voices" so readily to be translated as ghosts? Are there still ghosts?

A better question might be not whether ghosts survive, but whether there are ghosts again. Beckett's poem "Saint-Lô," first published in the *Irish Times* in 1946 (or roughly two years before he begins *Godot* in October, 1948),[10] is instructive here:

Vire will wind in other shadows
unborn through the bright ways tremble
and the old mind ghost-forsaken
sink into its havoc (4:38)

Eoin O'Brien has located this poem in Beckett's postwar experience of working in an Irish Red Cross hospital in the ravaged French town that gives the poem its name.[11] O'Brien writes: "The river Vire winding its way through the ruined city links the past … the destruction of the present, and the inevitable rebirth witnessed by Beckett, with the future havoc which all-forgetting humanity will just as inevitably inflict upon itself again" (337). One implication of O'Brien's paraphrase is that the company of ghosts prevents havoc. The poem's premise reverses the common association of the ghost and the primordial: some mind other than the old one would *not* be "ghost-forsaken." The new is haunted. Vladimir and Estragon then appear as haunted moderns who long to be old minds, "ghost-forsaken." Not for them the piety that ties the ghost to ethics.

If they could exchange silence, if not havoc, for the noise of "All the dead voices," they would. And their understanding of the noise made by the dead resembles some critical readings of their own speech: the dead talk not because they want to do something with their speech – these are not revenge ghosts with tales to unfold or tasks to assign – but because life and death are not enough, they need speech: "To be dead," complains Vladimir, "is not enough for them." The dead possess voices and yet are not quite ghosts. It is as though, after *Godot*, Beckett's drama turns from those who try, in a gesture all too familiar in postwar Europe, to silence or repress the dead, to representing dead voices that are not ghosts. Beckett's pivotal work for the stage may be *Play*, where three figures speak from the urns that contain them. It seems his characters – his speakers, his creatures, those beings, what have you – have, since *Play*, always spoken from beyond the grave.

Ghost Media

Even ghosts require media. If we recall Marshall McLuhan's formulation, media are extensions of the self. Small wonder, then, that we talk with ghosts via media: the medium speaks with that thing, the ghost, that exists only in its extensions. So, to revise: ghosts especially require media. The bodiless need extensions to speak. Smaller wonder, then, that (as many have noticed) – from the "ghost of 'lectricity" to *Phantasmic Radio* to *The Material Ghost* – the language of media and the language of ghosts so often mix.[12] The *locus classicus* is probably not as familiar as it once was:

> The electric light is pure information. It is a medium without a message, as it were, unless it is used to spell out some verbal ad or name. This fact, characteristic of all media, means that the "content" of any medium is always another medium. The content of writing is speech, just as the written word is the content of print, and print is the content of the telegraph. If it is asked, "What is the content of speech," it is necessary to say, "It is an actual process of thought, which is itself nonverbal."[13]

This passage (despite its blunt reminder of the linguistic turn that separates us from McLuhan) offers one way of reading the speaking of the dead in *Godot*: that speech is the medium for "an actual process of thought" which is the activity of the dead for whom to be dead is not enough. However unsatisfactory McLuhan's formulation will prove in the end for a reading of Beckett, McLuhan's central point that media become a set of extensions of man nevertheless illuminates Beckett. Indeed, Beckett's work presents McLuhan's theory with a set of limit cases. Those voices of the dead are exemplary. Is this speech a medium? Paradigmatically, speech in Beckett has no content beyond itself. Estragon and Vladimir are arguably like the dead voices in that their speech is not a medium for content, but a speech more closely resembling the purity of that "electric light," carrying not content but instead simply a sound. The medium of these dead voices is the message. And this in turn might explain why so often Beckett resists the word "ghost." The speech of the dead is not the extension of some body called a ghost. The dead exist as speech, but this speech proves nothing about the existence of ghosts.

I invoke McLuhan in part to acknowledge his continuing influence in discussions of media and in part because his example of electric light proves important to Beckett. In Beckett's late play, *A Piece of Monologue*, the lone figure of the piece – called, simply, Speaker – combines ghost and light: "Nothing stirring. Faintly stirring. Thirty thousand nights of ghosts beyond. Beyond that black beyond. Ghost light. Ghost nights. Ghost rooms. Ghost graves. Ghost … he all but said ghost loved ones" (3:458). "Ghost" aside, every part of this passage is a return to a refrain of the short text. Near the play's opening, the Speaker invokes "Funerals … he all but said of loved ones. Thirty thousands nights" (3:454). "Nothing stirring," "beyond": these, too, are refrains in the brief text. That reiterated "ghost," then, marks a difference. Suddenly, it seems, the ghost can modify anything and everything: nights, light, rooms, graves, loved ones. In a text that includes a refutation of totality to rival Adorno's lapidary epigram, "The whole is the false"[14] – "No such thing as whole" (3:456) – it seems that these ghosts may aspire almost to universality.

Recent valuable investigations of the generic status of the ghostly and of the psychoanalytic valences in Beckett have obscured aspects of the history of ghosts.[15] *A Piece of Monologue* is a play about ghosts and memory, and about theater as a privileged site for meditation on ghosts and memory. It is also one of Beckett's plays about technology, and about the theater as a technological site. "Ghost light": this meeting of ghost, technology, and theater has its emblem here. Beckett plays with a theatrical tradition: when theaters are dark, a single standing lamp is left burning onstage. Explanations for this tradition range from a measure to protect theater operators against a litigious intruder's falling into the orchestra pit to the thoughtful practice of lighting any nocturnal shows that might be performed by ghosts.[16] Each of these antithetical meanings plays a role in Beckett's play. Consider the opening stage direction:

Curtain.
Faint diffuse light.
Speaker stands well off centre downstage audience left.
White hair, white nightgown, white socks.
Two metres to his left, same level, same height, standard lamp, skull-sized white globe, faintly lit. (3:453)

On the one hand, the "standard lamp" is the customary furniture of the bourgeois home, or, for that matter, of the stage at night. (What the British call a "standard lamp" Americans call a "floor lamp"). On the other hand, these stage directions insist on a homology between Speaker and lamp: this Speaker is the measure of that lamp, which shares his height and features a "skull-sized white globe." (All skulls are the same size? Grammar resists common sense here.) No less than with the tape recorder in *Krapp's Last Tape* or the camera in *Film* or the searchlight in *Play*, Beckett examines the interaction of Speaker and technology. Technology produces the possibility of speech; speech produces ghosts; technology produces ghosts? Such transitivity or dialectic is already at work in the very name "Speaker," designating as it does at once a simple designation connecting person and speech, a privileged term in poetics, and a mechanical device for the transmission of sound.

Many critics have now followed Hugh Kenner's lead and charted Beckett's intense and idiosyncratic engagement with technologies.[17] *A Piece of Monologue* almost comically rehearses central concerns and tropes of Beckett's career. It also marks a kind of culmination in his examination of technology. If, in *Krapp's Last Tape*, Beckett was a pioneer in scrutinizing the potential of a new recording technology, in *A Piece of Monologue* he examines a technological force so taken for second nature as almost to become invisible: artificial light. That is, a lamp and a match are also technologies. What this means in *A Piece of Monologue* is that artificial light, like other technological prostheses, produces ghosts. Speaker describes a nightly ritual where the sun sinks, dark gains, and, then, "faint light from standard lamp." There follows the narration of a particular night:

> And now. This night. Up at nightfall. Every nightfall. Faint light in room. Whence unknown. None from window. No. Next to none. No such thing as none. Gropes to window and stares out. Stands there staring out. Stock still staring out. Nothing stirring in the black vast. Gropes back in the end to where the lamp is standing. Was standing. When last went out. Loose matches in right-hand pocket. Strikes one on his buttock the way his father taught him. Takes off milk white globe and sets it down. Match goes out. Strikes a second as before. Takes off chimney. Smoke-clouded. Holds it in left hand. Match goes out. Strikes a third as before and sets it to wick. Puts back chimney. Match goes out. Puts back globe. Turns wick low. Backs away to edge of light and turns to face east. Blank wall. So nightly. Up. Socks. Nightgown. Window. Lamp. (3:454)

The narrated scenario at once describes the situation the audience views – the Speaker, solo, staring east at the fourth wall between him and audience – and stresses the temporal disjunction between actions narrated and words spoken: "And now" nothing happens but narration. The staging or narration of narration is one of Beckett's great preoccupations, but what concerns me especially here is the careful description of the nightly slapstick involving three matches. The letter of the narration plainly insists that three matches are necessary every night: "So nightly." The first and second matches are themselves short-lived lamps to make the globe and chimney visible in the dark: Speaker, in a long line of skeptics, cannot know the lamp is in its place until the first match is lit. The faint comedy in the deliberate ritual of lighting the lamp is then matched by its pointlessness: there is nothing to see.

What the lit lamp now makes visible is a wall:

> Covered with pictures once. Pictures of … he all but said of loved ones. Unframed. Unglazed. Pinned to wall with drawing-pins. All shapes and sizes. Down one after another. Gone. Torn to shreds and scattered. Strewn all over the floor. Not at one

sweep. No sudden fit of … no word. Ripped from the wall and torn to shreds one by one. Over the years. Years of nights. Nothing on the wall now but the pins. Not all. Some out with the wrench. Some still pinning a shred. So stands there facing blank wall. Dying on. No more no less. No. Less. Less to die. Ever less. Like light at nightfall. (3:454)

Beckett rigorously refuses to specify what sort of pictures Speaker destroys. (Beckett's French version, *"adapté de l'anglais par l'auteur"* and tantalizingly strange as ever, is in this respect consistent: "Images de —— il allait dire d'êtres chers.")[18] In a passage marked by disavowals, this refusal to name the kind of image belongs to a similar logic. If we understand the disavowal of love as a backhanded confession of love, if we understand the hesitation to name the emotion that inspired the "fit" behind the destruction of images as the repression of an all but acknowledged passion, "Pictures" might seem self-evidently to mean, simply, photographs. The *OED*'s fascinating definition of "picture" certainly supports such a reading: "With *of* or genitive. A portrait, now *esp.* a photograph."[19] These "pictures" were, simply, photos of "loved ones." But the Speaker's name for these images nevertheless suggests the imprecision that might lie in decoding too quickly. The colloquial translation of "photo" into "picture" is of course at work here, but this translation is not self-evidently a matter of synonymy. Is a "photo" a "picture"?

Speaker's name for these destroyed things points to the ideality that comes in once an image, photo or otherwise, becomes a "picture." Even absent, they function still:

Could once name them all. There was father. That grey void. There mother. That other. There together. Smiling. Wedding day. There all three. That grey blot. There alone. He alone. So on. Not now. Forgotten. All gone so long. Gone. Ripped off and torn to shreds. (3:454)

The fragments survive as "Thousand shreds under the bed with the dust and spiders" (3:455). Two hesitations meet here, then: "ghost" and "photo" alike appear to be censored or unnamable. This coincidence evokes the fatality in every photograph that Barthes so influentially detected. Indeed, the thirty-eighth section of *Camera Lucida* startlingly aligns with the section of *A Piece of Monologue* I have been examining. The section begins with a discussion of photographers as "agents of Death," ponders the transformation of photos into trash along the way, and ends with a meditation of the destruction of photographs as the destruction of "sometimes—how to put it?—love," a love exemplified by that between dead parents to which the surviving child is the last able to testify.[20] Even that hesitation and its hyphenated interruption recalls Beckett's ellipses. Barthes invokes "what Edgar Morin calls the 'crisis of death' beginning in the second half of the nineteenth century," and calls for an inquiry into "the anthropological place of Death and of the new image." "For death," writes Barthes,

must be somewhere in society; if it is no longer (or less intensely) in religion, it must be elsewhere; perhaps in this image which produces Death while trying to preserve life. Contemporary with the withdrawal of rites, Photography may correspond to the intrusion, in our modern society, of an asymbolic Death, outside of religion, outside of ritual, a kind of abrupt dive into literal Death. *Life / Death*: the paradigm is reduced to a simple click, the one separating the initial pose from the final print. (92)

To link the photograph according to Barthes to Beckett is made tempting by the seeming fatality that marks photos in Beckett. Barthes's notion of an "asymbolic Death" might identify something like the horizon of so much of Beckett's work: death, the thing itself, unadorned. But that notion is not only questionable in itself – questionable because it belongs to no human anthropology – but also only doubtfully fits the case of Beckett.[21] Yes, the map could not be more banal or a more worn symbol. But its banality is the result of its dull claim to permanence. If Beckett's lamp exists in historical time, perhaps death, too, is dated?

Before turning back to Beckett's work for theater, I'd like to return to the poem "Saint-Lô." As with another poem Beckett published in the *Irish Times*, "Dieppe, 193?," "Saint-Lô" has consistently been republished shorn of its date. "Saint-Lô 1945," to give the poem its original title, also appears with a variant that may smack of a censor's fear that "ghost-forsaken" sounded too much like "godforsaken." But do we need the dates to guess that "Saint-Lô" is a poem about deaths that have happened in historical time and may happen again in historical time, in a time that has forgotten its history? "Saint-Lô," quite the reverse of a poem about "asymbolic" death, treats the symbols that even or especially death does not escape. For is there anything more historical than death?

Internalizations

Sara Danius has argued with particular force that certain monuments of high modernist prose fiction, and especially *Ulysses*, incorporate technology's increasing mediation of the "matrices of perception."[22] Danius criticizes earlier criticism for its tendency to treat technology as external to high modernist representation, as forming a structure against which art defines itself. Danius, then, describes an opposition between the externality called technology and a field separate from it called literature, which her own analysis strives to overcome: "technology and modernist aesthetics should be understood as *internal* to one another" (11). The very grammar of her argument, however, indicates a problem: however internal to each other, however inseparable, "technology" and "modernist aesthetics" remain separate, a pair of fields that do not, simply, cohere to form a whole. We can speak of their being internal to each other but, however intimately allied, they retain their separate names.

Even if we grant Danius's claim that *Ulysses* renders "the immediacy of lived experience" in terms of the "matrices of perception" offered by technological modernity and her argument that Joyce understands the mediation of the "sensorium" by these technologies, these "matrices" remain media outside of literature and available for appropriation. The logic of externality is hard to avoid. This is not, I think, simply a matter of the intransigence of language, of the difficulty of shaping a grammar for the full internalization of the technological into experience. A literal insistence on a certain externality legible even where the spirit of an argument insists on internality suggests instead that no internalization will be so thorough as to erase the distinction between technology and the self, or technology and experience. Danius asks us to replace the notion of technology as "*prosthesis*" with "*aisthesis*," thus moving from externalization to internalization" (3). But this movement, subsuming art into experience, however mediated, reflects a desire to erase the very mediation Danius describes. If the internalization of technology were indeed complete, then mediated experience would be, simply, immediacy's new name.

Even granting Danius's argument that Joyce represents the saturation of experience by technologized modes of perception to an unprecedented degree – and granting, even, that such saturation might have become a norm – questions remain. What if this technologized norm includes unexamined privileges? Where and when was it a norm? Who gets to experience his vision as like that of a camera? The labor with which Beckett separated himself from Joyce is familiar. Beckett wrote for, but not about, the privileged urban audience familiar to our formulations of modernism.[23] If the privileged city dweller, that cosmopolitan subject Danius is hardly unique in assuming as the subject of modernism, *might* sometimes experience what were once prostheses as simply the immediate instruments (or "matrices") of perception, some of Beckett's characters are often alienated from even the seemingly simple technologies to which they have access. Recall, in *Godot*, Pozzo's lost watch – "A genuine half-hunter … with deadbeat escapement" (3:38) – or, in *Endgame*, the instruments Hamm describes in his first-person narration: a "thermometer" (3:127), followed by a "heliometer" (3:128), an "anemometer," and a "hygrometer" (3:129). The humor in this precision about portable and household machines stems in part from the audience's mystification, and the point of this mystification may be to put the audience in the place of those subject to the structural deprivations for which variable access to "technology" has long been and remains a crucial measure. Hamm narrates a meeting between a man who owns and knows how to read machines to measure every climactic condition – "zero by the hygrometer" (3:129) – and another whose only "possession" is the child he wants to give away. One of the ways Beckett revises Joyce, or, it may be, modernism more generally, is by representing alienations from technology. Far from a reactionary inability to recognize the extent to which subjectivity had become inseparable from technological mediations of various kinds, far from staging reductions in the world of things as simply a transhistorical philosophical project in the long wake of Descartes, Beckett's theatrical evacuations of the world of things at once acknowledge technology's alteration of the terrains of spectatorship and aesthetic experience, and the uneven access to the mediation of technology that modernism, and some accounts of modernism, may assume.

Lisa Gitelman has argued persuasively for the need to think specifically and locally about particular technologies:

it is as much of a mistake to write broadly of "the telephone," "the camera," or "the computer" as it is "the media," and of now – somehow, "the Internet" and "the Web"

– naturalizing or essentializing technologies as if they were unchanging, "immutable objects with given, self-defining properties" around which changes swirl, or to or from which history proceeds. Instead, it is better to specify telephones in 1890 in the rural United States, broadcast telephones in Budapest in the 1920s, or cellular, satellite, corded, and cordless landline telephones in North America at the beginning of the twenty-first century.[24]

A title speaks volumes here: *The Quiet Revolution: The Electrification of Rural Ireland, 1946–1976*.[25] It is only coincidence that Beckett began to write *A Piece of Monologue* in the year following Shiel's terminal date for this "quiet revolution." Nevertheless, this thirty-year history of postwar rural electrification suggests part of the force of Beckett's play. To return to Danius's terms, what Beckett's play and Shiel's history alike expose is a set of assumptions about the even development of internalization. Even – or especially? – the lamp is not among those "unchanging, 'immutable objects with given, self-defining properties' around which changes swirl, or to or from which history proceeds." The lamp, that is, is not yet fully internalized. But to follow Gitelman is to ask: What lamp, in what place, in what time? Or, to use Beckett's phrase, what is a "standard lamp"?

Here it is worth recalling that for M. H. Abrams the lamp is the figure for a turn to expressive poetry associated with Romanticism: where the mirror figures a mimetic replication of the world, the lamp figures, so to speak, the light cast by the poet on the world represented.[26] It is, Abrams writes, "a radiant projector which makes a contribution to the objects it perceives" (vi). When Abrams is thinking of the lamp, he imagines a peculiar kind of instrument, what Bachelard called "the spirit that watches over every room"[27]: that is, in the more prosaic rendering of Wolfgang Schivelbusch, "the domestic oil-lamp" (28). Schivelbusch describes the psychic disruptions that followed the development of gaslights served by sources outside the home: suddenly the illumination of the home – earlier the site of independent sources of light – becomes linked to a system necessary to this light. Schivelbusch notes that many would turn off the gas at night so as to "restore the household's original autonomy for a few hours" (38). One might observe that, given the need for fuel, the autonomy of the household was always something of a mirage, but the important point is that Abrams's Romantic poet, and Schivelbusch's "paterfamilias" (38) shutting off the gas, both imagine an economy in which the illumination of the lamp needs, or needed, only what the inside can provide. The oil-lamp has figured both the autonomy of the household and the autonomy of the poet.

Abrams and Schivelbusch allow us, then, to specify what might easily pass as something more self-evident than it is in *A Piece of Monologue*. As is frequently true of Beckett's plays, this brief piece locates history in what might be mistaken for "immutable objects with given, self-defining properties." The contrast between Speaker and standard lamp no doubt returns us to some of Beckett's central epistemological concerns. Does the reduction of consciousness to the thinking mind leave Descartes's cogito as its solid residue? Is the mind Abrams's "radiant projector," or is it something else entirely, something more dependent on the externalities it seeks to dismiss than Descartes might have believed? I will not rehearse scholarly treatments of Beckett's ornery philosophical investments and disavowals here, but the essential point, that Beckett is concerned with the central philosophical problem (at least since Descartes) of thinking about consciousness, is important. From the pairing of Speaker and standard lamp in the opening stage direction onwards, Beckett bluntly presses on the parallel between narrating mind and lamp. Schivelbusch's history of the movement from the oil-lamp to gas lighting points to Abrams's reliance on a certain kind of lamp, without which his figure for autonomous poetic radiant projection cannot function. Beckett's play does something similar: Speaker describes the laborious ritual of lighting an oil-lamp, as though staging as a refrain a comic version of Abrams's privileged figure for autonomous creation: "Lights lamp as described" (3:456). Further, this deliberate return to the lamp will almost necessarily raise questions in performance, questions about the difference between the lamp Speaker describes and the lamp the audience sees, the "standard lamp" that is, on the face of it, so similar to Speaker. The gap between the stillness of Speaker and the actions Speaker narrates is one of the central devices of *A Piece of Monologue*. This gap extends beyond actions to things. Is this lamp to be lit with a match? Is it a "ghost light"? Beckett's French rendition is explicit on this point: the lamp is an oil-lamp. Artificial ghost of oil-lamps, the electrical source of the onstage lamp belies the parallel the text so vigorously establishes.

The Phantom of the Lamp

CLOV [*harshly*]   When old Mother Pegg asked you for oil for her lamp
and you told her to get out to hell, you knew what
was happening then, no?
[*Pause*]
You know what she died of, Mother Pegg? Of darkness.
HAMM [*feebly*]   I hadn't any.
CLOV [*as before*]   Yes, you had.
[*Pause*]
HAMM   Have you the glass?
CLOV   It's clear enough as it is. (3:146)

In this passage from *Endgame*, Hamm and Clov briefly consider the events that have left their world as it is. Hamm recalls nothing: "Absent, always. It all happened without me. I don't know what's happened" (3:146). Clov invokes the death of Mother Pegg, then, as a singular example that might disturb Hamm's more general amnesia. In this case, Clov implies, there is no not knowing what has happened: Hamm's withholding of oil leaves her in the darkness of which she dies. Hamm's feeble disowning of responsibility convinces no one, least of all Clov, but certainty that Hamm withheld oil does not explain what can only sound metaphorical: death of darkness, as though darkness were a communicable disease. To blame Hamm for this death does not alter the obscurity of the diagnosis – in French it is "Obscurité" that kills her (3S 300) – but it does point to a responsibility that even Hamm briefly acknowledges: "All those I might have helped" (3:141, 3S 292).

To return to McLuhan's terms, then, Mother Pegg's oil-lamp is an extension that has become, simply, necessary to life, which is to say, no longer an extension at all. In a play crowded with the necessaries without which, it turns out, one can nevertheless live – for instance, "painkiller" (3:143) – Mother Pegg's light is an exception. And it is important to stress Beckett's insistence on the particular technology here: Mother Pegg's lamp is a step beyond the "Grey light" (3:91) that illuminates *Endgame* – that is to say, the lighting designer's simulation of the dim "natural" light admitted by the two windows of their refuge – and if Hamm might once have had oil that he could have given to her, there is no sign that he has any to give now. (There is no lamp among *Endgame*'s props.)

A Piece of Monologue, in its contrary way belonging to the long tradition Abrams describes, asks: Where does the light come from? Early in the play, Speaker describes light before the lighting of the lamp: "Up at nightfall. Every nightfall. Faint light in room. Whence unknown. None from window. No. Next to none. No such thing as none" (3:454). The ideal of total darkness informing this passage is a corollary to the Romantic ideal of absolutely self-generating radiance. That is, Beckett's negation of the absence of light looks like the partner of the Romantic fantasy of light that has only itself for fuel. The absence of darkness might be ascribed to modernity's pollution of the sky by omnipresent light. In this context a comparison of the closing of *A Piece of Monologue* to that of *Solo* is illuminating:

The dead and gone. The dying and the going. From the word go. The word begone. Such as the light going now. Beginning to go. In the room. Where else? Unnoticed by him staring beyond. The globe alone. Not the other. The unaccountable. From nowhere. On all sides nowhere. Unutterably faint. The globe alone. Alone gone. (3:458)

Les mort et en allées. La vie qu-ils y mircnt. Dès le mot va. Le mot va-t'en. Telle la lumière maintenant. En voie de s'en aller. Dans la chambre. Où d'autre? Sans que s'en aperçoive l'oeil tout à l'au delà. Seule celle du globe. Pas l'autre. L'inexplicable. De nulle part. De toutes parts de nulle part. Seule celle du globe. Seule elle en allée.[28]

One phrase here, "La vie qu'ils y mirent," has no equivalent in Beckett's English text. It might roughly be translated, "The life that they stare at there."[29] If Beckett's text seems to encourage a one-to-one correspondence between Speaker and lamp and between Speaker and the object of narration on the one hand, on the other it consistently complicates the question of where Speaker's others, the "dying and the going," might find themselves. Nothing better embodies this uncertainty than that particle, "y," which so economically designates place. But where is this place? Who is staring at what life, and where? Similarly, "Sans que s'en aperçoive l'oeil tout à l'au delà" does not precisely translate "Unnoticed by him staring beyond." That unlocatable eye, "l'oeil," seems at once not to be perceived and not to perceive itself; like the "staring" in English, it might belong to Speaker or to some other eye. The grammatical reflexivity of French emphasizes the text's concern with seeing and being seen. In this way as in others, Beckett reprises a concern that spans his career.[30] To the eye of the Speaker and the light of the globe corresponds a light without source and an eye belonging to an unseen and unknown seer.

This dynamic leads into the heart of Beckett's experiments with self-knowledge and knowledge of others, with seeing and being seen. Perhaps no other corpus so thoroughly investigates the ways that self-consciousness involves the production of a spectral observer at once internal and external to the self. Beckett's engagement with the media and history of this production of interiority has, however, received less attention. (The problem with many philosophical accounts of Beckett, I believe, is that they are too often predicated on the erasure of these contexts.) To return once more to *Solo*:

L'oeil collé à la vitre dévore cette première nuit. S'en détourne enfin face à la chambre obscure. Là lentement une main fantôme. Tenant droit un tortillon de papier enflammé. (34)

Eyes to the small pane gaze at that first night. Turn from it in the end to face the darkened room. There in the end slowly a faint hand. Holding aloft a lighted spill. (3:456)

Solo introduces its "fantôme" long before *A Piece of Monologue* introduces its "ghost." This "fantôme," however, rather than a turn away from the ghostly letter of *A Piece of Monologue*, glosses its spectral logic. Why "fantôme," rather than other available French ghosts, rather than "revenant," "esprit," "spectre"? The English already suggests the alienation of Speaker from that "faint hand" that becomes an object in the visual field. The French "fantôme" stresses the ghostliness of this hand, but also introduces the medical term equivalent to the English "phantom limb." As with that eye, glued to the pane, "L'oeil collé à la vitre," *Solo* emphasizes the migration of limbs and organs outside the body. The sensation of the presence of an amputated limb stresses the logic of ghostliness here. This living hand, unmoving, held towards no one, becomes a phantom. The difference between the minima of the fragmentary present-tense narration and the stillness of the body onstage conjures a phantasm of spectral movement that might have belonged to this body.

Recall Schivelbusch's scene of the bourgeois homeowner cutting off the connection to the gas supply in order to assure the autonomy of the private home. In *Solo*, the specificity of gaslight, "un lampadaire à pétrole" (29), erases the ambiguity of the source of the standard lamp's fuel. Beckett evokes a technological shift so slow as not to be recognized: the fall back to the oil-lamp also evokes the desire to produce a space shielded from the outside. Speaker rises at dark so as to be in control of the sources of light, and in the light of that lamp destroys images that retain traces of his disavowed cathexes even in their absence. "No such thing as no light" (3:456). "Faint light in room. Whence unknown" (3:455). In *Solo*, the provenance of this light becomes stranger still: "Faible lumière dans la chambre. Indiciblement faible. D'où mystère" (33). This "ghost light," product as much of the electric light that almost illuminates the stage as of the oil-lamp the stage simulates, marks the modernity of Beckett's ghosts. That that "ghost light" is also a long-standing theatrical tradition suggests, too, the strange temporalities of Beckett's histories of ghosts and of theater, where ghosts come after electric light.

In *Scare Quotes from Shakespeare*, I examined the fortunes of the mid-nineteenth-century inventor Henry Dircks.[31] Dircks invented a phantasmagoria, strictly speaking an apparatus for the production of ghostly images onstage, in the hopes that this device would serve the purposes of enlightenment. Knowledge of the workings of the mechanism would produce an audience able to see through the illusions of less reputable and less capable illusionists, or so Dircks claimed to hope. Dircks's machine was, instead, taken over by the entrepreneur who made his name with it, Henry Pepper, and Pepper's Ghost produced what were, by all accounts, some of the most successfully spooky stage ghosts in theater history. Dircks himself felt he had been undone by quasi-supernatural agencies. The failure of this production of ghosts for the purposes of enlightenment, I argued, was symptomatic of the tendency of technologies of disenchantment to produce its opposite, re-enchantment.[32] Beckett's drama, and *A Piece of Monologue* and *Solo* in particular, is legible as a sequel to this history. If Pepper's Ghost prefigures the mediated splashes of a later era, Beckett's ghosts are the spirits of *slow* popular culture. Beckett's reduction of media to the lamp is a blunt test of the tendency of technologies of "enlightenment," these bright extensions of the selves, to produce what enlightenment is supposed to have banished: ghost light.

NOTES

1   Thanks to Lois Beckett for research assistance and to the Radcliffe Institute for Advanced Study for making her assistance and my work on this essay possible. I also thank the American Council of Learned Societies for a Burkhardt fellowship in support of the work in progress of which this essay forms a part. I have also benefited from responses at the modernism seminar at the Humanities Center at Harvard organized by John Paul Riquelme and Peter Nohrnberg and, as always, from Virginia Jackson.

2   Eric Hobsbawn, *The Age of Extremes: The Short Twentieth Century, 1914–1991* (London: Michael Joseph, 1994), 289.

3   James Knowlson, *Damned to Fame: The Life of Samuel Beckett* (New York: Simon & Schuster, 2006), 295. For a scintillating portrait of gleaning and other varieties of scrounging, which includes a relevant discussion of French law, see Agnès Varda, *The Gleaners and I* (Ciné Tamaris, 2000).

4   This is not to say that popular culture has not in certain ways claimed Beckett. My focus here, however, falls more on Beckett's registration of experience shared by many people rather than on popular culture as such.

5   Samuel Beckett, *The Grove Centenary Edition, Vol. 3* (New York: Grove, 2006), 54–55. Except where noted, all quotations from Beckett in English follow the four-volume Grove Centenary Edition, with volume preceding page number. Except where noted, all quotations from Beckett in French and German are from Samuel Beckett, *Dramatische Dichtungen in drei Sprachen* (Frankfurt am Main: Suhrkamp, 1981), abbreviated 3S.

6   Virginia Jackson's *Dickinson's Misery: A Theory of Lyric Reading* (Princeton:

Princeton University Press, 2005) and conversation with the author have informed my understanding of the history of the lyric.

7   Joseph Roach, "'All the Dead Voices': The Landscape of Famine in *Waiting for Godot*," in *Land/Scape/Theater*, ed. Elinor Fuchs and Una Chaudhuri (Ann Arbor: University of Michigan Press, 2002), 87.

8   Marvin Carlson, *The Haunted Stage: The Theatre as Memory Machine* (Ann Arbor: University of Michigan Press, 2001); Alice Rayner, *Ghosts: Death's Double and the Phenomena of Theatre* (Minneapolis: University of Minnesota Press, 2006).

9   Ruby Cohn, "Ghosting through Beckett," *Samuel Beckett Today/Aujourd'hui* 2 (1993): 1–2.

10   John Pilling, *A Samuel Beckett Chronology* (Houndmills: Palgrave Macmillan, 2006), 105.

11   Eoin O'Brien, *The Beckett Country: Samuel Beckett's Ireland* (Dublin: Black Cat Press in association with Faber & Faber, 1986). For other discussions of "Saint-Lô," see Lawrence Harvey, *Samuel Beckett: Poet & Critic* (Princeton: Princeton University Press, 1970), 179–82, and Marjorie Perloff, "'In Love with Hiding': Samuel Beckett's War," *Iowa Review* 35 (Spring 2005): 101–102.

12   Bob Dylan, "Visions of Johanna," http://www.bobdylan.com/#/songs/visions-johanna; Allen S. Weiss, *Phantasmic Radio* (Durham: Duke University Press, 1995); Gilberto Perez, *The Material Ghost: Films and Their Medium* (Baltimore: Johns Hopkins University Press, 1998).

13   Marshall McLuhan, *Understanding Media: The Extensions of Man* (Cambridge, MA: MIT Press, 1994), 8.

14   Theodor W. Adorno, *Minima Moralia*, trans. E. F. N. Jephcott (London: New Left Books, 1974), 50.

15   Phil Baker, "Ghost Stories: Beckett and the Literature of Introjection," *Journal of Beckett Studies* 5, no. 1–2 (Autumn, 1995): 39–65; Graham Fraser, "'No More than Ghosts Make': The Hauntology and Gothic Minimalism of Beckett's Late Work," in *Gothic and Modernism: Essaying Dark Literary Modernity*, ed. John Paul Riquelme (Baltimore: Johns Hopkins University Press, 2008); Jean-Michel Rabaté, "Beckett's Ghosts and Fluxions," *Samuel Beckett Today/Aujourd'hui* 5 (1996): 23–40.

16   The lighting designer Neil Peter Jampolis writes in an email: "The ghost light is still very much in use. For as long as I've been in the theatre, I've only known it as a safety measure, although the more romantic interpretation is certainly appealing. More to do now with insurance, I'm afraid. Every proscenium house I've ever worked in, on every continent, uses one – even when they put up a barrier at the apron to prevent falls. It's as much job insurance for the house electrician as anything. He has to stay until everyone's gone. Then he puts the light out onstage and goes home. Some overtime there as well."

17   Hugh Kenner, *The Mechanic Muse* (New York: Oxford University Press, 1987), 83–105.

18   Samuel Beckett, *Solo: Catastophe et autres dramaticules* (Paris: Minuit, 1982), 27–31.

19   *Oxford English Dictionary*, 1.c. And the OED definition for "portrait" further suggests that these images are not quite portraits: "*spec.* A drawing or painting of a person, often mounted and framed for display, esp. one of the face or head and shoulders; (also) an engraving, photograph, etc., in a similar style. (Now the usual sense.)" (1.b.). That is to say, unmounted, unframed, and "unglazed," these images are unusual portraits.

20   Roland Barthes, *Camera Lucida: Reflections on Photography*, trans. Richard Howard (New York: Hill and Wang, 1981), 92–94.

21   For a brilliant anthropology of particular practices surrounding death that has informed this essay, see Neni Panourgiá, *Fragments of Death, Fables of Identity: An Athenian Anthropography* (Madison: University of Wisconsin Press, 1995).

22   Sara Danius, *The Senses of Modernism: Technology, Perception, and Aesthetics* (Ithaca: Cornell University Press, 2002), 23.

23   The classic account here is Arno J. Mayer, *The Persistence of the Old Regime: Europe to the Great War* (New York: Pantheon, 1981).

24   Lisa Gitelman, *Always Already New: Media, History, and the Data of Culture* (Cambridge, MA: MIT Press, 2006), 8.

25   Michael J. Shiel, *The Quiet Revolution: The Electrification of Rural Ireland, 1946–1976* (Dublin: O'Brien Press, 1984).

26   M. H. Abrams, *The Mirror and the Lamp: Romantic Theory and the Critical Tradition* (New York: Norton, 1958). In a wonderfully suggestive and wide-ranging essay, Alan Ackerman anticipates this link: "If the Romantics replaced the mirror with the lamp, Beckett denies the lamp's efficacy" (424). See Ackerman, "Samuel Beckett's *Spectres du Noir*: The Being of Painting and the Flatness of *Film*," *Contemporary Literature* 44, no. 3 (2003): 399–441.

27   Quoted in Wolfgang Schivelbusch, *Disenchanted Night: The Industrialisation of Light in the Nineteenth Century*, trans. Angela Davies (Oxford: Berg, 1988), 28.

28   Beckett, *Solo*, 37.

29   Thanks to Mirabelle Ordinaire for correspondence about the French text.

30   See Peggy Phelan, "Lessons in Blindness from Samuel Beckett," *PMLA* 119, no. 5 (October 2004): 1279–1288.

31   Martin Harries, *Scare Quotes From Shakespeare: Marx, Keynes, and the Language of Reenchantment* (Stanford: Stanford University Press, 2000).

32   For a fuller account of Dircks and Pepper's Ghost, see chapter one of *Scare Quotes From Shakespeare*. In addition to the secondary material cited there, see Tom Gunning, "To Scan a Ghost: The Ontology of Mediated Vision," *Grey Room* 26 (Winter 2007): 94–127.

Chapter 3

Uncanny Marxism: Or, Do Androids Dream of Electric Lenin?

Peter Hitchcock

It is not much fun being a ghost. Unfortunately for Marxism much of its spectral promise has been compromised by its historical substantiation. The ghost, however, persists but this may be more than a nostalgic remnant, especially given its critical materiality in an understanding of contemporary capitalism. The idea for this essay began as an investigation of the concept of "world" as it informs a reading of global capital but, as a sign that the vocation of the public intellectual is confined to infinite regress (or perhaps, digress), I want to offer instead a prolegomenon to that concept, a logic of critique that lurks, haunts if you will, in a somewhat odd collocation of political, historical, and theoretical narratives. These could include one that leads from the worldliness of Marx and Engels in their effervescent manifesto to the prospect of worldliness in the equally prescient work of Said. Another would account for that symptomatic subculture of Marxism after 1989 that says all we have left is the specter haunting Europe and radicalism is as much about séance as it is about socialism in the present. A third trajectory leads from this spectral sclerosis to something a little more kinetic in the strangely familiar and has to do with the subject of automata for Marxism, bodies of Marxism, let us say, the better to understand the ghost in its shell: this is the place where my thesis lies, around the future of Marxism as a critical spirit, and it is a bridge to the second half of the discussion announced in the subtitle. The argument will place special emphasis on the term "like Lenin" and will, I hope, revivify only what is necessary to understand the struggle over "world" as a political imperative. Indeed, it is precisely at that point when "world" becomes automatic that the prehistory of automata uncannily undoes our measured allegiance to its assumption. In the spirit of Jameson's call for anti-anti-Utopianism the polemic may whisper anti-anti-Leninism of a sort, but the kind that finds Lenin himself strangely familiar or *Unheimlich* in the present.

Like Lenin? What's to like? What's not to like? Let us think of this first in terms of simile and what is proximate. A few years ago I embarked upon an uncanny sojourn. I gave back-to-back lectures in Beijing and Moscow and decided it offered a great opportunity to consider the husks of communism, the shells of my belief, in the form of two celebrated cadavers, Mao Zedong and Vladimir Ilyich Lenin. I approached my task with eerie trepidation. I had an easy answer for why Marxism-Leninism bred compulsive mummification but nothing quite prepared me for the shock of seeing my longtime heroes in the "flesh." Outside Mao's Mausoleum I joined maybe three hundred Chinese peasants and a few European students of Goth waiting for an audience with the round person from Shaoshan. Several of the peasants rented bouquets of plastic flowers to lay a few feet before his glass sarcophagus and once I saw the Great Leader I wished that I had had some flowers in hand. I liked the Mao Mausoleum – it was appropriately rendered as kitsch and as tatty as Mao's past could be. The Mausoleum store sold all manner of chotchky: there were packs of Mao cigarettes with no health warning except, ironically, for the picture of Mao himself; there were Mao lighters that when opened played the "East is Red" (which now perhaps only refers to the sarcophagus across the Korean border); there were Mao talismen to be hung from taxicab mirrors to ward off the strong possibility of hitting a cyclist (an everyday event in Beijing); and there were Mao t-shirts in suspiciously large sizes that opined "We miss you Chairman Mao." The Great Leader was bathed in light while all around *waidiren* (outsiders or non-residents) placed the plastic flowers before him. Once deposited, a scruffy uniformed chap would dash in, grab the floral simulacra and scramble outside for other punters to express this affective moment of *Maore* (Mao fever). We bustled about Mao as we would attempting to get into Beijing's main railway station. Pushing and shoving was no shame: it told of our vital humanity, our collectivity, our responsive co-experiencing, and a certain floating signification in the meaning of the mob. Mao was more porcelain than porcine and seemed about as organic as those flowers. He was heavily made up (a political truism I suppose) and reminded me of those wonderful paintings by Li Shan, who renders Mao as an erotic object with lipstick and his mole as a beauty spot (given Mao's alleged bisexuality his dead delectability was intensified). Nobody was allowed to look for very long or take pictures but in my mind's eye I had a snapshot of a figure eviscerated not by the desire for preservation but by the much greater historical force of commodification. One always detects the merest of grins on Mao's face, not because he knows he did all of the horrible acts attributed to his name, and not because he always believed more in his power than he did in his peasantry, but because he truly taunts erasure. Nobody over in the new and luxurious and bizarrely named Yosemite gated community loses sleep over Mao's carcass in Tiananmen Square; yet however empty his signifier he is nevertheless a ticklish trace. Caught between reminder and remainder he is a devilish doll: in Mao we recognize the measure of *méconnaissance* itself. It is not pretty but it laughs at attachment. It persists merely to accentuate aphanisis; the fading not of Maoism (Mao smiles also at Nepal) but of a certain subject reason. I was in awe of this special effect as much as I was of the peasants' sincere devotion.

The aura of affect was much more difficult to sense in Moscow where a couple of goosestepping guards had no time for the floral faithful. They were worried that we, Lenin's visitors, were not appropriately attired and I wondered about those peasant rags in Beijing. There was still the same air of materialism as mannequin, a reduction to exchange highlighted by Lenin's companion across Red Square, the renovated GUM, which my Moscovite friend informed me was the largest washing machine in the world (that is, by selling luxury goods at hugely inflated prices it attracts bad money that then becomes good: corruption gets a good rinsing at GUM and the Mafia and any number of oligarchs get baubles into the bargain including, by the way, the chance to be embalmed "like Lenin"). Lenin maintains his composure. He seemed a lot less waxy than Mao and of course more gaunt, yet his glow was warmer. He had no smile, in part because he wanted to be cremated and interred in St. Petersburg but Stalin had other plans. If socialism had no savior it at least had a saint and the bending light of social contradiction could be outshone by the cult of personality and rigid monumentalism. All these were my reminders as I stared into the shell of Lenin; he was frightening because his contours had been made available. The revelation of his body is simultaneously his *heimlich* state, the promise of a secret, the canny, the magical. The doll itself is *unheimlich*, my strangely familiar friend, my proximate other, the comforting cadaver. Here is the genius of revolution: the preservation of likeness.

It takes Olympian efforts (an operative term) to maintain Lenin and, whatever difference I noticed in the commodity logic of Mao and Lenin, the responsibility for their preservation falls on the same collection of mad scientists, the Dr. Frankensteins and Dr. Praetoriouses known as the Mausoleum Group (these purveyors of pickling are also responsible for "Uncle Ho" as in Ho Chi Minh, the third member of our ticklish trio). Every eighteen months Lenin is removed from his glass box and he takes a thirty-day bath in glycerol and potassium acetate. The glycerol is primarily to encourage hydration and plasticity but remember too its importance in the production of dynamite. Potassium acetate is also a conditioner, although mainly for textiles. It is a catalyst in the making of all kinds of polyurethane (the painting, perhaps, that Li Shan sees in Mao) and of course in the manufacture of glass crystal. If we were to eat Lenin he would taste rather rubbery and sweet. All of the major organs were removed. No one has revealed the fate of his heart but, as we know, his brain became the subject of an intense project to analyze genius, the very soul of socialism and thus Lenin's brain is preserved on over 20,000 dissection slides. Lenin's genitals are intact, as are Mao's, and, because of the delicate nature of the tissue, they are handled with extreme care. During Stalin's time the scientists attached to the Mausoleum Group were accorded all kinds of perks yet several were eventually imprisoned (incredibly on suspicion of spying; on what, you are free to imagine). At one point a flower of mold appeared on Lenin's right cheek, much greater than the empathic eruption of Mao's mole, and the group feared for their lives until one, Illya Zbarsky (the son of Boris Zbarsky, the original Lenin embalmer), managed to remove it with cotton swabs of bleach. Lenin was initially dressed in military garb but now, every three years, he gets a new suit made from his favorite Swiss fabrics, perhaps picked out at GUM. During the Second

World War Lenin was clandestinely removed from Moscow in an elaborate game of hide and seek from German bombers. In this operation Lenin was known only as "Object No. 1" and this object status, with its conceptual ambivalence, is crucial to the Marxist uncanny and its meaning for afflicted powers. The fate of Stalin's body was long since settled, and his remains remain hidden outside the Kremlin's walls. The fight over Lenin's shell has been protracted and has intensified since the collapse of the Soviet Union. Yeltsin tried on several occasions to have Lenin bundled off to St. Petersburg but the Communists defeated at the White House drew a pentagon around their Lenin until Putin came along to promote exhumation of another order. My point is not that you measure the winds of change in the post-socialist world by what happens to these Dead Reds, but there is a particular process of identification at play that animates their otherwise ghostly semblance.

Since 1989 – the year socialist states did not so much wither away as dissipate, like ether, in an instant – much leftist theory has been devoted to the life elixir in ectoplasm for, the logic goes, there is an indefatigable spirit in Marxist anti-capitalism that does not need the shell of actual existence for ghostly transubstantiation to occur. Derrida's *Specters of Marx* remains the most stunning contribution to this metaleptic autopsy (since Marx's *Gespenstergeschichte* haunts before the life of that which has putatively expired) and, while I have deep reservations about its contributions to Marxism, *Specters of Marx* still has the ability to conjure warring spirits on the political purpose of the revenant and its register in Marxian texts.[1] Not all people procreate, but every specter spawns and Derrida's lectures at Riverside in 1993 quickly bred collections by Magnus and Cullenberg, Sprinker, special issues of journals, and various strains of hauntology (including Gordon's and one by me).[2] I am not going to cover this ground again; I am interested, however, in Derrida's friendly reminder that Freud, in his essay on the "Uncanny," decides not to punctuate his exegesis with a ghost story because "the uncanny in it is too much intermixed with what is purely gruesome and is in part overlaid by it"; that is, the ghost story, *es spukt*, is the most striking example of the *Unheimlich* because it directly refers to our repressive compulsion about death.[3] Derrida repays the elision and notes that the subtitle of his address could be "Marx – *das Unheimliche*." Freud comes to the uncanny by writing about Hoffmann; Derrida comes to Marx by writing about Shakespeare. And there I was, pondering the cadavers of Mao and Lenin in all their uncanniness but their ghosts were nowhere to be seen, nor still their literary alibi. In the spirit of the supplement (and the supplicant) we must unpack the *Unheimlich* further to avoid the impress of pure *méconnaissance* – the ability to literalize the spectral as haunting. This latter tendency is perhaps best captured by the first English translation of the *Communist Manifesto* which appeared in a journal called the *Red Republican* in 1850 and began: "A frightful hobgoblin stalks through Europe!" Many of us are seduced by mourning but we cannot mourn this because, whatever its injunction, its trauma is located elsewhere in the name of communism and whatever it named it named also the bullet, the noose, the sword, the cannon, and the ice pick. No, I did not mourn in the presence of Mao and Lenin – there was something in the trauma of likeness itself that spurred me: "Ein Gespenst geht um in Europa – das Gespenst des Kommunismus." *Des*, of, that was it – that which is *of* disturbs, not that which is *is*. The uncanny in Marxism is not to be found in the horror of haunting. No. The disturbance in extent rests in the depth of the familiar, in the capacity to interrupt the identification as if some secret self was at stake.

Denisov-Nikolsky, one of the Mausoleum Group, ponders this in terms of reverence, and recalls shaking when he first worked on Lenin: "Not every expert is allowed to restore such treasured historical objects, like a Raphael or a Rembrandt. Those who do it, we tremble. I feel a great responsibility in my hands."[4] Obviously, his reverence is privileged and comes with the fear to which I have already alluded. Few others can feel this professional obligation and yet, if we reduce the presencing of Mao and Lenin to adulation, to hero-worship, then likeness itself is threatened, cheated by awe, cowered by power.

Derrida suggests that a secret always makes you tremble and this is as much about the responsibility to its charge as it is to the content of the secret itself. Denisov-Nikolsky shivers from the fear that comes with this responsibility, in part because he risks becoming the state he preserves. I would like to argue, however, that the secret is the strange familiarity of attachment and we tremble in the knowledge of this likeness. Denisov-Nikolsky certainly liked Lenin and the Lenin he maintained looked like Lenin, but the aura of approximation, the uncanny, the like Lenin-ness if you will, has a history at least as long as Marxism and its No. 1 object, capital, which paradoxically bears likeness only in relation and not as object *qua* object (so the Lenin of this discussion is always beside himself, doubled in the secret of likeness itself). This is also why Freud withholds the example of the ghost in his elaboration of the uncanny and instead begins with a suitably Derridean undoing of the secret of the *Unheimlich* in the *Heimlich*, in the similarity of one meaning to its supposed opposite so that they, in effect, coincide. We are concerned with the oppressed rather than the repressed, even as we maintain the injunction that after 1989 Marxism obsessed about its remains with the assumption that what remains, remains to come back like some hapless Casper with the giggles. Freud draws on Jentsch (without of course endorsing his position) that the uncanny exists for one where it is not certain the apparently animate is alive and the reverse, where the lifeless object may well indeed be animate. The examples in mind are waxwork figures, dolls, and automata. You say I knew Mao and Lenin were dead before my gaze, but was it merely confirmation I sought in proximity and was this death what the Mausoleum Group was charged with preserving?

Likeness is all. Freud is piqued by Jentsch to read E. T. A. Hoffmann's "The Sand-Man," but whereas Jentsch is primarily interested in Nathaniel's "blind love," let us say, of Olympia (hence Olympian), a life-like doll, Freud spies the uncanny in the figure of the Sand-Man himself, who tears out children's eyes (or rather, the sand causes the eyes to leap from their sockets and the Sand-Man subsequently collects the eyes to feed his beak-mouthed children). Nathaniel, as a child, works this traumatic tale into a substantive event and this, psychologically, prepares his eyes for trickery with regard to Olympia. Spalanzani has made himself a wooden daughter, Olympia, an automaton whose clockwork movements are precise enough to invoke Nathaniel's affection. But the eyes are the handiwork of Coppola, he who seems to be the Sand-Man of Nathaniel's youthful trauma and all this seeming precipitates eventually a fit of madness and Nathaniel's suicide, punctuated by the cry "fine eyes, fine eyes." Coppola has plucked out Olympia's eyes and kept the eyeless doll for himself and it is the possibility of her reappearance, or his, which spurs Nathaniel's demise. Freud, in this example, will of course push the function of infantile disorder, including the castration complex, in the experience of the uncanny (a particularly ironic emphasis, as Derrida avers, because it hinges on the literary that Freud, in the same essay, suspects is less than convincing on this point). A second conclusion Freud draws from this and other examples is that the uncanny also exists in the reappearance of primitive beliefs assumed to have been surmounted. Essentially, he drops Jentsch's initial point about dolls and automata yet this too has a deep structure in the consternation of semblance and is operative not just in the trembling that must preserve Lenin, but in the sense that what is not there is the subsumption of the human in technological extension. Automata are not just the look of the human in this example but the very process by which the labor of being human can be extended by extraction. Olympia is an automaton whose machinery is dedicated to likeness: the human shell forms the basis of an overinvestment not in the human but in the process that gives it object status. There is certainly room in this scheme for an analysis both of infantile disorder and of the re-emergence of primitive belief, but these are of secondary importance here. We will briefly leave Lenin and Mao in repose and ponder the meaning of automata in the reading of capital.

Marx, in *Capital: Volume One* clearly understood that mechanization *by* man meant the mechanization *of* man (where he must himself be an automaton, as Marx puts it) and thus he quotes from and of course criticizes Andrew Ure, who wrote of the factory as "a vast automaton, *composed of various mechanical and intellectual organs, acting in uninterrupted concert for the production of a common object*, all of them being *subordinated* to a self-regulated *moving force*."[5] Marx loves the fact that Ure wears his ideology on his sleeve and delights in his struggle to overcome the contradictions it lays bare. Ure contends that the major difficulty was "the *discipline* necessary to induce human beings to renounce their desultory habits of work, and to *identify themselves with the unvarying regularity of the complex automaton*" (549). He suggests that the capitalist must be diligent in acculturating children to this end because as "undeveloped human beings" they may be more easily broken in to become organs of the automaton. This diligence is increasingly nurtured in sweatshops all over the globe. Yet, at stake here is not just the diminution of labor specialization, labor capacity, or the intensification of alienation that accompanies it, but how to conceive labor in the absence of its body and, conversely, how to conceive the body in the absence of its labor. In *Capital* Marx develops this sense of the automaton and the automatic around his critique of the machine. Thus, in Chapter Fifteen we have: "A system of machinery, whether it reposes on the mere co-operation of similar machines, as in weaving, or on a combination of different machines, as in spinning, constitutes in itself a huge automaton, whenever it is driven by a self-acting prime mover" (502). He continues:

An organized system of machines, to which motion is communicated by the transmitting mechanism from a central automaton, is the most developed form of production by machinery. Here we have, in the place of the isolated machine, a mechanical monster whose body fills whole factories, and whose demon power, at first veiled under the slow and measured motions of his giant limbs, at length breaks out into the fast and furious whirl of his countless working organs. (503)

The machine has indeed taken on human form, and one of uncanny, monstrous proportions. Yet there is simultaneously, and in the same concept, a perspicuous reduction in scale to the very human who is, as it were, the dollmaker:

In the first place, in the form of machinery, the implements of labour become automatic, things moving and working independent of the workman. They are thenceforth an industrial *perpetuum mobile*, that would go on producing forever, did it not meet with certain natural obstructions in the weak bodies and the strong wills of its human attendants. The automaton, as capital, and because it is capital, is endowed, in the person of the capitalist, with intelligence and will; it is therefore animated by the longing to reduce to a minimum the resistance offered by that repellent yet elastic natural barrier, man." (256)

We have here several interpretations of the automaton whose interrelation is itself uncanny: shells of socialism, bodies without organs, bodies as machines, mechanized bodies, systems of automata, and capital itself as an automaton. The automaton is the function of likeness, but if it were simply a mimetic faculty it would not make us tremble. We can accommodate this likeness as a child will cradle his doll. The disturbance in likeness Marx anthropomorphizes in the factory becomes uncanny when all that is surface remains so, when the automaton becomes an autocrat (as Marx terms it) in the subsumption of labor. The logic of the reproduction of likeness is indeed subject to the falling rate of profit; yet the uncanny likeness of the automaton now emerges not in reproduction (seen in the spectrocentrism I noted in the afterlife of actual existence) but in the economy of replication, the virtual, the shade of likeness as commodified affection. There are no moving parts in Lenin. We are denied his eyes but, knowing their Freud, the Bolsheviks took care to leave his testicles. He remains still an automaton in that without machinic modulation (principally of humidity and light) Lenin would become human, and dissolve. Marx understands, more or less precisely, the affective embrace of automata and this lives on not just in the shell that is Lenin but in the paradoxically non-spectral ghost that animates him. This is more than nostalgia; the uncanny is the revelation of a real relation. And thus we move to the subtitle of my speculative gloss: "Do Androids Dream of Electric Lenin?"

A quarter-century ago Donna Haraway seized on the cyborg as a means to pry politics from the originary myth of wholeness that animates socialism and feminism.[6] As an historical document it has grown in importance not just because cyborganic systems saturate the socius, but because it marks a moment when an ironic cyborganic dream was possible in socialism, because of Reaganism, because of the Cold War, and because, most significantly, Haraway's irony had the benefit of large-scale actually existing socialism as a foil. Again, it is the dissolution of this complement that conjures the spectral uncanny of the Western theorati, but this has tended to suspend, like Freud, like Derrida, the articulation of the uncanny automaton whose semblance is now assembled in the discourse of replication. Haraway places her faith in the cyborg's illegitimate promise – it is not fettered by onerous Oedipalism even if many cyborg narratives, including Shelley's, offer science as the Law of the Father. The cyborg is our border being, an ontology that gives us our politics, says Haraway, for it troubles every essence that would discretely rationalize the modes of informatic domination and yet, for this is irony, as Marx's automaton goliath is reduced to the micron and the molecule the unseen itself becomes more nefarious and the promises of monsters carry too a predatory charm because of omniscience (omni-science). Thus, as Haraway puts it: cyborgs are ether, quintessence.

There is much more to Haraway's position than this but permit me to extrapolate her sense of the cyborg for the uncanny. Her manifesto, unlike that of Marx and Engels, does not unleash the ghoul on an easily spooked bourgeois sensibility but invokes the cyborg as something a little more everyday in its intimacy. It is a concept metaphor that challenges the dualisms of human and automaton by beginning from the supposition that the machine is us, as Haraway puts it. There is a border when one thinks of the organic, but technological integration makes it much more difficult to discern and thus, while we are not quite (with over 6 billion of us) past the human we are in the era of passing for human. The cyborg stares Janus-faced into the technological integration of the human into micro-circuits of power and at the dubious prospect any socialist experiment can persist outside this massive transformation of affective coding. I take it as axiomatic that the only state that would disavow the automaton is the one that articulates it yet finds it less than liberating from the realm of necessity. We might say this is the uncanny in what Marxism became rather than the uncanny Marx more or less projected in his Gothic renditions of the factory system. Haraway claims, perhaps not surprisingly, that the boundary between science fiction and social reality is an optical illusion and, while it is common to find this as a neon-lit doorway to metaphysics, it has proved fruitful in defamiliarizing essentialist tendencies in socialist feminism and indeed in Marxism. Yet what has become automatic is that the articulation of the techno-self simply renders the border inconsequential and thus the very frame of illusion is canceled. It is not so much that the cyborg is our ontology but its assumption. With the collapse of the Eastern bloc the eerie inconstancy of the border appeared to liquefy and science fiction itself marks the real of illusion as the being of the automaton. One could compare, for instance, the substance of the Terminator between Schwarzenegger's initial hyper-masculinity and the slick chrome CGI of the T1000 (we might call this the triumph of flow epistemology, although it was symptomatic before the break in Deleuze and Guattari and its subsequent canonization in Hardt and Negri); or, and this for me is decisive, compare the proletarianized obsolescence of Baty in *Blade Runner* with the Blue pill/Red pill conceit in *The Matrix* (politics begins where the fiction of choice is engaged – for the Wachowski brothers there is no film with the blue pill, yet by the time they cash out of the franchise with the cinematic claptrap that is *Matrix Revolutions* the series has become precisely that experience). On the other side of this border that is not one, the Berlin Wall, the difference between the real and the Real is a special effect and an accumulation strategy. Despite Negri's estimable critique of Derrida's specters I say the Blue pill/Red pill conceit is precisely hauntological. It is the apotheosis of "as if" rather than like and valorizes the gesture as *geist*. Thus, as Hardt and Negri aver, "This is the alternative implicit in Lenin's work: *either world communist revolution or Empire*, and there is a profound analogy between these two choices."[7]

It may be said with some credence that the delirium I offer here is a false one between the ghost and the cyborg that pivots on an ambivalent interpretation of the historical rupture represented by 1989. By figuring the uncanny in Marx's discussion of the automaton rather than in his spectral metaphors I am reducing Marxism itself to a Blue pill/Red pill stratagem that the theory, or the caesura, cannot possibly sustain. Even if the intricate process used to preserve Lenin's shell is symptomatic of the impasse that produced 1989, there is still the niggling suspicion I might turn the Mausoleum Group into a revolutionary vanguard by positing their cyber-Lenin as deathly dynamite; that is, Lenin might have wanted an ordinary burial but his obsessive scientism blossoms in his revolutionary preservation. In fact, to negotiate the difference within uncanny Marxism we must hold these symptoms, ghostly or cyborganic, in an impossible tension, for they animate a counter-narrative to the automaton that is capital and the organs it is compelled to proletarianize. Paolo Virno suggests the multitude has itself been rendered uncanny, such that the life of a stranger (*bios xenikos*) is experienced as ordinary.[8] While this does not simply recapitulate estrangement it nevertheless interpellates its central core, the dissimulation that riddles simulation or likeness in the experience of being human. As I looked at Lenin's shell I could not animate his ghost, perhaps out of the fear of reverence as nostalgia. Yet, 1989 did unleash Lenin, or at least his cyborganic semblance and thus we turn not to Lenin in Zurich, but to Lenin in Ljubjlana, Slavoj Žižek. The cyborg is always a special effect, so using this perspective, a parallax view, one can consider the prospect of uncanny repetition captured quite brilliantly on the cover of Žižek's book *The Parallax View*, where he reverses the perspective on Grigori Shpolyanski's painting of Lenin so that Lenin sits writing on the back cover while an empty chair is positioned on the front.[9] The answer to this absence is found in the text but much more immediately in the author photo. With the title, "Slavoj Žižek does not exist," we see Žižek sitting in the reflection of a mirror yet the seat is empty in the foreground. Thus, using the principle of the parallax view (think impossible point-of-view shot) Žižek exists in the empty chair both in the author photo *and* in Shpolyanski's painting. It is uncanny: the subject in the empty chair speaks and now Lenin appears to take dictation. Let us peruse his notes.

That which is like Lenin is not the scene of reproduction but nor is it, in Žižek's schema, the task of materialism to indulge in simple repetition (and recall that I am arguing the Lenin who is at stake in his likeness is the Lenin of replication). "Communism equals Soviets plus electrification" is a powerful formula as long as we understand electrification grounds replication. The homeostasis in which Lenin persists is electronic and every replicant takes only from the organic its capacity to signal electrically. This song of the body electric is sung by Shelley's creature and is replicated in Lenin. Two years before he died Lenin met Theremin and played his touchless instrument of electromagnetism. He could not have known that the principle of this instrument now plays him. I do not claim Lenin's shell is properly cyborganic but any position that takes Lenin as replicable is indeed cyborgian. To this extent Žižek is Lenin's cyborg.

That Žižek bursts onto the international theory scene in 1989 with the publication of *The Sublime Object of Ideology* is not a coincidence, of course, although I would not put this down solely to the desire for a post-socialist native informant, especially one so obviously out of sync with Western prerogatives: Hegel? Lacan? Hitchcock?[10] If Lenin's moment, according to Žižek, was the spring of 1917, the proper time of revolution, revolution's repetition in the cause of real revolution, then Žižek's came in the dissolution of Yugoslavia and in his run for President of Slovenia in 1990. When the second revolution did not occur Žižek set about writing it into existence and, while it would be unfair to cast this prodigious output as simply Žižek's *objet petit a*, there is an uncanny doubling in its troubling. No one can summarize Žižek, the content always exceeds the form, yet there are specific reasons why he likes Lenin and why, in this economy of uncanny semblance, he is like Lenin. First, is the obvious point that revolutionary politics necessitates a party, an organizational hub that is the organ of transformation (class is its machine). For those who prefer gestures, says Žižek, there is always revolution without revolution. Second, revolution is a condition of "world." The concept of building socialism in one country is not only Stalinist but idealist and has failed to heed the lessons of capital in its history. Third, the mechanism of revolution will not be liberal democracy because it has never separated itself from the axiom of private property; indeed, its long history has been dedicated precisely to its preservation. This sarcophagus is coterminous with capital itself. Fourth, Lenin was dedicated to the politics of truth, not as partial, but as a universal based exactly on the truth of partisanship. In all of this Žižek seeks not a return to Lenin, the substance of nostalgia for Object No. 1, but a repetition founded on the notion of Lenin-in-becoming.

That Žižek is "like Lenin but not" is redolent in his misapprehension of repetition that, in being true to Lenin, cancels his historical meaning for the present. There are two ways to understand this by-all-means uncanny resemblance. Žižek, of course, was a student of Jacques-Alain Miller and was also his analysand. Miller was Lacan's star pupil and one need not speculate what the Law of the Father means in that genealogy. Now Žižek does not repeat Lacan, or Miller for that matter; his procedure is based on the concept of formalization, which, by and by, is exactly what he claims Lenin does with Marx, Lacan does with Freud, and what Žižek theorizes through Lenin. We have then the classic Žižekian zig: that repetition, as in his article "Repeating Lenin," is not repetition; it is the dilemma of repetition that can only be sublated by rearticulation.[11] But in the same instant, which for Žižek is usually the same breath, this position is itself repeated and we have the zag of Žižekian peripateia. The article itself is both rearticulated and dispersed: we cannot say it begins with the version in *Lacanian ink*, but one can claim it is more than editing choices that render it as "Lenin's Choice" in Žižek's edited version of Lenin's writings from 1917, *Revolution at the Gates*.[12] The Marxist uncanny exists both in this version of ghosting as non-repetition and in the strangely familiar notion of using historical intervention as a model. Denouncing Leninism as Stalinism (which for all of Žižek's railing against political correctness is spot-on pc), Žižek's Lenin proliferates, copies itself without origin, replicates from "Lenin Repeats" to "Lenin's Choice" to "A Plea for Leninist Intolerance" to "Seize the Day: Lenin's Legacy" to *The Parallax View* in which, finally, Lenin only exists as a shell (the cover) and disappears into the ghost that is Žižek himself in the introduction titled "Dialectical Materialism at the Gates." The easiest way to understand this replication is to note that Lenin's choice has been radically suspended (I will return to this radical suspension in another example) in favor of Žižek's. Because the latter does not exist he exists everywhere, and particularly in Diamat that, predictably, has been reverse engineered as Lacan's tripartite scheme of the Real, the Imaginary, and the Symbolic yet is presented as the choice between *What is to be Done?* and the magisterial *State and Revolution*.[13] Just as Hobsbawm provocatively identifies the period between 1917 and 1989 as an interregnum,[14] we might call this the suspension of properly globalized capital, so Žižek underlines that what was held in place by the nostrums of *What is to be Done?* can now be unleashed by the collapse of state socialism that proffered the bad copy. Politics does not pour life into dead Lenin, it replicates the principle that did not allow him to be properly buried. By subscribing to the violent revolution advocated by *State and Revolution* two theoretical conditions are solved by one: false attachment can be annulled by burial and the ghostly deferral of capital's demise can be exorcised.

Since I do not wish to caricature by summary we might clarify by adding another Žižekian paradox: the advocacy of anti-anti-capitalism where anti-capitalism is posed as a rectifiable problem of the democratic state. This position is wonderfully displayed by the cover for *Revolution at the Gates*.[15] It features a photo of a statue of Comrade Lenin that graced a rooftop overlooking Houston Street in Manhattan. The low angle emphasizes Lenin's leadership pose but includes two other elements: first, in the foreground there are two outstretched hands (out of focus) that seem to cup Lenin in their embrace; second, in the right-hand corner of the photo one can just make out the U.S. flag. This last is the punctum of Žižek's argument, for the kind of gesture that freely permits gesture (after, of course, the collapse of the Soviet Union) is the kind that must be overreached by a dialectical sublation of the very practice of gesture only. Here again, we have repetition not as repetition but as the end of repetition; thus, "repeating, in the present world-wide conditions, the Leninist gesture of reinventing the revolutionary project in the conditions of imperialism and colonialism."[16] Repeating without repeating, gesturing without gesturing. This is the logic not just of the Lacanian-Hegelian but of the cyborg, the simulation, for which contradiction would require a home. The Tyrell corporation in *Blade Runner* promises 'borgs that are more human than human; here Žižek argues for a Lenin that is "in Lenin more than Lenin himself."[17] The Real of Žižek is like Lenin as the uncanny, "the almost nothing that sustains the gap that separates a thing from itself,"[18] but whereas Žižek continues to view this as a return "in the guise of spectral apparitions" I would say this can only rise to the level of caricature and we must undo the politics of this genealogy for the disruptive non-coincidence of likeness where the proximate is figured itself without ground, without the reassurance of gesture, without the guarantee that the political problems of dialectical resemblance might be sutured with a little touch of the Lacanian Real in the night. This may explain, as Eagleton puts it, why "Žižek's works are both familiar and unfamiliar, breathtakingly innovative yet *déjà lu*, crammed with original insights yet perpetual recyclings of one another."[19] The writings are uncanny, and no more so than when they like Lenin.

Since my critique is more about the necessity of a Marxian and cyborgian dream of Lenin than it is about Žižek I do not want to push the notion of semblance to the point of equivalence. Again what is tantalizing about Žižek's Lenin is his non-coincidence, his out of timeness, but a time out of joint that is essentially jointless (it is not Derrida's point, the scene, that is, of the phantasmatic). Yet Žižek's basic position is that Lenin had to think about how to reinvent a radical, revolutionary politics in this situation of total breakdown. This is, as he says, "the Lenin I like."[20] He continues: "What I like in Lenin is precisely what scares people about him – the ruthless will to discard all prejudices. Why not violence? Horrible as it may sound, I think it's a useful antidote to all the aseptic, frustrating, politically correct pacifism." It is the nasty goblin of Lenin again, the ghastly ghost, and not the ghost in the shell, the logic of the separable as replicable. On the one hand, Žižek is absolutely right to stress the parallax of historical and dialectical materialism, that they exist in tension not essential contradiction; on the other, Žižek will conceive of the parallax as the non-coincidence of the One with itself that, while it eschews the fatal flaw of reflectionism, internalizes likeness so that "the Lenin I like" borders on narcissism, filling the shell of subjectivity with a constitutive gap that nevertheless repeats its object as a material effect. Žižek repeats, but he cannot repeat like Lenin because for all of the tenacity of his reading of Lenin's crucial months in 1917, that space of political possibility is lost to the matrix of post-1989 and can only persist as baths of glycerine and potassium acetate.

So why not simply kiss Lenin goodbye and let his likeness wallow in obsolescence? Here a Western German fantasy, Wolfgang Becker's 2003 film *Goodbye Lenin*, shows how the life of automata survives the pesky simulacrum of Lenin, whose statues saturated East Germany before 1989 as a sign of the collective but now signal collectible to the discerning eye of accumulation. Briefly, the film follows the life of Alex Kerner in Berlin before and after reunification as he tries to understand the world of socialism evaporating before his eyes and those of its most dedicated acolyte, his mother. On the night of East Germany's fortieth birthday he joins a demonstration against Erich Honecker and the authoritarianism of his regime. Alex is beaten and arrested in full view of his mother who is on her way to collect yet another prize for her comradely devotion. She has a heart attack and goes into a coma. The premise of the film is that Alex's mother sleeps through the collapse of the East German state and the fall of the Berlin Wall but, because her heart is weak, Alex decides to gently introduce her to these changed circumstances by attempting to maintain socialism in one room, her bedroom at their flat. Alex and his sister Ariane (who now works for Burger King) stuff the room with socialist seeming, appropriate novels, drab furniture, and inoffensive *recherché*. Television programming is provided by Alex's friend Dennis, a West German worker, who plays tapes of old East German favorites but then experiments with original programming, fake news, to explain the odd effulgence of the West in East Berlin. The banners proclaiming the GDR's birthday are replaced by those of Coca Cola (news item: coke was actually invented by socialism and the Germans in their Leipzig soda factory) and suddenly East Berlin is teeming with West Germans (news item: West Germans seek asylum in the East to escape unemployment and neo-Nazi parties). The conceit is wonderfully flush with the uncanny in the ghostly sense, that the familiar can be strangely made present in the replenishment of old empty jars of Spreewald Pickles and scavenging for Mocha Fix Gold coffee. Alex's voice-over proclaims: "I did everything in my power to resurrect a full-scale East Germany" but as this ideological project of the simulacrum becomes more elaborate the aura of repressed desire is pronounced: "My scheme had taken on a life of its own. The GDR I had created for her [his mother] became the one I might have wished for." That is, the world sutured by reproduction becomes the lost object that never was, the state that existed in a desire with no original to copy. We are asked to bid farewell to a Lenin who was as fake as Dennis's news items, banalized and commodified by the force of state apparatus not freedom. Yet because the new Berlin is itself banalized and commodified, our eyes have been stolen (the story, by the way, is framed by the TV appearance of a character named the Sand-Man) and in this matrix, to borrow from Žižek, we face the other side of perversion, which, as I have argued, exists in Lenin's replicant.

Uncanny Marxism is defamiliarized in the film by an extraordinary scene of the *Unheimlich*. As Alex's mother wanders outside for the first time, past a picture of Jesus and an ad for IKEA, she enters Karl Marx Allee just at the moment when a statue of Lenin is being taken away from the new Berlin by helicopter. Lenin is suspended (radically) but moves through space and time and, shot from the mother's point of view, seems to beckon to her in a defining act of interpellation. Surely, however, this is a copy, produced by the automata of the state ideological apparatus? To the extent that in post-production Karl Marx Allee was digitally restored by replacing the grime that the West had removed and erasing the ads from 2001 when the sequence was shot, we might claim the technology of imaging, the cinematic apparatus itself, conspires with the nostalgia mode to rewrite history in the cause of forgetting. But, as Becker avers, "We underestimated the Lenin statue."[21] The first time they tried to shoot the sequence there was a massive thunderstorm and the camera crews ran for cover; the second time, the helicopter broke down and suddenly the time allotted by the city was up. Thus, Lenin was finally constructed on the computer using 3-D wire frame software and a computer model purchased on the Internet (interestingly, with no computer model of Lenin available, the CGI wizards used one of a businessman and digitally enhanced him). Once you have the wire model, you overlay it with skin. Then, by sampling pictures of bronze and scratched metal, you drape this sheen over the form. The problem was that the result did not look like Lenin. As Becker put it, his face is so well known he is difficult to fake, especially in close up. Digitally, Becker explains, "creating monsters and spaceships is not very problematic because we're not familiar with items or creatures like that." But Lenin? Becker: "It was very difficult for the designer to make it look *like Lenin*. It always looked a bit *like Sigmund Freud* or Gustav Mahler or whomever" (emphasis added). Uncanny, Lenin begins to merge with the very theorist of his strange familiarity (with a musical accompaniment). They brought in a professor of sculpture to help the designer but after four months this only served to underline the paradox of cyborg replication: "The Lenin statue got more expressive but unfortunately, in the end, it didn't look like Lenin at all, but like the professor." According to my history of automata for Marxism, this cyborg, this Lenin, this professor, may provisionally be called Žižek.

But that is not my point, even though I would contend the Marxism lost in darkness and distance can only return in the form of cyborgian replication from Eastern Europe, from those who experienced not the evolution of socialism but its involution fantastically exorcised from 1989–91. Here among the Western theorati we have no problem performing these last rites because, the logic goes, we are always already their very effect. I am not so sure. I think what is symptomatic is the *Unheimlich* as a skin-deep comfort zone, the ghost as a condition of proximate cathexis, the shade, as it were, uncanny enough to sustain the *geist* of a giggle. Marx, in his reading of Ure, sought to track industrialization through automatic reproduction, the extending and monstrous tentacles of an accumulation machine that makes organs of human bodies (indeed, makes organs without bodies). It would be as facile to say that this time is exactly with us still as it would be to say that Lenin and Mao, in their crystal sarcophagi, are the cyborgs who will lead us against the automata strata and their compulsive extraction faction, since this "us" is itself a simulacrum, the multitude as proximate identification, whose intelligentsia, as Žižek points out, is heavily invested in celebrating change as stasis, the ground that permits the party (small p) to subsist. Nevertheless, just as Haraway cogently argued for a socialist feminist politics that would tackle the informatics of domination and its dreams of replication, so now I would insist that if we believe in the *sur-vivre* of Marxism we must address the dreams of the replicant and replication, the question of the ghost in its seventh sense, a Leninism, for instance, that has no origin in Lenin. We know the world already as an impossible orb but this is a challenge for the sensate, not its sublation. This would mean keeping at a distance a spectral reading of *State and Revolution* not because it does not inspire but because it inspires too well. The task is less ghoulish recoding but uncanny transcoding.

On the first page of *State and Revolution* Lenin sees his future in the Red Square. He notes of "great revolutionaries" that

> After their death, attempts are made to turn them into harmless icons, canonize them, and surround their names with a certain halo for the "consolation" of the oppressed classes and with the object of duping them, while at the same time emasculating and vulgarizing the *real essence* of their revolutionary theories and blunting their revolutionary edge. (7)

He continues, "In such circumstances, the distortion of Marxism being so widespread, it is our first task to *resuscitate* the real teachings of Marx on the state." The lure here of the spectral and the spooky is tangible: we wrestle not with the angels but with ghosts to innure that which is dead for the ectoplasmic real. I have been reading this real as a ghost in the shell which is confusing because it is the other ghost, the very soul of revolutionary desire, that must be made up, fabricated, invented, replicated, and does not ultimately depend on the shell for substantiation. Perhaps this is the kernel of the Real as Žižek puts it, but the world does not quite conform to the logic of this proximate (or indeed, to Lenin's reading of Marx on the state). Thus, I believe I now understand the experience of the uncanny in the presence of Dead Reds: I would rather be a cyborg than a goblin.

NOTES

1   Jacques Derrida, *Specters of Marx*, trans. Peggy Kamuf (New York: Routledge, 1994).

2   Bernd Magnus and Stephen Cullenberg, eds, *Whither Marxism?* (New York: Routledge, 1994); Michael Sprinker, ed., *Ghostly Demarcations* (New York: Verso, 1999); Avery F. Gordon, *Ghostly Matters: Haunting and Sociological Imagination* (Minneapolis: University of Minnesota Press, 1998); Peter Hitchcock, *Oscillate Wildly: Space, Body and Spirit of Millennial Materialism* (Minneapolis: University of Minnesota Press, 1999).

3   Sigmund Freud, "The Uncanny," in *The Uncanny*, trans. David McLintock (London: Penguin, 2003), 124.

4   Mark McDonald, "Lenin Undergoes Extreme Makeover," *ArtUkraine.Com*, March 1, 2004, http://artukraine.com/historical/lenin_makeover.htm.

5   Karl Marx, *Capital: Volume One*, trans. Ben Fowkes (New York: Penguin, 1976), 544. Marx, in fact, had worked out this reading in the *Economic Manuscripts* of 1861–1863. See, in particular, Volume 33 of the *Marx/Engels Collected Works*, Part Three on relative surplus value: http://marxistsfr.org/archive/marx/works/1861/economic/ch35a.htm. *Capital* draws on these arguments, of course, almost verbatim.

6   Donna Haraway, "Manifesto for Cyborgs: Science, Technology and Socialist Feminism in the 1980s," *Socialist Review* 80 (1985): 65–108.

7   Michael Hardt and Antonio Negri, *Empire* (Cambridge, MA: Harvard University Press, 2000), 234.

8   Paolo Virno, *A Grammar of the Multitude*, trans. Isabella Bertoletti et al. (New York: Semiotext(e), 2004).

9   Slavoj Žižek, *The Parallax View* (Boston: MIT Press, 2006).

10   Slavoj Žižek, *The Sublime Object of Ideology* (London: Verso, 1989).

11   Slavoj Žižek, "Repeating Lenin," http://www.lacan.com/replenin.htm.

12   Slavoj Žižek, *Revolution at the Gates* (New York: Verso, 2004).

13   Lenin, V. I., *What is to be Done?* (Moscow: Progress Publishers, 1987); Lenin, V. I., *State and Revolution* (Moscow: International Publishers, 1969).

14   For this position, see E. J. Hobsbawn, *The Age of Extremes* (New York: Vintage, 1996).

15   Since I wrote this essay, *Revolution at the Gates* has appeared with a new cover, this time featuring alternating photos of Lenin and Žižek with the same "shade" and scale. It is not as subtle as a parallax view but the thesis is somewhat more explicit.

16   Žižek, "Repeating Lenin."

17   Žižek, *Revolution*, 310.

18   Slavoj Žižek, "The Rhetorics of Power," *Diacritics* 31, no. 1 (2001): 99.

19   Terry Eagleton, *Figures of Dissent* (New York: Verso, 2005), 197.

20   Slavoj Žižek, "I am a fighting atheist," interview with Doug Henwood, *Bad Subjects* 59 (2002). http://bad.eserver.org/issues/2002/59/zizek.html.

21   All Becker quotes are drawn from the production extras that accompany the DVD of the film produced by Westdeutscher Rundfunk/ARTE France/X-filme.

Chapter 4

Where Are the Dead?
A Genealogy of Mediumship in
Victoria Glendinning's *Electricity*

Justin Sausman

> I wept uncontrollably for Peter. Where was he? Was he crying for me, as I
> cried for him? Where was his spirit?[1]

Where are the dead? This is the question asked by Victoria Glendinning's *Electricity*
(1995), a novel that explores a central concern of late Victorian spiritualism, that of
tracing the physical location of the spiritual through hybrid theories that sought to
account for matter and spirit, the mechanical and the ghostly. For the investigators
of the late nineteenth century the physicality of the ghost, its material traces, and
corporeal symptoms were central to the experiments and theories developed to
explain phenomena occurring during the séance. First emerging in New York State
in 1848 with the Fox sisters, spiritualism arrived in Britain in 1852 with the medium
Mrs. Hayden, and continued to grow in popularity, exerting a fascination that spanned
social and intellectual divides, and in the latter half of the nineteenth century was
a source of public controversy as scientists debated the inclusion or exclusion of
the spirits from within the borders of scientific naturalism, as Janet Oppenheim has
argued:

> Intellectuals turned to psychic phenomena as courageous pioneers hoping to
> discover the most profound secrets of the human condition and of man's place in
> the universe. With psychology in its infancy, it still seemed in the late-nineteenth
> century that psychical research, if not spiritualism, might play a legitimate and
> important role in the growth of a new science.[2]

If today spiritualism no longer generates the public controversies of the nineteenth
century, the figure of the medium nevertheless remains a source of fascination,

50

following a broader upsurge of interest in the supernatural in the realm of popular culture that a recent article in *New Statesman* has dubbed, after the long-running television series of paranormal investigations, "generation X-Files."[3] Spiritualism has become a prominent feature of television shows such as *Medium* or *Ghost Whisperer*, which portray female mediums often struggling to come to terms with their abilities and seeking to help both the spirits and the bereaved, while the British series *Sea of Souls* and *Afterlife* depict the scientific investigation of the supernatural by university psychologists. When viewed from a historical perspective, it is striking that these themes appear to echo the explosion of interest in the scientific investigation of spiritualism that occurred in the late nineteenth century. This essay will explore the ways in which the present moment is haunted by the Victorian past, using *Electricity* as a medium through which to read contemporary representations of late Victorian spiritualism. I will investigate the ways in which the novel is haunted not by ghosts themselves, but by the language in which spiritualists and investigators of the late nineteenth century sought to represent and explain ghostly phenomena. *Electricity* explores this through the use of persistent electrical analogies to forge links between haunting, sexuality, and spatiality, displaying a carefully researched investigation into the debates surrounding spiritualism and science, and in turn drawing attention to the ways in which electrical science generates, rather than destroys, ghostly effects. The essay will firstly survey the flow of ideas between spiritualism and electrical science during the nineteenth century, demonstrating how the novel engages with questions of the materiality of the ghost crucial to late Victorian spiritualism. I will then suggest that the novel can be seen as a critical engagement with the history of psychical research, tracing a possible model for the central character in Ada Goodrich Freer, a controversial late nineteenth-century psychical researcher, arguing that the novel suggests a hidden narrative behind the figure of the deceptive medium.

Victoria Glendinning is primarily known as a biographer, and in addition to *Electricity* has published two further novels, *The Grown Ups* (1989) and *Flight* (2002). *Electricity* was a popular success, receiving praise in broadsheets and tabloids, and was adapted for a BBC radio play in 1997. Set in the late nineteenth century, the novel is written in the first-person narrative voice of Charlotte Mortimer, wife of Peter Fisher, an electrical engineer who receives a commission to install electric lighting at the country residence of Lord Godwin. The couple moves to a cottage on his estate, and while Peter oversees the electrical work, Charlotte begins an affair with Godwin. The grand unveiling of the new electrical system is celebrated with a party, of which the central attraction is a séance; whilst attempting to fix a problem with the circuitry Peter is electrocuted and dies. Charlotte then turns to spiritualism as a way of making a living, giving private séances, but remaining skeptical of the existence of ghosts. She uses electricity to simulate a series of shocks she claims are generated by the spirits, but is exposed at an investigation and disgraced; a last revelation occurs when she is, to her own surprise, contacted by the spirit of her dead aunt, at which point she abandons mediumship. She finally returns to Godwin's estate, the novel ending on a note of uncertainty as to her future. *Electricity* thus entwines themes of electrical science, spiritualism, sexuality, and class, suggesting that both the ghost and electricity can move easily across boundaries, disrupting intellectual certainties and forming new connections.

In turning to the nineteenth century, *Electricity* is part of the growing genre of the neo-Victorian novel, associated pre-eminently with A. S. Byatt's *Possession* (1990) and Sarah Waters's *Tipping the Velvet* (1998), which were popular literary successes in addition to being adapted for cinema and television. These novels adopt a Victorian setting and form, while self-consciously drawing attention to their historical distance. The ghost has become a key trope within the neo-Victorian novel, both as subject matter and as a way of exploring critically the turn to the past in those novels whose plots do not ostensibly explore spiritual themes. According to Hilary M. Schor, debates over science and faith during the nineteenth century "have opened new possibilities for discussion of the nature not only of fiction, but of material reality. The Victorian past has come to uncanny life in contemporary fiction."[4] Sally Shuttleworth has argued that the neo-Victorian novel reveals a "non-ironic fascination with the details of the period" and reads this through Fredric Jameson's argument in *Postmodernism: Or, the Cultural Logic of Late Capitalism* that our "historical deafness" manifests as a proliferation of dead styles and fashions in pastiche, symptomatic of a lack of genuine historical understanding.[5] In contrast, Cora Kaplan argues that the fascination with the Victorian past is animated by more than nostalgia for a past that never was or postmodern pastiche, and is instead a "self-conscious rewriting of historical narratives to highlight suppressed histories of gender and sexuality, race and empire, as well as challenges to the conventional understandings of the historical itself."[6] Both Shuttleworth and Kaplan place the turn to the Victorian in the context of the British Conservative government's exhortation of Victorian values during the 1980s and early 1990s, which promoted thrift, family values, national pride, and the value of work.[7] It is perhaps unsurprising that fiction which self-consciously draws on motifs of haunting should have turned to spiritualism as a theme, as in Byatt's *Angels and Insects*, Sarah Waters's *Affinity*, Melissa Pritchard's *Selene of the Spirits*, and *Electricity*.

Looking back on the developments of the nineteenth century, Alfred Russel Wallace, Darwin's co-theorist of natural selection and an ardent spiritualist, argued that advances in electrical science were perhaps the greatest scientific triumph:

> Of the various branches of human knowledge which have at once opened new vistas into the mysteries of the universe and furnished new and unexpected, and still unexhausted powers for the service of mankind, none can surpass, perhaps none can even approach, the science of electricity.[8]

Although not explicitly addressing spiritual matters here, Wallace's language nonetheless gestures towards them, suggesting that electricity moves beyond the boundaries of a strictly materialist paradigm, implying intangible forces that have expanded the range of scientific naturalism. Electricity would be put to a range of literal, metaphorical, or analogical uses during the nineteenth century, able to power everyday technologies, yet also to conceptualize mysterious ghostly phenomena, a tool simultaneously esoteric and mundane. It is this seemingly vague range of application which makes it such a strong and pervasive tool for theorizing spirit forces simultaneously with the domain of orthodox science, yet also undermining conceptions of a solid material universe.

Spiritualists and psychical researchers turned to electromagnetic science in order to conceptualize séance phenomena, with electricity functioning as both a theoretical concept and a practical tool in séance investigations. Focusing on America, Jeffrey Sconce has explored some of the early connections between spiritualism and electricity, noting how the telegraph served as a metaphor for spiritual communication:

> Spiritualism attempted to align itself with the principles of "electrical science" so as to distinguish mediumship from more "superstitious" forms of mystical belief in previous centuries. It was the animating powers of electricity that gave the telegraph its distinctive property of simultaneity and its unique sense of disembodied presence, allowing the device to vanquish barriers of space, time, and in the Spiritualist imagination, even death.[9]

Sconce links this to electricity's association with the vital force or spark of life, seen in the late eighteenth-century experiments of Luigi Galvani (1737–1798). Galvani realized that when he touched a frog's leg with a scalpel it triggered movement in the leg, and he believed he had discovered a specific animal electricity, stored in the muscles as a kind of battery, which the scalpel then released by completing the electrical circuit.[10] The language of flows, currents, and energy appears to undermine a strict materialism, suggesting that consciousness can be dispersed throughout a network rather than being fundamentally rooted in an individual body, and so by extension the personality can survive its bodily death.

Throughout the nineteenth century, spiritualism engaged in controversy with scientific naturalism, alternately challenging its claims whilst drawing on the authority of its theories to legitimate its own beliefs. Mediums generated hostility from scientists such as T. H. Huxley and Michael Faraday, as Roger Luckhurst has shown: "The insistent hammering on the absurdities of Spiritualism by scientific naturalists aimed to draw demarcations between empowering knowledge and disempowering superstition."[11] Other scientific figures threatened to erase these boundaries: William Crookes investigated the mediums Daniel Dunglas Home, who was reputed to have floated out of a window during a séance, and Florence Cook, who produced a full materialized spirit, "Katie King." In 1874 Crookes declared that he had absolute proof of Katie's existence.[12] The key moment in the scientific study of spiritualism came with the formation of the Society for Psychical Research (SPR) in Cambridge in 1882 by prominent Victorian intellectuals including poet and classical scholar Frederic Myers, philosopher Henry Sidgwick, and the chemist William Barrett. It continued to attract important figures throughout the late nineteenth and early twentieth centuries, including the physicist Oliver Lodge, and philosophers William James and Henri Bergson, all of whom served as presidents of the Society.

Historians of science have examined in detail the links between spiritualism and electrical technologies in mid-Victorian Britain. Richard Noakes has shown how the electrical engineer Cromwell Fleetwood Varley used his research into invisible electrical discharges in gases "to invent new ways of showing that the strange and frequently unseen manifestations of spiritualism had a 'natural' basis."[13] Varley was also responsible for the laying of the first transatlantic telegraph cable during the 1850s, and he used similar strategies for making both telegraphy and spiritualism credible to the public in the face of accusations of fraud.[14] Nineteenth-century spiritualism did not turn away from technology, but embraced machine culture, with investigators using scientific instruments to measure bodies during séances. Noakes details how the investigations of scientists, who privileged laboratory apparatuses and the testimony of scientific experts, came into conflict with spiritualists, who in contrast privileged the personal testimony of mediums.[15] This electrical thinking can also be seen at work in other aspects of the occult field. Alison Winter notes that in mid nineteenth-century mesmerism electricity was used as both an experimental tool and a speculative theory to explain mesmeric trance.[16] Luckhurst has noted the journalist W. T. Stead's enthused championing of electrical developments and Alexander Graham Bell's speculations on the possibilities of thought transference by electricity (138). As Iwan Rhys Morus puts it, "electricity appeared to promise a great deal to nineteenth-century people. The mysterious fluid seemed capable literally of performing wonders."[17]

The reciprocal flow of ideas between electromagnetic physics and spiritualism continued throughout the late nineteenth and early twentieth centuries. The physicist Oliver Lodge, a pioneer of radio and electrical science, used electricity as both a practical and theoretical tool in his investigations of the Italian medium Eusapia Palladino for the SPR in 1894. Palladino was famous for producing physical phenomena during séances, such as ghostly figures and ectoplasmic phantom hands that attacked investigators. In order to ensure that she was not cheating by using her own limbs, the medium was connected to an electrical circuit, "which rings an electric bell if either foot is raised, and which was tested many times during a sitting to see that it was working well, sometimes this apparatus was replaced by actual holding of the feet and legs."[18] Electrical technology here supplements, and is interchangeable with, the human body: the medium's body is transformed into a technological object, as are the investigators, whose holding of the medium's limbs can be exchanged for an electrical substitute. Lodge continues to draw on electricity when reflecting on how to understand the deformations of the ectoplasmic body that she produces:

> She is an instrument whose ways and idiosyncrasies must be learnt and to a certain extent humoured, just as one studies and humours the ways of some much less delicate piece of physical apparatus turned out by a skilled instrument maker. A bad joint in a galvanometer circuit may cause irregular and capricious and deceptive effects, yet no one would accuse the instrument of cheating. So also with Eusapia: it is obviously right to study the phenomena and exhibits in their entirety, so far as can be done, with such a complicated mechanism, but charges of fraud should not be lightly and irresponsibly made. (324)

Palladino was frequently caught cheating, yet remained a source of fascination for members of the SPR, who explained away her deception by arguing that any tricks were her own doing, motivated by a simple desire to please, while the spirits continued to act through her, producing genuine phenomena.[19] Marina Warner has argued that ectoplasm was seen as a physical substance that spanned the worlds of matter and spirit, and allowed investigators to move away from questions of individual souls to those of the physical structure of the spirit world: "Ectoplasm did not *haunt* its believers: it offered a solution to the problem of imponderables, and embodied a postulated *prima materia*" (290, emphasis in original). Lodge can be seen using electricity to theorize similar ideas, investigating the medium within the framework of the electrical laboratory. In addition, he draws on electricity to mark out his position in the debates surrounding Palladino: electricity does not cheat, and scientific instruments do not have will or intention. Thus, as a piece of electrical technology, the medium must be investigated, diagnosed, but not condemned for any failures that arise.

Electricity was also used to describe the physical sensations experienced during the séance. The *Proceedings of the Society for Psychical Research* contain numerous examples, of which one will suffice. Describing a séance with the famous medium D. D. Home, the sitter describes the sensations his body registered: "The last thing that occurred was that my chair began to vibrate rapidly in the most violent way; it gave me a curious tingling sensation up my arms to the elbow, and up my legs as though I was receiving an electric shock."[20] Home himself gave an electrical explanation for the raps which he claimed were caused by the spirits of the dead: "You may often notice, especially at the commencement of a séance, a whole volley of taps let off, that is a spirit discharging the electricity, to equalize the current; often until the whole is harmonized we cannot stop ourselves from making raps and cannot control them."[21]

Electricity thus provided a highly mobile set of analogies for thinking within spiritualism and psychical research. However, founding members of the SPR were also aware of the analogous nature of their speculation, emphasizing how the application of electrical language to psychical research did not automatically guarantee scientific legitimacy and represented a transformation and reinterpretation of ideas originally discussed within a scientific context. They suggested that they were "obliged by the very structure of language to make frequent use of terms which are primarily of physical import," but that nonetheless "electrical action, too – itself so unexplained – has furnished us with several parallels."[22] There seem to be two strategies at work here: firstly, they disclaim any naïvely direct application of electrical theory, suggesting that they are being forced into using electrical analogies through the attempt to explain and speculate on newly emerging powers of mind. Secondly, in noting that electrical action is unexplained in physics they suggest that electrical theories themselves are inherently analogical or metaphorical, and that scientific language itself can at best approximate the phenomena it describes rather than finding a direct linguistic correspondence for its observations. Electricity provided a basis on which to speculate about the nature of both physical and psychical forces, and a way of scientifically legitimating the existence of invisible forces. By extension, it legitimized the presence of the dead among the living. As Pamela Thurschwell puts it: "Electricity at this time is often portrayed as mysterious and commonplace, useful as an explanation for anything otherwise incomprehensible, but not easily explainable itself."[23]

Electricity displays a carefully researched portrayal of these debates through constant recourse to electrical language, and electrical imagery is used to highlight the uncertain boundaries between science and the supernatural. The physical apparatuses of wires and circuits are described in terms that suggest the spiritual: "Never let the unrolled cable have kinks or twists in it. Never step on it, never let it become damaged or damp. Peter treated the cable as though it were sacred snakes" (97). Peter speculates that religion may be a way of explaining hitherto misunderstood natural forces, which electrical science's explanations will now supplant: "What if he isn't a He but the Thing itself? The unseen force....Not the all-powerful but the power" (25). Similarly, at the party to celebrate the switching on of the electric lighting, the entertainment is a medium, staging the conflict and proximity between science and spiritualism. Godwin describes the medium as "the magnetic link between the sitters and the spirit world," to which Charlotte's unspoken reply is "that was how Peter defined electricity" (137).

After Peter's death by electrocution Charlotte turns to mediumship, but professes a belief not in the survival of spirit, but in electrical science: "It seemed inevitable, too, in order to preserve my connection with Peter. He had manipulated an invisible force for profit, and I intended to harness a rival force for the same purposes" (191). The emphasis here is not on the connection with the dead, but on the medium – electrical technologies – through which belief in that connection can be articulated. She uses electricity to generate physical phenomena during the séance, in terms which echo the nineteenth-century description referred to previously: "I was putting on an act now, thoroughly in control of everything, and the realization was like a power surge. I began to tap rhythmically with the fingernail of my right index finger on the tin beneath the table top. The effect was electrifying. (For once, imagery is precise)" (228). The sole encounter with a real ghost occurs when Charlotte's dead aunt begins to speak through her, much to her surprise: "Aunt Susannah short-circuited me. The contact was broken. The current did not flow. Energy drained from me daily, I could feel it ebbing" (244). If the novel has previously suggested that electricity is productive of ghostly effects, this now suggests that the ghost can in its turn destroy electrical thinking. The result of this haunting is to reconfigure the space of everyday life for Charlotte. Whereas electrical technology appeared to hold out the promise of spirit connections, it is, paradoxically, this proof of life after death that removes all trace of spirit from everyday objects: "life could be understood as nothing more than irrational rearranging of matter, whether dust, printed words, ingredients of meals, cups on shelves, ourselves from place to place" (244). The novel thus suggests that the actual presence of haunting is less significant than its potential, which allows speculation on a future state and a forging of connections between spiritualism and electrical science. Once the ghost appears it is reduced to the status of another material object, devoid of supernatural properties.

If electricity as spiritual energy is here destroyed through the presence of the ghost, it is also associated throughout the novel with sexuality, used to express modes of intimacy that appear at once corporeal and spiritual: "I thought about Peter, Godwin and myself. I imagined them as two electrified rods, and myself as a filament between them, binding them together and holding them apart" (105). As well as directly figuring sexual connections, electricity is also used to express the connections that occur between medium and sitter: "The concentration, and the current of feeling between us, made me light-headed" (210). If electrical imagery appears to articulate a sense of sexual power for Charlotte, it is also used to reinforce prescriptive gender roles in the séance room: "It is desirable that at least two be negative, passive persons, preferably female, and that so far as possible male and female should sit alternately, and negative-passives should alternate with positive-actives" (153). This suggests another metaphorical significance of electricity and spiritualism – that of power, as Alex Owen has argued:

The ultimate irony of spirit mediumship, and the measure of its adherence to prescriptive norms, lay in the fact that it operated around a fundamental power/ powerlessness duality. The medium's power lay in her ability to absent herself in order to become the vessel for spirit possession, and this was a species of power which must remain … contained.[24]

However, as Owen goes on to note, and as *Electricity* demonstrates, "whilst at one level her renunciation of self often facilitated specific gains in the public world, the séance also permitted the medium to play out her refusal of fixed gender meanings and behaviour" (12).

This persistent use of electrical analogies has been criticized by Kathryn Harrison, who in her review of the novel argued that "in 1995, to evoke physical passion with the language of electricity – with currents and jolts and sparks – is both risky and unoriginal."[25] Harrison suggests that the novel has uncritically replicated electrical metaphors from the nineteenth century. However, it is precisely the persistent use of electrical language that self-consciously draws attention to the ways in which the present moment is haunted by the language of late Victorian ghosts that emerged from psychical research, explicitly drawing the reader's attention to the ways in which electrical terms circulate between different fields. This can be read as demonstrating Bruno Latour's "chains of translation" within scientific and technological projects, which link together disparate elements. He argues against the diffusion model that views a scientific concept or technology as emerging fully formed from its creator, "as if it were 'endowed from the start with automatic and autonomous power.'"[26] In its place he proposes the translation model, in which "the initial idea barely counts. It's a gadget, a whatchamacallit, a weakling at best, unreal in principle, ill conceived at birth" (119). So the new technology can only become a center of interest through translation: "every time a new group becomes interested in the project, it transforms the project – a little, a lot, excessively, or not at all. In the translation model there is *no transportation without transformation* – except in those miraculous cases where everybody is in total agreement about a project" (119, emphasis in original). *Electricity* foregrounds this process of translation, suggesting that the alliance of spiritualism and technology is the result of scientific progress, that enlightenment here produces the ghostly, whilst also complicating this by suggesting that the appearance of the ghost is productive of scientific materialism: there is therefore a constant process of mutual translation between the scientific and the spiritual.

This might suggest that the novel is to be read as a kind of displaced cultural history, simply foregrounding those elements already implicit in late nineteenth-century spiritualism. However, it functions as a critical intervention into the history of psychical research as well, and is not the first occasion that Glendinning has shown an interest in late nineteenth-century spiritualism. In 1980 she reviewed Trevor Hall's biography of Ada Goodrich Freer in *The Times Literary Supplement*.[27] Freer is a controversial figure within the history of psychical research, and Hall's biography appears to function mainly as a character assassination, exposing her deceptions and manipulations of the eminent Victorians of the SPR. Freer was a key member of the Society, who claimed a sensitivity to phantasms and automatic writing, and was initially championed by Frederic Myers, a classical scholar and one of the founding members, who supported her with monetary loans. Myers introduced her to the journalist W. T. Stead in 1891 and, under the name Miss X, she became Stead's editorial assistant on *Borderland* (1893–1897), his periodical that aimed to popularize the study of the occult in its diverse manifestations, including spiritualism, psychical research, hypnotism, palm-reading, and theosophy. Stead claimed that he communicated telepathically with Miss X,

> as accurately and as constantly as I receive telegrams from those with whom I do business without the employment of any wires or any instrument. Whenever I wish to know where she is, whether she can keep an appointment, or how she is progressing with her work, I simply ask the question and my hand simply writes out the answer.[28]

Stead's body is here controlled by the female, suggesting a mode of psychological intimacy that functions analogically with recent developments in electrical communications technologies, a link that Thurschwell has explored:

> As well as both being handy if mystifying explanations for transmission, telepathy and electricity share other characteristics. They both inspire fantasies of community – instant access to others. If the world becomes a smaller place because of telecommunication, telepathy too is imagined to create connections with even more startling potential effects. (25)

Miss X herself appeared more circumspect on occult matters than her employer, noting in the final issue of *Borderland* that "I am not a Spiritualist any more than I am any other *ist*," and that séance investigations should be "carefully recorded and considered without any haste as to conclusion or deduction."[29] This contradiction in attitudes can also be seen in her attitude to professional mediums, declaring that "professional mediums are out in the market as are other goods, and are open to the same criticisms. I have never been to any professional séance that was not dull, or vulgar, or both" (369). This disdain for the commercialization of the occult appears somewhat ironic, given its appearance in a commercial (albeit unsuccessfully so) publication, and is bolstered by Hall's claim that the lady advertising psychic services in *Borderland*, to be contacted via the office of Miss X, was in fact Goodrich Freer herself (17, n3).

In addition to her work on *Borderland*, Freer also embarked on two investigations of haunted houses, funded by the Marquess of Bute, vice-president of the SPR, who installed her in residence with a staff of servants. Both cases caused controversy: Hall suggests that in her investigation of Clandon Park, Surrey, in 1895, she based her reports on servants' testimonies rather than her own direct experiences (66). Her investigation of Ballechin House, Perthshire, in 1897, erupted into controversy in the pages of *The Times*, with one of the party suggesting that ghosts were seen due to Freer's suggestions. This in turn prompted Myers to disclaim the authenticity of the phenomena. It subsequently precipitated a falling out between Myers and Freer, although Hall suggests there were more personal reasons, citing rumors that they were having an affair and that Freer objected to Myers taking a female medium to Ballechin house while she was absent (103).

The view that emerges from Hall's portrait is of someone who exploited the desire of the SPR to find proof of life after death, obtaining funding from the members to investigate phenomena that may have had no ghostly origins. This uncertainty is also seen in her personal life, as Hall notes that mystery surrounds her personal life and family background, that she claimed a number of different dates of birth spanning a twenty-year period (Hall traced her actual year of birth as 1857), and that her claimed connections to distinguished families were entirely fabricated (5). Whether these accusations are justified is outside the scope of this essay; what is more significant is that psychical research allowed Freer to move within the circles of a number of eminent public figures whose patronage enabled her to take up residence in country estates while carrying out investigations into ghostly presences. She thus appears as a figure who can move deftly between classes and, crucially for my argument, Hall sexualizes her connections with these figures, noting her "personal attractions which seem to have been almost hypnotic in their effect, and which she used irresistibly and ruthlessly upon those whom she thought could be of use to her" (3). *Electricity* also explores the ways in which spiritualism allows a crossing of class boundaries: "Were it not for our psychical work we should not be invited to Morrow Hall. I realise that. I do. Our very special work has enlarged our social range. It opens a door to the most desirable milieux" (146). The description of the séance suggests a space in which sexual liaisons can be covertly carried out, while at the same time drawing attention to the anxieties this mixing of classes could prompt:

I shifted the finger of my left hand an inch and touched Godwin's. For appearances' sake, I did the same with my right hand, and made contact with Mr Moss. Glancing around I saw that the only gap in the circle was between the little fingers of Mrs Carney and Lady Cynthia. Perhaps it was a question of social class? (154)

Glendinning's review notes Hall's severe tone, of "a judge towards a jury whom he suspects of not attending properly to his summing up" and praises the openness this leaves for the reader, noting enigmatically that "there are more things in heaven and earth than are dreamt of in Dr. Hall's philosophy."[30] This reference to *Hamlet* most obviously suggests that despite Hall's suggestion that Freer defrauded the SPR for her own ends, this does not preclude the possibility of genuine haunting. In more metaphorical terms this comment draws attention to uncertainty within the narrative, suggesting a kind of ghostly quality to writing. This is further supported by Glendinning's comments on biographical writing, which emphasize a refusal of final narratives: "As long as there is human variety and fallibility there will never be a definitive version. There is no end to any story."[31]

With these comments in mind, *Electricity* can be read as an implicit critique of Hall's biography, rewriting Freer's story from the perspective of the female medium's voice that Hall excluded. This is emphasized by the form of the novel, which is presented as Charlotte's own narrative written in her notebooks, as if Glendinning wished to present a biography without the mediation of the biographer and to explore answers to the question (prompted by Hall's account) of why eminent men "came to lend themselves, to give themselves over rather, to such transparently childish experiments, and still suspend their disbelief?"[32] Further links with Freer are suggested by Charlotte, who uses a crystal in her speculations on life after death. Immediately after Peter's death she gazes into it, hoping for an answer: "Where *was* Peter? I set my piece of amethyst beside me on the pillow and gazed at the shining purple peaks from close range, looking for something hidden in the central hollow" (170). Later, when she becomes a professional medium, the amethyst becomes her central prop, noting that it allowed the women to talk, "opened to their secrets and closed off to their ordinary lives" (211). The emphasis here is not on spirit communication, but, as with electricity, on the ways in which the crystal is a catalyst that allows repressed or hidden thoughts to emerge.

Freer also practiced crystal gazing and, like Charlotte, stresses that there may be no ghostly origins of the phenomena it reveals, but that it may simply act as a stimulus to the imagination, "a convenient vehicle for bringing to the surface what might otherwise never rise from the unconscious stratum into which it has been received, or to which it has sunk."[33] Hence, when Charlotte is accused of cheating during séances, her unspoken answer is: "Was I? I cannot say" (223). The question of deception is muddied by the psychological truths that the crystal releases: the spirits may not be real, but the séances achieve the same effect as if they were. This is a view also suggested by Freer, who maintains an ambivalent view on the reality of ghosts:

My own theory, so far as I have any, being that the phenomenon of so-called "Haunting" is one on which our chief duty is to provide evidence more abundant and more varied. I have seen too many "ghosts" – I won't say to believe in them, but most certainly to dogmatise about them. (73)

This passage resonates with uncertainty, as Freer distances herself repeatedly from the hypothesis she is exploring: "so far as I have any," "so-called," "I won't say," and the quotation marks all suggest that her theory is in fact cancelled out by her own (dis)belief. This uncertainty is seen throughout *Electricity*, whether it is in the unstable boundaries between physical and spiritual forces or in the crossing of class boundaries. It is also apparent in the novel's ending, which sees Charlotte returning to Godwin's estate and taking up residence in her former house, while avoiding encountering Godwin himself, who ultimately leaves a note for her. The language of the closing paragraph continues to express this uncertainty, setting out a series of questions: "Shall I go to meet him? Shall I wait for him to come to me? ... Shall I leave here at dawn, take the train to London, and make my own way" (250). The final line, while it seems to counteract this indecision, still leaves the outcome unknown to the reader: "I shall go to bed, and when I wake up, my mind will be made up" (250).

The ghost thus remains an uncertain presence in *Electricity*, marked through its absence: it is only ever encountered analogically or metaphorically through electrical language. If the Victorian medium remains a figure of interest, she has become so not because of what she can reveal about the reality of the afterlife, but because of the critical possibilities she embodies for rethinking the ways in which science and the supernatural are productive of each other, rather than being diametrically opposed fields. Peter Buse and Andrew Stott have argued that today, "even though it is frivolous to believe in ghosts, they cannot shrug off the specter of belief: it is simply that now they have been consigned to the task of representing whatever is not to be believed."[34] *Electricity* appears to confirm this view, being not so much a ghost story as a story about the language of haunting. It is the medium herself who becomes ghostly, haunting the narratives of the past, undermining class boundaries and the divisions between science and belief. If the present moment appears to replicate questions that obsessed late Victorian spiritualists, in asking the question of where the dead might be located, it does so with a self-consciousness that, in Latour's terms, "translates" the ghost into an entity that is less the presence of the dead than a critical presence that enables the rewriting of the past: it is the ghost itself which now becomes haunted by the present.

NOTES

1   Victoria Glendinning, *Electricity* (London: Arrow, 1996), 166.

2   Janet Oppenheim, *The Other World: Spiritualism and Psychical Research in England, 1850–1914* (Cambridge: Cambridge University Press, 1985), 4.

3   Stephen Armstrong, "Generation X-Files," *New Statesman*, August 7, 2006, http://www.newstatesman.com/200608070028.

4   Hilary M. Schor, "Sorting, Morphing, and Mourning: A. S. Byatt Ghostwrites Victorian Fiction," in *Victorian Afterlife*, ed. John Kucich and Diane F. Sadoff (Minneapolis: University of Minnesota Press, 2000), 234.

5   Sally Shuttleworth, "Natural History: The Retro-Victorian Novel," in *The Third Culture: Literature and Science*, ed. Elinor S. Shaffer (Berlin: Walter de Gruyter, 1997), 253.

6   Cora Kaplan, *Victoriana: Histories, Fictions, Criticism* (Edinburgh: Edinburgh University Press, 2007), 3.

7   Shuttleworth, "Natural History," 253; Kaplan, *Victoriana*, 5.

8   Alfred Russel Wallace, *The Wonderful Century: Its Successes and Failures* (London: Swan Sonnenschein, 1903), 211.

9   Jeffrey Sconce, *Haunted Media: Electronic Presence from Telegraphy to Television* (Durham: Duke University Press, 2000), 28.

10   Gerrit L. Verschuur, *Hidden Attraction: The History and Mystery of Magnetism* (Oxford: Oxford University Press, 1993), 45–48.

11   Roger Luckhurst, *The Invention of Telepathy, 1870–1901* (Oxford: Oxford University Press, 2002), 27.

12   Ibid., 28.

13   Richard Noakes, "Cromwell Varley FRS, Electrical Discharge and Victorian Spiritualism," *Notes and Records of the Royal Society* 61 (2007): 7.

14   Richard Noakes, "Telegraphy is an Occult Art: Cromwell Fleetwood Varley and the Diffusion of Electricity to the Other World," *The British Journal for the History of Science* 32, no. 4 (December 1999): 421–459.

15   Richard Noakes, "'Instruments to Lay Hold of Spirits': Technologizing the Bodies of Victorian Spiritualism," in *Bodies/Machines*, ed. Iwan Rhys Morus (Oxford: Berg, 2002), 125–163.

16   Alison Winter, *Mesmerized: Powers of Mind in Victorian Britain* (Chicago: University of Chicago Press, 1998), 120.

17   Iwan Rhys Morus, *When Physics Became King* (Chicago: University of Chicago Press, 2005), 156.

18   Oliver Lodge, "Experience of Unusual Phenomena Occurring in the Presence of an Entranced Person (Eusapia Palladino): Report to the President and Council of the S.P.R.," *Journal of the Society for Psychical Research* 6 (November 1894): 314–315.

19   Marina Warner, *Phantasmagoria: Spirit Visions, Metaphors, and Media into the Twenty-first Century* (Oxford: Oxford University Press, 2006), 294. See also Oppenheim, *The Other World*, 149–152.

20   Quoted in Oliver Lodge, "Introduction to the Earl of Dunraven's record of experiences with D. D. Home," *Proceedings of the Society for Psychical Research* 35 (1925): 52.

21   Ibid.

22   Edmund Gurney, F. W. H. Myers, and Frank Podmore, *Phantasms of the Living* (London: Trubner, 1886), 315.

23   Pamela Thurschwell, *Literature, Technology and Magical Thinking, 1880–1920* (Cambridge: Cambridge University Press, 2001), 157, n57.

24   Alex Owen, *The Darkened Room: Women, Power and Spiritualism in Late Victorian England* (London: Virago, 1989), 11.

25   Kathryn Harrison, "Power Sources," *New York Times Review of Books*, October 22, 1995, http://www.nytimes.com/1995/10/22/books/power-sources.html.

26   Bruno Latour, *Aramis, Or the Love of Technology*, trans. Catherine Porter (Cambridge, MA: Harvard University Press, 1996), 118.

27   Trevor Hall, *The Strange Story of Ada Goodrich Freer* (London: Duckworth, 1980).

28   W. T. Stead, "How We Intend to Study the Borderland," *Borderland* 1 (July 1893): 6.

29   Miss X, "After Four Years, A Retrospect by Miss X," *Borderland* 4 (October 1897): 369.

30   Victoria Glendinning, "Phantasms and Frauds," *The Times Literary Supplement*, July 8, 1980, 867.

31   Victoria Glendinning, "Peter Le Neve Foster Lecture. Biography: Choice and Gender,"
      RSA Journal 142 (May 1994): 69.
32   Glendinning, "Phantasms and Frauds," 867.
33   Ada Goodrich Freer, *Essays in Psychical Research* (London: George Redway, 1899),
      112.
34   Peter Buse and Andrew Stott, "A Future for Haunting," in *Ghosts: Deconstruction,
      Psychoanalysis, History*, ed. Peter Buse and Andrew Stott (Basingstoke: Macmillan,
      1999), 3.

Chapter 5

The Skeptical Ghost: Alejandro Amenábar's *The Others* and the Return of the Dead

Colin Davis

At first glance, skepticism and the belief in ghosts would seem to be polar opposites of one another. One doubts the existence of the external world; the other asks us to believe in what is most doubtful: the survival of the dead. What they have in common, though, is the suggestion that what we know is not all that there is: there may be less or there may be more to the world than we thought. This essay examines the connection between skepticism and film, particularly filmed ghost stories, with reference to the thought of Stanley Cavell and Emmanuel Levinas, and then to Alejandro Amenábar's *The Others* (2001). The link between skepticism and ghosts is suggested by Levinas in *Autrement qu'être ou au-delà de l'essence*, when he argues that "Le scepticisme est le *réfutable*, mais aussi le revenant" (Skepticism is the *réfutable*, but also what returns/the revenant).[1] Even after it has been dismissed, skepticism keeps on returning; like a ghost, it survives its own death. The ghost can serve as a privileged figure to approach the two central questions of skepticism: what can I know of other minds, and what can I know of the external world? And ghost stories are a site where popular culture reflects and explores the skeptical insight that the world is not what it seems.

The connection between death and the technologies which make film possible has been extensively discussed. As Roland Barthes, Susan Sontag, and others have argued, photography brings the dead back before us, reminding us of their living selves whilst recalling us to our own inevitable mortality.[2] Photograph albums are, as Friedrich Kittler puts it, "realms of the dead,"[3] all the more so given the nineteenth-century practice of postmortem photography to which *The Others* alludes.[4] As for sound recording, from its earliest years it was envisaged as allowing us to hear once again the voices of the dead. In 1878 Edison suggested that one of the applications of his newly invented phonograph might be the ability to preserve "the last words of dying persons";[5] and in 1902 recording machines were described as making it possible for us to listen to the dead: "Cherished loved ones, dear friends, and famous individuals who have long since passed away will years later talk to us again with the same vividness and warmth."[6] Combining photography and sound, motion pictures enable the dead to walk and talk in front of us, still apparently animated even though also tantalizingly distant. However, film does not just faithfully record what is or was before the camera. The first filmmakers quickly learned that the new medium could also deceive its spectators. Kittler recounts the accidental discovery of trick cinematography by Georges Méliès:

> It is said that the Lumière brothers documented simply and incessantly what their lens could record and what the type of projection they developed could reproduce. Legend has it, however, that Georges Méliès, the great film pioneer, ran out of celluloid while shooting a street scene. He left the tripod and camera in position and loaded a new reel, but in the meantime so-called life went on. Viewing the fully spliced film, the director was consequently surprised by the magical appearance and disappearance of figures against a fixed background. Méliès, who as former director of the Théâtre Robert Houdin had already projected many a magical trick onto the technological screen, had accidentally also stumbled upon the stop trick. (115)

So if film gives back to us what was once there to be seen, heard, and touched, it does not present it in a form that can be taken as precisely and only what it seems to be. Discussing the complex relation of film to reality in his book *The World Viewed*, Stanley Cavell links the issue of filmic realism to skeptical doubt concerning the existence or intelligibility of the world: "Film is a moving image of skepticism: not only is there a reasonable possibility, it is a fact that there our normal senses are satisfied of reality while reality does not exist – even, alarmingly, *because* it does not exist, because viewing it is all it takes."[7] Looking at the screen, we have an experience of the senses which meets our expectations and requirements of external reality, yet that reality is not fully present to us. This presence-absence of the world, and our absence from the world that seems present unto itself, encapsulates the skeptical dilemma insofar as it realizes the fear that the world we hope to know is unavailable to us as we are unavailable to it. It puts reality in front of us, but keeps us separate from it.

This is not to say that for Cavell there is no representation of reality in film; such a view is in his opinion a "fake skepticism" (188), since it is blatant to him that photography, painting, or film may represent reality. To deny it is to deny the obvious. But this does not mean either that film refutes skepticism by offering to us a world which is available for us to know and to possess; that would be, as it were, a fake realism as flawed as fake skepticism. Film is a moving image of skepticism precisely because it does not resolve the stand-off between the desire to know the world and a sense of its retreat from us.

Cavell declines to defuse the tension between skepticism and realism. It is what he calls "a farce of skepticism" to deny "that it is ever reality which film projects and screens" (189).[8] Both *projects* and *screens* here are (at least) double-edged. Film projects reality by putting it up before us, but *as a projection*: something constructed rather than merely reflected. And reality is *screened*: both presented to us on a screen, and screened from us, made inaccessible even as it is offered to us. This play on *screening* is picked up in the following paragraph in a key sentence which perfectly encapsulates the complexity of Cavell's position. "In screening reality," he says, "film screens its givenness from us; it holds reality from us, it holds reality before us, i.e., withholds reality before us" (189). The screen puts reality before us and bars our way towards it; film "withholds reality before us" because reality is at the same time held up for our attention and withheld from us. Film gives us a world, but it is a world which we do not possess, and to which we do not belong.

The challenge of skepticism, for Cavell, is not to find arguments which will prove or refute it once and for all. As he puts it, "philosophy left to itself has been unable to determine whether skepticism is refutable (Descartes, Kant, Moore) or irrefutable (Hume, Wittgenstein) or unworthy of refutation (Husserl, Heidegger, Quine) or self-refuting (Austin, Strawson, Dewey)."[9] To conceive of skepticism as either definitively unanswerable or finally disproven is to miss the force of its standing threat: that is, the brusque, unexpected, and shocking revelation that the world as we thought we knew it is not what we believed it to be. At least concerning the insistence that skepticism will always return, Cavell is in agreement with Levinas.[10] For Levinas, skepticism can be refuted.[11] There are perfectly good arguments which can be used against it even if, as Robert Bernasconi comments, he shows little direct familiarity with them.[12] But as we have seen, Levinas describes skepticism as a ghost which keeps on returning from the dead, or a shadow which cannot be dispersed: "La philosophie ne se sépare pas du scepticisme qui la suit comme une ombre qu'elle chasse en le réfutant pour la retrouver aussitôt sur ses pas" (Philosophy is inseparable from skepticism which follows it like a shadow which it chases away by refuting it only to find it immediately back at its heels) (260).

Levinas's point is that if reason, self-presence, and consciousness presided tranquilly over a fully knowable world, then the refutation of skepticism could be achieved once and for all; but this is not the case. Skepticism does not belong to the same order as reason – it cannot be refuted on reason's terms – because what it contests is precisely the order which reason occupies. It speaks for non-coincidence and fractured temporalities rather than a stable, unified plane of intelligibility to which everything can be reduced. It is like a ghost because it comes from a domain which reason cannot entirely capture or dominate. It is disturbing, disruptive, ungraspable. It survives its refutation because it radically negates the dominion of knowledge to which reason tries to make it conform. As Levinas puts it, it is "inénarrable" (unnarratable, incredible) (258): it cannot be thematized, described, recounted, or written down. It resides *in proximity* to philosophy, but it cannot be made to coincide with it or to obey its rule. Reason does not account for everything; there is also something Other which is an affront and a challenge to reason, and as such it is at the very core of what is for Levinas the question of ethics: how do we learn to abide peacefully, in generosity and justice, with that which will not be reduced to the order of the Same? How do we live with the Other without seeking to annihilate it?

Skepticism has typically been a question for epistemology; Levinas's key move is to turn it into an ethical issue.[13]

The general point I am making is that skepticism might look as if it asks us to reject the belief in ghosts, but in fact it asks us to be willing to suspend *all* our beliefs, including the belief that ghosts do *not* exist. The relevance of this to ghost stories and in particular to *The Others* barely needs to be spelled out.[14] If, as Cavell argues, film is a moving image of skepticism, ghost films illustrate the point in a particularly self-conscious form. They confront us with questions of what is real or imaginary, and of how far we can trust our senses. They ask us to believe – or at least to suspend our unwillingness to believe – that the world we think we know is haunted by presences which belong to another realm. What we know of reality is not all that reality is. And Levinas's ethical take on the skeptical problem asks whether we can learn to coexist with the uncanny Others with whom we find ourselves sharing our world. In Amenábar's film the living and the dead occupy the same space, in proximity to one another and for much of the time in welcome ignorance of each other. As the housekeeper Mrs. Mills tells Grace, the Nicole Kidman character, "sometimes we'll sense them, other times we won't. But that's the way it's always been." In fact, in the film the ghosts succeed in ousting the "intruders" from their home, though it is suggested that others will follow them; the living will return to haunt the world of the dead. The ethical core of the film is enunciated by Mrs. Mills when she tries to explain to Grace what she calls "the new situation." The point is neither for the living to exorcize the dead nor for the dead to frighten away the living, but to find a means of coexistence: "We must all learn to live together, the living and the dead."

Levinas's notion of skepticism involves the proximity of two separate, reciprocally contesting realms, one commanded by reason and consciousness, the other traversed by what exceeds reason and consciousness. One is the knowable world which accords with familiar laws of causality and temporality; the other is fractured, anarchic, and chaotic, impervious to logical explanation. My claim, in making of *The Others* a manifesto of skepticism, is that these two realms can be mapped onto the respective worlds of the living and the dead in the film. Each denies the priority of the other; they compete with one another for occupancy of the haunted house, but neither can ultimately dismiss the other.

It is of course not unusual for a ghost story to revolve around the interpenetration of the worlds of the living and the dead. On the contrary, that is one of their defining features. What distinguishes *The Others* from most popular ghost stories, though, is the insistence that this interpenetration is permanent and ongoing, however fraught or unfathomable it may be; and it confuses our initial perceptions about who is alive and who is dead. Typically, the ghost story recounts a *temporary* incursion of ghosts into the land of the living. This is the case, for example, in the "unfinished business" model of the return of the dead: ghosts appear, as the historian Keith Thomas puts it with reference to pre-Reformation Europe, "to confess some unrequited offence, to describe the punishment which lay in wait for some heinous sin, or to testify to the rewards in store for virtuous conduct," or "to denounce an undetected evil-doer."[15] The dead return because their business on earth is not over. Once their business is finished they can go away again, this time forever.

The predominant popular model of the ghost story, then, entertains the possibility that the dead may impinge on the world of the living, but only for a specific purpose or a limited period. This is the case, for example, in Joseph Mankiewicz's classic *The Ghost and Mrs. Muir* (1947). Mrs. Muir, a young widow played by Gene Tierney, discovers that her cottage by the sea is haunted by a cantankerous ghost (Rex Harrison). After initial conflict, the two eventually find that they are able to coexist. The ghost even dictates his memoirs to Mrs. Muir, who publishes them under her own name and thereby ensures her financial security. However, the harmony between the living and the dead breaks down when a potential suitor begins to court Mrs. Muir, and the jealous ghost withdraws from the world of the living. Only years later, when Mrs. Muir herself dies, can the couple be reunited as ghosts. The film ends with Mrs. Muir, restored to her youthful beauty, being welcomed to the afterlife by the ghost who had haunted her house. The lesson is clear: the ghost and Mrs. Muir may be meant for one another, but they can only be together when they belong to the same realm. The transgression of the barriers between life and death cannot and should not be sustained.

M. Night Shyamalan's *The Sixth Sense* (1999) equally insists on the separation of the living and the dead even if it also allows for their provisional interpenetration. The film is often, understandably, regarded as a companion piece to *The Others*. Released shortly before Amenábar's film, it is another intelligent reworking of the filmic ghost story, and it hinges on the same (to most audiences: unexpected) twist by which a character who appears to be alive – here, the psychiatrist played by Bruce Willis – turns out in fact to be a ghost. The superiority of *The Others* over *The Sixth Sense* is explained by the latter's replication of the conventional "unfinished business" model. Despite its tricks and feints, *The Sixth Sense* follows a well-established pattern. Ghosts return because their dealings with the living have not been settled. They need the living; they have a message to deliver or a task to perform. Once they have achieved what they returned to do, they can depart once again, this time permanently. The ghost of the child psychiatrist returns because he wants to make amends for mistakes committed during his lifetime, and to speak for a final time to his grieving wife; towards the end of the film another ghost appears in order to reveal a murder which has gone unpunished. Once the ghost has delivered its message or fulfilled its mission, its place among the living can be relinquished; it can be laid to rest so that the proper moral and epistemological order is restored. The child who sees dead people comes to understand that his role is to listen to them and help them so that they can at last find peace.

The ghosts of *The Others* certainly also have unfinished business. Grace has not yet learned to grieve for her husband, who was lost in the Second World War; nor has she confronted and atoned for the terrible crime of killing her children. She has not won or been granted the grace which her ironic name tells us is hers. But the film does not conclude with any sense that her haunting is a temporary interruption of normality. On the contrary, at the end of the film, when she has finally accepted that she is dead and understood that her children died by her hand, she insists, "No one can make us leave this house." Whereas *The Sixth Sense* uncritically follows the "unfinished business" model according to which separate domains must only temporarily interfere with one another, *The Others* alludes to that model but breaks from it, leaving us with the unresolved and irresolvable coexistence of competing orders.

If *The Others* is a "moving image of skepticism" in something like Cavell's sense, it is because it asks fundamental questions about the existence and nature of the world and of other minds. What is the world? Who is living and who is dead? Who are the "Others" and what can we know of them? After the opening credits, the film begins with a shot of Grace screaming in her bed, though we do not know whether she is awakening from a nightmare or responding to the horror of her everyday life. Mystery and uncertainty permeate the film. The outside world is always shrouded in fog; the inside rooms are usually ensconced in darkness because Grace's children (she believes) cannot tolerate the light. Grace's previous servants have, she says, "disappeared"; they vanished "into thin air." As she shows the new servants around she warns them to move carefully because "most of the time you can hardly see your way"; it is often difficult, she says, to make out if there is a table, a chair, a door, a sideboard, or a child playing hide and seek. This is surely a skeptic's world: people appear out of nowhere and vanish into thin air; we cannot be sure what this world contains because the absence of light makes it impossible to see properly; doors open and objects move without apparent cause; voices are heard where no person is visible. As an essay in skepticism, the film probes the uncertain distinctions between knowledge, belief, and superstition. Grace believes that her children will be harmed by the light; but as the housekeeper Mrs. Mills points out, "If you never expose them to daylight, how do you know they're not cured?" How do you know what you believe you know? How does Grace reconcile her distrust of books with her insistence that everything in the Bible is true? Why is it necessary to believe in God but unacceptable to believe in ghosts? At the end of the film Grace asks, "What does all this mean? Where are we?"; and Mrs. Mills points out that these were the exact final words of the now mute servant Lydia on finding herself dead.

The dialogue in *The Others* often consists in the juxtaposition of contradictory beliefs or truth claims, where nothing allows us to choose between competing assertions. Some of the exchanges between the children Anne and Nicholas illustrate this perfectly:

Nicholas: Nothing happened.
Anne: Yes it did.
Nicholas: No it didn't.
Anne: Yes it did.

Or later:

Nicholas: I don't believe you saw that boy.
Anne: Believe what you like. …
Nicholas: You're lying. I'm going to tell mummy.
Anne: So I'm a liar, am I?
Nicholas: Yes.

On other occasions, Grace participates in the conflict of claims about and perceptions of the world. She trusts her senses rather than what her children tell her:

Grace: Why were you crying?
Anne: I wasn't crying.
Grace: I heard you a moment ago. …
Anne: His father's with the others in the Hall.
Grace: But I've just been in the Hall. There's no one there.

This conflict reaches an extreme point when Anne appears to her mother, and to us, as a wizened old woman:

Grace: Where is my daughter? What have you done with my daughter?
Anne/Woman: Are you mad? I am your daughter.
Grace: No! You're not my daughter.

Who or what are we to believe here? The person before Grace is visibly not her daughter, yet she speaks with the daughter's voice and claims to be the daughter. If Grace is hallucinating – this being one of the many indications that she may be mad – then we are being made to share her hallucination. We may be as mad as she is.

From the standpoint of the philosophical problem of skepticism, these exchanges from *The Others* raise the same issues as those considered by Ludwig Wittgenstein in his meditations on the possibility and limitations of doubt. Wittgenstein's reflections, published posthumously as *On Certainty*, repeatedly return to the question of what can be doubted.[16] The fragments waver between maintaining that it seems senseless to doubt some things and envisaging the possibility that the systems which underpin our certainties may be historically and conceptually unstable. *On Certainty* attempts to formulate a refutation of skepticism as well as sketching reasons why that refutation cannot be definitive. It is not quite true to say, though, that the resolution of these two strands is, as one commentator has put it, "fudged."[17] The different aspects of the work do not so much contradict one another as offer an open-ended probing of what we mean by certainty and how we might endeavor to justify it. One observation bluntly asserts that some claims seem beyond doubt: "I cannot at present imagine a reasonable doubt as to the existence of the earth during the last hundred years" (261). If I doubted this, what would be left for me to be certain of? The conviction that the world has been around for a long time is so deeply embedded in our thinking that it is beyond question. Even so, the qualification "at present" ("I cannot *at present* imagine a reasonable doubt") leaves a loophole in the speaker's certainty, however minimal it may be. Our most fundamental convictions form a system, but systems may change. Moreover, what people consider to be reasonable or unreasonable varies: "*Very* intelligent and well-educated people believe in the story of the creation in the Bible, while others hold it as proven false, and the grounds of the latter are well known to the former" (336; emphasis in original). Intelligent people may believe incompatible things; and this is not because they have not been exposed to the evidence and arguments which contradict their beliefs. They believe what they believe in full knowledge of the reasons why they should not.

Wittgenstein is not trying to put an end to skepticism; rather, he describes the conditions under which some convictions appear to be beyond reasonable doubt, while preserving the awareness that they may nevertheless be susceptible to pressure which will destroy them: "But might it not be possible for something to happen that threw me entirely off the rails? Evidence that made the most certain thing unacceptable to me? Or at any rate made me throw over my most fundamental judgments? (Whether rightly or wrongly is beside the point)" (517). Wittgenstein acknowledges that under such circumstances "a doubt would seem to drag everything with it and plunge it into chaos" (613); but this does not mean that it could not happen. It may not seem reasonable to doubt some things, yet they may nevertheless be thrown into doubt. This is effectively what happens to Grace in *The Others*. The world as she believed it to be is shaken to its foundations by events in the film. And Wittgenstein adds a further point which elucidates the problematic dialogue of *The Others* when he refers to the deadlock which arises when someone bluntly contradicts a fundamental belief: "If someone doubted that the earth had existed a hundred years ago, I should not understand, for *this* reason: I would not know what such a person would still allow to be counted as evidence and what not" (231; emphasis in original). If an apparently reasonable person denies a belief which I do not think it is reasonable to doubt, we witness the erosion of the very grounds on which discussion might take place and agreement might be achieved. Wittgenstein *does not* say that the existence of the world a hundred years ago has been proven and is therefore beyond doubt. What he says is both more modest and more disruptive: it does not seem reasonable to doubt it, but if someone does doubt it – and doubts at the same time the system of convictions which sustains the claim – then he would not know how to argue in favor of his belief.

This argumentative deadlock is repeatedly rehearsed throughout *The Others*. If Anne states that there are people in the Hall, and Grace insists that she has just passed through an empty Hall, there is no accommodation between their contradictory convictions. The conflict of irreconcilable claims reaches its most terrifying point in the exchange "I'm your daughter / You're not my daughter." Wittgenstein's observation that a doubt may plunge everything into chaos becomes most apposite and most visceral at this point. If a mother cannot recognize the person claiming to be her daughter, the order of the known world collapses. There is no possibility of dialogue, persuasion, or consensus when competing claims about reality do not accept each other's underlying assumptions: "Nothing happened / Yes it did," "I don't believe you saw that boy / Believe what you like," "Why were you crying? / I wasn't crying." Sometimes, the most fundamental questions are unanswerable, and all that can be done is to change the subject:

Anne: Mummy, when people die in the war, where do they go?
Grace: Oh what a question. It depends.
Nicholas: On what?

Grace: Well, on whether they fought on the side of the goodies or
                 the baddies....
Anne: How do you know who the goodies and the baddies are?
Grace: That's enough questions. Eat your food, children.

The Others records a collapse of faith in the very terms with which we might talk
about the world. The erosion of conceptual certainties is matched by the confusion
of perceptual data, as the film plays tricks on its viewer. When Grace is searching in
a dark room, for example, we see a spectral face hovering menacingly above her;
but it soon becomes apparent that it is only part of a portrait hanging on the wall.
Such tricks, though cleverly done, are part of the standard fare of suspense films; the
frequent use of mirrors in the film, though, adds a further dimension to the disruption
of the spectator's sense of what is real and what is not. One sequence involving Grace
and Anne turns out to have been shot through a mirror, so that spatial perspectives
are inverted. In another sequence Grace talks to her husband who is sitting on a
bed whilst the mirror on the wardrobe door apparently fails to show his reflection.[18]
Things are not as they seem or where they seem. And on a couple of occasions the
stakes of trickery and reflection are raised unnervingly when the camera itself comes
close to looking at a mirror head on. In one sequence, the camera moves towards
a mirror to the point that it seems almost inevitable that we will see its reflection,
before at the last moment an abrupt cut saves the day. Later, the camera remains static
as Grace opens a mirrored wardrobe door towards it. The tension here is pushed to
its limit; surely we are about to see the camera reflected in the mirror, and behind the
camera should be *ourselves* watching the film. We are saved only by the rapidity of
the shot and the frosting of the glass. The danger here, for our comfort as spectators,
is extreme. If the mirror points straight at us, and we cannot see ourselves, where are
we? Do we exist? The whole film revolves around the questions of what is real and
what is not, who is dead and who is alive, are we haunted by Others or are we the
ghosts? At these points, the film's questions exceed the frame of the screen and throw
them back at us. Perhaps it is we who are the ghosts. Perhaps we are not real.

There are plenty of explanations on offer for the strange goings-on in the house
which Grace occupies with her children and servants. Anne, the daughter, may be a
fantasist who makes up stories to frighten her brother Nicholas; or, as Anne suggests,
Grace may be a madwoman who wants to kill her children; or there may be some
mysterious plot between the three servants who appear out of nowhere and accept her
offer of work; or it may be that there really are ghosts in the house. The problem with
these explanations is that they all turn out to be true. Anne *does* make up stories to
frighten her brother;[19] Grace *is* a madwoman who kills her children; the servants *do*
conspire together, hiding gravestones from Grace and not telling her all they know;
and the house *is* haunted, even if it turns out that it is the protagonists who are doing
the haunting.

This overlayering of explanations is reminiscent of nothing so much as Freud's
anecdote of the borrowed kettle. Accused of returning a borrowed kettle in a
damaged state, a man comes up with a number of contradictory defences: the kettle
was damaged when you lent it to me; the kettle wasn't damaged when I returned it

to you; you never lent me a kettle.[20] Each of these solutions makes sense on its own, but together they amount to an excess of explanation which suggests that something else is in play. In Freud's anecdote that excess is the trace of unconscious desire; in *The Others* it marks a fracturing of totalized knowledge. It is not that nothing can be known in the skeptic's world; it is rather that there is too much knowledge, too many solutions, instead of a settled "answer" that will put an end to enquiry. If all explanations are true, we perhaps end up knowing less than before we started. So the film narrates the erosion of certainty about external reality and the nature of the others who share our world. The final twist of *The Others* is that, ethically, this erosion turns out to be a positive step forward. The words which haunt the ending of the film are Grace's repeated "I don't know"; or, as she tells her children, "I'm no wiser than you." Rather than a traumatic loss of knowledge, we might hear in this a definite advance on the closeted and dogmatic certainties with which she began the film. She might now be able to welcome an unknown future. The film does not recount the defeat of skepticism; it shows on the contrary the possibility of survival in a world refreshed by doubt.

The brilliance of *The Others* lies in part in the remarkable level of self-consciousness with which it explores its own medium, as it probes the links between film, skepticism, and the return of the dead. If film in general is a moving image of skepticism, *The Others* is a work which takes that insight to its heart. Its ethical force lies in its willingness to maintain in proximity two separate, reciprocally challenging worlds. As Levinas has it, the ghostly return of skepticism disrupts the dominion of reason and makes us traumatically, ethically, aware that the world that we know is not everything there is of reality. Levinas's and the film's lesson is that we learn something worth knowing when we learn that we do not know enough. At the end of *The Others*, the living owner of the house, who wants to coexist with the dead even if his wife will not allow it, resists the impulse to rid the house of the ghosts or to flee from them: "We know nothing about them yet." The final "yet" contains a brave commitment. It both concedes the skeptical point (we know nothing about the Others) and it refuses any final victory to that insight (we know nothing about them *yet*). Knowing nothing does not mean giving up, though the possibility of radical, disastrous misunderstanding will always return, as a ghost, to haunt our endeavors. And who are the Others anyway? What we see on film does not exist, though it is almost palpably real. Perhaps, as we imagine that we see the specter of the real, it is we who do not exist, our disappearance being reflected back to us in the filmed mirrors that we would not dare to look into. What does all this mean? Where are we?

NOTES

1   Emmanuel Levinas, *Autrement qu'être ou au-delà de l'essence* (The Hague: Martinus Nijhoff, 1974; Livre de Poche edition), 261; emphasis in original.

2   See Roland Barthes, *La Chambre claire: Note sur la photographie* (Paris: Cahiers du Cinéma-Gallimard-Seuil, 1980); Susan Sontag, *On Photography* (Harmondsworth: Penguin, 1979). For discussion of these and other works in relation to *The Others*, see Susan Bruce, "Sympathy for the Dead: (G)hosts, Hostilities and Mediums in Alejandro

Amenábar's *The Others* and Postmortem Photography," *Discourse* 27, no. 2–3 (2005): 21–40, to which the present essay is indebted in numerous ways.

3   Friedrich Kittler, *Gramophone, Film, Typewriter*, trans. Geoffrey Winthrop-Young and Michael Wutz (Stanford: Stanford University Press, 1999), 11.

4   For discussion, see Bruce, "Sympathy for the Dead."

5   Quoted in Kittler, *Gramophone, Film, Typewriter*, 12.

6   From a German monograph written by Alfred Parzer-Mühlbacher, quoted in Kittler, *Gramophone, Film, Typewriter*, 55.

7   Stanley Cavell, *The World Viewed: Reflections on the Ontology of Film, Enlarged Edition* (Cambridge, MA and London: Harvard University Press, 1979), 188–189.

8   On the resonance of the word *projection*, see Stanley Cavell, *Cavell on Film*, ed. William Rothman (Albany: SUNY Press, 2005), 285–286, commenting on the French translation of *The World Viewed* as *La projection du monde*.

9   Stanley Cavell, *Disowning Knowledge in Seven Plays of Shakespeare* (Cambridge: Cambridge University Press, 2003), xv.

10   The issue of the similarities and differences between Levinas and Cavell has not, to my knowledge, been examined at any length. Cavell himself has shown some awareness that there may be a degree of significant concordance between his thought and that of Levinas, but the detailed working out remains to be done; see in particular Cavell's comments on Levinas in *Philosophy the Day After Tomorrow* (Cambridge, MA and London: Harvard University Press, 2005), 144–152.

11   See Levinas, *Autrement qu'être*, 256–266. On the issue of skepticism in Levinas, see Robert Bernasconi, "Skepticism in the Face of Philosophy," in *Re-Reading Levinas*, ed. Robert Bernasconi and Simon Critchley (Bloomington: Indiana University Press, 1991), 149–161; Simon Critchley, *The Ethics of Deconstruction: Derrida and Levinas* (Oxford: Blackwell, 1992), 156–169; B. C. Hutchens, *Levinas: A Guide for the Perplexed* (New York and London: Continuum, 2004), 55–66.

12   On Levinas's apparent lack of knowledge of the history of skepticism, see Bernasconi, "Skepticism in the Face of Philosophy," 150.

13   Hutchens denies that this is particularly innovative on Levinas's part; see *Levinas*, 57. In my view he underestimates the originality of Levinas's ethical interpretation of skepticism.

14   In *The Others*, Grace (played by Nicole Kidman) lives in a large house on Jersey in 1945. A mysterious trio of people turns up at the house, and Grace employs them as servants. She explains that the house is kept largely in darkness because her two children, Anne and Nicholas, are harmed by light. A series of events suggest that the house is haunted; it turns out, though, that Grace and her children are themselves dead, as are the three servants who died years previously in a typhoid epidemic. Grieving over her husband, who had not returned from the war, Grace had suffocated her children and then taken her own life. They remain in their former home, and the living family who had taken residence in it decides to leave because the house is haunted.

15   Keith Thomas, *Religion and the Decline of Magic: Studies in Popular Beliefs in Sixteenth- and Seventeenth-Century England* (London: Weidenfeld & Nicolson, 1971), 597. For discussion of the "unfinished business" model of haunting, see my *Haunted Subjects: Deconstruction, Psychoanalysis and the Return of the Dead* (London: Palgrave, 2007), especially 1–4.

16   Ludwig Wittgenstein, *On Certainty*, trans. Denis Paul and G. E. M. Anscombe (Oxford: Blackwell, 1969); paragraph numbers to this work are given in the text.

17   A. C. Grayling, *Skepticism and the Possibility of Knowledge* (London and New York: Continuum, 2008), 114. My comments on Wittgenstein are heavily influenced by Cavell's discussions of him, and of skepticism more generally; see for example Cavell, "The Availability of Wittgenstein's Later Philosophy," in *Must we Mean what we Say?* (Cambridge: Cambridge University Press, 2003; updated edition), 44–72, and *The Claim of Reason: Wittgenstein, Skepticism, Morality, and Tragedy* (Oxford: Oxford University Press, 1979).

18   This sequence is analyzed in Bruce, "Sympathy for the Dead," 20–21. As the sequence progresses it turns out that the part of the bed reflected in the mirror is on the other side from where the husband is sitting. He is not invisible, as we might have guessed, because he is a ghost (when ghosts traditionally have no reflection), but because of a trick of perspective.

19   In the scene where Anne tells Nicholas that a ghost called Victor keeps opening the bedroom curtains, she turns away from her brother and from the camera when Victor speaks, and the suggestion of movement around her mouth implies that it may in fact be she who is speaking. In any case, her claim that she has seen ghosts wearing white sheets and carrying clanking chains is not supported in the film.

20   See Sigmund Freud, *Jokes and their Relation to the Unconscious*, trans. James Strachey (Harmondsworth: Penguin, 1976), 100.

Part Two

Spectral Politics of the Contemporary

Chapter 6

National Hauntings: Specters of Socialism in *Shree 420* and *Deewar*

Caroline Herbert[1]

> The ghost is not simply a dead or missing person, but a social figure, and investigating it can lead to that dense site where history and subjectivity make social life.[2]

> Long years ago we made a tryst with destiny, and now the time comes when we shall redeem our pledge, not wholly or in full measure, but very substantially. At the stroke of the midnight hour, when the world sleeps, India will awake to life and freedom. A moment comes, which comes but rarely in history, when we step out from the old to the new, when an age ends, and when the soul of a nation, long suppressed, finds utterance.[3]

At midnight, August 14, 1947 – an apt hour for a haunting – Jawaharlal Nehru inaugurated India's independence with language evocative of specters, of souls resurrected and bodies come to life. On the cusp of an eternal past and "the challenge of the future," the Indian nation – which is new, but also ancient – is offered as a spectral becoming-body, a community in the process of substantiation, rising from a long sleep to redeem the emancipatory promise of democracy.[4] This essay examines cinematic engagements with the legacy of this promise, exploring how two iconic Hindi films, *Shree 420* ("Mr 420"; Kapoor, 1955) and *Deewar* ("The Wall"; Chopra, 1975), mobilize ghostly narratives and instances of haunting to interrogate India's postcolonial urban modernity, offering ambivalent representations of what Pheng Cheah terms the "spectrality of the postcolonial nation" within the city-space of Bombay.[5]

India's (re)birth is haunted; the possibilities of Independence troubled by the ghosts of Partition and memories of colonial oppression. Nehru's optimistic rhetoric of national becoming is therefore tempered by a tone of mourning: "our hearts are heavy with the memory," he admits, of the "pains of labour" (208). In a printed address, published on August 15, 1947, Nehru similarly remembers the "unknown volunteers and soldiers of freedom who ... have served India unto death," unable to "share at present in the freedom that has come."[6] As Leonard Lawler notes, for Derrida, while "the ghost refers to possibility," it also evokes "the problem of the promise," appearing as a reminder of the unfulfilled pledge of social justice.[7] In *Specters of Marx* Derrida "speak[s] of ghosts ... in the name of *justice*":

> Of justice where it is not yet, not yet *there*, where it is no longer ... where it is no
> longer *present*, and where it will never be, no more than law, reducible to laws or
> rights. It is necessary to speak *of the* ghost, indeed *to the* ghost, and *with it*, from
> the moment that no ethics, no politics, whether revolutionary or not, seems possible
> and thinkable and *just* that does not recognize in principle the respect for others who
> are no longer or for those who are not yet *there*, presently living, whether they are
> already dead or not yet born.[8]

A specter, then, articulates social justice as urgently necessary, but necessarily impossible, a promise of democracy that has always already failed and is always yet "*to come*."[9] Similarly, Nehru offers an ambivalent articulation of independence as a pledge that must be endlessly repeated, but whose fulfillment is endlessly deferred. "The achievement we celebrate today," he claims, "is but a step, an opening of opportunity, to the greater achievements that await"; only a restless, "incessant striving" will allow partial redemption of the possibilities of freedom that "may be beyond us."[10]

Drawing on the duality of the ghost as a "missing person" and marginalized "social figure,"[11] postcolonial studies has recognized the figurative possibilities of specters as "witness[es] to the erasures in the 'living present,'" and a "spectral ethics"[12] informs what Spivak terms the "attempt to establish the ethical relation with history as such, ancestors real or imagined."[13] If, as Ghosh argues, "[g]hosts are literary devices that return us to those ethical questions of historical, cultural, and economic violence" (217), then my essay suggests that the spectral is important to cinematic attempts to bear witness to exclusions within the postcolonial city's past and present. In reading for the specters of the city, I take a cue from Arjun Appadurai's work on postcolonial Bombay. Locating that city as "one of the most dramatic scenes of urban inequality and spectral citizenship," Appadurai draws on Derrida's *hauntology* to interrogate the impact of global capitalism, deindustrialization, and ethnic violence on Bombay.[14] Specifically concerned with the intersections between the city's spatial crisis and the rise of Hindu nationalism in the 1980s and 1990s, Appadurai deploys the notion of "spectral citizenship" to embody subjectivities materially and imaginatively unhoused by the violent rewriting of Bombay as "ethnically pure but globally competitive" (644) – destitute, house poor, and non-Hindu bodies. For Appadurai, spectrality offers a way of mediating "between the steady dematerialization of Bombay's economy and the relentless hypermaterialization of its citizens" through urban violence and poverty (635). Drawing on Appadurai's work, I trace how moments of spectrality are employed in filmic representations of Bombay to articulate the dilemmas of postcolonial citizenship and bear witness to uneven experiences of capitalist modernity.

Released in 1955 and 1975 respectively, *Shree 420* and *Deewar* trace a significant historical trajectory from the idealism of the immediate post-Independence years to the crises of later decades. The 1950s were characterized by optimism regarding the possibilities of the Nehruvian nation – modern, industrial, socialist, secular – and film projected Bombay at the center of the popular imaginary and its understandings of postcolonial citizenship.[15] The declaration of an authoritarian State of Emergency in 1975 signaled a crisis in the Nehruvian ideal which had been in decline throughout, and arguably before, the 1970s.[16] In both *Shree 420* and *Deewar*, instances of spectrality trace the material failures of the developmental state to address issues such as homelessness, child poverty, and worker exploitation. Juxtaposing these films brings into view an intertextual dynamic of haunting and mourning. Although *Shree 420* offers an ambivalent representation of the city, caught between the attractions of capitalism and the commitments of socialism, it nevertheless reaffirms Bombay as a site of social(ist) possibility. Reading *Deewar* alongside *Shree 420* reveals its complex engagement with the earlier representation of Bombay, as well as its performance of a process of mourning, both for the lost potential of Nehruvian socialism and for the optimistic faith in socialism that the earlier film evinces.

Shree 420 provided a foundational narrative of Bombay, revealing postcolonial subjectivity to be painfully split between capitalist modernity and its socialist other. Once a poor migrant to the city, hopeful of accessing its reputation of social mobility and economic prosperity, Raju (Raj Kapoor) reinvents himself as a successful, but fraudulent, businessman. In an iconic scene, Raju stands before a mirror, dressed in an expensive tuxedo, only to be haunted by a reflection of his former vagrant self, clothed in a tattered two-piece. An uncanny moment of doubling, the scene emblematizes a city ambivalently caught between socialist past and capitalist future-present, and the identity of the "real" Raju becomes confused; as Virdi notes, "what appears in the mirror, 'image,' is purported to be the 'real' self, while the 'real' self standing before the mirror is the ephemeral chimera."[17] The reflection offers a spectral embodiment of the city's marginalized destitute community, with which Raju was allied when he arrived. The "real" Raju's wealthy urban subjectivity is confronted here by its exclusions, the discrepancy in attire foregrounding the uneven distribution of Bombay's capitalist economies and the broken relationship between the body that labors and the body that profits. The dialogue emphasizes the emptiness of individual prosperity when thus disconnected from community: "Aren't you happy?" the spectral Raju asks his future-present other; "No, Raj, I'm very sad," comes the reply. This scene of haunting is also a moment of mourning for a former self; "Raju, where have you disappeared?" he asks, reaching for the fading image of an earlier ideal of social responsibility and individual integrity.

A key characteristic of the Derridean specter is its liminal position as a simultaneous embodiment of a past promise and an (im)possible futurity, a "living past or a living future" (123). The appearance of Raju's reflection is similarly ambivalent; presented as a moment of mourning, the apparition nevertheless performs a paradoxically affirmative function, emphasizing film's role in recuperating the "twin pillars" of Nehruvian nationalism: socialism and secularism.[18] As Corbridge and Harriss explain, Nehru "understood socialism in the broader sense of uplifting the poor" and believed that "the *raison d'être* of government in modern India … was to liberate the minds and bodies of ordinary Indians by purposeful acts of economic and social transformation."[19] Planned economic development, industrialization, and the well-planned city were central to his vision of Indian modernity and would be tied to secular equality, and equal access to education, employment, and social welfare.[20] Virdi explains that 1950s social films "are self-conscious in their commentary about the formative years of the nation and the responsibility to build it" (93), and as Khilnani suggests, Raj Kapoor's productions, scripted by K. A. Abbas, "staged and sang a nationalist vision of India that was recognizably Nehru's own," screening "a democratic, outward-looking and secular nationalist sentiment, and affirm[ing] the city as the most likely place to cultivate this" (137).[21] Such films did not unequivocally celebrate the city, presenting Bombay as Janus-faced, foregrounding its exploitative and corrupt machinations. Thus, the social combined a "critical appraisal" of the developmental state with an often contradictory faith in its potential.[22] As Varma records, Kapoor made clear the relationship between his cinematic project and Nehru's nationalist vision: "[Nehru] said that he wanted every Indian in this country to do something for the nation, to build it up into the beautiful dream he had. He was a visionary and I tried to follow him, to do my best, whatever I could, through films" (68).

The mirror scene draws attention to the actively nationalist role Kapoor envisioned for film, and Raju/Kapoor is confronted by both an older self and a cinematic self. The mirror is transformed into a screen projecting its critique of the exclusions of postcolonial modernity back onto its capitalist other, producing a "mobilization-effect" which is doubly-directed.[23] The dialogue extends across the cinematic frame of both mirror and film, the "image" Raju reminding his diegetic and extra-diegetic audiences of the need to recuperate the promises of independence. Close-up shots of each Raju's face draw the viewer into the scene's interrogatory dynamics, positioning spectatorial subjectivity – the Indian citizen-viewer – at the center of the crisis between a fading socialist past and a predatory capitalist future-present. The "virtual space of spectrality" of the mirror coincides with the cinematic space, with cinema privileged as a form capable of embodying the lived experiences of the city's spectral selves and, crucially, of mobilizing spectators to renew the promise of democracy.[24]

The mirror scene has gained iconic status and commensurate critical attention,[25] but its mobilization of spectral mourning as a mode of critique is anticipated in an earlier scene. Rejected by his fiancée's preference for honest poverty over duplicitous wealth, Raju – drunk on the proceeds of a night of gambling – cynically warns Vidya (Nargis) to "Remember, you and others like you who laud honesty will perish with hunger. I won't starve." Invoking the constitutional pledge to secure for Indians "work, a living wage, [and] a decent standard of living,"[26] Raju castigates a government that "did not care when [he] was starving," claiming that he has been forced to invest in private capitalism's exploitations as the nation-state fails to offer the basic rights of citizenship – food, work, shelter.

Having delivered his verdict on India's postcolonial progress, Raju leaves, producing an extraordinary scene that foreshadows his later negotiation of the tensions between the city's possibilities and its exclusions. As Vidya watches Raju retreat, a ghostly figure – pale, transparent, glittering – emerges from her body, a psychic projection of her conflicting desire for her fiancé and her suspicion of his wealth. As Vidya looks on, paralyzed by and yet steadfast in her ideals, her ghostlike self frantically vacillates between her body and Raju's, urging him to remember his commitment to community rather than cash. The specter embodies the fraught tensions between Vidya's socialist faith in collective commitment and Raju's claims that prosperity will follow from individualist capitalist pursuit. For both Raju and Vidya, however, the capitalist fetishization of cash renders subjectivity spectral; it is after Raju thrusts fistfuls of rupees towards Vidya, visually placing her within a frame of excessive wealth, that doubles of both characters are introduced. The traffic between these spectral figures highlights the material consequences of an ideological failure; while Vidya's spirit incarnates an ideological crisis, Raju's more substantial, but no more "real," reflection offers a paradoxical incorporation of the realities of that failure, bearing witness to the corporeal materiality of those made destitute while the city prospers.

Vidya's spirit, like the film's conclusion, reincorporates itself into the body of socialist idealism, Vidya. But as it does so, the scene positions Raju's cynical capitalism within a framework of mournful nostalgia: "Forget that old Raj," Raju pleads, "What's past is past. Don't look back. We're entering a new world." Vidya's spectral self refuses such irresponsible forgetting, all the while mourning a promise that Raju once embodied. Directly rejecting the amnesiac impulse of capitalism, voiced elsewhere by the seductive Maya (Nadira) in the song "Mud Mud Ke Na Dekh" ("Don't Look Back, Don't Think of the Past"), Vidya's specter implores Raju to do precisely that in "O Jaanewale Mud Ke," urging him to "look back" and remember a past promise.

That promise is one in which postcolonial modernity is built upon shared dreams and shared resources. This is clear in Raju's earlier marriage proposal, in a scene which promotes community as a mode of survival in the city. With his paltry income, Raju feels unable to dream of a good life – marriage, shelter, children, education; Vidya's response evinces socialist pragmatism: "A man alone cannot," she replies, "but if both of them [husband and wife] work together ..." While the preceding song complicates this faith, with the lyrical ambivalence of "Pyaar Hua, Iqraar Hua" and a rainstorm intimating difficulties ahead, the playful use of a black umbrella allows the scene to resolve into an ideal of mutual responsibility. Raju opens up Vidya's umbrella and passes it to her; she in turn draws Raju underneath it in a move at once erotic and ideological, a gesture of recognition of Raju's labor and his need for shelter. The playful sharing of the umbrella signals an affirmation of mutual responsibility as the foundation of equitable citizenship. Nevertheless, while the lyrics express hope for future prosperity, such futurity is already embedded within a tone of nostalgia. While Raju sings that "The youth of tomorrow will sing our melody," Vidya, gesturing towards some passing children, intones, "Neither you nor I will remain, but the tokens of our love will reign." Here, an optimistic articulation of inclusive modernity is repositioned as a spectral ideal, not yet arrived and always already deferred.

Despite these ambivalences, *Shree 420* remains heavily invested in the Nehruvian nationalist vision, and its final scenes resurrect – quite explicitly – the possibility of a utopian future. After discovering Seth Sonachand Dharmanand's fraudulent development scheme, Raju renounces his pursuit of individual prosperity and renews his commitment to Bombay's house poor. In a lengthy speech, Raju critiques private capitalism *and* the developmental state, before reiterating the importance of collective commitment in achieving social transformation:

> Don't lessen your strength. No home can be made with a hundred rupees. But with a hundred thousand rupees, several homes can be made. You could go to your government and tell them, "Here's a hundred and fifty thousand rupees. Give us land and we'll build our own homes." ... [T]he solution to poverty and unemployment is not greed and deceit but courage and hard work. The solution is the nation's development and the people's unity.

Virdi reads this speech as a "last-ditch effort to reinstate the official rhetoric" and "plead – against the grain of the entire film – for a truce with status quo" (93), and the populist endorsement of a nationalist utopia is certainly problematic.

However, even as he reiterates official rhetoric, Raju exposes its inadequacies. Reading the speech alongside instances of spectrality elsewhere brings into view the ambivalence of Raju's injunction to his fellow citizens to resuscitate the nation. Indeed, this becomes clear in the moments preceding the speech, in which Raju appears to rise from the dead. Shot by the defiant and callous Seth, Raju dramatically falls down, to be mourned immediately by Vidya and the gathering crowd, a process that reincorporates his body back into Bombay's less privileged communities. Having played "dead" for several minutes, Raju spontaneously resurrects himself, revealing that the gun was loaded with blanks. It is at this point that he launches his call to action, collapsing "Raju," fictional character, and Raj Kapoor, auteur and "star text,"[27] and again collapsing diegetic and extra-diegetic audiences.

Caught between his (faked) death as a capitalist and his resurrection as a socialist, Raju is located as a spectral "becoming-body."[28] According to Derrida, the specter reminds us that democracy is a "concept of a promise that can only arise in a ... *diastema* (failure, inadequation, disjunction, disadjustment, being 'out of joint')," articulating justice as "a future modality of the *living present*" (81, emphasis in original). In Spivak's terms, "the 'end' of the ghost dance ... is to make the past a future ... the future anterior, not a future present, as is the case with the 'end' of most narratives of social justice" (70). Raju's resurrected body, a symbol of simultaneous failure and possibility, similarly recasts past ideals as future possibilities. *Shree 420* may well offer what Virdi calls "an idealized longing for a nationalist spirit" (92), but it does so self-consciously. Raju's body emphasizes the incomplete project of independence and, in his spectral injunction to his fellow Bombayites to follow his lead and resurrect their own nationalist spirit through acts of collective responsibility,

Raju articulates (and embodies), as Nehru did in 1947, the postcolonial citizen as a becoming-body, whose achievement of social and economic justice remains yet to come. Reading *Shree 420* for ghosts reveals the use of spectrality to embody the dilemmas of postcolonial citizenship in the newly independent nation. *Shree 420* became a "master narrative,"[29] establishing Bombay as the ideal site for negotiations of citizenship and modernity. Engaging with this master narrative, *Deewar* returns to material spaces traversed in *Shree 420* – the footpath, bridge, and housing development – to continue its examination of discrepant experiences of postcolonial modernity. A narrative of haunting can be discerned on a number of levels: structurally, an extended flashback presents the contemporary nation-state as haunted by its criminalized other. More centrally, an intertextual haunting of *Deewar* by *Shree 420* combines with the representation – through the wandering body of the father – of socialist nationalism as spectral, at once a future (im)possibility and an anachronism. *Deewar*, I suggest, is both haunted by, critiques, and mourns the loss of (faith in) the promise held out in the earlier film.

While, in the mid-1950s, *Shree 420* strained to offer optimism, suggesting that the nationalist utopia of social equality could, with collective effort, be revived, in the mid-1970s, Yash Chopra's *Deewar* performs a more equivocal process of mourning for lost possibilities. It is, Mazumdar suggests, "in many senses the film that marks the acknowledgement of the crisis of postcolonial nationalism."[30] Virdi explains that, in the 1950s, "Nehru's 'tryst with destiny' held promise, even if the future seemed daunting," but as "uneven development, overpopulated cities, false electoral promises, and worker-peasant-student unrest" became increasingly visible, the "placatory tone" of Kapoor's films gave way to anger as a key trope (14). In films such as *Zanjeer* (1973), *Sholay* (1975), and *Deewar*, Amitabh Bachchan's "angry man" articulated the disenchantment of a generation that was not part of the nationalist movement, but that perceived the discrepancy between the promises of independence and its experience two decades later.

Deewar narrates the divergent fortunes of two brothers, Ravi (Shashi Kapoor) and Vijay Verma (Bachchan), a police officer and dockworker/smuggler respectively. As boys, the pair travel to Bombay with their mother (Nirupa Roy), destitute and ostracized after their activist father, Anand (Satyendra Kapoor), disappears, following his betrayal of his fellow miners to the landowner. Vijay's body is marked by the burden of Anand's betrayal, having been forcibly tattooed with the statement "My Father is a Thief." A powerful "signifier for marginality and social displacement,"[31] the tattoo acts as a persistent reminder of the failure of the Nehruvian nation's socialist principles.

In Bombay, Vijay joins the city's toiling communities, funding Ravi's education and progress as an "exemplary citizen"[32] by working on the streets as a child shoe-shine and, as an adult, as a coolie at the docks. Increasingly frustrated by the inequalities of the city, Vijay resists the exploitation of dockworkers by extortionists, before becoming a leading figure in the mafia underworld. Assigned to his case, Ravi pursues and finally shoots and kills Vijay. In these narratives, *Deewar* offers conflicting versions of postcolonial Bombay, Ravi's official, but abstract citizenship conflicting with Vijay's illicit, but "lived" experience of urban subjectivity.[33] At the same time, the film demonstrates Ravi's apparently ideal citizenship as dependent upon – and compromised by the presence of – a laboring body it consistently criminalizes. *Deewar* is frequently read as allegorizing "a civil war between state and community,"[34] citizen and subject, the brothers embodying distinct modes of being in the city.[35] Similarly, critics situate the film's attention to Bombay's social and spatial crises as offering a powerful "sociology of urban poverty" and violence, and a prescient narrative of nation-state authoritarianism.[36] Social protest, especially in cities, was strident through the 1970s, as dissatisfaction with developmentalism grew. The 1973 rail workers' strike is particularly significant to *Deewar*, in which trains accommodate the spectral body. Effectively halting the economy, the unprecedented nationwide strike was "brutally repressed" by the central government.[37] Student, peasant, and worker strikes followed through 1973–75 and, in the face of growing opposition to the Congress government, and accusations of electoral malpractice, Indira Gandhi declared a State of Internal Emergency. The Constitution was suspended, opposition activists jailed, the media censored, and draconian anti-poor policies such as mass sterilization, forcible resettlement, and slum demolition implemented. While the Emergency marked a derailment of the Nehruvian vision, popular protest, rising poverty, and authoritarian government throughout the 1970s highlighted the failure to "transform India into either the socialist, industrial society of Nehru's ... dreams, or into a dynamic capitalist society" and "to provide for the basic, minimum needs of most of its people."[38] By reading for spectral bodies, I seek to open up new angles on *Deewar*'s engagement with India's crisis, but also with its own cinematic contexts; reading for its haunted and haunting narratives extends our understandings of the traffic between the material and the imagined city, and between its various cinematic selves.

Deewar's central narrative is presented in extended flashback. The film opens with a ceremony in which Ravi is honored for bravery, achieved through Vijay's death. Interrupting this ceremony, the flashback functions as a mode of haunting, in terms of structure and content. Ravi dedicates his award to those who "go unnoticed and unknown," "whose name is not printed in any book, paper or gazette," before asking his mother to receive the medal. Doing so, the mother gazes beyond the frame, her grief prompting the flashback. Prasad reads the flashback as presenting an "'unofficial' history" that is "doubly erased":

> The flashback structure codes the narrative as a mother's memory hidden from public view, evoking a powerful sense that the film will tell an "unofficial" history, one which the audience can share in, although no official record will include it. (148)

Once the flashback ends, with Vijay's death, the film returns to the ceremony where the applause for the ideal representative of the nation-state (Ravi) is "partially re-allocated to the rebellious son" in an "imaginary and unofficial elevation of the resistant subject to a place of honour in the community's informal memory" (148). Prasad's understanding of Vijay's story as "doubly erased" informs my reading, and I agree that *Deewar*'s sociology of resistant criminality at once takes center stage and is subsumed within a reassertion of nation-state authority. However, I want to suggest that the flashback frames Vijay's story as spectral – a ghost story of the nation or national ghost story – a move that brings into view further complexities in *Deewar*'s engagement with marginalized subjectivities, as well as with official discourses of the nation.

Vijay is always already dead; the award ceremony commemorates – indeed, celebrates – his death, which concludes the flashback. Positioned between two deaths, Vijay's biography performs a haunting that disrupts the nation-state's authority. Vijay's spectral presence within the ceremony hall has multiple functions. His narrative demands recognition of his criminality as the direct consequence of the failures of the nation-state, which is, in turn, urged to remember an earlier promise of social justice. Vijay's experiences of urban poverty and childhood exploitation make flesh the inadequacies of the developmental state, and his body becomes a narrative prosthesis for Bombay's "unnoticed" subjectivities, inadvertently conjured by Ravi's dedication. Vijay's ambiguous ontological condition, meanwhile – at once the nation's past and its future-present – locates his narrative as both memory and cautionary tale. For Derrida, "one can never be sure if by returning [the specter] testifies to a living past or a living future, for the revenant may already mark the promised return of the specter of a living being" (123). Vijay's spectral narrative offers a warning of future civic unrest, the possible (violent) return of a resistant subjectivity. Emphasizing the symbiosis between ideal citizenship and fratricide, the flashback exposes citizenship and national unity as always already disrupted by their violent erasures, haunted by their failures.

While the flashback haunts the nation-state's present, it is itself haunted by the vagrant father, Anand. Via Vijay's tattoo, critics have given Anand implicit significance in *Deewar*'s negotiation of a patriarchal nation-state[39] and urban masculinity,[40] but have paid little attention to Anand himself. A trade union activist, Anand first appears leading a mineworkers' strike, demanding improved pay and working conditions. In the face of threats to his family, Anand signs a disadvantageous settlement, a betrayal for which his fellow workers attack him. Humiliated and guilt-ridden, Anand disappears. Critics tend to abandon Anand's narrative precisely when he abandons his family, limiting him to a plot device or catalyst for the family's move to Bombay.[41] However, as Bannerjea briefly notes, Anand continues to make sporadic appearances, "liv[ing] as a destroyed vagrant, traveling endlessly on the railways as a man with no name" (167–168).

Anand is important because his actions provide the context for *Deewar*'s central dilemma, but also because he leads us to an implicit intertextual engagement with *Shree 420*, not least through Vijay's tattoo: "420" refers to the Indian Penal Code, in which the number signals small-scale fraud and, more popularly, "the more significant villainy of politicians and businessmen."[42] Vijay's tattoo takes us, via Anand's absent presence, to the "master narrative" of the earlier film and, while Vijay negotiates the legacy of his father's compromised socialism, *Deewar* negotiates the legacy of the faded ideals of its cinematic ancestor.

In *Deewar*, as in readings of it, Anand is a crucial absent presence. Just as memories of him interrupt the lives of his family, he visually interrupts the film's progress and, like Vijay, is ambivalently poised between life and death. On three occasions, the film cuts away from the city to reveal Anand's ghostly figure occupying train carriages and railway stations, anonymously traversing the nation's liminal spaces. Anand travels "nowhere," the only word he speaks after his disappearance. Anand eventually dies, his corpse reported as an "unknown" body that "nobody has claimed," until Ravi recognizes a family photograph amongst the possessions. The brothers' responses to Anand's death reposition his earlier appearances as moments of haunting, and he is retrospectively caught between the corporeal and the phantomic. Ravi asserts authority over Anand's corpse, stating that "[t]his body is not unclaimed." Vijay, meanwhile, identifies Anand as always already dead, telling his girlfriend Anita (Parveen Babi) that "my father died twenty years ago. Today he was cremated, that's all."

Locating his body between their different experiences of urban modernity, these counter-claims similarly position Anand between official history and unofficial memory, nation-state and local community. This is important if we consider the nationalist vision that Anand articulates before his disappearance. Protesting against the advance of exclusionary private capitalism, Anand evinces a Nehruvian socialism that echoes Raju's final speech in *Shree 420* in its demands for wealth redistribution and equal access to welfare and education. Evoking Nehru's "Tryst with Destiny," Anand speaks of a "new dawn" "when the workers get the right and proper share for their efforts, a hospital to treat them, and a good school for their children." There is a significant overlap between Raju and Anand, who are probably of the same generation, and Anand resurrects Raju's call to action, responding, perhaps, to *Shree 420*'s "mobilization-effect." There is, however, a shift in tone; that Anand repeats Raju's call reveals the continuing failure of the nation-state to substantiate its constitutional promises. In turn, the optimistic tone of Kapoor's film gives way to a more oppositional stance, as Anand declares that "this strike will not be over as long as there is strength in us."

There are further overlaps and shifts between the films. During a second protest, Anand signs the agreement that caps pay, but also renders future strikes illegal. Gathered outside the landowner's bungalow, protesters hold black umbrellas against torrential rain. The prominence and number of these umbrellas potentially evokes the umbrella of the proposal scene in *Shree 420*, and there is an interesting overlap in its use as an icon of hope and disappointment. I suggested that the playful umbrella-sharing in *Shree 420* transformed it into a symbol of social responsibility, in a moment where familial and broader civic responsibilities are placed in symbiosis. The umbrella's reappearance in *Deewar*, when Anand must choose family over community, suggests a shift away from the earlier optimism. *Shree 420* resurrects such optimism in its final scenes, suggesting continued faith in the possibility of social and economic justice, even as that possibility is always already deferred; in Anand's betrayal, *Deewar* seems to foreclose the possibilities of an equitable society in its early moments.

Shree 420's proposal scene also offers *Deewar* a key location within Bombay: the bridge. Raju and Vidya sing the final refrains of "Pyaar Hua, Iqraar Hua" as they walk across a bridge and down its steps. This bridge resembles the one underneath which Vijay and Ravi grow up. Upon it, Vidya and Raju cast passing children as present surrogates for a future utopia of inclusive modernity and equitable citizenship. Underneath the bridge twenty years later, Vijay and Ravi translate that future into the conflicted reality of the present. In a much-discussed scene, the brothers meet at the bridge, where Vijay urges Ravi to transfer out of Bombay. As Mazumdar notes, the confrontation "shows two visions of the metropolitan experience. One brother wants to move on, leaving the past behind, the other wants to recall the experience of homelessness in the past, to emphasize the burden of lived experience" (21). Thus, Vijay urges Ravi to remember their shared experiences, but Ravi, "emancipated from the past" by his elevation "to the position of a representative of the law,"[43] resists the pull of shared experience in favor of the performance of ideal citizenship, refusing to leave. Echoing Raju's drunken rant in *Shree 420*, Vijay boastfully points out the discrepancy between his illicit prosperity and that offered by the nation-state. As Ravi reminds him, however, his criminality casts him beyond community; Ravi "has mother," while Vijay has merely the memory of family. Underneath the bridge, the future held out by Raju and Vidya is presented in ruins: ideal citizenship and mutual social responsibility have become incommensurate; the "tokens" of Vidya and Raju's love have become, in Ravi and Vijay, "tokens" of a failed social contract.

Significantly, after Ravi delivers the devastating line "I have mother," the film cuts to the train containing Anand's corpse pulling into Bombay's Victoria Terminus Station. The engine's noise plays over the final frames of the scene, relocating its representation of the dilemmas of citizenship within a betrayal of the nation's proclaimed socialist principles. While the nation-state (Ravi) appears willing to forget the material inadequacies of developmentalism, it similarly overlooks its founding ideological moorings, rejecting the connections between contemporary civil unrest and its own broken promises. Ravi's reclamation of Anand's body – an attempt, perhaps, to reappropriate socialism back into official discourse – would seem disingenuous given his refusal of responsibility for Vijay. Notably, despite their centrality to Nehru's nationalist vision, the terms "socialist" and "secular" were only written into the framework of the Constitution in 1976, during the Emergency.[44] This "cynical amendment,"[45] which belied the authoritarian implementation of anti-poor policies, is prefigured by Ravi's official documentation of Anand's socialist body. Derrida suggests that the specter is conjured "in order to chase it away, to exclude it, to exorcise it" (124). Ravi's claim perhaps similarly works to appropriate Anand's ideological legacy in order to conjure it away, to seal off its relevance from the present.

The return of Anand's corpse on a train reiterates an association made throughout *Deewar* between his spectral vagrancy and technologies of industrial modernity. While in Indian film trains tend to signal the promise of "progress and modernity," they often do so ambivalently, "expos[ing] another side of modernity."[46] "[I]mages and sounds of trains," Lalitha Gopalan argues, frequently "amplify urban despair, poverty, and ... alienation" (87). *Deewar* positions trains at the center of a nexus of visual and sonic symbols of urban despair. Anand consistently appears at moments of trauma – immediately before Vijay is tattooed; after Vijay strikes the construction manager who sacks his exhausted mother; immediately after the bridge confrontation – and his appearances are framed by close-ups of technologies of modernity: an electronic tattoo pen, machinery on the construction site, trains bearing down on the camera.

Anand's first speech establishes this association between modernization and dematerialized bodies, technology mediating his oration in a way that reiterates his socialism as always already ghostly. Anand's speech is disrupted by a cutaway to the landowner who listens to a recording of the protest in his bungalow, switching it off before it reaches its conclusion. Anand is momentarily refigured as a disembodied voice, haunting a nation being rescripted by private capitalism, interrupting its private spaces to remind it of its public responsibilities. Technology, however, allows the landowner to reject this responsibility by silencing the speech. The repeated juxtaposition of Anand's vagrant body with technologies of modernity – and the role that technology plays in rendering him spectral – highlights his significance as, to borrow Gordon's term, a "phanto[m] of modernity's violence" (19). The industrial modernity that Nehru hoped would help India's citizens substantiate their freedom is, in *Deewar*, represented as violently rendering them spectral again.

When Ravi shoots a boy on a railway line for stealing bread, the connections *Deewar* builds between the violence of modernization and the machinations of an authoritarian nation-state become clear. Connected to this moment of civic violence, Anand's wandering spectrality serves a dual function. Traveling outside Bombay, but consistently associated with the violence within, his ghostly figure embodies the corporeal materiality of subjectivities unhoused by capitalist modernity and criminalized by an authoritarian nation-state, acting as a narrative prosthesis for identities excluded from its public narratives and public spaces; at the same time, he symbolizes an unfulfilled national promise, a socialist vision that is no longer accommodated within Bombay. His dual homelessness – at once corporeal and ideological – draws our attention to real and imagined exclusions of the postcolonial city, emphasizing the urgency of re-reading Bombay for the bodies who live within its spaces, but remain "unnoticed," unknown and unclaimed by capitalist modernity.

Bombay's history since *Deewar* has made the urgency of reading for spectral bodies all the more real. From the late 1980s, the uneven distribution of the profits of Bombay's globalization has coalesced with its remapping as Mumbai, a city at the heart of a Hindu nationalist geography. In the horrific events of 1992–1993, spatial crisis combined with ethnic conflict, with Mumbai's poor and, more specifically, its Muslim poor suffering the worst excesses of the struggle over material and imaginative belonging.[47] Meanwhile, recent violence in high-class hotels and railway stations has once more cast Mumbai in the (international) popular imaginary as fatally caught between competing discourses of modernity, in which commitments to global capitalism and local community intersect and grate against each other. If *Deewar* offers a prescient narrative of the coincidence of spatial conflict, deindustrialization, organized crime, and communal violence, then the continuing uneven experience of being in Mumbai serves as a stark reminder that the promises of Independence are yet to be fully realized for many of its spectral citizens. And, while the self-congratulatory fêting of *Slumdog Millionaire* (Boyle, 2008) obscures earlier, as well as more recent, filmic depictions of Bombay/Mumbai's Janus-faced modernity – and indeed *Slumdog*'s own referencing of *Deewar* – the film and the surrounding debate on child poverty highlight the continued relevance of Kapoor's earlier staging of the dilemma of postcolonial citizenship, even as they demonstrate the inadequacy, if not naivety, of its optimism.

As India descended towards the Emergency in 1975, Chopra could not raise such optimism. Anand's corpse is cremated midway through *Deewar*; Vijay is shot at the close of the flashback. Unlike Raju in *Shree 420*, these bodies do not rise again. *Shree 420* mobilizes spectrality in order to resuscitate a Nehruvian nationalist vision, fleshing out postcolonial citizenship as a becoming-body whose emancipation is always yet to come. Even as they mark a failure, spectral figures here offer an optimistic faith in the possible resurrection of an earlier ideal. *Deewar*'s ghosts are more troubling, emphasizing an ongoing crisis in the nation. Here, the citizenship of marginalized subjectivities appears to *become spectral*, their corporeality becoming less, rather than more, substantial. Even as it asserts the authority of the nation-state in its closing moments, the ideal citizen is anxiously haunted by a resistant, marginalized other. The specter in *Deewar* does not resurrect a promise, but rather a threat, and the future evoked is not one of emancipation and social justice, but of civic unrest and authoritarian rule. *Shree 420* offers the spectral as a modality of becoming; in *Deewar* the specter marks an ending, the drawing in of a haunted night, after the "new dawn" of Independence.

NOTES

1   This essay is part of a project generously supported by a Canadian Commonwealth Postdoctoral Research Fellowship, funded by the Department of Foreign Affairs and International Trade, Canada, and a Postdoctoral Fellowship funded by *Figura: Centre de Recherche sur le Texte et l'Imaginaire*, based at Concordia University, Montreal. I would like to thank Jill Didur for her comments on earlier versions of this piece.

2   Avery Gordon, *Ghostly Matters: Haunting and the Sociological Imagination* (Minneapolis and London: University of Minnesota Press, 1997), 8.

3   Jawaharlal Nehru, "Tryst with Destiny," Speech in the Constituent Assembly, August 14, 1947. Reprinted in *The Oxford Nehru*, ed. Uma Iyengar (New Delhi and Oxford: Oxford University Press, 2007), 207.

4   Ibid., 208.

5   Peng Cheah, "Spectral Nationality: The Living on [*sur-vie*] of the Postcolonial Nation in Neocolonial Globalization," *boundary 2* 26, no. 3 (1999): 227.

6   Jawaharlal Nehru, "The Appointed Day," Message to the Nation printed in newspapers on August 15, 1947. *The Oxford Nehru*, 209.

7   Leonard Lawler, *Derrida and Husserl: The Basic Problem of Phenomenology* (Bloomington: Indiana University Press, 2002), 217, 212.

8   Jacques Derrida, *Specters of Marx: The State of the Debt, the Work of Mourning, and the New International*, trans. Peggy Kamuf (New York and London: Routledge, 1994),

xviii, quoted in Bishnupriya Ghosh, "On Grafting the Vernacular: The Consequences of Postcolonial Spectrology," *boundary 2* 31, no. 2 (2004): 207, emphasis in original.

9   Derrida, *Specters of Marx*, 81.

10   Nehru, "Tryst with Destiny," 208.

11   Gordon, *Ghostly Matters*, 8.

12   Ghosh, "On Grafting the Vernacular," 207, 208.

13   Gayatri Chakravorty Spivak, "Ghostwriting," *Diacritics* 25, no. 2 (1995): 70. For more recent interest, see, for example, John McLeod, "Business Unbegun: Spectral Subjectivities in the Work of Jackie Kay and Pauline Melville," in *Postcolonial Ghosts*, ed. Mélanie Joseph-Vilain and Judith Misrahi-Barak (Montpellier: Presses Universitaires de la Méditerranée, forthcoming 2009).

14   Arjun Appadurai, "Spectral Housing and Urban Cleansing: Notes on Millennial Mumbai," *Public Culture* 12, no. 3 (2000): 649.

15   Sunil Khilnani, *The Idea of India*, 3rd edition (New York: Farrar, Straus & Giroux, 2003), 136; Rashmi Varma, "Provincializing the Global City: From Bombay to Mumbai," *Social Text* 22, no. 4 (2004): 68.

16   Aijiz Ahmad, *Lineages of the Present: Ideology and Politics in Contemporary South Asia* (London and New York: Verso, 2000), 180.

17   Jyotika Virdi, *The Cinematic ImagiNation: Indian Popular Films as Social History* (New Brunswick, NJ: Rutgers University Press, 2003), 95.

18   Ahmad, *Lineages of the Present*, 228.

19   Stuart Corbridge and John Harriss, *Reinventing India: Liberalization, Hindu Nationalism and Popular Democracy* (Cambridge, UK: Polity Press, 2000), 29, 20.

20   Corbridge and Harriss, *Reinventing India*, 29.

21   See also Varma, "Provincializing the Global City," 67–68.

22   Virdi, *The Cinematic ImagiNation*, 92.

23   M. Madhava Prasad, *Ideology of the Hindi Film: A Historical Construction* (New Delhi and New York: Oxford University Press, 1998), 131.

24   Derrida, *Specters of Marx*, 11.

25   Varma, "Provincializing the Global City," 69; Virdi, *The Cinematic ImagiNation*, 95.

26   Quoted in Corbridge and Harriss, *Reinventing India*, 30.

27   Vijay Mishra, *Bollywood Cinema: Temples of Desire* (London and New York: Routledge, 2002), 201.

28   Derrida, *Specters of Marx*, 5.

29   Virdi, *The Cinematic ImagiNation*, 93.

30   Ranjani Mazumdar, *Bombay Cinema: An Archive of the City* (Minneapolis and London: University of Minnesota Press, 2007), 2.

31   Ibid., 13.

32   Prasad, *Ideology of the Hindi Film*, 145.

33   See Mazumdar, *Bombay Cinema*, 24.

34   Prasad, *Ideology of the Hindi Film*, 145.

35   Mazumdar, *Bombay Cinema*, 14.

36   Ibid., 15, 22.

37   Ibid., 6.

38   Paul Brass, "The Strong State and the Fear of Disorder," in *Transforming India: Social and Political Dynamics of Democracy*, ed. Francine R. Frankel et al. (New Delhi: Oxford University Press, 2000), 74.

39   Prasad, *Ideology of the Hindi Film*, 144–153; Virdi, *The Cinematic ImagiNation*, 119.

40 Koushik Bannerjea, "'Fight Club': Aesthetic Hybridization and the Construction of Rogue Masculinities in *Sholay* and *Deewaar*," in *Bollywood: Popular Indian Cinema Through a Transnational Lens*, ed. Ramindar Kaur and Ajay J. Sinha (New Delhi and London: Sage, 2005), 167–175; see also Mazumdar, *Bombay Cinema*, esp. 24–27.

41 Rachel Dwyer, *Yash Chopra* (London: BFI, 2002), 76–77; Rachel Dwyer and Divia Patel, *Cinema India: The Visual Culture of Hindi Film* (London: Reaktion, 2002), 34; Mazumdar, *Bombay Cinema*, 13–14; Prasad, *Ideology of the Hindi Film*, 145; Virdi, *The Cinematic ImagiNation*, 115.

42 Srinivas Aravamudan, "'Being God's Postman is No Fun, Yaar': Salman Rushdie's *The Satanic Verses*," *Diacritics* 19, no. 2 (1989): 7.

43 Prasad, *Ideology of the Hindi Film*, 151.

44 Corbridge and Harriss, *Reinventing India*, 21.

45 Ibid.

46 Lalitha Gopalan, *Cinema of Interruptions: Action Genres in the Sociological Imagination* (Minneapolis and London: University of Minnesota Press, 1997), 85, 87.

47 See Appadurai, "Spectral Housing," 649.

Chapter 7

Shadow of the Colossus: The Spectral Lives of 9/11

Georgina Banita

The power of these haunted things would also explain why the remains of
the World Trade Center – its wrecked steel and ductwork and piping and
shiny aluminum cladding – would never be dealt with quite rationally. The
immeasurable importance of those remains, the preciousness of the messages
they carried from the inferno on September 11, could not be confronted squarely
without facing the howls of the dead in every buckled strut or beam that had
once sheltered humanity.[1]

Introduction: Twin Colossi between Shadow and Light

As a video game, *Shadow of the Colossus* does all the wrong things. The title is unusually
elaborate and abstract, the game itself contains no weapons orgy, explosions, or an edgy
soundtrack, and the color scheme is exceedingly subdued.[2] The hero's composure borders
on autism. He is a man of few words, whose meager body betrays his lack of interest
in training and fitness regimes. Yet *Shadow* is nonetheless a masterpiece of its genre.
Its two protagonists – a young man (Wander) and his horse (Agro) – drift through an
expansive landscape sprinkled with ruins that seems to stretch forever. They are energized
only by the hero's task of defeating sixteen giants in order to bring his comatose beloved
(Mono) back to life. Primarily a visual feast of paradoxical austerity, *Shadow* consists of
a series of majestic, melancholy images worthy of Caspar David Friedrich (1774–1840)
or Giovanni Battista Piranesi's nightmarish *Carceri* (1760s), punctuated not by the usual
paraphernalia of video games but by the howling wind and Agro's rhythmical hoof tap.
The colossi are the only dynamic elements of the scene, but even they seem eerily lifeless:
their bodies are a fusion of muscles, wood, and rock. They tower over their traipsing
opponent, behaving in the manner of unruly architectural structures.

In Mike Binder's 2007 film *Reign over Me*, former dentist Charlie Fineman
retreats from his life after losing his wife and daughters in the 9/11 World Trade

Center attacks. Now residing alone in the apartment he once shared with his family, Charlie renovates it compulsively, practices playing drums, and cannot get enough of *Shadow of the Colossus* on a gigantic TV screen. Significantly, his family had been on one of the planes that crashed into the Twin Towers, suffering a violent death that haunts Charlie years after the attacks. Like Wander, Charlie attempts to revive his lost love through a process of gradual alienation and severance of his ties with the world. Whereas Wander enters the Forbidden Land populated only by him and the giants he is chasing, Charlie breaks contact with his remaining family, placing himself squarely in the shadow of the twin colossi that were his wife and daughters' crime scene and resting place. To find each colossus, Wander must raise his sword while in a sunlit area to reflect beams of light, which converge when the sword is pointed in the right direction of the next encounter. The two light beams pointing at the sky that mark the anniversary of the 9/11 attacks each year never converge, though, and their striking parallelism echoes Charlie's failure to dislodge himself from the trappings of memory and trauma. The immaterial light beams commemorating the towers also epitomize the complex nature of the towers' continued presence even after their collapse, both as symbols of a prelapsarian paradise lost beyond recovery, and as specters of a new world that haunts us – not as the past conventionally haunts the present, but as the uncanny footprint of a future yet to come.

In the segment directed by Sean Penn in the collective project released as *11'09"01* (2002), an elderly widower haunted by the presence of his wife, whose spectral existence he preserves with pathological abandon, experiences an epiphanic enlightenment when the towers collapse and remove their shadow. The flower on the widower's sill can finally bloom again, bringing daylight into a life that had succumbed to permanent shadow. Instead of dispelling the spirits that inhabit his mind, as we might expect, the invasion of light into the old man's life only deepens his belief that a miracle has occurred, which he hastens to share with his wife. Notwithstanding the ambiguity of the segment and its subversive, almost absurd suggestion that some good might have evolved from the carnage, the film poignantly reveals the inescapable grip of spectral haunting as a compulsive reaction to grief. Even an event that promises to break through preconceptions and make room for genuine insight only aggravates the illusions that each of us had entertained. The fall of the towers, I shall argue, erected a much larger shadow than they eradicated.

This essay draws on Jacques Derrida's concept of the hauntology of terror to point out the spectrality of the images we associate with terrorism and with 9/11 in particular by focusing on such popular culture staples as the portrait of Osama bin Laden, the terrorist as invisible ghost – "the enemy within" – and other spectral conceptions of evil and criminality. In doing this I hope to challenge received notions of haunting in relation to spatiality and futurity in the context of a particular form of hauntology related to a specific locale – here the Twin Towers in Manhattan – which, however, becomes diluted through its infinite mechanical reproduction in the media. My interest is divided among several layers of popular attention to post 9/11 "apparitions."[3] First, I look at the haunting presence of the WTC victims in the popular imagination, victims whose bodies were never recovered and whose photographs were scattered in a traumatized city that learned to associate presence with image rather than with concrete corporeality. Second, I consider the proliferating metaphors linking terrorism to ghost-like invisibility and tenacious haunting. Since the terrorist attacks of September 11, 2001, Osama bin Laden has often been likened to a specter that resists "capture" – both in the sense of retrieval and visual representation. Third, I investigate several explicitly post 9/11 mainstream films that not only mention the attacks but offer an unsubtle reification of the events. While *Cloverfield* (Reeves, 2008) points to the attacks as its unstated backdrop, as the reality that always inhabits a portion of the viewer's mind but does not receive any explicit mention in the film itself, other productions such as *Reign over Me* and *25th Hour* (Lee, 2002) contend with 9/11 trauma as a hidden tumor written into the fabric of the film's narrative and artistic strategies. I conclude that the imbricated layers of media representation itself have performed a kind of spectral haunting by reiterating images that have become ingrained in the popular perception of an event which still seems to derive its potency from hauntic repetition, involuntary memory, and a subtle process of post-mortemization. The attacks, I argue, have not claimed a position in popular memory as an event, but rather as a post-event – less as the happening of one September morning and more as the era it ushered in through its abrupt disruption of everyday life and normality.

It's Only by Our Lack of Ghosts We're Haunted

In a brief comment entitled "Where Are the Ghosts of 9/11?" published shortly before the 2008 presidential elections in the U.S., David Simpson – author of *9/11: The Culture of Commemoration* – writes: "Seven years after 9/11 one of the strangest things is that there are no ghosts. There never were."[4] To some extent this failure of the attacks to haunt and harass those they did not kill can be traced back to the rapid responses of the authorities and of the media toward a patriotic eulogization of heroism and a dismissal of the more troubling consequences of the attacks. "The photographs that appeared day after day in the *New York Times*," Simpson continues,

> seemed ... flagrantly dishonorable in their very effort to commemorate. They left little to be haunted by as they reconstructed the lives of the dead as Disneyfied icons of optimistic upward mobility, dreams achieved, selfless happiness, and civic virtue amidst an energetic and responsive democracy. No one was cruel, unhappy, or disappointed, no one unappeased.

Simpson astutely argues that by preventing the work of mourning implicit in the act of being haunted, post 9/11 political games manufactured a pervasive fear of the exterior "other" while paying too little attention to the otherness within – the confrontation with uncanny remnants and specters of the attacks: "Except for the immediately bereaved who have hardly been allowed to speak but are constantly spoken for, we have continued to be kept (do we keep ourselves?) from our own hauntings, our own Godzillas or jungles of screaming souls."

Put differently, the shadow of the attacks was taken as an external projection rather than a presence that is integral to the event itself, a confusion that calls to mind what has been described as the "shadow stage" in the recognition of identity. As Victor Stoichita has shown, drawing on Jean Piaget's theory of the child's relationship to its shadow, at the first stage the shadow is subsumed to the concept of alterity until the individual perceives the intimate relation between an object and the shadow it throws.[5] Seen in this perspective, the failure to engage with the intrinsic aspects of the tragedy that Simpson diagnoses corresponds to the failure of the child to admit the inextricable connection between the self and its projected shadow. To remedy this dissociation, we must admit that the shadow resides as much outside us as it does within. The shadow of the colossus, then, is not an external obstacle to be overcome but the internal hubris of a soul bent on destruction and permanent battle – as Wander's tragic death makes patently clear at the end of the allegorical video game I invoked at the outset of this discussion.

The salutary engagement with a benign form of haunting does not, however, entail a self-absorbed preoccupation with selfhood and trauma, but a healthy respite from history and a meditation on the profound interruption caused by the attacks. Paradoxically enough, to indulge in post-traumatic haunting acts as a prerequisite for overcoming trauma and its impairing effects on the affective stability of all involved. As Simpson notes, although "(t)he rhetoric of trauma was everywhere in the months after 9/11," it concealed "the absence of trauma itself, of deep trauma's imperative toward introversion and arrestation. We did not stop the clock for deep reflection." While I agree with this verdict, in the following pages I seek to reveal how this blockage of haunting does not go against the grain of ghostly practices, nor does it completely preclude the therapeutic effects of mourning as prescribed by trauma theory. To make this point I rely on Derrida's concept of hauntology – a typically deconstructive multi-layered term that merges haunting and ontology to reflect on their relationship. Simply put, hauntology contrasts the spirit or essence of a thing with its countless materializations or specters, which allow for the persistence of spirit as memory. I want to probe the ways in which the multiple specters of the WTC attacks haunt the popular culture and the collective unconscious of contemporary America. These specters, I argue, represent nothing but the heterogeneous afterlives of the American spirit scattered by the 9/11 attacks, a spirit which, precisely by choosing not to linger in the traumatic moment, has remained forever ensconced in it. At the same time, these spectral reverberations of 9/11 intertwine and play off each other to produce a hybrid homage not to a supposed terror "original" but to a schizophrenic, transtraumatic culture that is both marked by the 9/11 tragedy and unmoved by it, both obsessed with recovering the innocence of "before" and intensely anticipating a redeeming "after." This is not to say, however, that 9/11 cannot be legitimately examined as a historical event. Yet my deep purpose here is to stipulate that the attacks relinquished their historical stringency and segued into a more diffuse hauntology. The status of the attacks as a single, unified event is contradicted by the very modes of contemporary production and dissemination of such visual incidents. As a heterogeneous "archive," however, 9/11 is a "spectral a priori: neither present nor absent "in the flesh," neither visible nor invisible, a trace always referring to another whose eyes can never be met."[6] The archive of 9/11 specters illustrates various forms of "return" and has become far more important than accurate historical descriptions of the attacks as ways to diagnose and attenuate trauma. Ultimately, then, in an uncanny gesture of reversal, the specters of 9/11 transhistorically haunt their source and reframe the attacks in a more ambiguous register than purely historical accounts would permit.[7]

Spirit Photography Today

The first visible ghosts of the WTC attacks – the photographs of the missing persons – problematize the notion of a direct relationship between spirit and specter, pointing to the ways in which the specter not only supplements but eventually supplants the original spirit.[8] Although couched in the guise of empathy and ethical concern, the images ostensibly work to train the viewer into replacing the painful absence of the WTC victims by their soothing pictures, usually taken at festive or generally more pleasurable moments of their lives. The effect of these spectral presences plays upon the assumptions of the spectators that despite the terrorists' brutal intentions, the humanity of the dead was in no way diminished, but possibly even enhanced by their status as innocent victims. Such attitudes are the source of what Simpson deplores as a premature interruption of mourning, precipitated by a prevalent sense of self-righteousness and the right to take vengeance.

Further, the transition of the 9/11 events from original spirit to manifold specters is nowhere more evident than in Diane Schoemperlen's dissociation of real 9/11 victims from the lives she describes in her elegiac portraits collected in *Names of the Dead*.[9] In answer to both the photographic records of the attacks and the *Portraits of Grief* published in the *New York Times*, Schoemperlen detaches the victims' lives from the names of the victims, suspending her anecdotes and brief prose poems in a spectral vacuum as indefinable and unnameable as any otherworldly visitation: "In reading about the victims," she writes,

> I found that many things were mentioned over and over again: taking the children to the park, buying a new house, going grocery shopping, renovating, and so on. I decided I had to find a way to write about these common activities without mentioning any one person by name, thereby telling the story of an individual while at the same time using that small story to represent the stories of many others. Therefore, each narrative fragment appearing in a separate paragraph does tell a specific story, but it is not intended to refer directly to the name that immediately precedes it. (xii)

The narrative fragments created by Schoemperlen's "haunting elegy" (book blurb) are imaginative rather than factual, reconstructing the dreams, thoughts, and preferences of the dead and including scenes that are wholly the product of the author's fantasy, ranging from descriptions of ordinary objects on the kitchen table to scenes of lovemaking. Such creativity almost inspires voyeurism. It also suggests that far from being replicas of the victims' elusive spirit, the spectral profiles of the dead become a reflection of the minds they are haunting.

The same can be said about the photographs of missing people, displayed all over Manhattan in the aftermath of the tragedy. Not only the victims but also the hijackers were equated with visual approximations of their faces, which mirror less the past reality of the dead and more the present actuality of their viewers. The effects of these images on New Yorkers can be studied in the book *Lamentation 9/11*, a collection of such photographs which documents the city's telephone poles, subway stations, fences, and building walls where people hung posters of missing loved ones.[10] The accompanying prose poem by E. L. Doctorow embeds these images into the collective consciousness of the city itself, where they mingle with the faces of the living. What the pictures – together with the pleas for information, messages to family members, and children's drawings – ultimately project is an injunction to vision as a way to counterbalance the physical disappearance of the missing and as a clue to the similar thinning out of the living observers, now walking the streets of the city as mere specters of themselves, only marginally visible to each other yet subliminally present as the very pulse of the city:

> We would appear on the perimeters of one another's consciousness, in one another's sightlines, on any given day, passing in the street, riding the subway, shopping for our families, going to the ballgame, waiting on the same street corners for the light to change, heading home to the joy of our children, taking the same holidays … all of us doing the same things in our different ways, mirroring one another's daily lives as we flowed through the streets or rode under them, always intent on our business within the dimensions of our city. (63)

The Terrorist as Poltergeist

In his interview with Giovanna Borradori, Derrida expresses a view of terrorism as a function of the fantasmatic and spectacular character of the media; "the real terror," he insists, "consisted of, and, in fact, began by exposing and exploiting … the images of this terror by the target itself."[11] The specter of terror as media reproduction thus supersedes the authentic terrorist attack, shifting the focus from an easily traceable ideology of terror to a hauntology, or even clonology of terror – to radicalize W. J. T. Mitchell's theory of clonophobia,[12] or the fear of terrorism seen as the spectral reproducibility of an indeterminate and invisible danger. As an insidious force that infiltrates a social organism without announcing its presence, terrorism is a perfect example of the embedded spectrality I am illustrating here. In extreme cases, the distinction between a host and its ghost is fully obfuscated, as numerous instances of so-called homegrown terror have revealed. Defining terrorism as a form of visual warfare, Mitchell suggests that the war on terror is "a war on a projected specter or phantasm, a war against an elusive, invisible, unlocatable enemy, a war that continually misses its target, striking out blindly with conventional means and waging massive destruction on innocent people in the process" (185). Resembling shadow-boxing more than an act of self-defense carried out with moral scrupulousness and precision, the war on terror can be seen as the struggle of a possessed person to ban the spirit that they are possessed by – a struggle that damages the self more than it banishes the parasitic spirit.

Perhaps the most symptomatic embodiment of the terrorist as poltergeist is the symbolic head of Al Qaeda, Osama bin Laden, whose frequent video appearances, coupled with the impossibility of tracking him down, have bestowed upon him the aura of a demon, a supremely evil figure who appears and disappears at will. Many of the audio and video segments purporting to represent bin Laden have been fraught with inconsistencies and sparked debates over whether the recording was authentic and when/where it had originated. The intervals between the releases of such recordings in turn fuel speculation about bin Laden's well-being, or his ability to remain active as the head of Al Qaeda in the midst of the largest-ever campaign to hunt down a single individual. Further, a constant and constantly remarked upon feature of these recordings is the ghostliness of bin Laden's appearance. One BBC report aptly described him as Al Qaeda's "spectral anchorman."[13] As Andrew Hill has noted, bin Laden's pallor "is further enhanced by the low quality of portions of this footage, which calls to mind the association of poor picture quality in television during the 1950s as evidence of the presence of phantoms inhabiting the medium."[14] Bin Laden's extreme malevolence and his ability to inhabit our imagination – as in Langlands & Bell's computer-generated projection *The House of Osama bin Laden* (2003), shortlisted for the 2004 Turner Prize, which reconstitutes and displays one of the leader's former abodes – are evocative of his status as a specter haunting the U.S. and its allies. Yet while the specters of the towers emphasize the depth of the shadow, Osama's haunting pinpoints the demonic power and agency of the colossus, despite its somewhat distorted visual profile. Instead of aiming to defeat this colossus, though, the U.S. seems to nourish and further its menacing existence for strategic purposes in the war on terror. This ghost, then, is not repulsive and exorcised, but actively entertained, confirming Derrida's claim that the secondary specter – i.e., bin Laden's fantasmatic image as global apparition – has supplanted the original and proven that despite their initial attachment to a specific locale (here, primarily the WTC), such haunting images possess "a transcendental relationship to space and time."[15] Consequently, killing bin Laden would be superfluous, in that his death would only reinforce his presence as the abject undead or revenant, the media acting as the "medium" that conjures him. The paradox of bin Laden's ubiquitous persona can be aligned with the one I discussed earlier. Bin Laden is both indispensable to post-9/11 American politics and excluded from it in moral terms, just as the ghosts of the 9/11 dead are obscured in the collective consciousness of the nation only to resurface as a subliminal factor in the public legitimization of the war on terror.

A Filmic Hauntology of 9/11

This dialectic of presence and absence forms the premise and artistic strategy of several mainstream films released since 2002, which draw variations on trauma and repression on the larger canvas of a post 9/11 world, partly obscuring the attacks themselves. *Cloverfield*, for instance, produced by the Hollywood entertainment czar J. J. Abrams, reached its target demographic through a canny viral marketing campaign that deliberately obfuscated the film's plot and its violent premise. The obvious apocalyptic undertones point to the movie's blatant debt to 9/11.[16] Yet the vacuousness of the characters, the implausible narrative, and emotionally numbing special effects not only trivialize the most dramatic single day in recent American history, but also manipulate and abuse real-life fears of terrorism, as well as the audience's refined palate for authenticity, trained in the course of what John Ellis has called "the century of witness,"[17] facilitated by contemporary technologies of instant transmission of images and digitalities. *Cloverfield* depicts a giant monster attack on Manhattan entirely through the video camera of an impromptu documentarian following a group of twenty-somethings on the run from a reptilian creature with a slithering tail that coils its body around skyscrapers and the war machines of an army rendered useless and confused. As the monster wreaks havoc in the urban canyons, clouds of dust billow down the street, silently carrying shredded paper – an image that instantly invokes the 9/11 cloud of dust and debris. In a further instance of reciprocal haunting, *Cloverfield* draws on the Japanese monster movie *Godzilla*, created in response to fears of U.S. nuclear power. Star producer J. J. Abrams spells out his intention to fashion the movie as a catalyzer for pent-up emotions sparked by the terrorist attacks and effectively sublimated during the subsequent Bush years:

> When *Godzilla* came out, the idea of doing a movie about the destruction of a city because of a radioactive man-made thing must have had a similar feeling. On the one hand, it's a silly man in a rubber suit. On the other hand, it's a way to process these fears that are mostly bottled up. … With *Cloverfield*, we were trying to create a film that would be entertaining and, as a by-product of the subject matter, perhaps be a catharsis. We wanted to let people live through their wildest fears but be in a safe place, where the enemy is the size of a skyscraper instead of some stateless, unseen, cowardly terrorist.[18]

The specters of the 9/11 events, then, have the additional function of attenuating the emotional impact of the attacks.[19] Moreover, their cathartic role is greatly enhanced by the infinite dispersal of perception occasioned by the attacks, which occurred precisely at the historical juncture effecting the transition from analog to digital representation.[20] *Cloverfield* embraces this culture of endlessly alert visual attention, or what Abrams calls "the YouTubification of things," offering a shaky view of how 9/11 ghosts are mediated and the precarious spectatorship involved in the process.[21]

The most explicit treatment to date of post-traumatic symptoms associated with the 9/11 attacks, especially in their original urban context, is Mike Binder's *Reign Over Me*, a genuinely sympathetic film that occasionally teeters on the brink of clichéd melodrama. Charlie's renewed camaraderie with his former college roommate and dental-school pal Alan Johnson helps him recapture that free-wheeling period of his life when he could roam free, before he settled into a blissful family life that was painfully snatched away from him on September 11, 2001. What the film manages to convey, despite its somewhat awkward negotiations among the characters' emotional bonds with each other, is a sense that 9/11 trauma has often been appropriated and vicariously inhabited in inappropriate ways by individuals that did not immediately partake in the loss. To some extent, most of the people that Charlie interacts with abuse his situation to address their personal grievances. Alan uses his liberating relationship to Charlie to become more responsive in his marriage and more assertive in his professional life. Charlie's own in-laws, who try to commit him to a psychiatric hospital because his mourning is less demonstrative than theirs, clearly use him as a projection screen for the emotional void that their daughter's sudden death has left behind. Alan's patient Donna Remar, who suffers from severe abandonment syndrome after her lover's departure and throws herself indiscriminately at other men (including Alan), sees Charlie as a potential peg to pin her own frustrations on. Despite their avowed sympathy, Charlie's friends regard his situation as largely self-inflicted and see themselves in a position to jolt him out of it. Most indicative of their vested interests is a scene in which Alan is accused of secretly coveting Charlie's millions, received in compensation for his loss.[22] In between these exploitative attempts to share in the glamour of 9/11 trauma – the characters could even be said to suffer from a pernicious form of trauma envy – we are offered an overly romantic glimpse into Charlie's own style of accommodating his grief. Next to the escapist indulgence in the expansive emptiness and catatonic lethargy of *Shadow of the Colossus*, Charlie relaxes by scooting through nighttime Manhattan on streets that are unencumbered by traffic, like a shadow of his former self, or a haunting spirit circling around the spot where his life (his family) was taken away from him. The single pivotal scene of the film shows Charlie having a tear-jerking meltdown in the waiting room of his therapist's office. The moment lacks subtlety, force-feeding rather than inspiring compassion. In the end we prefer Charlie as a mute ghost, swallowing his pain with discretion like a communion tablet.

Better able to contain emotion is Edward Norton's character (Monty Brogan) in Spike Lee's 9/11 elegy *25th Hour*, based on the 2001 debut novel by David Benioff, who also wrote the script. The film documents a convicted drug dealer's last night on the town before he begins serving seven years in prison. Although the plot in no way requires a direct engagement with the 9/11 events (Benioff completed his book before September 11), the film was shot in New York in the months following the attacks so Lee decided – wisely, I believe – to include brief sequences showing how the city responded to the disaster.[23] The cinematographer (Rodrigo Prieto) envelops New York in bleached colors to convey the pale veneer of a city covered with ashes. The title sequence features the twin memorial searchlights piercing the New York skyline. Ground Zero also forms the backdrop of a conversation between two of Monty's friends before going to meet Monty at his favorite club. The score by Terence Blanchard swells at this point into a full-throated choir to invoke the spirits unearthed by the excavating machines that crawl over the site like beetles. In the course of their conversation, the two friends come to face the fact that Monty has most likely been handed a death sentence, and admit that he probably "had it coming." The statement applies to Monty as much as it does to America itself as a dealer in questionable values that finally receives a punishment that rattles its self-confidence and faith in the future. Monty's own anticipatory fear of prison life thus resonates with the sense of impending terror that swamps the city. Far from taking 9/11 as an incentive to idealize New York and its glamorous American-ness, Lee allows Monty to take a violent verbal swipe at the city's melting pot – a bile-ridden invective that drew critical attention to the film – and completes the movie with a fantasy of escape into the western part of the country in a land of mountains and deserts, which are better equipped than steel and concrete to repel contemporary terror.

Epilogue: Spectral Portraits of Grief

On the morning of September 11, 2001, a florist and volunteer Emergency Medical Technician named Mickey Flowers grabbed his digital camera and drove the few blocks from his store to the WTC after the first plane hit the north tower. The images that Flowers took became the basis of a collaboration with the artist Kevin Clarke, whose studio was also near the WTC.[24] Since 1987, Clarke has been making unique portraits combining photographic images and his subject's DNA sequences to create what W. J. T. Mitchell calls "biopictures" or "biodigital pictures."[25] His usual method is to take some time to get to know his subject, then carefully select a setting in which he recognizes the individual. He then photographs this object or scene, digitally manipulates the color and image, and overlays it with the subject's genetic code, which is sequenced by a laboratory from donated blood. For this collaboration, Clarke used Flowers's images of 9/11 and its aftermath for portraits of people who survived the attacks or were involved in the rescue effort. A view of smoke billowing from the ruins is overlaid with the DNA sequence of a child who was evacuated from a school near the towers. Another image of the smoldering remains is paired with the genetic code of a fire fighter. Of course, gene sequences codify the nucleotides in each DNA molecule and thus demonstrate the way in which individual genomes differ from each other. The sequence of letters is distinct in the genome of each individual, as we all possess our own genetic code. Clarke's 9/11 portraits thus convey the idea that the invisible victims of the attacks, reduced to a state that renders them not only indistinguishable from each other but also unequal to themselves, i.e. unidentifiable, as well as hard to separate from dust and trash, do have their own personal uniqueness reflected in their genetic coding. By creating images of the crumbled towers that contain visible fragments of the victims trapped inside, this photographic project harks back to nineteenth-century ghost photography, whereby spirits were captured by the camera that made them visible. It also epitomizes what Mitchell describes as "the fusion of the older 'spectral' life of images (the uncanny, the ghostly) with a new form of *technical* life" (181, emphasis in original). Rather than reclaiming a "biological reanimation," as Mitchell would have it, I believe the DNA portraits illustrate what I have tried to unravel: that far from producing no ghosts, as David Simpson insists, the 9/11 events exists only spectrally, to the point where even the biological remains of the victims are relegated to the fantasmatic realm of the visual.

Instead of a ghostly spirit interrupting post 9/11 life, the spectral memory of the attacks has become the very condition of our existence and the shadow of a future colossal in its destructive potential.

NOTES

1   James Glanz and Eric Lipton, *City in the Sky: The Rise and Fall of the World Trade Center* (New York: Henry Holt, 2003), 336.

2   *Shadow of the Colossus* is a Japanese-developed video game for PlayStation 2, released in North America and Japan in October 2005.

3   My understanding of ghosts in this context is not coextensive with the conventional definition of the term as a specific person who has died but nevertheless appears visibly or aurally as a recognizable entity; see also Katherine A. Fowkes, *Giving Up the Ghost: Spirits, Ghosts, and Angels in Mainstream Comedy Films* (Detroit: Wayne State University Press, 1998). Although certainly retrieved from a site of death and destruction, 9/11 specters are a product of collective imagination and act collectively as a ghost mob or chorus, with a symbolic rather than frightening power.

4   David Simpson, "Where Are the Ghosts of 9/11?," http://pressblog.uchicago.edu/2008/09/11/where_are_the_ghosts_of_911.html.

5   See Victor Ieronim Stoichita, *A Short History of the Shadow* (London: Reaktion Books, 1997); Jean Piaget, *The Child's Perception of Physical Causality* (Paterson, NJ: Littlefield, Adams, 1960).

6   Jacques Derrida, *Archive Fever: A Freudian Impression*, trans. Eric Prenowitz (Chicago: University of Chicago Press, 1996), 84.

7   For a somewhat related argument in the context of film adaptation see Shannon Donaldson-McHugh and Don Moore, "Film Adaptation, Co-Authorship, and Hauntology: Gus van Sant's *Psycho* (1998)," *The Journal of Popular Culture* 39, no. 2 (2006): 225–233.

8   Photographic figures have been associated with the hauntic and spectral by several critics: Siegfried Kracauer, *The Mass Ornament: Weimar Essays* (Cambridge, MA: Harvard University Press, 1995), 56; Roland Barthes, *Camera Lucida: Reflections on Photography* (London: Vintage, 2000), 14; Susan Sontag, *On Photography* (London: Penguin, 2002), 9. While photographic criticism revolves around the semiotic indexicality of the image in relation to its referent, my own approach throws into question the stability of this relation, reframing it as a double haunting that produces Derrida's spectral archive.

9   Diane Schoemperlen, *Names of the Dead: An Elegy for the Victims of September 11* (New York: Viking, 2004).

10 E. L. Doctorow, *Lamentation 9/11* (New York: Ruder-Fin Press, 2002).

11 Giovanna Borradori, *Philosophy in a Time of Terror: Dialogues with Jürgen Habermas and Jacques Derrida* (Chicago: University of Chicago Press, 2003), 108.

12 W. J. T. Mitchell, "Cloning Terror: The War of Images 2001–4," in *The Life and Death of Images: Ethics and Aesthetics*, ed. Diarmuid Costello and Dominic Willsdon (Ithaca: Cornell University Press, 2008), 179–207.

13 Andrew Hill, "The bin Laden Tapes," *Journal for Cultural Research*, 10, no. 1 (2006), 41.

14 Hill, "The bin Laden Tapes," 41. See also Jeffrey Sconce, *Haunted Media: Electronic Presence from Telegraphy to Television* (Durham: Duke University Press, 2000), 124–166.

15 Hill, "The bin Laden Tapes," 45.

16 As Manohla Dargis suggests in her review of the film, the fact that its director, writer, and producer all live in Los Angeles rather than New York may explain their failure to intersperse the 9/11 allusions with more economy and tact. Manohla Dargis, "We're All Gonna Die! Grab Your Video Camera!" *New York Times*, January 18, 2008, 10.

17 John Ellis, *Seeing Things: Television in the Age of Uncertainty* (London: I. B. Tauris, 2000).

18 Lev Grossman, "Apocalypse New," *Time*, January 28, 2008, 111.

19 Wes Craven's *Red Eye* (2005) is haunted both by the spirit of Alfred Hitchcock and the 9/11 hijackings. A spectacular terrorist attack against the Chief of Homeland Security carries the otherwise underdeveloped plot, mostly condensed in that half of the movie taking place in the claustrophobic environment of an aircraft. Unlike the desire of *Cloverfield*'s makers to force the viewers through an affective purgatory that would purge their post 9/11 anxieties, *Red Eye* is content to provide leisurely entertainment without Freudian complexity or political critique.

20 See also Georgiana Banita, "The Tragedy of Technology: Raymond Williams and Online Video," in *About Raymond Williams*, ed. Lawrence Grossberg, Roman Horak, and Monika Seidl (London: Routledge, forthcoming 2009).

21 Many viewers suffered from motion sickness or headaches during the screenings.

22 On the ethical issues involved in the efforts of the 9/11 victim fund to compensate grieving families for their loss, see Kenneth R. Feinberg, *What Is Life Worth? The Unprecedented Effort to Compensate the Victims of 9/11* (New York: Public Affairs, 2005).

23 Spike Lee counts as one of New York's most celebrated cinematic poets, alongside Woody Allen and Martin Scorsese, courtesy of such Big Apple gems as *Clockers* (1995), *Summer of Sam* (1999), and *Do the Right Thing* (1989).

24 Mickey Flowers, *Ashes to Ashes, Dust to DNA* (New York: ars genetica, 2002).

25 Mitchell, "Cloning Terror," 180.

Chapter 8

Everyday Ghosts and the Ghostly Everyday in Amos Tutuola, Ben Okri, and Achille Mbembe

Esther Peeren

In many Western ghost stories the appearance of a ghost causes surprise, shock, and fear, and represents a rupture in the everyday – an interruption by the unfamiliar and frightening of the familiar, the comfortable, and the routine. The plot of such ghost stories tends to focus on turning the unknown back into the known, on restoring order through finding out what the ghost wants and how it can be laid to rest or exorcized. The everyday and the ghostly are thus presented as irreconcilable realms that ought not to encroach on each other, an adage that works in both directions: just as the ghost is perceived as an undesirable intruder when it makes its appearance in everyday life, living human beings are not supposed to enter the supernatural ghostly realm, mostly because this would threaten their life or sanity, but also because such a visitation would disturb the everyday of that other realm, *its* commonplace and routine practices. This reciprocal prohibition receives poignant illustration in Alejandro Amenábar's 2001 film *The Others*. Even when, as happens there, the two worlds overlap and ghosts are imagined to exist alongside the living in the same house, interaction is not supposed to take place and, when it does, it is conceived of as a problem to be solved only by one of the parties relinquishing its claim on the property. Generally, it is the ghost who is eventually made to disappear, yet sometimes, as in *The Others*, the living depart instead. What has to be re-established at any cost, however, is the everyday, the ordinary state of being either of the living or of the dead. Only very occasionally in Western ghost stories is the possibility of a harmoniously shared everyday realm envisioned, as for example in Tim Burton's 1988 film *Beetlejuice*. There, two reluctant and inexperienced ghosts – a recently deceased couple – first attempt to drive a living family out of what used to be their house with the help of a bio-exorcist (a "humanbuster" as it were), but when the latter turns malignant they decide to help the living family exorcize him and everyone ends up living happily ever after as a mixed human–ghost family in a re-established everyday realm of domestic bliss.

In the context of the convention of perceiving the ghost and the everyday as mutually exclusive realms, an exception like *Beetlejuice* reminds us of Freud's insistence that the *unheimlich* (uncanny) does not signify the opposite or absence of the *heimlich* (homely, familiar, comfortable) but is part of it, being "that class of the frightening which leads back to what is known of old and long familiar."[1] Paradoxically, however, Freud's text is preoccupied with purifying a concept that he himself characterizes as fundamentally ambiguous. Thus, the reason the ghost is not explored as a prime example of the uncanny is that "the uncanny in it is too much intertwixed with what is purely gruesome and is in part overlaid by it" (218). It appears that the uncanny has to be sanitized precisely because it manifests as the undesirable return of the as-yet undifferentiated: either the ego that "had not yet marked itself off sharply from the external world and from other people" (212) or primitive humanity associated with an "animistic conception of the universe" (216). The return of such indistinction in the developed self or society is frightening and somehow improper. Thus, although Freud establishes a close link between the uncanny and the everyday (some of his examples – especially those involving "an unintended recurrence of the same situation" (213) – are positively mundane), the fact that he persists in associating the uncanny and ghostly with the regrettable return of non-separation sees him partaking in the tradition that would ideally banish the ghost from daily life.

The harmoniously hybrid household depicted at the end of *Beetlejuice* resonates in a more affirmative way with Jacques Derrida's injunction, in *Specters of Marx*, to "learn to live *with* ghosts."[2] Of course, what Derrida is speaking of is not the literal ghost (the dead demonstrably returned to life), but the ghost or specter as a signifier of absolute alterity and of the way such alterity disturbs established notions of presence, identity, and history. Derrida urges us to treat the metaphorical ghosts of our society (immigrants, foreigners, victims of historical injustices like colonialism and slavery, but also a supposedly surmounted thinker like Marx) in a way that respects their otherness. Through the principles of absolute hospitality and the messianic, we should allow this otherness to disrupt the rigid categorizations (presence/absence, life/death, past/present/future) that govern our day-to-day practices, thus transforming ontology into *hauntology*. For Derrida, then, the everyday is inevitably suffused by numerous forms of otherness so that in it we can never expect to find ourselves on solid ground, unambiguously present or "at home." Whereas Ben Highmore calls the idea that the everyday "is haunted by implicit 'others', who supposedly live outside the ordinary, the everyday" the "underside" of everyday life studies, which leads to assertions of dominance for specific ways of life,[3] Derrida considers it an ethical opportunity. Rather than taking recourse in acts of exorcism that negate alterity or acts of assimilation that convert it into identity (which, to an extent, is what happens in *Beetlejuice*, where the ghosts can be accepted as part of the everyday because they are in fact more "normal" and traditional than the human family they end up domesticating), he challenges us to accept this haunting and live *with* it, thus moving towards the realization of Highmore's stated purpose of "questioning the transparency of the daily" (1).

Nonetheless, because Derrida links the specter to the "unheard-of interruption" (37) of the messianic that signals "an alterity that cannot be anticipated" (65), it remains something that is (at least initially) emphatically *extra*-ordinary. Though no longer valued negatively, the ghost is still that which disturbs the everyday space and puts time out of joint. Living *with* ghosts, moreover, does not come naturally; the formulation "it would be necessary to *learn* spirits" (xviii, emphasis added) underlines its status as an acquired skill, an adjustment (this time desired) to the ordinary that remains a future project(ion).

Michel de Certeau, one of the founders of everyday life studies, considers the everyday as always already unsettled and haunted, famously declaring that "haunted places are the only ones people can live in."[4] For him, spirits or ghosts stand for the communal memories and histories that create a place's habitability in the face of its definition and disciplining by the dominant spatial order. Unlike Freud, who seeks to overcome superstition, de Certeau conceives of "*superstitions*" as desirable cracks in the system (106), nascent political tools capable of countering the panoptical gaze. Still, not only does the knowledge these ghosts possess remain mostly unspoken, but much like Derrida, who never explicitly acknowledges that the ontology he seeks to displace is not a universal structure but the product of a distinctly Western philosophical tradition, de Certeau leaves his ghosts as unspecified as the "anonymous hero" (v) to which his account of the everyday is dedicated (who, of course, is not anonymous at all, but decidedly French, urban, and male).

Just as the ghost's function and significance should be historically and culturally specified, so should the everyday, but this is often neglected. By linking the everyday with the "mundane, 'boring' aspects of the daily," Joe Moran's *Reading the Everyday* already defines it in a way that presupposes a particular way of life where people designate their daily activities as repetitive and validate them as dull.[5] Further on, Moran acknowledges that this concept of the everyday, taken from Lefebvre and de Certeau and applied to contemporary Britain, is tied to "the relative comfort of Western consumer societies" and that we do not tend to question the normativity of what we consider to be the everyday (23). Significantly, the latter point is reiterated in the course of a discussion of the 9/11 attacks as having been particularly "haunting" in the West because they targeted people going about eminently recognizable daily routines (166). Moran poignantly adds that "it is more difficult to make a similar imaginative connection with Iraqis or Afghans killed by bombs dropped from fighter planes, because their daily lives are not so easily recognizable or represented" (167). What he does not concede is that death and bombings are not necessarily external to the everyday but, in some contexts, part of it, if we define the everyday more generally as "occurring every day" or "commonplace, usual."[6] What occurs regularly and is thought ordinary differs from place to place and is not inevitably dull. Recognizing this opens the way to radicalizing and particularizing Derrida's and de Certeau's insights in order to come to consider the ghostly as a potentially inherent part of the everyday and vice versa, a possibility I will explore by looking at two ghostly novels from Nigeria – Amos Tutuola's *My Life in the Bush of Ghosts*[7] and Ben Okri's *The Famished Road*[8] – and the theorization of the everyday realm of ghostly violence by Cameroonian political theorist Achille Mbembe.

There are many non-Western (and marginal Western) traditions of the ghost where its status as part of the everyday is not seen as something extraordinary or problematic and where the ghost is not reduced to a metaphor. In such traditions, ghosts do not have to be *learned*, nor do they necessarily oppose or disturb the reigning ontology. Instead, they are simply *there* as part of everyday life. Many cultures feature a strong belief in the continued presence of and ongoing communication with those who have died, and/or a constant interaction with spirits and other so-called "supernatural" beings.[9] Contact with dead ancestors, ghosts, and spirits may be highly ritualized, take place only on designated occasions, or be reserved for certain people (shamans, mediums) or places (usually marginal, like the bush or forest), but the notion that these spectral beings play a concrete role in everyday life is accepted: the "belief in the existence, the facticity, of the spirits" is "consensually validated, and often ritually confirmed."[10] Ghosts also do not tend to be confined to a completely separate world. Although Levy, Mageo, and Howard in *Spirits in Culture, History, and Mind* argue that the "numinous" describes a spooky realm that is "more or less separated from the natural or ordinary," they stress that the division is permeable and that "numinous beings and human beings ... do not generally exist in two absolute, discrete realms, but move between realms of experience."[11] Furthermore, while ghosts and spirits in these cultures can take on a disturbing role, unlike in Western cultures it is not generally their presence in itself that shocks and surprises, but rather their specific actions. And while individual presences can be bound, banished, or exorcised, the drive to exorcism that Derrida traces in Western philosophy and literature is not necessarily the default position when encountering a ghost.

The specific ghostly traditions represented in the novels of Tutuola and Okri are those of Nigeria (of the Yoruba and Igbo in particular). A common belief represented by both authors is the *abiku* (Yoruba) or *ogbaanje* (Igbo), which designates a child that is repeatedly born only to die young every time because it remains tied to the spirit world that is its true home and to which it has pledged to return. This tradition is not confined to folklore or myth, but plays an active role in everyday Nigerian life. Peter O. Ogunjuyigbe provides recent statistics that show belief in the existence of *abiku* is widespread and, more importantly, directly impacts on the treatment of sick children.[12] Anthropologist Misty L. Bastian focuses on the Igbo, establishing the participation of spirits in the everyday realm by noting that "in Igbo, both spirits and humans are said to be *ndi*, people."[13] Within this system, the *ogbaanje* is considered a special, but by no means rare case in which action needs to be taken to bind it to the human world and cut its connection to the spirit realm. Crucially, what occurs is not a driving out of the spirit, but, since the child *is* the spirit, an acceptance of the spirit into the human kinship system. Neither in the occurrence of *abiku* nor in its cure is the notion of living *with* ghosts seen as particularly different from living with other people. In fact, Bastian argues that from an anthropological perspective the *ogbaanje* can be seen as a way to symbolize increasingly complex kinship relations in a globalizing culture. She warns, however, that for the people involved the spirits form part of everyday reality and cannot therefore be dismissed as "only abstractions and mystifications" (131).

To further explore this non-polarized relation between the ghostly and the everyday I turn to the two novels. In Tutuola's *My Life in the Bush of Ghosts*, a seven-year-old boy fleeing a group of armed slave-traders accidentally enters the Bush of Ghosts, which he describes as "so dreadful so that no superior earthly person ever entered it" (22). In the Bush, the boy-narrator encounters a variety of ghosts – some having been alive before, like the burglar ghosts (Tutuola's version of the *abiku*) and a deceased cousin, but most having always existed in the form of spirits and even able to die as such. Although the majority of the ghosts he encounters treat him horribly – enslaving him, attempting to sacrifice him, almost eating him, etc. – he also befriends certain ghosts and even marries two. Through his adventures, however, the boy retains the wish to be reunited with his mother and brother, which finally happens at the end of the novel. Okri's *The Famished Road* is also narrated by a young boy, Azaro, who is an *abiku*. Azaro, however, decides to stay with his earthly parents and ignores his spirit-companions' ongoing ruses to lure him back to their world. The novel, which won the 1991 Booker Prize, tells the story of the precarious life Azaro and his parents lead in the face of hunger, squalor, political corruption, and violence in Nigeria around the time of Independence (1960), and of the way ghosts and spirits form a central part of this life.

In *My Life in the Bush of Ghosts*, there appears at first to be quite a rigid separation between the earthly world and the Bush of Ghosts. Olatubosun Ogunsanwo notes that "the extraordinary world of spirits and demons" is presented as separate from "the mundane world of history, stability, morality and order where there is a comprehensible interplay of deities and ancestors and humanity."[14] While Ogunsanwo significantly includes deities and ancestors as actors in the mundane world, he excludes the ghost world in which the boy-narrator becomes trapped. Mbembe, however, suggests a less stable division, calling the Bush of Ghosts a "lateral space" which "constantly spills over its assigned time and space."[15] Although there is clearly in the novel a sense that the Bush of Ghosts *should* remain distinct from the world of earthly persons – the bush is "banned to be entered by any earthly person" (22) – there are many signs that the two worlds are fundamentally interlinked. Several ghosts, most notably the burglar ghosts, move in and out of the earthly world, earthly wizards and witches regularly visit the Bush of Ghosts, and the episode where the boy-narrator meets a Television-handed Ghostess who shows him live images of his mother in the earthly world suggests not only communication but also equivalence between the two worlds: the cure he sees his mother practice on a baby with sores also works on the Television-handed Ghostess.

Moreover, although it features strange practices, the Bush of Ghosts is not completely alien. It shares many institutions with the earthly world: a system of towns, marriage, kings, a judicial system, schools, and commerce. Thus, whereas Ato Quayson argues that "it is the world of spirits that embodies the chaotic and anxiety-generating forces of nature,"[16] the Bush of Ghosts also includes many aspects of the cultured world and functions not as an irremediable otherness without any order but as a place with which one can familiarize oneself by following *its* everyday practices. In the beginning, the boy-narrator is a stranger to this world, but once he learns its language and customs and gets close to a number of ghosts, he becomes one of them: "nobody could identify me again that I am not a ghost, because I was then nearly become a full ghost and was doing everything that ghosts are doing and also speaking the language of ghosts fluently as if I was born in the Bush of Ghosts" (136). Quayson's assertion that the Bush is "the crucible of a nightmare" that generates only "extreme anxiety" (50) ignores both the acclimatization to violence that occurs and how the Bush also offers the boy-narrator hospitality, friendship, love, a son, a happy reunion with his dead cousin, and even a position as head of the court system. Significantly, after returning to the earthly world, the boy does not turn his back on the Bush of Ghosts, but tells his mother and brother that he would like to attend the "SECRET-SOCIETY OF GHOSTS" in order to "bring some of its news to them and other people" (174) and preserve the link to the other world which has also become his own. In the end, therefore, the Bush of Ghosts emerges as more of a foreign country with unusual yet apprehensible mores than a totally otherworldly realm.

And just as the ghostly shares in the everyday, the everyday shares in the ghostly. The horrible violence to which the boy-narrator is subjected in the Bush is not particular to it but virtually identical to what he experiences in the earthly world. Even before he enters the Bush, the boy-narrator is surrounded by brutality, noting that "there were many kinds of African wars and some of them are as follows: general wars, tribal wars, burglary wars and the slave wars which were very common on every town and village" (17–18). War is "common" and therefore constitutive of the everyday. A form of warfare even governs the domestic sphere, where multiple wives and children compete for prominence. The boy does not wander into the Bush on a casual walk or out of curiosity, but in a desperate act of flight after he and his brother are chased out of their village by slave-traders of whose approach the other wives and their daughters deliberately neglected to warn them. The earthly world's everyday is therefore far from a stable, dull, and comforting environment; instead, it is a zone always already uncanny and out of joint.

The notion that the Bush of Ghosts and the earthly realm are mirror worlds rather than separate realms is reinforced by the far-reaching similarities between two episodes. When the boy-narrator finally escapes the Bush after many adventures and 24 years, he is immediately captured by slave-traders in a re-enactment of one of his adventures early on in the Bush, when his use of a juju to escape one ghost transformed him into a cow, to be caught, mistreated, sold by "cow-men," and later nearly sacrificed by his new owner. Almost exactly the same happens upon his return to the earthly realm as he is taken, tied up, enslaved, and, after he becomes sick and breaks out in sores, sold as a religious sacrifice to a slave-owner. The boy-narrator drily notes the irony of the equivalence: "It is a great pity that I was lost in the Bush of Ghosts for twenty-four years with punishments and when I came out of it I am caught and sold again as a slave" (169). His escape from what seems a death sentence is also similar in both cases: he uses trickery. In the Bush, the boy-narrator escapes when the ghosts holding him do not pay attention and, after turning back into himself, he misdirects the ghosts chasing him. In the earthly realm, it turns out the slave-owner who bought him is his brother, who does not recognize him because 24 years have gone by and because a slave-owner does not interact with his slaves. To make his brother recognize him, the boy-narrator sings a song that contains his name, using the prohibition on slaves mentioning their master's name to be brought before his brother and then forcing the moment of recognition (the song is the same one they sang before being chased out of their village by the slave-traders at the beginning of the story). There is thus a clear relation of correspondence between the Bush of Ghosts and the everyday realm, with both realms partaking in acts of violence as well as in acts of kindness and certain social institutions.[17] Neither, therefore, can be read in terms of the univocality implied in the definition of the everyday as the space of dull monotony and the Bush as the embodiment of pure anxiety.

At the beginning of *The Famished Road* it again seems that there is a spirit world distinct from the "world of the Living" (3). However, the very nature of the *abiku* is to take advantage of the possibility of passage from one world to the other and to straddle the border: "We are the strange ones, with half our beings always in the spirit world" (5). After he breaks his bond with the spirit world by burying his "objects of identity" (10) somewhere and deliberately forgetting the location, Azaro briefly imagines that the worlds are indeed disconnected, until one day at the market he perceives several strange-looking spirits. When they realize he can see them and come after him, he reacts much like a character in a Western ghost story would: he is afraid, runs away, and concentrates furiously on not seeing them. But soon he realizes this is futile and acknowledges their presence: "That was the first time I realized it wasn't just humans who came to the marketplaces of the world. Spirits and other beings come there too. They buy and sell, browse and investigate" (19). What is noticeable here is that the spirits are doing the same things at the market as its human visitors; they may look different (they walk backwards, have breasts on their backs, or eyes on the sides of their faces), but they are essentially joining in the same everyday activities. Rather than disturbing or threatening the everyday, they partake in it and, as such, appear as quite mundane beings.

In *The Famished Road*, despite all the deformed and malignant spirits Azaro encounters, it is ultimately the everyday that is most disturbing, and the living who most closely resemble ghosts.[18] In the context of Independence-era Nigeria, it is not learning to live *with* ghosts that constitutes the difficult yet necessary task, but living, period. There is no taking for granted presence, identity, or home when disease, hunger, and war continually threaten to obliterate your body and self, when corruption and poverty can make the roof over your head disappear at any moment, and when even an act of hospitality (a feast with a wild boar for the entire compound to celebrate Azaro's rescue from a haunted house) is repaid with destruction and immediate demands from ruthless creditors. The horrors of the spirit world are matched by the horrors of everyday life – misshapen spirits by amputees, malignant and scheming spirits by politicians who poison the people, starving spirits by homeless beggars – and at many points in the book Azaro, as well as the reader, cannot be sure whether he is dealing with a human or a spirit, with folklore or reality.

With the two worlds and beings so thoroughly enmeshed, the ghost can no longer function as an unproblematic signifier for absolute alterity (the spirit world in Okri's fictional universe is many things, but it is not the complete unknown or unanticipated – at least no more unknown and unanticipated than the vicissitudes of everyday life) or be easily reduced to mere metaphor. This is why K. Anthony Appiah insists on a distinction between magical realism and the "spiritual realism" of Okri's work: "for Okri, in a curious way, the world of spirits is not metaphorical or imaginary; rather, it is more real than the world of the everyday. And so tales of that world have, like tales of our own, their own justification."[19] I suggest that in *The Famished Road* the spirit world is not *more real* (except perhaps to Azaro), but *as real* as the everyday world, because the two constantly feed into each other. Also, the justification of the tales in the two realms is not as distinct as Appiah implies, since both realms are governed by similar kinds of injustices (the strong preying on the weak, false seductions, fixed fights, etc.) and no guarantee that good will triumph over evil. In the end, the everyday of *The Famished Road* comprises the ghostly and is in turn comprised by it, so that the distinction becomes porous, as does the related one between the folkloric and the everyday.

This hybridity of the ghostly and the everyday amounts to an insistence on what Quayson calls the "essential 'ghostliness' of reality" (136). He cites Okri, who grew up during the Biafra war (1967–1970) in a ghetto surrounded by corruption, as saying that "you can't write about Nigeria truthfully without a sense of violence. To be serene is to lie. Relations in Nigeria are violent relations. It's the way it is, for historical and all sorts of other reasons" (147). Life in Nigeria is violent and disturbing and this violence and disturbance, incarnated by the ghosts and spirits of oral tradition and folklore, does not remain separate from the practices of everyday life but forms a constitutive *part of* them, prompting a reformulation of the everyday as not necessarily uneventful and dull or divorced from imagination and storytelling, and not invariably defined through capitalist consumerism and its accompanying work/leisure opposition either.[20] For everyday life studies this would mean having to theorize not only how to make normally unnoticed and trivialized aspects of existence visible, but also how aspects that from one perspective appear extra-ordinary or even excluded from reality altogether may from a different perspective be all there is to the everyday.

In this way, Freud's uncanny and Derrida's specter become insufficient models with which to think through the ghostliness of the everyday, since they explicitly oppose the ghost to order and routine as an unexpected, surprising figure of disturbance, the return of the repressed, and absolute alterity. Where the ghostly everyday *can* be found is in the work of Achille Mbembe, whose description of the African postcolony positions itself against Western models of thought that rely on valuated dichotomies and thereby exclude "[t]he world of instincts and animality."[21] As an alternative for thinking subjectivity through notions of reason, self-possession, and identity, he proposes emotion, capture, and metamorphosis, which he connects with a specifically African history, culture, and spirituality. Disturbingly, however, the primary emotion referenced is fear, metamorphosis is seen as agonizing and terrifying, and capture is always being captured rather than capturing. This negative subjectivity is produced by a form of sovereignty, which, in Mbembe's Foucault-inspired definition, exerts an ungraspable, ghostly violence and is predicated on full control over mortality: "My concern is those figures of sovereignty whose central project is not the struggle for autonomy but *the generalized instrumentalization of human existence and the material destruction of human bodies and populations*" (14, emphasis in original).

What these figures of sovereignty generate is a postcolony characterized by "forms of social existence in which vast populations are subjected to conditions of life that confer upon them the status of living dead (ghosts)" (1). Here, the ghost *defines* the everyday as a realm in which only *specular experiences*, experiences associated with transparency (insignificance), mediated perception, and the illusionary wholeness and misrecognition of the Lacanian mirror stage, are possible. These experiences are firmly rooted in an everyday horror of hunger, poverty, riots, corruption, civil war, and dictatorship. Mbembe also describes the living-dead subjects of ghostly power as *wandering subjects*, which appears to indicate a certain agency, freedom of movement, and possibility of escape. However, Mbembe is quick to dissociate his ghostly wanderers from celebratory accounts of fragmented subjectivity, including Derrida's.

With the ghost standing both for the ungraspable terror employed by the African sovereign to subjugate the population *and* for the impotent insubstantiality to which this population is thereby reduced, Mbembe firmly includes the ghost in the everyday. His ghostly everyday is typified by a phenomenology of violence to the extent that "the violence of death ... has become the normal state of things" and it has become possible to speak of "everyday forms of torture, harassment, fatigue, and execution" as well as of "the brutality and uncertainties of everyday existence."[22] Whether or not this is a factually accurate description of the (entire) African postcolony, it makes thinkable a situation where there is no longer an everyday *outside of* violence and terror, if these are wielded over entire populations and if their ongoing nature has long since made it impossible to think of them as mere interruptions to a normalcy bound to return. The bleak everyday realms of Tutuola's and Okri's fictions actualize this possibility: they no longer oppose a quiet, undisturbed everyday to the shock of the ghostly interruption, but present an everyday in which this interruption has become routine, thus prohibiting any sense of stability and any straightforward opposition of ghosts and the living.

Yet, Tutuola and Okri not only show the everyday infected by the ghostly, but also the ghostly infected by the everyday, signaling that no world, not even the spirit realm, is likely to be totally devoid of a sense of ordinariness or a set of practices that can be inculcated (as what Bourdieu calls a *habitus*)[23] in order to function within it and make it livable. Mbembe reads Tutuola's Bush of Ghosts as a realm in which "[g]hostly power harasses the subject, screams, beats him mercilessly, starves him for an instant, and then in the next instant forces him to eat exactly as one feeds an animal, and makes him drink his own urine."[24] The subject here appears totally passive and ineffective in the face of the ghost and the ghost necessarily cruel and oppressive. As we have seen, there are also benign ghosts in the Bush and although the boy-narrator is certainly at a disadvantage in most of his adventures, he repeatedly escapes the ghosts trying to capture and kill him by using their own techniques against them. In Okri's novel, too, Azaro's *abiku* home is not a world of horrors but a "world of dreams" (22), and excursions into the spirit world, though draining, frequently yield agency and insight.

While Mbembe usefully points to the terrible ghostliness of certain everyday realities, thus questioning Derrida's association of the ghost with justice and the messianic and the suggestion that time cannot be too out of joint or subjectivity too unsettled,[25] in reading Tutuola selectively he also interprets the ghost in a rather one-sided manner that leaves little room for agency and resistance.[26] It could be argued that Mbembe ends up reducing the everyday to the ghostly, where the latter is – ironically, as in many traditional Western ghost stories – equated with pure oppression and danger, rather than seen as the more ambiguous, more everyday realm we find in Tutuola and Okri.

This essay has argued for the need to culturally specify the ghost and its possible functions in relation to the everyday, as well as for moving beyond theorizations that rely on a dichotomous separation between an everyday seen as orderly and devoid of wonder, and a ghostly interruption (whether through the spectral or the uncanny) that is invariably unsettling. Reading Tutuola, Okri, and Mbembe has enabled me to conceptualize the notions of a ghostly everyday and an everyday ghostliness in the African context. With the recent appearance of more and more "ordinary" ghosts, whose haunting consists of participating in the mundane activities of everyday life (this includes the ghosts in *Beetlejuice* and those in *The Others*, with the latter taken for the living even by themselves), it will be vital to reconfigure the relation between the ghostly and the everyday not just in cultures that have always considered these realms as more or less intertwined, but also in the Western imagination.

NOTES

1   Sigmund Freud, "The Uncanny," in *Writings on Art and Literature* (Stanford: Stanford University Press, 1997), 195.

2   Jacques Derrida, *Specters of Marx: The State of the Debt, the Work of Mourning & the New International*, trans. Peggy Kamuf (New York and London: Routledge, 1994), xviii.

3   Ben Highmore, "Introduction: Questioning Everyday Life," in *The Everyday Life Reader*, ed. Ben Highmore (London and New York: Routledge, 2002), 1.

4   Michel de Certeau, *The Practice of Everyday Life*, trans. S. Rendall (Berkeley: University of California Press, 1988), 108.

5   Joe Moran, *Reading the Everyday* (London and New York: Routledge, 2005), ix.

6   "Everyday," in *The Concise Oxford Dictionary*, 9th edn, CD-ROM (Oxford: Oxford University Press, 1999).

7   Amos Tutuola, *The Palm-Wine Drinkard and My Life in the Bush of Ghosts* (New York: Grove Press, 1994). Original publication 1954.

8   Ben Okri, *The Famished Road* (London: Vintage, 2003). Original publication 1991.

9 On the category of the supernatural as an essentially Western construct, see Benson Saler, "Supernatural as a Western Category," *Ethos* 5, no. 1 (1977): 31–53.

10 Vincent Crapanzano and Vivian Garrison, "Introduction," in *Case Studies in Spirit Possession* (London: John Wiley, 1977), 11. See also John W. Burton, "Ghosts, Ancestors and Individuals Among the Atuot of the Southern Sudan," *Man* 13, no. 4 (1978): 600–617.

11 Richard I. Levy, Jeannette Marie Mageo, and Alan Howard, "Gods, Spirits, and History," in *Spirit in Culture, History, and Mind*, ed. J. M. Mageo and A. Howard (New York and London: Routledge, 1996), 13.

12 Peter O. Ogunjuyigbe, "Under-Five Mortality in Nigeria: Perception and Attitudes of the Yorubas towards the Existence of '*Abiku*'," *Demographic Research* 11, no. 2 (2004): 43–56. Ogunjuyigbe outlines how it is believed that *abiku* will not respond to modern (Western) medical care and should be treated by a traditional healer.

13 Misty L. Bastian, "Married in the Water: Spirit Kin and Other Afflictions of Modernity in Southeastern Nigeria," *Journal of Religion in Africa* 27 (May 1997): 122.

14 Olatunbosun Ogunsanwo, "Intertextuality and Post-Colonial Literature in Ben Okri's The Famished Road," *Research in African Literatures* 26, no. 1 (1995): 46.

15 Achille Mbembe, "Life, Sovereignty, and Terror in the Fiction of Amos Tutuola," *Research in African Literatures* 34, no. 4 (2003): 6.

16 Ato Quayson, *Strategic Transformations in Nigerian Writing: Orality and History in the Work of Rev. Samuel Johnson, Amos Tutuola, Wole Soyinka and Ben Okri* (Oxford: James Currey, 1997), 56.

17 Quayson describes the mother and brother's sufferings from slavery in the real world as "analogous to that of the boy in the bush of ghosts," yet insists that "the adventures in the spirit-realm, which form the core of the narrative, are framed within social referents that have no direct relationship to the spirit-realm" (55). I suggest that the parallels between the two worlds in fact point to a quite direct link. For an account of how events in the Bush mimic the slave trade, see Laura Murphy, "Into the Bush of Ghosts: Specters of the Slave Trade in West African Fiction," *Research in African Literatures* 38, no. 4 (2007): 141–152.

18 Azaro's mother acquires ghostly characteristics (blank eyes, speaking in an "unnatural language," and surrounded by a mysterious mist) when she suffers from malaria (63–6); his father is turned into "a tall ghost" after working as a load-carrier and getting covered in white dust (70); and Madame Koto, an unscrupulous businesswoman and wine bar owner, acquires more and more monstrous and miraculous characteristics as her association with corrupt politicians becomes deeper.

19 K. Anthony Appiah, "Spiritual Realism," *The Nation*, August 3–10, 1992, 147. Quayson describes Okri's work as "animist realism" (148). What is important is not the precise terminology, but the fact that neither animist realism nor spiritual realism is, in the African context, a contradiction in terms: the marvelous is *part of* the real and not separated from it, as it is, for example, in Tzvetan Todorov's Western model of the fantastic. See Tzvetan Todorov, *The Fantastic: A Structural Approach to a Literary Genre* (Ithaca: Cornell University Press, 1975).

20 It is telling that the "Everyday things" section of Highmore's *The Everyday Life Reader* (293–351) contains essays on a trade exhibition, plastic, interior design, cooking, television, supermarkets, and bags, all associated with capitalist consumer culture.

21 Mbembe, "Life, Sovereignty, and Terror," 2.

22 Achille Mbembe, *On the Postcolony* (Berkeley: University of California Press, 2001), 173, 197, 167, 199.

23   See Pierre Bourdieu, *The Logic of Practice*, trans. Richard Nice (Cambridge, UK: Polity Press, 1999).

24   Mbembe, "Life, Sovereignty, and Terror," 15.

25   Derrida acknowledges that disjointure risks "the evil, expropriation, and injustice (*adikia*) against which there is no insurance" (27), but seems to consider the taking of this risk as a choice to be made freely (as in the decision whether or not to offer absolute hospitality), something which is manifestly not possible for the populations described by Mbembe.

26   For eloquent critiques of Mbembe's pessimism, see Jeremy Weate, "Achille Mbembe and the Postcolony: Going beyond the Text," *Research in African Literatures* 34, no. 4 (2003): 27–41; Mikael Karlström, "On the Aesthetic and Dialogics of Power in the Postcolony," *Africa* 73, no. 1 (2003): 57–76. Mbembe has envisioned some avenues of subversion in practices of stylization and syncretism. "On the Power of the False," *Public Culture* 14, no. 3 (2002): 629–641, for example, transforms the ghost into a "heretical spirit"; even here, however, Mbembe warns that if this spirit is taken too far it will result in a disabling lack of stability.

Chapter 9

The Gentle Irruption of the Hereafter in This Life: Jean Echenoz's *Au piano* and Robin Campillo's *Les revenants*

Michael Cuntz[1]

The Dead Walk Among Us

When at the end of the first of the three parts of Jean Echenoz's 2003 novel *Au piano* Max Delmarc, the book's protagonist, dies, this comes as a surprise to the reader who is unprepared for this turn of events.[2] Up to this point, nothing in this seemingly "realist" novel, neither its title nor any genre conventions, has hinted at the fact that the equation "death of hero" = "end of story" does not apply. On the contrary, upon learning on the very first page that Max has only 22 days left to live, one expects the text to be an account of the last portion of his existence lying ahead of him. The reader is perplexed to learn that, instead, Max crosses the threshold separating life from death only to come back, after a short stay in an accommodation center in the "next world," to "this world" as a revenant. If, in Echenoz's novel, *perplexity* is an effect of the story imposed on its reader, it is imposed on the living characters within the story in Robin Campillo's movie *Les revenants* (2004) when, for no apparent reason, a plethora of dead people – about 70 million, deceased over the last decade – deserts the cemeteries and calmly returns.[3]

In both cases, the realm of the living and the realm of the dead interact in a very concrete manner: the boundary between "this life" and the "hereafter" is blurred, thus pointing to the fact that despite the temporal semantics of the English terms, in modern Western culture this separation is, of course, also conceived of as spatial. In *Les revenants* the "transgression" soon turns out to be a mass phenomenon: like zombies, myriads of dead walk among the living, but unlike zombies, they behave in a more silent, discreet, and inoffensive manner; these revenants do not come after the living. And yet, what Echenoz's and Campillo's un-dead have in common with zombies is their concrete materiality, their corporeality. They have real bodies and real physical needs resembling more or less those of living human beings. Their desire is not to eat living flesh or transform living persons into their un-dead likes. Instead, their corporeality allows for less violent physical and even erotic contact between those dead and those alive.

Thus, both temporal-eschatological overtones of doomsday and supernatural connotations are avoided and replaced by a bio-political attitude that makes the encounter with the dead no less odd or disturbing. In both cases, the intersection of space causes perplexity[4] because it raises problems of agency and its redistribution: it is the number of dead that necessitates the posing of the question, and it is their nature that makes this redistribution so problematic. Are they human or not? Or could the whole mindset that attributes agency only to living human beings be called into question? Do the dead have to be granted agency even though they are different? And how and why is it that they are (eventually) denied the status of actors on the political scene and thus as members of society – even if they might outnumber the living? At stake are the community of the living and the community of the dead, their respective "police orders," and the possibility of a community of the dead *and* the living in spite of a disagreement that cannot be overcome.[5]

This is where temporality comes back into play, because what is opened up through the return of the dead is not only a spatial, but also a temporal breach. In the nameless French town where *Les revenants* takes place, the mayor, who as a political representative is the first to speak in this movie, describes his state of mind in the following terms: "Je suis stupéfait. L'impensable vient de se produire" ("I am amazed. The unthinkable has happened"). *Stupéfaction*, the French term for amazement, designates a state of paralysis: there is an interference or an interruption in the normal processes of perception and (re)action, of the sensory-motor link. What happens is simply too much to be dealt with for the characters, who from actors turn into spectators. This is a symptom of the crisis that, according to Gilles Deleuze, leads to the transformation of the movement-image into the time-image.[6] The characters cannot react to the excessive situation of the *encounter* with the beloved dead – their parents, lovers, husbands and wives, or children – which is simultaneously horrible, wonderful, and a puzzle without solution and which for this reason thwarts the very possibility of simultaneity. The inscription of multiple temporalities within the time-image coincides remarkably with Derrida's description of the effect of the *chose*, the thing called specter: "It de-synchronizes, it recalls us to anachrony."[7]

It is the tardiness both of the revenant's motion and of the shots that affects the living. They lose their own rhythm but remain unable to synchronize with the dead. Here, Deleuze's "dead time" (24) is provoked by the time the dead evolve in. For the film's spectators, this impression is reinforced by the music of the soundtrack flowing and pulsating without a clearly defined measure. The flux of time seems to be congested. This tardiness of motion clearly establishes a resemblance between these revenants and cinematographic zombies. From the very first sequence, Campillo is referring to George Romero's famous *Trilogy of the Dead*, which serves as frame of reference for the whole movie.[8]

For a shot of the revenants moving along the main street of the French town, filmed in extreme bird eye's view, one of the first shots of *Day of the Dead* (1985) can be clearly identified as model.

Figure 1: Film still from Robin Campillo, *Les Revenants* (2004), © Haut et Court, France 3 Cinéma, Gimages Développement.

Figure 2: Film still from George Romero, *Day of the Dead* (1985), © Arrow Films.

Other sequences showing the movements of the crowd of the returned dead rely on shots from *Dawn of the Dead* (1978), the film in which Romero most consistently stages the zombies as a multitude moving through a banal space of everyday life, the shopping mall.

Figure 3: Film still from George Romero, *Dawn of the Dead* (1978), © Arrow Films.

Figure 4: Film still from Robin Campillo, *Les Revenants* (2004), © Haut et Court, France 3 Cinéma, Gimages Développement.

In Romero's film, they are spurred by the megaphones of the helicopter crews, which arouse their need to eat the living. For the spectator, the extra-diegetic element of the driving rhythm of the soundtrack adds to the effect. The zombies move jerkily past signs of chaos and decay in a ghost town where crashed or burnt-out cars are scattered along the streets like garbage to indicate the entropy of apocalypse.

By contrast, Campillo's revenants are not moved by attraction to an exterior, living source, but follow their own impulse. Only their slow motion distinguishes them from living persons. Their flowing movement and regular distribution on the lanes and pavements rather conjure up associations of a traffic stream that has to be controlled or of the motion of regularly distributed elementary particles, forming a pattern of even distribution in space where entropy and order paradoxically coincide and which points forward to the wish to dissolve the mass of the dead in the body politic of the living. It is the coagulation of this flux, the clotting together of the dead, that will worry the living. The irruption of the living dead into everyday life takes on the quality of a traffic jam – and, in fact, the reflux of such a large population that seemed to have drained away into the hereafter forever, causes a major demographic perturbation. It is not the social order that has broken down, but the normal flow of traffic and population movement. Consequently, the view from the rooftop has changed its meaning. In Romero, it was the view of a human being that found a safe place to hide from the zombies. In Campillo, it is the place where a surveillance camera has been installed to control the revenants.

Unexpected Encounters or Arranged Meetings?

In contrast to meetings that are arranged in advance, encounters cannot be planned; they come unforeseen. One can desire an encounter, but whether it happens or not is left to chance. But chance also means risk. The word "encounter" thus encloses a semantic ambiguity between, on the one hand, what is simply unexpected and, on the other, a scene of conflict and violence. "To encounter," then, means to collide with something dangerous or threatening – an enemy. Encounters between the dead and the living are a *challenge* and Echenoz and Campillo show how institutions and individuals cope with this challenge and try to reduce the risks. Campillo focuses on the administration of this life – by the city council, police, scientists, health system, etc. – which seems to be completely unprepared when confronted with the dead. In Echenoz, on the other hand, we see the workings of the administration of the hereafter. It comes as no surprise that, unlike the authorities of this life, they know how to deal with the newly deceased. This fact calls into question the whole concept of the encounter. Even if the dead and the living mingle, is there really a place or a scene for encounters? To describe this situation, one can take up the term *mixed zone*, currently used in the domains of sports and show business to designate an area accessed by heterogeneous groups, usually sportsmen (or VIPs) and reporters, to talk to each other. It suggests the freedom of an unconventional and unconstrained contact, but the very fact that such a zone is established on purpose contradicts unconventionality. The encounter in the mixed zone turns out to be an arranged meeting obeying preestablished rules with clear regulations as to who is authorized to have contact with whom. The term is thus suitable to characterize the topographical and topological, but also the chronological situations conceived by Echenoz and Campillo.

Both designs differ considerably from Sartre's drama *Huis clos* (*No Exit*), a hypotext for *Au piano*, as well as from recent movies like *The Sixth Sense* (M. Night Shyamalan, 1999) or *The Others* (Alejandro Amenábar, 2001), which show the postmortem[9] state as a private affair. In all these works the question of the number of the dead remains irrelevant. Both movies are about the "social nucleus" of the family and the responsibility of the father or the mother towards wife and/or children, while Sartre's drama concerns a triangular constellation where a third person interrupts the imaginary relation of desire and self-deceit between two persons attracted to each other. Sartre, Amenábar, and Shyamalan restrain considerably the spatial and temporal zone where an encounter or just a faint unilateral contact between the dead and the living can occur. Corresponding to traditional conceptions, this contact is a merely transitory phenomenon. Instead of revenants or ghosts condemned to haunting, the protagonists are recalcitrant dead who, once they understand and accept their new status, let go of the living. Contact with the hereafter is normalized by its temporariness: it swiftly converts into a definite separation of the spheres that goes along with the insight of the dead that they no longer have any impact on the living. In *Au piano* and *Les revenants*, on the contrary, there are no personal, local or temporal limitations. The generalized mixed zone is no heterotopy, but it is coextensive with the world of the living. If there is no local constraint, no *renfermement* of the dead in the hereafter or in controllable spots and areas of this world,[10] this does not automatically mean greater freedom, but rather the substitution of the circulation of the dead under the conditions of the society of control for the disciplinary *incarceration*. If this world and the next world overlap, this requires governmental regulation. If it is impossible or just undesirable to prevent spatiotemporal interference, it can *very well* be controlled, camouflaged, and corrected.

Reconfiguring the Hereafter: *Au piano*

In his update of the hereafter, Echenoz is referring clearly not only to *Huis clos*, but also to Dante's *Divina Commedia*. In order to understand Echenoz's modifications, one has to be aware of the way Dante regulates the economy of the hereafter and the communication between the dead and the living in this text (in his earlier *Vita Nova* the situation is different: Beatrice returns to this life). Both spheres are sharply separated; only the chosen few – Aeneas, Christ (who is alive *and* dead at the same time), and Dante – are permitted to transgress the boundary, and this works only in one direction. In his fleshly body, Dante exceptionally gains access to the realm of the dead, who in return are denied entry to the sphere of the living.[11] No mixing between both realms takes place; the transition zone of the *selva oscura* is not localized and seems to be set up exclusively for Dante. Yet, spatial separation is not synonymous with the impossibility of cross-border communication, from which only the inhabitants of hell are cut off. Quite on the contrary, the spatial segregation of the dead goes along with the explicit exhortation of the living to communicate with them directly or indirectly, by mediation of God. Thus, the hereafter does not constitute a "gated community" of the dead hedged off from the living. The perfect order of the hereafter also integrates the living in a community of true life, assembling all Christians around God and the work of salvation. Pointing to the importance of purgatory in the establishment of this economy of salvation, Jacques Le Goff speaks of the colonization of the hereafter.[12]

With purgatory, we find installed in Dante's hereafter what according to Foucault emerges much later in this world: the dominating feature of the disciplinary. If the power over the body, the right to take life and to give death, is what characterizes sovereign rule,[13] in Dante this is only true of Hell, where irredeemable sinners suffer the endless repetition of ever-identical torture and punishment. Purgatory, on the contrary, is a place of discipline where the bodies of the purified, although submitted to severe and painful punishment, labor within time, thus working for their salvation. This disciplinary *renfermement* of the otherworldly subjects only finds its sense in the release of the repentants into the eternal life in Paradise as the goal of their purification. Moreover, in his hereafter Dante realizes perfectly the ideal of addressing each and every individual that Foucault claims underlies the pastorate.[14] If Foucault states that the transition from the sovereign to the disciplinary is performed by shifting from reigning over a territory to governing its inhabitants, in Dante the *singulatim* governance comes into being *via* space. Each inhabitant of the hereafter coincides exactly with the position of his body in space. It is his very localization that pronounces – and visualizes – judgment on him, and only from this precise point in space that defines his true identity can he speak as a member of the group of sinners or saints that God has assigned him to or that he ascends to during the course of his purifying itinerary. Thus, what emerges with Dante's hereafter is the order of a perfect police where every subject can be localized and identified through an individual address.[15] There is no space left for a scene of disagreement in this topography.

The hereafter to which Max arrives after his assassination consists of three sections, too. But the fact that from the *centre de tri* the deceased can join either the *section urbaine*, a sullen grey Paris, or the idyllic *section parc*, where one lives in hermit-like isolation, clarifies that these are not just renamed analogies of Dante's *inferno*, *purgatorio*, and *paradiso*. There, once you enter either purgatory or hell, judgment has already taken place. In *Au piano*, judgment still lies ahead. In fact, the procedures of the *centre* have little in common with those of purgatory. Old-fashioned Max, who lived his life according to disciplinary principles, fails to notice the discreet hints to this modification. Twice he examines his conscience and his past comportment by the moral standards of Christian faith. In doing so, he errs doubly. First, because he believes that the examination of his conduct has come to an end with his life. However, one of the basic principles of the society of control is that nothing ever stops.[16] Thus, Max ends up in an assessment center. The innocuousness of the place, the comic contrast between the hypermodern medical treatment of the "patients" and its old-fashioned elements, from the Hollywood movie characters of the fifties – Max is attended by Doris Day and Dean Martin – to its bureaucracy, is deceiving. The director's fiddling about with yellowed documents in front of Max is pure comedy, a façade designed to meet Max's level of expectations. His personal file is meaningless because he is not judged for his life in this world, but assessed on the basis of a series of behavioral tests he goes through unawares. Very much unlike Beatrice, Doris Day only leads him into temptation, seducing him to spend a "fatal" night of love with her that will send him to *section urbaine* and thus back to Paris. And yet it is all but clear if this is to be considered a punishment. This is because, secondly, Max goes wrong when he expects a *moral* judgment on a comportment meeting or failing divine law. The judgment on the good or bad nature of man is replaced, as Foucault states for the dispositifs of security, by the foresighted taking into account of the nature of things. This seems to allow for more freedom insofar as decisions are based on individual wishes and interests within these dispositifs.[17] But in the end, the two sections are populated according to *quota*. Both have their pros and cons, as Max is assured. The plain values of the *judgment*, good and bad, are replaced by the problem of *distribution*. The administration of the hereafter does not punish or reward, it merely assesses and regulates the streams of the newly deceased.

The organization of space in the *centre* follows the same principles. If space in the *Divina Commedia* is a rigid *moule* wherein the shadow bodies of the dead are formed, the *centre de tri* proceeds by *modulation*, the constant mutual adaptation of space and the *dividuels*.[18] In contrast to Dante, Max is allowed to move freely, without guidance. Yet one should not forget that for Dante, guidance was necessary to prevent him from making fatal mistakes in an unknown environment where he would never have been able to find his way on his own. This might shed a less favorable light on the center's central values: initiative and responsibility of one's own. The more Max moves around, the more the space around him becomes unstable. In this *centre*, there is no need for piled up files and data storage anymore, because it acts and reacts in real time. Based on information generated from Max's thoughts and acts, it constantly modifies its shape and appearance in order to generate new experimental designs. Within the dispositifs of security examined by Foucault, the classic sanctions on action through punishment and prohibition are replaced by a more discreet technology of power based on a clearly defined concept of freedom: "the possibility of movement, change of place, and processes of circulation of both people and things. I think it is this freedom of circulation, in the broad sense of the term, it is in terms of this option of circulation, that we should understand the word freedom."[19] The manipulative experiments invented by Echenoz show how this discreet technology of power that regulates rather than inhibits these movements uses the supposed autonomy of the individuals to control them.

Modulation is also the underlying principle of the *section urbaine*, which does not work with old-fashioned barriers, but informs the "*matière 'dividuelle*" with passwords (and denials of access) in order to guarantee permanent control of the (in)dividuals based on their dispersal in space. When Max returns to Paris as a revenant, it is seen to that he moves among the living (and other dead) without being recognized by former friends and acquaintances. His situation as a revenant does not differ radically from what it was when he was alive, but is altered by minimal modulations, which, combined with subtle forms of surveillance, unfold a maximum effect. These modulations are necessary to prevent Max from transgressing certain interdictions. The most important are: he must not enter into contact with any person he knew in his lifetime and he must not practice his former profession as a pianist. His fate as a revenant consists not, as one might expect, in endlessly repeating elements of his former life, but in making a new life. He thus receives a new civic identity and his face is modified. It is interesting to notice how Echenoz uses the motif of the new face by plastic surgery, which is a familiar element of genre movies, for in this case the modification takes place in an imperceptible and indiscernible manner:

> Nice work. They hadn't made a mess of it. While Max was patently unrecognisable, you couldn't attribute his transformation to anything in particular ... Rather, it was the arrangement of these features, the relationship between them, that had been imperceptibly altered, although Max himself couldn't have said exactly how, in what order or which direction. But the fact was he wasn't the same any more – or rather, he was the same but incontestably someone else: his face might appear vaguely familiar to someone who had known him, but it would surely go no further than that. (127)

Given this conditioning, it is unnecessary to let Max's return among the living take place in a new environment. The deserted hotel bar where he works as a bartender lies near the square where he used to live. But here, too, a minimal local displacement yields a maximum effect. When returning to his ancient quarter, not even his own sister recognizes him. Right in the center of Paris, which thus turns itself into a "zone," Max finds himself leading a shadowy existence that equals the total exclusion from his social milieu, since his lodging in the hotel is no better than one in the *banlieue*. In his circulation, Max is not stopped by gates or walls, but nevertheless micro-boundaries and mechanisms separate him from his former life.

This society-of-control's hold on the revenant is only possible because for his needs, too, it is true that nothing ever stops. As in his lifetime, Max is in need of money, food, lodging, clothing, etc., and thus has to earn his living. Mortality as a limit and an ending is replaced by the endless horizon of needs that can only be satisfied by further labor. Another prerequisite for this governance is the indiscernibility of the dead and the living. Not only are living human beings unable to tell that Max is a revenant, but, more importantly, the dead cannot identify each other as being of the same kind. Although they certainly outnumber the living, they are, in Deleuze's terminology, not only stripped of the possibility to become major, but also of the chance to act as a minor majority.[20] The dead's supposed freedom of movement is highly regulated, because the treatment by which each of them is singled out thwarts the very possibility of contact with each other in the awareness of sharing the same condition. They remain without a common voice, because they cannot constitute themselves as a "part des sans-part," i.e. as part of society that has no part in society.[21]

But Max does not put up with the place to which he has been assigned. He takes advantage of a failure in the control system to escape: Bernie, his former factotum, recognizes and helps him. Transgressing the main interdictions imposed on him, Max moves in with Bernie and starts to perform as a pianist in a bar. Béliard, a representative of the hereafter in charge of Max, shows up promptly, but after initial indignation, "calming down a bit too quickly," he gives in to Max's unruliness (167). The ineffectiveness of control seems to lead to a dénouement in the key of comedy. But Béliard's scarce resistance should have aroused suspicion. For the official of the hereafter also mentions that he actually came to *section urbaine* as a kind of postmortem blade runner to look for a woman who managed to escape from *section parc*. This woman is Rose, Max's unfulfilled love whose memory has haunted him for a lifetime. Max finally encounters her, seemingly by chance, in a department store, and despite her modulated features, he recognizes her immediately. Before he has the opportunity to address her, however, Béliard shows up, by coincidence as it seems, and engages Rose in an intimate conversation. He introduces Max to her, but recognition remains unilateral: "Max bowed clumsily to Rose, who, as anticipated, gave him merely a slight nod without showing the least sign of recognition" (178). Max protests Béliard's intention to take Rose back to the park, but it is in vain:

> "Wait just a minute," said Max. "Excuse me, but this person – I think *I'm* the one who was supposed to find her."
> "Yes," Béliard said with a cold smile, "I know. I'm perfectly aware of all that, but I'm still the one leaving with her. You see, this is what it's like in the urban zone. This is what it consists of. In a sense, it's what most of you call Hell." (178)

Max is left behind, "plus mort que jamais,"[22] literally "deader than ever." The encounter with the beloved person takes place and yet is prevented at the same time. At the end of the story it is obvious that this was just another experimental design. It becomes clear that the punishment of *section urbaine* has nothing to do with the intrinsic quality of the place, but that it is a question of regulating distribution. Hell is the certainty of being where the loved one is not – for eternity.

The Making of Zombies: *Les revenants*

Les revenants depicts a well-meaning police of this world that also functions as a care and counseling dispositif regulating the dealings with those who came back. As in Romero's *Trilogy*, the army and scientists are at the frontline when it comes to encountering the un-dead. In Campillo's movie, though, they do not act isolated and in a totalitarian, anti-civic manner, but are part of a network binding them together with the political administration. This network operates in the mode of the *humanitarian*, following UN guidelines for the treatment of war and disaster refugees.

Faced with the state of emergency caused by the return of the dead, authorities at first have recourse to the disciplinary strategy of incarceration. Armed forces and the Red Cross intern the revenants in camps that in humanitarian newspeak are baptized "structures d'accueil" (welcome centers). Uncontrolled encounters between the living and the returnees are thus prevented to a large extent. What has to be achieved next is the transformation of the amorphous plethora into a structured population that undergoes census, classification, and identification. Repartition by age, sex, and ability to work, and the recording of each "home-comer" needs to be reconciled with death registers. All this is supposed to lead to reintegration into their families and their previous employment.

Whereas Romero's movies depart from the radical difference between humans and the zombie "things" in order to deconstruct this opposition progressively throughout the *Trilogy*, Campillo traces the reverse process. Absolute identity between the returnees and "normal" humans is the initial assumption. The living treat the revenants as of their own kind, as fully-fledged fellow citizens whom they grant equal rights and duties. The measures taken by authorities are aimed at permitting the returnees to take up their lives right at the point where they were interrupted – just as if they had never been away.

Their "inconceivable" new existence can only be rationalized and conceived of as congruent with their former one; reinsertion presupposes that they can still be addressed in the same way as when they were living members of society and when they were put to "eternal" rest. It presupposes a continuity of biography beyond death that looks at the afterlife of the dead from the point of view of their surviving relatives. But to think of them as "home-comers" is the first and fundamental misunderstanding that thwarts a situation where disagreement could lead to a fertile displacement of the status quo. The problem is that the dead and those left behind have evolved in time – in different times. The strategy of the living seems to be to ignore or erase the lapse of time in which asynchrony has emerged. Careful re-adaptation aims at the restoration of synchrony in order to return to a coexistence in a common temporality – that of the living. The movie shows the failure of this attempt; the hypothesis that after a transitional period the returnees will finally wake up and speed up turns out to be illusive. As soon as the un-dead are perceived as irredeemably out of sync with the living, they appear as strange and threatening – an impression that comes as a result of scientific examination. The living are unable to find a way to build a community with the dead based on asynchrony and finally return to their usual temporality instead, thus widening the gap that separates them from the revenants.

The inhabitants of the French town evaluate the behavior of the living dead by their own standards and thus only in terms of deficit: what they perceive is that the revenants do not re-adapt to "human" language, patterns of action, and spatiotemporal schemes. What is inconceivable for them is not so much the return of the dead, but the possibility that they have evolved and continue to evolve *in their own condition*, pursuing their own interests and projects and speaking their own language.

Scientific observation and comment are central in this process of estrangement, because they help the living to absorb their perplexity, to re-establish the automatic sensory-motor link and restore conventional agency. In Campillo's movie, science as an institution that visualizes and verbalizes "knowledge" about the un-dead replaces entirely the mass media that were central in Romero's *Trilogy*. In his groundbreaking redefinition of the zombie genre, Romero reduced the genre effect by shooting in black and white, thus adapting his images to those of contemporary TV of the sixties;

TV images are included in his movie to create an effect of authenticity. Campillo's strange poetics of demography relies on a visual aesthetic simulating scientific image-guided procedures that become part of a surveillance *dispositif*. Moreover, in this expertocratic climate, scientists take on discursive authority from the mass media that in parts one and two of Romero's *Trilogy* sent out ever-new interpretations of events to their audience. In *Les revenants*, scientists report their findings to the city council, their explanations turning repeatedly into voice-over commentaries accompanying images of the returnees that mark the phases of their *othering*. In this process, nobody explicitly makes the decision to exclude the revenants from the political community. The "humans" are acting in obedience to the "objective constraints" of the hard data and facts they are constantly producing. From the very start, the scientists try to rationalize the phenomenon of mass revenance by pathologizing the returnees, whose bodily functions are not entirely normal. For instance, their brain functions are compared to those of trauma patients.

If the dead appear more and more as dysfunctional, the rights that are meant to guarantee their full reintegration quickly turn into constraints. The un-dead prove unable or unwilling to take their former places. Instead, they enter into relations with each other according to affinities incomprehensible to the living. To the great dismay and bewilderment of a dead boy's parents, an elderly man who is a complete stranger to them starts to look after them and wins his confidence. Groups of un-dead gather together in the street and in workplaces for no apparent reason. Sleepless at night, they go against the logic of *revenance* and haunting of familiar places and persons: an irresistible urge to move makes them flee their homes and relatives.

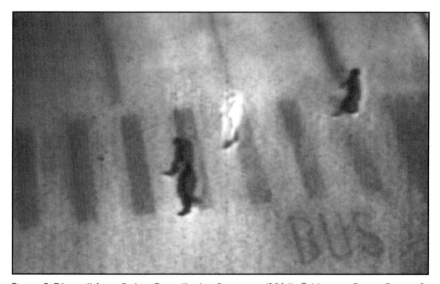

Figure 5: Film still from Robin Campillo, *Les Revenants* (2004), © Haut et Court, France 3 Cinéma, Gimages Développement.

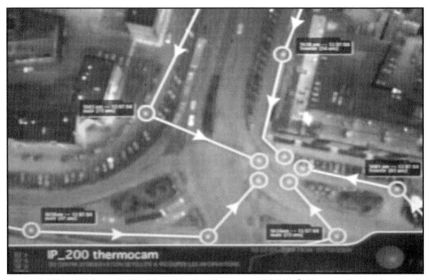

Figure 6: Film still from Robin Campillo, *Les Revenants* (2004), © Haut et Court, France 3 Cinéma, Gimages Développement.

This urge to move – a physician speaks of the excessive vitality of the un-dead – is answered by locking them in and administering psychotropic pharmaceuticals. But since their nomadism cannot be stopped, another step is taken: instead of trying to understand their (pathological) motives and healing them ("why?"), their migratory motion is treated as an objective phenomenon of traffic ("what and how?"). Taking advantage of the lower body temperature of the un-dead, thermal cameras are installed everywhere in town, showing warmer, red living persons and cooler, blue revenants. Sequences shot with these cameras are inserted repeatedly into the movie. The images serve as a basis for diagrams visualizing movement patterns and thus for the collecting of information on the mysterious circulation and gatherings of the observed individuals.

But despite all scientific efforts, in Campillo, even more so than in Romero, the revenants remain a strange and incomprehensible multitude whose appearance, movements, and actions are beyond any discernible pattern of causality. As with all other endeavors to find explanations, to understand their motivation, or to control their moves, pattern recognition that aims to visualize the underlying structures of their actions or organization fails. In *Les revenants* this inability to understand eventually leads the living to conceive of the revenants as zombies.

In the end, the "returnees" decide to move on and escape the community of the living. Their destination is a system of tunnels, a kind of Hades that guarantees freedom of motion and the encounters they prefer to the orderly *renfermement* of the cemetery where each dead can be localized by the living in the isolation of his grave. But because of the town's failure to deal with disagreement and the construction of a political scene, escalation of conflicts and overt hostility to the revenants is pre-programmed. In order to elude the constant control of the living, the dead organize their collective flight and try to divert attention by a series of explosions all over town. Although no one is harmed, this is immediately seen as an act of aggression by the living and, like in Romero, the army deploys to open fire – even if its grenades only contain a narcotic substance.

Some manage to escape, but most of the revenants end up where it all began: they are retransferred to the disciplinary order of the cemetery, into a spatial arrangement where they can be localized and addressed as dead citizens and family members. By returning them to the cemeteries, the afterlife of the dead is erased. The only special effect of the movie occurs here: the bodies of the unconscious dead, when laid upon their graves, dematerialize into translucent ghosts before they vanish completely. The "haunting" and revenance that was only produced by the behavior of the living has come to an end. Even more so than Echenoz, Campillo shows us the dead who have an afterlife and who are not concerned with the living as an object of their care (as in *The Sixth Sense*) or of their lethal desire (*Trilogy of the Dead*). The obstinacy and autonomy of the dead who refuse to be reinserted into the police of the living becomes the lesion to our narcissism that *Les revenants* inflicts on us: they did not come back, not to us.

NOTES

1   For a more detailed treatment of this subject, developing further aspects and containing extensive bibliographical references, see Michael Cuntz, "Mixed zone – Wie man den Toten begegnet," in *Unmenge – Wie verteilt sich Handlungsmacht?*, ed. Ilka Becker et al. (München: Fink, 2008), 191–226.

2   Jean Echenoz, *Au piano* (Paris: Minuit, 2003); English translation: Jean Echenoz, *Piano* (London: Vintage, 2005). Subsequent quotations are from the English edition.

3   The film was released for the English market under the title *They Came Back*.

4   "Perplexity" is the term Bruno Latour employs to describe the reaction of those who consider themselves as actors – i.e. human beings – when confronted with other entities aspiring to this status they had not taken into account: "Let us say that, under the name of fact, new entities appear in the form of that which leaves those who are discussing them perplexed." Bruno Latour, *Politics of Nature: How to Bring the Sciences into Democracy*, (Cambridge, MA: Harvard University Press, 2004), 104. In the glossary to this book, he defines perplexity as one of the seven tasks by which the collective becomes attentive and sensitive to the presence of a multitude of propositions on the outside that might want to form part of the common world (246).

5   For this concept of the political scene where neither the rules, the setting, nor the number and nature of the actors or a common language are established in advance but emerge in a polemic political process of *disagreement*, thus allowing for the building of a new community (as opposed to the order of the police where the roles, identities, and localization of actors are fixed), see Jacques Rancière, *La mésentente. Politique et philosophie* (Paris: Galilée, 1995); for the concept of police in Foucault see Michel Foucault, "'Omnes et singulatim': vers une critique de la raison politique," in *Dits et écrits II, 1976–1988*, ed. Daniel Defert and François Ewald (Paris: Gallimard, 2001), 953–980.

6   Gilles Deleuze, *Cinéma 2. L'Image-temps* (Paris: Minuit, 1985), 29–30.

7   Jacques Derrida, *Specters of Marx: The State of the Debt, the Work of Mourning, & the New International* (New York and London: Routledge, 1994), 7.

8 Campillo himself names *Night of the Living Dead* (1968) along with Don Siegel's *Invasion of the Body Snatchers* (1956) as major references. See Philippe Mangeot et al., "La parenthèse hantée. Entretien avec Robin Campillo," *Vacarme 30*, http://www.vacarme.eu.org/article_462.html.

9 On postmortem cinema see Thomas Elsaesser, "'Zu spät, zu früh.' Körper, Zeit und Aktionsraum in der Kinoerfahrung," in *Kinogefühle. Emotionalität und Film,* ed. Matthias Brütsch et al. (Marburg: Schüren, 2005), 415–439; and Elsaesser, "Was wäre, wenn du schon tot bist. Vom 'postmodernen' zum 'post-mortem'-Kino am Beispiel von Christopher Nolans Memento," in *ZeitSprünge. Wie Filme Geschichte(n) erzählen,* ed. Christine Rüffert et al. (Berlin: Bertz, 2004), 115–125.

10 On the historical evolution of the topography of death in funeral practices see Philippe Ariès, *L'homme devant la mort* (Paris: Seuil, 1977).

11 Exclusion of the dead from the world of the living is one of the central goals of the Church in late antiquity and the Middle Ages. See Edgar Morin, *L'homme et la mort* (Paris: Seuil, 2002).

12 See Jacques Le Goff, *La naissance du purgatoire* (Paris: Gallimard, 1981).

13 For the distinction between sovereign rule and disciplinary governmentality see Michel Foucault, *Surveiller et punir* (Paris: Gallimard, 1975).

14 Foucault, "'Omnes et singulatim'," 965.

15 This seems to confirm Giorgio Agamben's assumption that modern governmentality is a direct result of Christian theology as developed since late antiquity and centered on the notion of *oikonomía*. See Giorgio Agamben, *Il Regno e la Gloria. Per una genealogia teologica dell'economia e del governo* (Vicenza: Neri Pozza, 2007).

16 See Gilles Deleuze, "Contrôle et devenir," in *Pourparlers 1972–1990* (Paris: Minuit, 2003), 237.

17 See Michel Foucault, *Security, Territory, Population: Lectures at the Collège de France 1977–1978* (New York: Picador, Palgrave Macmillan, 2007), 48.

18 For the concept of *dividuel* see Gilles Deleuze, "Post-scriptum sur les sociétés de contrôle," in *Pourparlers 1972–1990* (Paris: Minuit, 2003), 240–247.

19 Foucault, *Security, Territory, Population*, 48–49.

20 "He continued to look at all the people he came across in the street, wondering about each one's status: maybe there were others like him, who had passed through the Centre before coming back here; maybe there were many of them, maybe, when you go down to it, they were even in the majority" (148). For the concepts of major(ity) and minor(ity), see Deleuze, "Contrôle et devenir."

21 Jacques Rancière, *La mésentente. Politique et Philosophie* (Paris: Galilée, 1995), 31.

22 Echenoz, *Au piano*, 223. The English translation has: "a crushed Max watches as Rose and Béliard proceed towards the glass doors" (178).

Chapter 10

Specters of the U.S. Prison Regime: Haunting Tourism and the Penal Gaze

Benjamin D'Harlingue

In Crest Hills, Illinois, across the street from Stateville Correctional Institute – a roundhouse prison run by the Illinois Department of Corrections that comes closer architecturally than any other currently operational U.S. prison to Jeremy Bentham's panopticon – sits a mock double called Statesville Haunted Prison. Statesville is not, nor has it ever been, an actual prison. Open during the month of October, it is an amusement park-styled haunted house, a plastic fantasy where actors donning ghoulish costume and make-up pretend to be prisoners. Nevertheless, Statesville's geographical proximity and metonymic nomination point its representational and spatial configurations toward an actual prison and its prisoners. Indeed, the subtleties of location and spelling in the designation of the two sites – official state institution and its ostensible parody – were missed by a September 10, 2003 *Chicago Tribune* article, titled "Stateville Inmate Attacks Officer," which reported: "A corrections officer from Stateville Correctional Center … was hospitalized … after being attacked by an inmate."[1] Not only do current events at Stateville get described under the sign of Statesville, but Statesville's spectacular haunted productions also call up the biographical case histories of deceased persons who had been sequestered by the Illinois Department of Corrections. An October 9, 2003 article in *Courier-News* (based in Elgin, Illinois), titled "Statesville's haunted prison beckons you to Hell," is clearly about the haunted tourist site, and even gives admission prices. Yet the article also reports, as if factually:

> The former home of John Wayne Gacy and Richard Speck, Statesville has been named the number one haunted house by HauntedHouseChicago.com for the last three years. Convicted serial killer Gacy died there by lethal injection in 1992. Speck, convicted of murdering eight nurses in 1966, spent 19 years at Statesville, then died of a massive heart attack in 1991.[2]

This article, functioning as advertisement, furthers a discursive slippage that Statesville Haunted Prison proliferates and upon which it relies. It might be said that, in part, it is the trope of haunting that allows for the possibility of such a slippage. Statesville's official website's video trailer advertisement for the haunted prison opens with the text, in all red caps: "STATESVILLE PRISON PERMANENT HOME FOR OVER 200 OF THE MOST VIOLENT CRIMINALS IN HISTORY."[3] In this rendering, incarcerated bodies from across multitudinous spaces and times of imprisonment can be thought as dislodged from their historical locations and gathered together, as ghosts, within the walls of this spectacle of haunting entertainment. The conditions of possibility for this spatio-temporal figuring in the mode of haunting are to be found in a prison regime historically organized through the creation of the figure of the criminal. The idea of a permanent haunting domicile for criminals tropes on contemporary terms of incarceration, whereby prisoners are indefinitely sequestered; the construction of prisoner psychobiography, whereby administrative case histories produce prisoners' souls as targets for reform; and the social ontology of prison as a mode of civil death, whereby prisoners become dead in law.

This essay is an inquiry into both haunting tourism and certain popular cultural configurations of the prison industrial complex.[4] Haunting tourism includes travel to places for the purpose of encountering or investigating supernatural or paranormal phenomena, such as ghosts, monsters, zombies, spirits, vampires, and the like. Such tourism might entail physical travel to a haunted destination, or it might entail more virtual travel like browsing websites about haunted places, reading a ghost hunter's guidebook, or watching the Travel Channel's programs *Ghost Adventures* and *Most Haunted*. While haunting tourism boomed as a popular, mass practice in the U.S. in the last decade of the twentieth century, it is noticeable at earlier moments.[5] Haunting tourisms often fixate on violent events or legacies, such as slavery, colonization, immigration exclusion, sexual assault, or war. Institutional settings such as houses, prisons, hospitals, or military installations frequently provide sites of interest. Focusing on contemporary haunting tourism of prisons, this essay is concerned with the modes of violence and the oppressive legacies that the prison as an institution mobilizes and instantiates in popular culture.

Some haunted prison tours, such as a radio-broadcasted, fundraising investigatory tour of New Mexico State Penitentiary recently conducted by the Southwest Ghost Hunters Association, claim recourse to scientific method and enlightenment reason, and seek evidence of the presence of actual ghosts. Other prison tours are less explicit about their theme of haunting, such as at Alcatraz Island, where the genre of official tours is historical reportage, even as former administrators and current Park Rangers who preside over the defunct prison-turned-museum occasionally testify to ghostly experiences for tourist guidebooks and film documentaries on ghosts.[6] Several haunted prison tours, like that of Statesville, are of the Halloween haunted house type. Tourism of Eastern State Penitentiary (ESP), in Philadelphia, PA, combines elements of all three.

Whatever the variety, haunted prison tourisms can be described as tourisms focused around prisons, marketed or discussed largely through tropes such as ghosts, spirits, zombies, and the undead. These figures have emerged against the backdrop of a legal situation whereby prisoners have been constituted as civilly dead. Civil death is a condition in which an individual is stripped of all civil rights, including the right to own property, to make contracts, and to vote. As Caleb Smith notes, at its very founding, the penitentiary's route to reform as a redeeming rebirth required that the prisoner first go through a death of sorts, a "mortification" that causes the prisoner to become "a divided figure: a redeemable soul, but also an offending body; a citizen-in-training, but also an exile from civil society; a resurrected life, but also an animate corpse."[7] Smith traces this splitting of the prisoner to the constitutive contradiction grounding the social contract. The founding of the very category of the human, the would-be citizen, entails a sacrificial violence that splits the human and the polity from monstrous nature and animality: "in the political imagination of the societies that built the first great penitentiaries, the citizen was a double figure, an enlightened subjectivity rising from the remains of a sacrificed beast" (252). The peopling of the body politic with the humans it was to represent required an inscription of the monstrous death-in-life from which citizenship would distinguish itself: "the prisoner was ... a figure at the threshold, the sacrifice of life through which the citizen-subject's transcendent humanity was born" (252). Yet, the social contract was to be distinct from and maintain rule over nature and death, so that those living dead forced to inhabit these spaces were not outside the force of law, even as they were without political representation.

This production of national citizen life through penal-instituted death is traceable in haunting tourism. Encouraging leisurely travel in pursuit of ghosts, a guidebook called *Haunted Holidays* explicitly claims the imbrication of the ghostly in the elaboration of the national: "So why not go find some? You probably won't even have to travel far, since ghosts seem to be everywhere in America, tangled in the roots of the nation's history."[8] It also binds the national imaginary to the imagery of death: "When we look into the mirror of death, ghosts are what we see" (27). If the prison is bound to a constitutive crack in subjectivity – between citizen life and the cast-off, disavowed monstrosity of death – that crack is imaginarily projected and misrecognized in the visual relations of penal democracy. Operative on the very boundary between life and death, the law's violent demarcation comes to appear as a divine inscription at haunting tourism sites, and it does so precisely in the register of the gaze.

Contemporary U.S. haunted prison tourisms naturalize and sanctify the reigning penal order by nothing less than the apparent gaze of God. In the racial order that organizes and is reproduced by this gaze, Whiteness demarcates the prison's outside from its inside, founding an abject civil death against which citizenship is constituted. In Foucault's well-cited genealogy of penality and the modern soul on trial, the expert gaze produces the figure of the criminal and the panoptic gaze of disciplinary power tied to the prison produces docile subjects.[9] In tourism studies, the notion of the "tourist gaze," developed by John Urry and adopted widely throughout the field, draws upon Foucault's account of the disciplinary gaze as it developed in the clinic.[10] Like this clinical gaze, the tourist gaze is buttressed and directed by institutional power and expertise, as it enacts a probing that produces objects' surfaces and their imagined inner depths. Foucault's genealogy of imprisonment and Urry's attention to tourist cultures provide important platforms from which to theorize the historical whereabouts of the gaze at the point of intersection between penality and tourism. Yet, to adequately account for the gaze's operation in excess of the ocular and imbricated with the symbolic order, the psychoanalytical dimension of haunted prison tourism also requires consideration.

Tourism of prisons is not a new phenomenon. As John Sears has shown, prisons were major tourist attractions in the U.S. in the early nineteenth century, drawing reformers, writers, specialists, and leisure travelers from across the country and Europe to view and assess the conditions, architecture, inmates, and modes of reform.[11] Travel to penitentiaries afforded a first-hand viewing experience that authorized members of the upper class to enter into public discussions over the significance of these relatively new institutions. According to Sears, prison tourism became less popular around the 1860s, as potential visitors grew less optimistic about the promise prisons held to reform people. He notes that tourist attention became directed at other sites, such as cemeteries and parks. In the late twentieth and early twenty-first centuries, however, prison tourism picked up again, and haunted tours constituted a substantial component of this new boom.

In an episode of Travel Channel's *America's Scariest Halloween Attractions* focused on ESP, Sean Kelley, ESP Program Director, provides some clues as to why so much of prison tourism is haunted prison tourism:

> It's incredibly eerie. We're talking about a building that's 178 years old where 75,000 men and women spent their lives, sometimes dying here of natural causes, sometimes leaving to be executed. There's just a lot of energy in this building. You know people think Eastern State Penitentiary's haunted, so whether you believe in ghosts or not, you would have to agree that if they exist anywhere in the world, they would exist here. The building after all was designed to intimidate. That was its whole purpose.

The violence of state-sponsored death produces an eerie affect that sticks to the very materiality of the prison building, making itself felt through haunting by the logic of architectural semiotechnique.[12] The history and architecture of state violence and intimidation become indistinguishable in the production of the affect and rationale that demand the knee-jerk recognition that if there is a proper place of haunting, it is the prison. It is not counter-intuitive to consider that the misery born of a project of state coercion as large as the prison would produce substantial fallout of emotion, haunting, or trauma. But would these be limited strictly to the inside of the prison?

Evidence of the extent to which prison has been constitutive of persons existing outside of the prison building can be found in its mobilization of tourists. A 2007 *New York Times* article entitled "In the Big House ... Just Visiting" reported that, in the U.S., "three dozen prisons and jails [are] now collectively drawing millions of visitors each year around the country."[13] The article notes that ESP drew 150,000 visitors in

2006. ESP's largest source of revenue is its Halloween attraction, "Terror Behind the Walls," which now runs for nearly two months of the year. While the Halloween event uses special effects and live performances typical of amusement parks or fairs, these appear as mere dramatizations or accompaniments to actual paranormal activity. ESP holds daily historical tours throughout the year, and official statements from ESP's program director continually assert a commitment to historical preservation. Nonetheless, a placard displayed for the historical tour, complete with audio listening station, asserts: "Many people argue that if ghosts exist, they must be found here." Moreover, a quick glance at tourist texts – whether guidebooks, news articles, or blogs – reveals widely circulated beliefs that ESP is in fact haunted by the guards and prisoners who once lived and/or worked there.

Whereas the prison tourism of old was mostly a practice of the bourgeoisie, this new tourism has a more mass cultural character. Additionally, whereas earlier prison tourism was aimed toward enlightened attention to the penitentiaries' social project, its contemporary version seems largely geared toward entertainment. Popular tourism of prisons still includes modes of reflecting on the shifting historical project of prisons and its social implications, but the new mass entertainment does not articulate this reflection in the same terms of explicit public debate that earlier prison tours engaged. Nevertheless, the implications of this tourism for politics cannot be underestimated, as the social text of haunting tourism evinces the ideology of the prison industry and its carceral regime as distilled in the form of mass commodity spectacle.

In *Discipline and Punish*, Foucault sketches penal intervention's new target, the soul, as a primary object upon which power would act in the wake of its shift from sovereignty to discipline. Judgment would now reference the soul as it crafted new identities, namely the delinquent or the criminal. Foucault carefully explores power's shifting investments in the body and the techniques by which the body was apprehended through varied, dispersed mechanisms that disciplined the body precisely through knowledge of the soul, which was simultaneously power's very product. The production of the criminal's soul was not accomplished exclusively through juridical measures, but involved medicine, psychiatry, criminology, anthropology, pedagogy, and architecture. Myriad specialized gazes thus descended upon the criminal, as well as upon the means and environment by which the criminal was to be reformed. This also involved the tourist gaze, the early refinement of which might be said to have taken place at prisons. Thus, while John Urry's oft-cited theory of the tourist gaze analogizes it to the clinical gaze that Foucault describes in *Birth of the Clinic*, we should also think of the tourist gaze as operating in conjunction with, or as an instance of, the disciplinary gaze busy at work on the soul of the criminal.[14]

If disciplinary power brought forth the prisoner's soul, or the soul as prisoner, the soul would be made to linger in the haunting of tourist sites, endlessly fulfilling its task for the prison regime. Haunting tourisms' itineraries, which gravitate around prisoners' souls, now render these souls through the figures of the ghost and the undead. Their privileging in contemporary haunted prison tourism is linked to a recent shift in penal practice, whereby the focus is no longer reform but incapacitation, or what some have called warehousing or entombment. The rationale for the incapacitation tied to the biggest prison proliferation in human history is that, as reform is not necessarily possible, it is best to hold prisoners in cages for as long as possible, thus preventing them from committing new crimes outside the prison.[15] Still, knowledge formations derived from earlier reform-oriented penal practice continue to scrutinize the status of the prisoner's soul. At retired prisons hosting haunted tours, there remain architectural arrays imbued with a visual economy that directs attention toward probing the inner depths of prisoners. Now lacking an object, these remnants direct the tourist gaze toward the shadow of a present/absent soul, which takes the form of a ghost. The corporeal bodies of prisoners no longer appear, but it may be said that through the haunting phantasm, the specters of prisoners' souls are nonetheless raised.

The direction of the penal gaze, however, spills over the sightline routed strictly to the prisoner's soul. In the power relations that produce ESP's tours, prisoners, guards, and tourists are discursively triangulated. At the base of the crack in citizenship – which imagines itself through a fantasy of wholeness and transcendence by casting off monstrous death by projecting it onto the bodies of prisoners and racialized bodies imagined always as potential prisoners – is the installation of a guard–prisoner relationship, which is not simply between individuals but also resides *within* individuals. This ambiguity is evidenced in "Terror Behind the Walls," inasmuch as tourists passing through ESP's haunted enactment are at times stalked by characters meant to be threatening guards and at other times by characters meant to be prisoners. Still, the privileged position the tourist is implicitly asked to occupy is that of guard, evidenced in a part of the tour in which visitors walk down a dark hall holding a flashlight, as if to experience what guards in the prison might have lived through. But what one must guard over too is one's own self, since the operation of panoptic power is such that for both guard and prisoner it installs a feeling of being watched by an unseen other.

At sites like Statesville and ESP that do not house prisoners, supernatural phenomenalization is supplemented with the work of actors playing ghosts and the undead. At prison sites that still house prisoners and also have haunting tours – such as Santa Fe State Penitentiary in New Mexico – it can be argued that the appearance of prisoners as ghosts may occur even when the bodies of prisoners are nearby, for those "real" bodies are not recognized as corresponding to souls that can be redeemed for tourist review. While Foucault's theory of the soul tracked the attempt to locate something behind, deep inside, or in excess of the body, this variety of haunting tourism allows for the appearance of souls at some temporal or spatial distance from the bodies they ostensibly reference. Thus, some prison tours focus on the spectral – a phantom (non)appearance or spirit *sans* corporeality – which can only be detected with electromagnetic-, sound-, or temperature-recording devices; others perform a monstrous, bloodied embodiment in the abject scene of acting out the undead, where the body is horrific precisely because of its detachment from a redeemable soul, or because of its complete elaboration of an evil irredeemable soul. In either case, what is dramatized is a ghostly unhinging of the body from the soul, or perhaps an unhinging of both from the time and space of civic life.

If the discourse of the soul relentlessly worked to modulate the inner depths of the prisoner toward desired social or transcendent ends, the reform has almost always failed.[16] This is acknowledged even in the legitimating texts of prison tourism. In the 1990s, when public debate about the fate of ESP considered the merits of turning the building into condos, a shopping mall, or a tourist site, articles in the *Philadelphia Inquirer* and the *Philadelphia Daily News* bemoaned the failure of the well-intentioned penitentiary to reform souls. They most typically suggested, however, that the problem was not prisons themselves, but the immutability of the corrupted, evil, or monstrous criminals who enlightened reformers had so admirably attempted to change. The apparatus of the soul, then, maintained one of its key features: the construction of a psychobiography that profiled the criminal type, the personality destined to become criminal.

The criminal soul was centrally subtended by race. As James Bernauer has noted, for Foucault the soul is a profoundly theological production, inasmuch as Christianity, in the sixteenth century if not earlier, would take on as a primary task the direction, circumspection, and confession of souls.[17] With the rise of the great disciplinary techniques, church officials were authorized to penetrate and bring forth souls at a variety of institutional sites, including prisons, schools, asylums, and military ranks. The techniques of soul craft were notably developed early on through colonial conquest. Whether in missionary conversion or genocidal warfare, the Christian demarcation of souls along civilizational and then racial lines provides the backdrop against which penal discipline in the U.S. must be analyzed. The soul as a theologically inflected penal target carries the epistemologies of colonial chattel slavery that either denied the possession of souls to non-white persons or only figured the salvation of non-white souls through their separation from the bodies thought to be their inevitable downfall.

In the U.S., until the early 1870s, prisons housed primarily working-class white men and sought to better synchronize the behaviors of convicts with the mandates of law and industrial capital.[18] According to Ruth Wilson Gilmore, in the wake of the official abolition of slavery, prisons soon became a new means to control black labor. With laws against vagrancy and loitering aimed specifically at black persons, their spatial movement was criminalized.[19] Criminal law thus became a means of preventing black participation in civic space. The laws that would increasingly imprison and define the penal treatment of black subjects arose from slavery provisions that equated Blackness with civil death. For Colin Dayan, civil death refers to the situation whereby contemporary U.S. prisoners bear, in many ways, a legal status comparable to the slave, and a political position short of human, which I argue affiliates them with the ghostly.[20]

The inscription of prison as a spectral site of death-in-life thus turns out to be founded on the nation-state's history of slavery and the contemporary production of the citizen as free and white against the foil of the prison, which is marked by an unfree blackness. Dylan Rodríguez argues that prisons constitute a forced passage through the space of death, recalling the transport of slaves across the middle passage.[21] For Rodríguez, the ontology of the citizen-subject is dependent on the denial of being and the extension of black unfreedom and civil death to the prisoner. In a penal democracy like the U.S., the citizen is granted certain rights that are defined in direct opposition to the situation of those experiencing civil death. The sense of being that is allotted to the citizen thus rests on an opposition drawn between what is outside prison and what is inside it. Moreover, racialization processes produce a seemingly inescapable metonymic link between black subjects and the interiors of prisons. The haunted figures that appear in certain prison tourisms arise from this interdependency between citizenship and civil death, between a fantasy of being and mattering and the deprivation of humanity against which this fantasy constitutes itself.

Haunted prison tours are involved in the designation of identities as either suited for imprisonment or not. In one instance of collaboration with the state and clear support for technologies of policing and surveillance, West Virginia Penitentiary's website advertises ghost hunts through a rotating photographic display of electric chairs, fences, and shimmering persons.[22] Above this ad, the website once featured a search engine where you could "find predators in your area": by clicking on a state, you are taken to government, police, and court websites documenting the location of actually registered sex offenders. This technology of explicit juridical surveillance mobilizes at the liminal site of the ghost tour to connect the prison's interior with its exterior through policing the domestic space of neighborhoods, marking some residents as inextricably tied to the prison. As racial profiling disproportionately brings the law's punitive weight and incarcerating capacities to bear upon persons of color, and as the prison is constructed as a home to sexual offenders (and as extending to their homes in the outside world), racialization before the law also designates sexual threats, reviving the virulent myth of the black rapist that, since slavery, has been used to rationalize brutal repression against black communities while skewing the sources of sexual assault.[23]

While tabulating knowledge about prisoners, prison tours proffer a gaze that normatively determines tourist populations. Statesville Haunted Prison's website reads:

> Come, let the prisoners of STATESVILLE HAUNTED PRISON® take you on a tour into the underbelly of this house of evil. You will find your way through these dark ancient walls, into thirty (30) of the prison's maximum-security cells. In this darkness, you will encounter over 200 of the most dangerous monsters ever imprisoned.

As Jasbir Puar and Amit Rai point out, the "monster" is one figure in Foucault's genealogy of "abnormals," an exception to both natural and juridical law. In the current context of the so-called War on Terror, the monstrous formulation of the terrorist signals a racialized sexual perversity.[24] Statesville's enticement to a dark encounter with "the most dangerous monsters ever imprisoned" calls forth the sexual and racial dangers of abnormality that bind and threaten subjects' relations to civil life. The tantalizing offer of entry into a "City of the Dead" establishes racial and sexual proximities between prisoners and tourists by playing on the tenuous border between civil life and death that prison walls seem to demarcate: "you must descend into the hallowed halls of City Of The Dead. The Tomb of Statesville has risen from the hell, and you must find your way above ground before you become a member in this army of the undead." However, even as the tour encourages a fantasy of haunted entry into the position of the prisoner, the ostensibly free position of the un-incarcerated citizen remains the ideal. Valorized life comes to be marked by tourist mobility through this ghoulish display. In a piece on tourism at Alcatraz Island, Mimi Nguyen writes,

> the pretense of inhabiting the lifespace of an inmate serves the display of power, if only to impress upon the visitor the totality of the disciplinary regime.... But the fantasy breaks apart. Occupying that imaginary space is impossible because the cell door is open; as a visitor you can always step outside the confines of cinderblock and steel bars to see yourself from the side of power.[25]

Escaping identification with abject imprisoned populations is no doubt easier for some than for others. As subjects are interpellated into varying positions within the assemblages of race, gender, sexuality, class, and spectrums of life and death denoted through the monster and ghost figures, particular identities get pinned to the figure of the prisoner, imposing uncomfortable identifications with some of penal democracy's most haunting imagos. Prisoners thus seem to be held up as objects of desire and fantasy within the very field of power that restricts them precisely from the circuits of normative kinship, property ownership (including their own labor), religious salvation (they are in "hell"), and inclusion in the category of the human citizen (the proper recipient of biopolitical life investments in the field of the national).

When Charles Dickens visited ESP, he was appalled by the way Quaker reformers had designed the prison to incite in inmates a reaction of penitence and submission to God. Like other early critics of the prison, he commented on its cruel, invisible manipulation of the psyche: such "ghastly signs and tokens are not so palpable to the eye."[26] This statement strikes at the ways that the symbolic order of prison escapes an analysis limited to power's constitution of surfaces and ways of looking. How to decipher the processes of subjectivation and the demarcation of zones of confinement and freedom, of carceral inside and civic outside, at work in the haunted social text of imprisonment? Maura Casey's aforementioned 2007 *New York Times* article on haunted prison tours reads: "adults exhibit a kind of nervous relief, never happier to be law-abiding citizens." What is this nervousness that draws such a mass of mostly American tourists? In the same article, Nicholette Phelps, who directs visitor programs at the Golden Gate National Parks Conservancy (which includes Alcatraz) is quoted as saying: "Everyone has a macabre interest in what could occur if you don't stay on the right side of the law.... We always think of what happens on the other side of that gate." In Casey we see nervousness, one might even say anxiety, around the law of prison that constructs its interior outside. In Phelps's take, that law and fascination are depicted as macabre. This affective complex can be explored in relation to a gaze that complicates the panoptic schema outlined by Foucault and Urry's directed tourist gaze.

Introducing a collection of Bentham's writings, Miran Božovič shows, in a Lacanian reading, how Bentham's panopticon worked to create the fiction of God: emanating from the guard tower was an opaque presence, omnipotent, omnipresent, omniscient.[27] For Bentham, God could only exist as an imaginary non-entity, but the paradox was that his power would lie precisely in being an imaginary non-entity. If his existence were to be verifiable, he would either lose his power or be found to be nothing more than a fabrication of prison-design. While this imaginary God disciplined the prison's inside through the all-seeing gaze, it was the appearance of the prison itself as a sign of punishment that would work toward deterrence on the prison's outside. In Foucault's later model, panoptic sight would come to exceed the purview of the prison's inside and become paradigmatic of power and surveillance as such.

Stateville's roundhouse and the wheel-shaped ESP both drew inspiration from the panoptic model, and ESP inspired hundreds of penitentiaries around the world. These varied architectural forms worked to simulate the all-seeing gaze that could be felt by prisoners and today by tourists. While the roundhouse's architecture varied only slightly from the panopticon formula, ESP's model employs a guard tower at the center of radiating spoke-like roofs with skylights installed by Quaker reformers so that prisoners could indeed feel God was looking down on them. This is a different formulation of God from Bentham's, one in which any God-like qualities the guard in the watch tower might seem to possess would be only derivative from and deferred to a God above.

As a counterpoint to Bentham's raceless theological penal formation, it is useful to turn to Kalpana Seshadri-Crooks's Lacanian discussion of Whiteness as transcendental (though historicizable) signifier.[28] According to Seshadri-Crooks, while subjectivity has only an absent center, the circuit of desire circling around Being is organized by a political and symbolic order that posits Whiteness as if it provided access to Being. Because Whiteness appears as a lack of a lack – seemingly filling in where there ought to be and can only be lack – racial vision invests the body as a site of racial difference, in order to provide an object to quell the anxiety caused by the appearance of Whiteness as Being where Being ought not to appear. This argument can explain how in prisons a symbolic ordering of racial difference reproduces the penal law that makes the racialized prisoner into something less than human.

Prison architectures that render a visual regime that appears to sanctify the reigning penal order by nothing less than the gaze of God can be understood as reconstituting Whiteness as Being, so long as the crucial binary between prison's exterior and interior is maintained. Yet, when tourists enter the prison, the architectural structuring meant to mimic the gaze of the Other directs these subjects toward the reality of incompletion, of lack. That is, the subject is incomplete, severed, and split by the very power that founds law and subjectivity. When one tries to pair this lack with the common sense of race, the ghost as object of sublimation and disavowal offers itself up. The ghost, then, comes to signify an object severed from the body politic, and between soul and body, under the scrutiny of the gaze. Two kinds of ghosts offer themselves up here. On the one hand, the ghost as supernatural apparition, sensed as a disembodied soul, unhinged from the body.

On the other hand, a horrifying body, played by an actor, gesturing at the monstrousness of prisoners reduced to irredeemable corporeality. Both are cast out of the civil order. The first functions as a figure unable to transcend law; it remains sequestered in prison despite its release from bodily encasement. By thus imagining ghosts as the proper non-entity residents of prison, the prison's potential to house humans is disavowed. The second functions as a body onto which ghoulish bodily difference is projected and coded as non-white, allowing potential access to Whiteness and citizenship for those fortunate enough to feel they have a chance of falling on the "right" side of the penal/racial/national divide.

At Eastern State, nearly one hundred actors embody haunting. The bodily difference that codes race in the performance is accomplished through signifiers of monstrosity, such as fake blood or mangled flesh. This can be said to signify the bodily, racialized difference of all prisoners as such. But there is excess within this difference. As prison statistics will testify, some prisoners are in fact white, even if their access to Whiteness has been called into question. With make-up and costumes cast aside, nearly all the Eastern State actors read as white; a few, however, read as black, and as part of their "ghostly" character and costume their faces are painted white. Some of the white actors also put white powder on their face, but none is as dramatically matted with white paint as the black actors, who still have some skin exposed around the edges of their faces and necks. Could one reason for this be that if the black actors were not to don whiteface, the exposure of who is actually in prison would point to the cruel mandate of the baseless moral law of Whiteness and its profiling legal attachments?

Facing what underlies the prison system might therefore cause different feelings than those the entertaining tours at ESP seek to elicit. That is, into the explicitly dramatized haunting, the disavowed foundation of citizen life seeps back in: what comes to haunt tourists is a vague awareness of the construction of their own subjectivities and the scripted death upon which citizenship rests. Inasmuch as current U.S. penal law constitutes prisoners as dead to law and civic life, and inasmuch as prisoners "are usually, and definitively in the United States, considered in law and in social practice an inferior race in and of themselves"[29] or as metonymically linked to blackness,[30] it appears that the prison's inside–outside binary, and that binary's tracking onto bodies, is crucial to the maintenance of what Seshadri-Crooks describes as the symbolic order of race.

Stage effects at work in contemporary haunted prison tours thus complicate a Benthamite logic that naturalizes the work of power and makes the gaze of a dominant symbolic order seem transcendent and unshakeable. While one could argue that these tourisms might work to unravel the reified images of the reigning prison order by drawing into relief the sustaining fictions as precisely fictions – stage effects that can be shown up and made amusing – the Benthamite model works to absorb the recognition of fictitiousness back into the workings of power. Because the omnipotence of power *might not* be real, it is also not confirmable that it is *not* real. This is what causes the anxieties attendant to haunted prison tourism and routes considerations of subverting that power back into the circuit of pleasure that prevents large-scale resistant confrontation with the totality of the prison order.

To conclude this essay, I propose to examine a brief passage from the writings of a political prisoner who has written extensively on questions of the spirit, the soul, religion, and prison democracy. I do this not to make a voice heard, but to locate the operation of state violence on a prisoner, and to gesture at the itinerary of a possible subjectivity for a person scripted for literal and figural death. Many of the political debates about Mumia Abu-Jamal's imprisonment are linked to local politics of law and order in Philadelphia, the site of ESP. The frequent portrayal of Abu-Jamal as a monster and the refusal by many to allow or struggle for Abu-Jamal's release from prison must be thought in relation to the dominant cultural formations to which such reaction is tied. As I suggested earlier, if the articulated focus of the prison has shifted from rehabilitation to incapacitation, the politics of incapacitation are anchored in a figuring of the black soul that posits its importance after life. Yet, while haunted tourisms imagine playing in the space of hell and death-in-life, in Abu-Jamal's text we find a description of the ongoing historical project to extract a soul from a black body abandoned to a life sentence. In "Spirit War," an aptly titled essay that discusses the Christian clergy who push prisoner conversion and repentant salvation, Abu-Jamal writes:

Though they profess to care deeply about where the objects of their missionary zeal will land after death, few spare a thought for how they may spend the rest of their earthly lives. While their piety is concentrated on a Hereafter, it forgets the Here. Their writers, it seems, are so intoxicated with the thought of heaven, they are content to close an eye to the simmering hell they have helped create on earth.

Often, a tract's content makes it almost impossible for the reader to escape a deeply felt suspicion that those who have sent it to him are fixated wholly on the state of his hereafter – that they couldn't give a damn about his living flesh and living soul.[31]

Today, tourists are comfortable with prisoners as ghostly disembodied souls or as actors metaphorically representing prisoners. Indeed, tourist adventures of haunted prisons are thought to be pleasurable in their sheer horror, offering an opportunity, for some, to revel anxiously in their distanced proximity from Abu-Jamal's shimmering hell on earth. As hundreds of thousands of people (myself at times included) flock to haunted prison tours each year to engage the image of the soul produced by penal power, Abu-Jamal's text writes the possibility of another soul, not reducible to the psychobiographical matrix: the notion of a living soul, not separate from living flesh but still held in captivity, while archiving, from the place of prescribed death, a potentially legible subjectivity and the potential of another social matrix.

NOTES

1   "Statesville inmate attacks officer," *Chicago Tribune*, September 10, 2003, 6, RedEye Edition.
2   Kathaleen Roberts, "Statesville's haunted prison beckons you to Hell," *Courier-News*, October 9, 2003, D1.
3   http://www.statesville.org/.
4   For more on the notion of the "prison industrial complex," see Angela Davis, *Are Prisons Obsolete?* (New York: Seven Stories Press, 2003), 84–104.
5   The Winchester Mystery House – famed for the story of Sarah Winchester, who thought herself haunted by the ghosts of Native Americans killed by the Winchester rifle and, on the advice of a medium, continued adding to her house to ward off or accommodate spirits – began in the late 1920s to hold tours that were largely hyped through suggestions that the house was built by ghosts. An earlier history of a haunting tourism of sorts can be located in the travel that people involved in the spiritualist movement undertook in the nineteenth and early twentieth century.
6   See, for example, Lynn Stevenson (dir.), *Ghosts of California*, DVD (Los Angeles, CA: Delta Entertainment Corporation, 2003); and Robert J. Wlodarski, Anne N. Wlodarski, and Michael J. Kouri, *Haunted Alcatraz: A History of La Isla de los Alcatraces and Guide to Paranormal Activity* (West Hills, CA: Ghost Publishing, 1998).
7   Caleb Smith, "Detention without Subjects: Prisons and the Poetics of Living Death," *Texas Studies in Literature and Language* 50, no. 3 (Fall 2008): 248.
8   Laura Foreman, ed., *Discovery Travel Adventure Haunted Holidays* (Singapore: Discovery Commications, 1999), 18.
9   Michel Foucault, *Discipline and Punish: The Birth of the Prison*, trans. Alan Sheridan (New York: Vintage Books, 1979).
10 John Urry, *The Tourist Gaze: Leisure and Travel in Contemporary Societies* (Thousand Oaks, CA: Sage Publications, 1990); Michel Foucault, *The Birth of the Clinic: An Archaeology of Medical Perception*, trans. A. M. Sheridan Smith (New York: Vintage Books, 1975).
11 John F. Sears, *Sacred Places: American Tourist Attractions in the Nineteenth Century* (Amherst: University of Massachusetts Press, 1998).
12 Semiotechnique has been a way of arranging signs of punishment. Foucault argued in *Discipline and Punish* that the shift to surveillance and discipline indicated a move away from semiotechnique as a privileged technology of penal power. To Bentham, semiotechnique, staging, and performance were important ways to impact an impression of prison that would deter offenses.
13 Maura J. Casey, "In the Big House ... Just Visiting," *New York Times*, May 11, 2007.
14 The medical gaze that Foucault describes in *Birth of the Clinic* is one in which the discursive and the visual achieve a certain unity. Aiming for the soul, the disciplinary gaze of *Discipline and Punish* differs from the medical gaze, which always narrated disease as the yet-to-be revealed to vision's light, in that it could only ever narrate an ephemeral interiority's trace on the body. In a follow-up article to *The Tourist Gaze*, Urry outlines how he departs from Foucault by positing "ways of being a tourist that do challenge and disturb dominant constructions." John Urry, "The Tourist Gaze 'Rivisited'," *American Behavioral Scientist* 36, no. 2 (1992): 178.
15 This may be the rationale, but as Ruth Wilson Gilmore indicates, incapacitation is part of the broader geographic solution that prisons present to capitalism's crisis of surplus

at a particular moment in globalization. Ruth Wilson Gilmore, *Golden Gulag: Prisons, Surplus, Crisis, and Opposition in Globalizing California* (Berkeley: University of California Press, 2007).

16   See Edgardo Rotman, "The Failure of Reform: United States, 1865–1965," in *The Oxford History of the Prison: The Practice of Punishment in Western Society*, ed. Norval Morris and David J. Rothman (New York: Oxford University Press, 1995), 111–129.

17   James Bernauer, "Confessions of the Soul: Foucault and Theological Culture," *Philosophy and Social Criticism* 31, no. 5–6 (2005): 557–572.

18   In the early nineteenth century, women prisoners (most of whom were white) made up only a small part of the U.S. prison population – approximately 4 to 19 percent, according to Lucia Zedner, "Wayward Sisters: The Prison for Women," in *The Oxford History of the Prison: The Practice of Punishment in Western Society*, ed. Norval Morris and David J. Rothman (New York: Oxford University Press, 1995), 329–361. Today, the majority of women prisoners in the U.S. are women of color, who, according to INCITE! Women of Color Against Violence, represent the fastest growing prison population in the country.

19   Ruth Wilson Gilmore, in conversation with Trevor Paglen, "From Military Industrial Complex to Prison Industrial Complex," Recording Carceral Landscapes, http://www.paglen.com/carceral/interview_ruth_gilmore.htm.

20   Colin Dayan, *The Story of Cruel and Unusual*, Cambridge, MA: MIT Press, 2007.

21   Dylan Rodríguez, "Forced Passages," in *Warfare in the American Homeland: Policing and Prison in a Penal Democracy*, ed. Joy James (Durham, NC: Duke University Press, 2007), 35–57.

22   http://www.wvpentours.com/.

23   Angela Davis writes: "The myth of the Black rapist renders people oblivious to the realities of rape and to the fact, for example, that over 90 percent of all rapes are intraracial rather than interracial." Angela Davis, *Women, Culture, Politics* (New York: Vintage Books, 1990), 43.

24   Jasbir Puar and Amit Rai, "Monster, Terrorist, Fag: The War on Terrorism and the Production of Docile Patriots," *Social Text* 20, no. 3 (Fall 2002).

25   Mimi Nguyen, untitled article, *Punk Planet* 42 (March/April 2001), http://www.worsethanqueer.com/slander/pp42.html.

26   Charles Dickens, *American Notes for General Circulation* (Kessinger Publishing, 2004): 91.

27   Miran Božovič, "Introduction," in *The Panopticon Writings*, by Jeremy Bentham (New York: Verso, 1995), 1–27. For another, earlier Lacanian analysis of Bentham's panopticon, see Jacques-Alain Miller, "Jeremy Bentham's Panoptic Device," *October* 41 (Summer 1987): 3–29.

28   Kalpana Seshadri-Crooks, *Desiring Whiteness: A Lacanian Analysis of Race* (New York: Routledge, 2000).

29   Avery Gordon, "Methodologies of Imprisonment," *PMLA* 123, no. 3 (May 2008): 651–657.

30   Angela Davis, *Abolition Democracy: Beyond Empire, Prisons, and Torture* (New York: Seven Stories Press, 2005).

31   Mumia Abu-Jamal, *Death Blossoms: Reflections from a Prisoner of Conscience* (Farmington, PA: Plough Publishing House, 1997), 41.

Part 3

Chasing Ghosts
In(to) the Twenty-first Century

Chapter 11

The Liveness of Ghosts: Haunting and Reality TV

Karen Williams

Reason would suggest that the ghosts of the supernatural are not a logical subject for reality TV. Reality TV's subjects have largely centered around the "real": documenting "real" people caught in common and uncommon situations, and depicting "real life" through moments both everyday and exceptional. In literature, any hint of the supernatural would immediately place a work outside the parameters of realism. But, in television, the supernatural was a part of reality TV from its earliest formulations, having been a recurring segment on the true-crime magazine show *Unsolved Mysteries* (NBC, 1987–1997; CBS, 1997–1999; Lifetime, 2001–2002; Spike, 2008–present). The supernatural itself, though, has long been a documentable subject for many believers armed with a variety of media and recording devices, a practice which began with spirit photography in the mid-1800s.[1] In the case of photography, the resulting "evidence" was often less convincing than intended – more likely poking holes in photography's claims to the real than serving as proof of a "real" not otherwise visible to the naked eye. While reality TV suggests similar tendencies to those of spirit photography, as many paranormal reality shows also claim to be documenting ghosts, the supernatural of reality TV participates in another genealogy as well: the ghost show or phantasmagoria, public performances dating back to the eighteenth century in which proto-cinematic devices such as the magic lantern were used to create spectral spectacles under the guise of demonstrating new technologies in optical science. In such performances, ghosts were rendered as a deceptively real visual entertainment, but also as an illusion of lenses and light intended to fool the senses.[2] While the visual marvels achieved were always declared an illusion, the fear they provoked was meant to be quite real. The paranormal reality show is in some respects a reality ghost show – relying on optical illusion and legerdemain, which make the eye see what it knows cannot be so. As spirit photograph or ghost show, the paranormal reality show harbors two intentions: one of earnest authenticating and the other of spectacle and effect.

Perhaps, then, it is in the troubling of reality claims that the ghost and reality TV find their greatest similarities – each being at once a medium for the revelation of an unseen real and a sensational form of entertainment. Each mediating form "blurs boundaries" – not only in terms of factual and fictional, real and unreal, subjective and objective, but also in terms of what is private and what is public, what is personal and intimate, and what is for general display and common spectacle. Indeed, ghosts themselves can range from the most public to the most private of entities, manifesting the horrors of national histories and the grumpiness of dead grandfathers. Ghosts make public spectacles of unspeakable historical trauma and unspoken family disputes. The ghost itself, though, often remains unsubstantiated, its presence charted through acts of haunting registered only as a series of phenomenological experiences – raps heard, cold spots felt, shadows glimpsed. Reality television has also relied on subjective representation, using first-person testimonials, video diaries, and hand-held cameras. Reality TV has been used to unveil and capture a range of intimate relations and personal moments, granting access to homes by sensationalizing the domestic lives within. As such, reality television has been witness to the increasingly indistinct boundary between the private and the public, as its documenting authority mediates the intimate for public display.

Reality TV, though, traffics in immediacy and contemporaneity, which would suggest that the form's abiding present-tense-ness would not be the temporality needed to represent the ghosts of the past. Mary Ann Doane has noted that television's tense and temporality are different from those of film and photography, and, in fact, television relies on this construction of time to create its predominant form of realism.[3] Film and photography are media that uncannily represent a now absent presence, signifying what Roland Barthes called the *"That-has-been,"* "which ensures the reality and the 'pastness' of the object."[4] In this way, such media, according to Doane, are "always haunted by death and historicity" (222). Television's tense, on the other hand, "would seem to be that of an insistent 'present-ness' – a *'This-is-going-on'* … a celebration of the instantaneous." "Death and referentiality" still find their way into television: rather than the dead of the past, though, television tends to represent "the potential trauma and explosiveness of the present," as epitomized by its live broadcasts of crisis and catastrophe (222). Televisual reality is generated by creating a feeling of simultaneous and continuous time – liveness – not through live broadcast, but through strategies of form and discourse such as loosely edited raw footage or direct address to the viewer. This liveness gives "the impression of a unity of 'real time'" and allows television to transform "record into actuality or immediacy," absorbing temporal difference into its flow of segmented texts (228, 227). Reality TV embodies the insistent present-ness of televisual realism, celebrating the instantaneous, the momentary, the transient. The temporality constructed in reality TV gives the impression of immediate "real time," of a simultaneous present tense to our own and the inevitable unfolding of natural time. Reality TV relies on what Jane Feuer calls the "ideology of liveness" to maintain its seeming coherence, the false unity of the hours of fragmented footage contained in each episode.[5] The past for reality TV is at most the segment before the last commercial break. The ghost, then, in its mediation of pastness, would confound the logic of reality television's liveness, and disrupt the de-historicizing effects of television's flow.

And yet, reality TV does articulate haunting, and at present the paranormal reality show is a reliable standard for many cable networks, including the Travel Channel, Discovery Kids, SciFi Channel, and A&E, each tailoring the subject matter to their own branded network identity. While reality TV might not supply its ghosts with the temporal structure of pastness, the ghost has still found a home somewhere in its machine. The medium of television and the modes and uses of documentary appropriated by reality TV seem to ideally suit the subject of haunting. Like a haunting, television is a domestic form which transmits images and sounds from the "ether" into the home, and like a spiritual medium, it collapses everything into the temporality of its present tense flow and maintains a constant direct address to the home's inhabitants. Like a ghost show, reality TV has always drawn on the more affective and sensationalist uses of documentary techniques rather than their referential and recording capacities, borrowing the "reality effect" of documentary to render the melodramas of marriage and family. In fact, reality TV demonstrates how documentary's recording strategies and formal structures can easily be put to the purpose of representing the very unreal subject of ghosts. The trope of haunting exploits the reflexive questioning of authenticity already found in reality TV and its reception, as paranormal reality shows rely on the undecidability of their represented phenomena. And, reality TV's emotional spectacle of subjects engaged in intense personal dramas is readily restaged as the paranormal reality show's display of terrified subjects confronting their ghosts. Haunting, though, also has metaphoric potential, which recent paranormal reality shows are beginning to tap. In such shows the ghost has come to figure private pathologies and traumas, and reality TV's camera is then endowed with the power of both revelation and recovery as it teaches "real" people how to live with their very "real" ghosts.

After the success of *Big Brother* (CBS) and *Survivor* (CBS) in 2000, reality TV went through a transformation as its budgets increased and it moved onto the major networks. As Su Holmes and Deborah Jermyn note, while initial definitions of reality TV "emphasised the importance of a focus on 'real life' and 'real people' as the crucial criteria" (found, for example, in 1980s law-enforcement shows like *Cops* (Fox, 1989–present), *America's Most Wanted* (Fox, 1988–present), and *Unsolved Mysteries*), "the more recent proliferation of Reality TV has witnessed a move away from an attempt to 'capture' 'a life lived' to the televised arenas of formatted environments in which the more traditional observational rhetoric of documentary jostles for space with the discourses of display and performance."[6] Paranormal reality TV went through a similar transformation, from *Unsolved Mysteries*' re-enacted real-life stories of the "unexplained" to elaborately staged, performed encounters with haunted places. During the period of reality TV's transformation, though, paranormal reality shows were equally influenced by a popular motion picture: *The Blair Witch Project* (Myrick and Sánchez, 1999), a mockumentary horror film which presented itself as recovered footage of student filmmakers who disappeared while making a documentary on the supernatural. After the success of *Blair Witch,* itself influenced by MTV's *The Real World* (1992–present), a new form of paranormal reality television emerged with shows like *MTV's Fear* (2000–2002), *Scariest Places on Earth* (Fox Family Channel and ABC Family, 2000–2006), *Ghost Trackers* (YTV, Canada, and HBO Family, 2005–2008), and most recently *Paranormal State* (A&E, 2007–present), which documented teens or young adults encountering and investigating haunted places. As was the case with *Blair Witch*, these shows suggested a youth culture practice called "legend trips," in which teens, typically boys, go to places with grisly pasts to "defy superstition" and test their own capacity for fear, "all in an effort to invoke – and then successfully escape – the wrath of the ghost."[7] *MTV's Fear* (*Fear*) most closely followed this model, and the horror genre, by having the pleasure of its show be almost entirely based on watching teens in various states of terror. As the paranormal youth show has developed alongside reality TV more generally, however, this focus on spectacles of teen fear has shifted to a far more narrative use of the supernatural to depict a kind of paranormal citizenship for young adults, as found in *Paranormal State*.

While *Fear* often required its young participants to engage in mediumistic activities and to use specialized equipment to contact and document possible ghosts, the show always did so in the context of a dare, making it more a legend trip than an investigation of paranormal phenomena. In fact, both *Scariest Places on Earth* (*Scariest*) and *Ghost Trackers* (*GT*) continued to use *Fear*'s dare format. In *Fear*, six *Real-World* style young people endured two nights alone in abandoned "haunted" spaces (prisons, mental institutions, plantations), completing increasingly frightening dares given to them through a website. Participants could drop out at any time, but whoever successfully completed their dares and lasted the two nights received five thousand dollars. *Scariest* continued the dare format, but instead dared young people and their families to spend the night alone in, again, abandoned and "haunted" places. Finally, *GT* placed the dare into a competitive format, having teens compete to become "Ultimate Ghost Tracker"; in each episode, two competitors investigated a purportedly haunted place alone and were then judged on their performance by fellow competitors. Therefore, unlike more recent paranormal reality shows, such as *Ghost Hunters* (SciFi Channel, 2004–present) and *Ghost Adventures* (Travel Channel, 2008–present), the shows which involve teens and young adults are not as focused on creating indexical proof of paranormal phenomena by using the reality camera and more specialized recording devices to capture evidence of ghosts. Rather, the youth paranormal shows focus on creating a far more figurative link between the represented – quick reacting hand-held camera movements, frightened young faces looking offscreen – and the unrepresented – ghosts. Each of these shows documents the young people's experience, both phenomenological and mental, of haunted spaces, more so than they do any actual paranormal phenomena.

Beginning with *Fear*, and continuing with *Scariest* and *GT*, these shows follow *Blair Witch*'s production technique of having the participants be alone and therefore film themselves. To increase visual variety, though, two documentary camera techniques were added to the self-filming hand-held cameras which captured the participants' points of view: surveillance cameras to capture wide shots of the setting and clam-shell cameras directed at the participants' faces to capture, in close-up, their reactions. These three camera techniques essentially represent the experience of the investigators rather than the paranormal: the apprehensive and agitated framing of the POV camera, the anxious and hesitant movements within creepy and cavernous spaces, and the wide-angle close-ups of hyper-vigilant looks offscreen and terrified responses to perceived sounds and movement. In the shows, the investigators are also given devices to aid in their investigation: EMF detectors (to gauge the electromagnetic energies of ghosts), directional thermometers (to track temperature changes caused by ghosts), and even dowsing rods (to indicate the presence of ghosts). More determining than any of these devices, though, is each participant's own visceral and sensory experience, as their bodies and their reacting first-person cameras become the main instruments by which unseen phenomena are registered. Reacting bodies and performance, then, become central to these experiential ghost shows. For example, in *GT*, the teens are given heart-rate monitors which measure their fear through heart rates of up to 150 beats per minute; also, the teens are judged based on how well they communicate their experience through radio contact: host Joe MacLeod instructs one contestant in "The Ghosts of the Performing Arts Center," "Notice how you are feeling as you are moving around the place." To return to Holmes and Jermyn's point about recent reality TV, these performative experiential shows are examples of "the televised arenas of formatted environments in which the more traditional observational rhetoric of documentary jostles for space with the discourses of display and performance" (5).

While the spectacles of orchestrated youthful terror continue in *Scare Tactics* (SciFi Channel, 2003–2004, 2008–present) and most recently *13: Fear Is Real* (CW, 2009), A&E's *Paranormal State* (*PS*) returns the reality ghost show to the public display of the intimate dramas of "real life" and "real people" found in earlier reality TV. In this program, the young participants of the previous shows have been replaced by a recurring group of college students (the Paranormal Research Society at Penn State, known as PRS) led by Ryan Buell, who investigate cases of the paranormal. Rather than haunted places, this group ("students, seekers, warriors," as they call themselves) investigates haunted people. *PS* does include a segment similar to the legend trip of earlier shows, "dead time" in which the young people sit alone in the most "active" spaces of the client's home asking to be contacted by its ghosts. *PS*, though, returns to the third-person observational cameras of law-enforcement shows like *Cops*, and the focus of the show is the group's intervention in the lives of their haunted clients. In this way *PS* participates more in a genealogy that goes back to the interventionist crime shows of the 1980s rather than to the horror mockumentary roots of *Blair Witch*. The trajectory from *Fear* to *PS* suggests a movement from a mockumentary-like play with the affective devices of documentary to a more earnest use of documentary form to both record authenticating paranormal evidence and depict situations of haunted subjectivity.

In this way the realities being claimed by these shows suggest the different ways that they are using their ghosts – as objects of their young investigators' fear or as pathologies that must be cured. While the earlier shows declare that their ghost-tracking youth's fear is "real," *PS* claims that the fear of their clients is "real," regardless of its actual source. Holmes and Jermyn further break down reality TV's claim to the real into discursive, visual, and technological claims (5). The discursive claims of the paranormal reality shows are typically delivered in first-person, highly subjective testimonials which report on seeing, hearing, and feeling "things." The shows pose questions without answers and possibilities without proof, as *Scariest*'s host Linda Blair asks at the conclusion of "The Cursed Monastery Dare," "So what is it that makes a place scary? Is it knowing that terrible things have gone on in that place? Is it believing that evidence of evil spirit activity has been found? Is it the difficulty of coming face to face with what you fear most?" The visual claims of these shows are equally ambivalent, as their images cannot serve as a direct window on real events, but instead must represent evidence just missed by a panning camera or just offscreen at the other end of a terrified gaze. Finally, the technological claims of these shows are complicated by the reflexive use of paranormal recording techniques within the shows, which claim to document the unseen and the unheard: heat-sensitive cameras, infrared and night-vision photography, parabolic microphones and EVPs (electronic voice phenomenon, in which recorders capture the inaudible sounds made by spirits). Within the shows, these represented forms of recording claim to capture that which cannot be seen by the naked eye – and by extension the naked documentary camera. Recording equipment comes to be seen as a medium both technical and spiritual, creating a logic by which the documentary apparatus, the paranormal research equipment, and the participants' bodies make competing reality claims. Ultimately, documentary technique records bodily responses to otherwise undocumentable phenomena. What these shows suggest, in their lack of documentable paranormal reality, is that the power of reality TV lies as much in its depiction of the *experience* of reality as it does in the depiction of reality itself. Both the experiential and the interventionist paranormal reality shows demonstrate two contradictory aspects of the documenting claims of both reality TV and paranormal research – the desire for proof of the "real," and the demonstration of the alarming real-ness of affective suggestion in the absence of such proof.

There is a paradox, then, at the heart of the paranormal reality show. The reality it claims to depict is at least equivocal if not fundamentally undocumentable. Invariably, the "unexplained" can only be documented as such if it remains as such – unexplained. While using the techniques and conventions of documentary, a form defined by the claim to the truth of its depicted reality, the paranormal reality shows follow a different epistemological criterion: they represent doubt and equivocality as their reality. In order for their subject to remain within the parameters of the paranormal – meaning without real-world explanation – or even hypothetically supernatural, they must use documentary to produce proof which paradoxically demonstrates that a phenomenon remains unexplained. The shows use documentary practice as a phenomenological apparatus which can structure the perceiving subject necessary to the reality ghost show – in their capacity to document, they may not render the ghost, but they do render the subjective experience of haunted spaces and haunted people. They rely on *not* being able to unambiguously identify something as either fact or fiction; the audience's equivocal position (both perceptual and cognitive) is intentionally constructed. Rather than "claiming the real," these shows are claiming the *possibly* real, and they do so by generating and recording specific affective responses in their subjects.

Such issues have been a central binary of documentary criticism for decades, beginning with John Grierson's 1933 formulation of documentary as "the creative interpretation of actuality."[8] In both the theory and practice of documentary a tension exists between "the capturing of some aspect of the real world and the people who inhabit it" and "the inevitable use of aesthetic and representational devices to achieve that aim."[9] The traditional debate about the two sides of documentary's "representing reality" – the actuality being depicted and the style and forms of representation – is not entirely applicable in the case of factual programming about ghosts. In paranormal reality shows, the "reality" being represented is under question long before the camera intervenes. And, in fact, it is only *in* "representing" that the "reality" of these shows can come into being at all; like the ghost, the reality of the paranormal show requires a medium and "creative interpretation" to be known. As John Corner has pointed out, traditionally the term "documentary" indicated that a text "was to be regarded primarily as a 'document,' a text whose interest lay in its referentiality, in what it indicated about the world through its sounds and images."[10] He goes on to argue, though, that "the core mode of documentation from the 1930s through to today is the employment of the *recorded images and sounds of actuality* to provide the viewer with a distinctive kind of 'seeing' and 'hearing' experience, a distinctive means of knowledge. Documentary was grounded in an appeal to *sensory evidence*" (208, emphasis in original). This is exactly the basis of proof presented in these paranormal reality shows. Recently, documentary scholars have tried to accommodate the "creative interpretation" side of documentary more effectively, and to do so they have focused on the performative aspects of the mode.

The experiential shows, and their representation of embodied perception, draw on these more performative and subjective forms of documentary. In documentary theory and criticism the term "performative" has taken on different meanings: that the film itself is performative, foregrounding its own techniques and devices;[11] that the filmmaker reflexively poses their documentary as the filmed record of their enacted encounter with their subjects;[12] or that the subjects acknowledge the documentary camera and self-consciously perform themselves. Bill Nichols introduced the category of the "performative mode" to his schema of documentary modes (the other four modes being expository, observational, interactive, and reflexive)[13] to accommodate documentaries which are as much about their "texture and tone" as about the historical reality they depict.[14] Nichols finds that these documentaries may be reflexive in their foregrounding of style and technique, but they also try "to represent the experiential" in that they "embody, through their form, an existential situatedness."[15] While Nichols is actually discussing avant-garde documentaries which attempt to render marginal identities and experience, his definition fits the experiential paranormal reality show remarkably well. Stella Bruzzi has critiqued Nichols's category, arguing that all documentary could be seen as performative: the documentary form records *and enacts* "a perceptual negotiation between the real event and its representation" (9). When filmmakers self-consciously foreground aspects of this negotiation, Bruzzi argues, they are acknowledging that any attempt to represent reality inevitably includes "falsification and subjectification" (155). Finally, in terms of the performative and the subject of documentary, Corner asserts that documentary's conceit of "unseen observation" is an "enabling fiction," a performed unawareness on the part of the subject (215). In addition, with the shift from film to digital and the introduction of cheaper and simpler cameras, first-person self-documentation has radically increased in the last two decades. Marsha and Devin Orgeron argue that in the era of cell-phone cameras and YouTube, a "pandocumentary culture" has emerged in which "the recorded event has become a dominant form of communication."[16] Due to the "creative interpretation" necessary in representing its real, the paranormal reality show collapses all these levels of performance; paranormal reality TV's real *is* performance – the variety of expressive camera techniques, a reflexivity about documentation in its staged use of ghost-tracking equipment, and the enacted fear of its subjects.

If the experiential shows are merely bodies and performance, then what is the ghost that is being enacted? The performative experiential shows present the ghost as TV's "unrepresentable," the material past. These shows propose that liveness does not efface the dead; rather, it represses them. They use reality TV's documentary techniques to produce affect, and ground this affect in the possible return of liveness' repressed. The participants' fear, then, becomes evidence of the uncanny traces of history in the present, encouraging an affective historical consciousness. The shows feed their participants a steady stream of horror stories – historical anecdotes of cruelty, exploitation, and death – before sending them to investigate if the places which housed these ghastly events are haunted. For the participants a fear of ghosts is equated with a fear of the angry revenants of history: one young *Fear* investigator observes in "Hacienda Tabi," "You don't go to a place where people were raped, pillaged, killed, and not have some of that history still remain there. There's definitely something out there." In *Fear* and *Scariest* this perception of the past is fostered by video documentaries which the participants and viewer watch together. The videos reflexively present the past through a documentary of the place, combining the "expert" knowledges of historians, local residents, and clairvoyants, mixing official and unofficial histories, and evidentiary and affective histories. As the shows progress, the footage of the investigation is intercut with clips from the video, functioning as flashbacks but also foregrounding how the videos were ultimately not about what should be known about the past, but what should be *felt* about the past. *GT* represents history in a similar manner: as the young trackers report sensations and perceptions, the host validates these feelings by reporting either historical information or paranormal encounters which correspond to the trackers' own. Much like the shows' filming techniques, their discursive histories are based in affect. The evidentiary image and historical information needed to ground claims of the real are dematerialized in these shows, as subjective experiences of fear stand as documents for the otherwise "unrepresentable" of history.

What these shows seem to be formulating is an affective historical subjectivity which can occupy even the most present-tense of temporalities. Such a formulation is related to Nichols's reading of the progressive possibilities of the performative documentary. He finds in the performative documentary suggestive and poetic forms of expression that are "less directed at proving what 'really happened' than in reframing what has been remembered" and promoting within the viewer a "social subjectivity" that "remains unattached to a logical explanation."[17] For Nichols, this social subjectivity is "a category of collective consciousness" with the potential to break down self/other binaries, evoking instead "a discourse of visceral, existential affinity." He warns, though, that social subjectivity can easily lapse into "the solipsistic terms of a privatized consciousness."[18] Such a lapse, in fact, suggests Nichols's trenchant critique of reality TV, a critique which undoubtedly applies to the experiential ghost show and its use of affect. For Nichols, the "very intensity of feeling, emotion, sensation, and involvement that reality TV produces is ... discharged harmlessly" in liveness' flow, as the "historical referent" and the "magnitudes that exceed the text" actually become absorbed into television's intentionally dematerializing circuit of "endless flux."[19] The affective devices of these shows actually produce the unrepresentable, making their haunted spaces and their histories more spectral, and televisual, than real. Also, with their game show structures and their "formatted environments," they turn real places into televisual spaces, the stories of which end when the dares are completed.

Paranormal State, while it does retain some of the performative techniques of the experiential shows, has in fact returned to more traditional modes of documentary to articulate its version of the ghosts of reality TV: the expository voice-over defining the experiences, the interactive interview which attempts to lay bare "the truth," and an observational camera which documents from an objective position. The head of PRS, Ryan Buell, is given a voice-over "director's log" in which he classifies and qualifies the phenomena he and the viewer encounter. The paranormal is also contained through a series of investigative interviews: beginning with the tour of the haunted home and an interview with the haunted family; continuing with a series of interviews with expert informants, such as a medium or town historian; and concluding with a "re-interview" of the haunted family, armed with new information culled through "research," either validating their unexplained experiences or demanding further revelation in order to fully free them from their ghosts. The narrative structure of the show in fact follows that of a police procedural drama, in which the enigma of a crime is posed and then resolved through a segmented investigation. *PS* follows this narrative structure quite closely, as each episode contains a repeated sequence of titled investigative steps: "Case Briefing," "House Tour," "Interview with Clients," "Psychic/Medium Arrives," "Historical Research," "Dead Time," "Evidence Evaluation," and "Final Meeting with Family." The show's adaptation of this procedural narrative structure serves as a rhetorical device which maps out cases as if they were crimes to be solved. This narrative strategy continues across the show's larger synergetic intertexts: in a DVD extra, Ryan tells his paranormal research students to "think of [themselves] as a detective or as a cop, who can solve a crime – the crime here is that there is something going on that shouldn't";[20] and an interactive game on the show's website invites users to test their skills as paranormal investigators, requiring them to click through clips of investigative steps in the proper order.[21] And, finally, the show's "third-person" observational camera returns to the transparency claims of the "fly-on-the-wall" documentary, and removes the reflexive and performative subjectivity which self-filming brought to the experiential shows. Like the experiential shows, Ryan and his team use surveillance and hand-held cameras during "dead time," but the footage which results – surveillance cameras capturing doors opening on their own, heat-sensitive cameras registering the chill of a team member's "goose bumps" – is evaluated as potential objective evidence.

PS does not use its liveness, then, to create an affective history in the present. The shaky and jerking movements of its dead-time first-person cameras capture moments of confrontation between Ryan and the ghost, rather than his moments of fear. The liveness which the show constructs is based more on the discursive space of television than on the immediacy of experience. Margaret Morse argues that television's forms of "talk" (in the news, talk shows, and commercials, for example) construct discursive positions ("I" and "us") from which the viewer is addressed (as "you") and relationships of discourse within the television text ("us" and "them"), thereby creating "not intersubjectivity, but *the impression of discourse.*"[22] For example, Ryan's voice-over log acts as a form of indirect address to the audience, and interviewee responses are for both the PRS investigator and the viewer. Morse argues that this "fiction of discourse" allows television to have "a subjective presence" in the home which addresses the viewer and "show[s] us the world as it happens" (5). Since television's realism is based on creating the impression of "real time," it does not need to construct the impression of "real space." Television's discourse, instead, constructs space through a series of communicative relations: between the television speaker and the viewer, and between interviewers and interviewees within the text. This virtual networked space becomes an ideal form for articulating haunting in *PS*, as it creates the possibility for correspondence between materially, and temporally, separate spaces. In Ryan's approach to his haunted clients, he presents the "healing of haunting" as a process which renders the ghost discursive – which makes the ghost speak in and to the present. Ryan's discursive approach also poses the healing of haunting as a kind of talking cure, containing the ghost within reality TV's therapeutic discourses of intervention and recovery.

PS has taken the performative experiential paranormal reality show and realigned it with the discursive intervention of its law-enforcement reality TV roots. As Ib Bondebjerg has argued, U.S. "true-life-story" genres have become an increasingly hybrid form, mixing fact and fiction as shows represent "crime themes and investigation of social distress in melodramatic form," shaping public issues to appeal to private fascination and packaging private trauma as public spectacle.[23] The branded supertext of the show's network, A&E, demonstrates this as well. As *PS* is aired, the network runs promos for related reality shows like *Intervention* (2005–present), in which the producers help a family stage an intervention for an addicted loved one, *The First 48* (2004–present), in which the first forty-eight hours of a murder investigation are documented step by step, and even *The Exterminators* (2009), which follows a family of pest-control experts as they go to different homes and remove the insects and animals which infest them. Even A&E's branding tagline suggests this hybridization: "A&E. Drama. Real Life." Recently, reality TV theorists have argued that this blurring of the boundaries between the private and the public within reality TV participates in the forming of "idealized" citizen-subjects. Such citizen-subjects are "ideal" in that they have adapted to the privatization of public life brought about by the increasingly neoliberal policies of a government that leaves citizens to fend for themselves more and more.[24] In reality TV, subjecting oneself to surveillance and discipline and putting one's struggles on public display has been presented as not only an active form of self-expression, but also as a means by which self-improvement and even self-revelation can be achieved.[25] Laurie Ouellette and James Hay argue that "by aligning viewers with a proliferating supply of techniques for shaping and guiding themselves and their private associations with others, reality TV has become the quintessential technology of advanced or 'neo' liberal citizenship": reality TV depicts privatized experts intervening in the lives of troubled families and people in distress to teach them the mindset and skills needed to manage and protect themselves (4). This form of neoliberal "caring for the self" is actually a way of governing at a distance, a kind of tele-governing, which Ouellette and Hay associate with Michel Foucault's "governmentality," one of the more occulted ways by which power can be exercised, as subjects come to internalize the interests of the state as their own desires (10).

In *PS*, the domestic, personal, and subjective aspects of haunting are made subject to the "neoliberal technology of everyday life" as it is enacted within the interventionist reality show. Ryan and his group present themselves as experts who perform paranormal interventions; the opening titles of each episode read: "Each year, PRS receives hundreds of reports of paranormal activity … only responding to the most severe. / This is one of those cases." Also, Ryan's opening introduction explains that his group's purpose is to "help those who are haunted." In the "case briefing" segment, Ryan not only introduces the forms of haunting in the client's home which the group will confront and try to contain, but also reviews the troubling domestic issues they will encounter. As each episode progresses, Ryan continually notes the ontological slippage of the investigated phenomena between the experience of real haunting and the experience of what he calls "real world" issues, making the ghosts of *PS* as metaphoric as they are undocumentable. For example, in "The Devil in Syracuse," a family has become vulnerable to a demon because they let their trailer-home and their life get out of control, and Ryan advises the wife, "the house – symbolically, it's saying everything's a mess in your life. [Demons] feed on that, [the] house needs to be cleaned"; in "Hell's Gate," a recovering drug addict who was severely injured in a factory accident hears voices telling him to kill his new family, and Ryan arranges for an exorcism and counseling. At the end of each episode Ryan notes that while PRS may not have definitively uncovered the true source of the haunting under investigation, they have helped the family who asked for their services. As Ryan expounds in his final director's log for "Smoke & Shadows," an episode involving a Vietnam veteran's paranormal experiences, "Whether we're dealing with post-traumatic stress or poltergeist phenomenon, the cure begins with therapy.... Like the fog of war, paranormal cases aren't always clear." The idea of the "ghost" is always blurred, as each situation PRS encounters is rife with a network of symbolic hauntings already: family disputes, violent death, suicide, molestation, domestic abuse. The ghost functions as an apparition of the past, but also as a recurring emotional and mental state which the client must, as a good neoliberal citizen, recover from in order to move forward. *PS*'s young investigators, however, also use the idea of haunting to formulate an intimate and spiritual model of their own citizenship, for being in and of the adult neoliberal world. They find domestic life and family relations haunted, whether this is based in "real world" issues or the paranormal; and they have internalized the ghost, viewing social and interpersonal relations as fraught with unknown forces that must be faced and conquered. Their blurring of distinctions between the psychological and paranormal, the scientific and spiritual, and the public and private is based on a formulation of haunting which transcends the private, allowing them to reconceptualize their affective social relations to "those who are haunted." In haunting, they find a transcendental intimacy that creates a paranormal public in place of the lost public of today's neoliberal state. In this paranormal public, fear is more real than anything else: it generates the emotional affinities needed to recreate missing social bonds and it inspires social consciousness and public service without addressing the complexities of the material world. PRS's neoliberal strategies, though, also construct a "paranormal state" that occults the true causes of "real world" problems, incorporating the social and economic issues of the material world into the imaginary of the unexplained.

In both the performative experiential and the discursive interventionist paranormal reality show the liveness of television somehow dematerializes the ghost and the past it represents. In the former, liveness drains historical spaces of their objective reality and endows them with subjective affect instead. In the latter, liveness transforms the past into personal problems and private traumas that must be mastered and overcome in the present. There is a reason no "real" ghost is represented in these reality shows. Neither the medium of television nor its forms of reality TV could ever represent its "reality": death and disconnection.

NOTES

1   See, for example, Clément Chéroux et al., *The Perfect Medium: Photography and the Occult* (New Haven: Yale University Press, 2005).

2   See Terry Castle, *The Female Thermometer: 18th-Century Culture and the Invention of the Uncanny* (Oxford: Oxford University Press, 1995) and X. Theodore Barber, "Phantasmagorical Wonders: The Magic Lantern Ghost Show in Nineteenth Century America," *Film History* 3, no. 2 (1989): 73–86.

3   Mary Ann Doane, "Information, Crisis, Catastrophe," in *Logics of Television*, ed. Patricia Mellencamp (Bloomington: Indiana University Press, 1990), 222–239.

4   Roland Barthes, *Camera Lucida: Reflections on Photography* (New York: Farrar, 1981), 77, quoted in Doane, "Information, Crisis, Catastrophe," 222.

5   Jane Feuer, "The Concept of Live Television: Ontology as Ideology," in *Regarding Television*, ed. E. Ann Kaplan (Los Angeles: AFI, 1983), 12–22.

6   Su Holmes and Deborah Jermyn, "Introduction: Understanding Reality TV," in *Understanding Reality Television*, ed. Holmes and Jermyn (London: Routledge, 2004), 4–5.

7   Lynn Schofield Clark, *From Angels to Aliens: Teenagers, the Media, and the Supernatural* (New York: Oxford University Press, 2003), 102.

8   John Grierson, "The Documentary Producer," *Cinema Quarterly* 2, no. 1 (1933), 8, quoted in Paul Ward, *Documentary: The Margins of Reality* (London: Wallflower, 2005), 10.

9   Ward, *Documentary*, 5.

10 John Corner, "Civic Visions: Forms of Documentary," in *Television: The Critical View*, ed. Horace Newcomb (New York: Oxford University Press, 2000), 208.

11 Bill Nichols, "Performing Documentary," in *Blurred Boundaries* (Bloomington: Indiana University Press, 1994), 92–106.

12 Stella Bruzzi, "The Performative Documentary: Barker, Dineen, Broomfield," in *New Documentary: A Critical Introduction* (London: Routledge, 2000), 153–180.

13 See Bill Nichols, *Representing Reality* (Bloomington: Indiana University Press, 1991).

14 Nichols, "Performing Documentary," 93.

15 Ibid., 98.

16 Marsha and Devin Orgeron, "Familial Pursuits, Editorial Acts: Documentaries after the Age of Home Video," *The Velvet Light Trap* 60 (Fall 2007): 50.

17 Nichols, "Performing Documentary," 99.

18 Ibid., 105.

19 Bill Nichols, "At the Limits of Reality (TV)," in *Blurred Boundaries* (Bloomington: Indiana University Press, 1994), 57.

20 "Behind the Scenes," *Paranormal State: The Complete Season One*, DVD, A&E Television Networks, 2007/2008.

21 http://www.aetv.com/paranormal-state/interactive-investigation.jsp.

22 Margaret Morse, "Talk, Talk, Talk," *Screen* 26, no. 2 (1985), 3, emphasis in original.

23 Ib Bondebjerg, "Public Discourse/Private Fascination: Hybridization in 'True-Life-Story' Genres," in Newcomb, *Television: The Critical View*, 384–385.

24 Laurie Ouellette and James Hay, *Better Living Through Reality TV* (Malden, MA; Blackwell Publishing, 2008).

25 Mark Andrejevic, *Reality TV: The Work of Being Watched* (Lanham, MD: Rowman & Littlefield, 2004).

Chapter 12

Ghost Hunters:
Simulated Participation in
Televisual Hauntings

Alissa Burger

The SciFi Channel original series *Ghost Hunters* (2004–present) follows The Atlantic Paranormal Society (TAPS) as they investigate haunted spaces, from private homes and businesses to local and national historical sites. Led by founders Jason Hawes and Grant Wilson, *Ghost Hunters* has grown from a small group of people interested in scientific investigation of the paranormal to an enormously popular phenomenon with a devoted fan following: at the start of the 2008 summer season, the SciFi Channel reported that a record 2.5 million viewers tuned in to see where the *Ghost Hunters'* next investigation would take them.[1] From the homes of frightened families to infamous haunts such as the Stanley Hotel, Mansfield Reformatory, and Waverly Hills Sanatorium, viewers keep watching to see what the *Ghost Hunters* will find this week and to learn the latest and most advanced trends in ghost-hunting technology from the TAPS team. However, the majority of fans do not passively watch *Ghost Hunters*, but instead actively engage with the footage from each investigation, watching for video evidence and listening for electronic voice phenomena (EVPs). This establishes a critical discourse of simulated participation surrounding the series, in which viewers actively engage with the show. However, while the viewers metaphorically "haunt" the show, always situated within the present discourse of the featured investigation, fan participation remains mostly virtual.

One of the unique hallmarks of the series and a reason viewers keep tuning in week after week is the encouraged interactivity extended to fans, which creates a simulacrum for personal experience in a number of ways. As Henry Jenkins has argued, over the past few decades popular culture fans have been developing more complex, critical, and interactive relationships with the materials before them, a trend which is influenced in part by "[n]ew tools and technologies [which] enable consumers to archive, annotate, appropriate, and recirculate media content."[2] Technology has been integral in constructing the participatory sense of *Ghost Hunters* fans as they watch and interact with the program.

First, in *Ghost Hunters,* the intersection of haunting and modern televisual technologies works to construct the ghost as a figure of futurity, drawing upon Jacques Derrida's notion of the ghost as "always a *revenant.* One cannot control its comings and goings because it *begins by coming back.*"[3] This discourse of the ghost as always returning pulls the paranormal out of the past by instead emphasizing the immediate and future nature of such hauntings and investigations. Framed within the possibility of the imminent and inevitable return, the ghost becomes a preoccupation of the present and future, rather than remaining contained within the discourse of the past, its more traditional position.

In addition, the centrality of advanced and specialized technologies in the growing field of paranormal research again points toward ghost hunting and the ghost itself as a figure of futurity amid a discourse of digital technologies, such as video and voice recorders, electromagnetic field (EMF) readers, and thermal imaging cameras. In tandem with this technological mediatization is the contemporary scientific approach to paranormal investigation, which is the trademark of *Ghost Hunters* and TAPS researchers. Of course, TAPS is not the first group to take a scientific approach in investigating the paranormal. In 1882, Henry Sidwich, an "eminent philosopher at Cambridge, founded the Society for Psychical Research with a group of friends and colleagues who wished to apply scientific principles to the investigation of unexplained phenomena."[4] Technology was a central concern of the SPR, with the group's inquiry "intersect[ing] at the vertex of the new technologies, especially photography," using cameras to record séances in the hope of capturing visual evidence of the paranormal.[5] Those interested in the paranormal also attempted to establish audio proof of ghostly presences. With the advent of wireless communication came the practice known as "DX fishing," through which the curious would listen to the ether of "silence and static" over the wireless in hopes of catching a ghostly message;[6] in 1922, with the boom of radio, "dead air" caught by a microphone within a sealed, empty booth was broadcast for the same purpose.[7] Researchers involved in this mode of inquiry throughout the twentieth century include Thomas Edison in the 1920s, artist Attila von Szalay in 1936, and documentary filmmaker Friedrich Jürgenson, who in the late 1950s reportedly captured his deceased wife's voice while recording birds in his garden.[8] The practice surrounding EVPs, as understood in contemporary discourses of paranormal research, was established by Konstantin Raudive, who "used a microphone and tape recorder to record the ambient sound in an apparently empty room," and then played the recording back to listen for ghostly voices and messages.[9] The grounding of paranormal research in scientific discourse seeks to remove discussions of ghosts from the realm of superstition and unsubstantiated ghost stories, a tradition which has often blurred the lines between personal experience, urban legend, and fictional creation. Instead, *Ghost Hunters* and the TAPS team draw upon this history of scientifically based paranormal investigation to replace campfire story spookiness with a critical approach, educated skepticism, and the high-tech equipment to both support and surpass personal experiences.

To reinforce this shift, viewers are offered the chance of simulated participation. Each individual investigation featured on *Ghost Hunters* is presented chronologically to viewers, from introductory case information through the investigation itself and concluding with "The Reveal." This experience is of course heavily mediated through the process of televisual editing and onscreen representation. However, the combination of crew cameras and hand-held video cameras carried by individual team members *simulates* participation by creating a sense that viewers are positioned alongside the TAPS team members throughout pivotal moments of the investigation, "experiencing" the suspense of the hunt and the thrill of witnessing paranormal activity. Featuring actual footage from investigations rather than the re-enactments or speculative recreations offered by similar shows, such as Discovery Channel's *A Haunting* and History Channel's *Monster Quest*, viewers feel a part of the investigation through the purported authenticity of the video and audio before them, as well as the investigators' frequent direct address to the camera itself, often in the form of one-on-one interviews with the crew or their fellow team members and, by extension, the fans. While editing is integral in allowing the key moments of each case to be showcased in the short period of time allowed by each episode, *Ghost Hunters* also features short montage sequences of team meetings, as well as evidence review and discussions, a structure which invites viewers to see themselves as part of the team and see the investigative process in its entirety, promoting active rather than passive viewing patterns among fans.

Finally, in addition to the simulated interactive participation of viewers, *Ghost Hunters* has also invited formal engagement with fans on a number of occasions. For the past three years, the TAPS team has staged a large-scale Halloween special, with live video feeds over the course of Halloween night. As part of the 2007 *Ghost Hunters Live* show from Kentucky's Waverly Hills Sanatorium, an interactive technology center was set up for fans to send messages to TAPS investigators about potential paranormal activity heard and seen onscreen, as well as on raw video running live online, inviting fans to "play at home," in a manner of speaking. In addition to the technological communication offered to fans during the 2007 Halloween investigation, the team also invited three amateur paranormal investigators along on the case, the finalists of the *Ghost Hunters* "Hunt for the Hunter" competition. Therefore, viewers were offered simulated participation on a number of levels, through watching the investigation live, having validated technological means for interactively sharing their own observations, and being asked to self-identify with other fans featured onscreen.

In exploring the way *Ghost Hunters* viewers have the paranormal experience mediated and mediatized for them in a way that encourages simulated participation, I will examine the ways in which the scientific discourse of technology, as well as the visual presentation and editing of investigation footage work to place fans in a position of interaction and involvement. I will then provide an extended consideration of the *Ghost Hunters Live* 2007 Halloween special from Waverly Hills Sanatorium in Louisville, Kentucky. Finally, I will conclude with a discussion of the ways in which *Ghost Hunters* renegotiates discourses of science, the paranormal, and fandom.

Technology, Science, and TAPS

Integral to establishing a simulated participation among *Ghost Hunters* fans is the transformation of the image of the ghost from a tale of the past to a figure of futurity. Jeffrey Andrew Weinstock has argued that "[t]he ghost is that which interrupts the presentness of the present,"[10] disrupting the surrounding world and creating a chasm between past, present, and future which must be addressed. The ghost's position as a figure of futurity is established in the program through the knowledge that the haunted spaces under investigation continue to be haunted after the cameras have stopped rolling, with the chance of ongoing activity, future investigations, and the potential for evidence of the paranormal to accrue indefinitely. Therefore, the image of the ghost must be removed from its archaic origins, brought into the present, and projected forward into the future, acknowledged as a dynamic and immediate paranormal force. As the TAPS team argues with each investigation, ghosts are not the remnants of a superstitious and undeveloped social structure, but are rather beings with the power to affect the everyday lives and change the futures of the places and people around them.

The paranormal has an immediate influence on the contemporary world and within this highly rational, skeptical, and technologically advanced context, establishing the ghost as an element of modern society requires scientific proof, which the TAPS team regularly gathers through the use of high-tech equipment and an investigative process grounded in the scientific method. TAPS founder Jason Hawes explains this approach to paranormal investigating:

> Scientific knowledge comes from systematic and objective observations, which help us make deductions we can trust. It also means we have to test those deductions through controlled experiments that can be repeated by others under the same conditions. After subjecting phenomena to recording, measurement, and experimentation, we may realize that our initial observations were in error, or we may see more evidence to support our hypothesis. But the point is to try to debunk it first.[11]

Rather than basing the claim of haunting on personal experience alone, as evidenced in long traditions of ghost stories throughout American popular culture, the TAPS team uses these rigorous scientific standards to bring the discourse surrounding the paranormal into the twenty-first century, often debunking and finding alternate explanations for reports of ghostly activity. This scientific approach has two effects on *Ghost Hunters* viewers, believers and skeptics alike: first, with all material coming under such critical scrutiny, any apparently non-dismissible evidence of the paranormal becomes that much more compelling. Second, viewers are critically and intellectually engaged with *Ghost Hunters* and the team's investigations because they are actively questioning rather than passively watching the program play out before them, creating a sense of simulated participation. While skeptics may refuse or attempt to debunk purported evidence, the struggle over paranormal proof is occurring around an agreed-upon set of scientific questions and critical discourse.

This engagement is furthered by the wealth of technological equipment used by TAPS in conducting their paranormal investigations, which again moves the team past mere collection of personal experiences to provide scientific proof of hauntings. As James Hibberd points out, *Ghost Hunters* uses "enough high-tech gadgets to fill a Radio Shack – including infrared and night-vision cameras, digital voice recorders and electromagnetic field detectors – to provide a scientific backbone while renewing a classic TV genre."[12] While the fascination with the paranormal previously addressed by sensationalist programs such as *In Search of ...* and *Ripley's Believe It Or Not* remains consistent with the aims of the TAPS team in attempting to find evidence of the unexplained, *Ghost Hunters'* approach is more rigorous and scientifically based, which creates a sense of fan participation on numerous critical levels. Through the increasingly advanced technological equipment, viewers are getting clearer and more compelling evidence of the possibly paranormal than ever before. However, this high-tech evidence is also open to interpretation and each piece of video or audio evidence presented is contested and critically debated. For example, a cold spot, defined as "[a] place that is cooler than the surrounding area ... thought by some to be an indication of a supernatural presence drawing energy from its environment in order to manifest,"[13] on its own could be evidence of paranormal activity, or it could be just a cold spot. That cold spot becomes more compelling, however, when it occurs in tandem with a significant temperature fluctuation (measurable by an ambient temperature thermometer), a change in the surrounding energy fields (which can be picked up by an electromagnetic field, or EMF, detector), or a visual anomaly, caught through video, still photography, or personal experience.

In addition, fans now have a wealth of technological tools at their disposal for independently considering the evidence as well, through their own paranormal investigations with similar equipment. As Carrie Kirby points out, paranormal research groups are springing up all over the country, which "is evidence of one thing: Ghost hunting has grown in the past two decades from a little-known hobby to a much more popular pursuit. Ghost hunters say that, judging from the number of ghost-hunting organizations with websites, there are hundreds of groups with thousands of members in the United States ... And technology is a major force behind the trend."[14] As TAPS and *Ghost Hunters* have been working to legitimize the field of paranormal research, the technology integral to these investigations has become more accessible and affordable. In fact, a 2005 *Business Week* report indicates that "[c]ompanies selling ghost-hunting gear – such as electromagnetic field detectors and infrared cameras – are booming due to the show."[15] Ghost hunting has thus become an economic activity; contemporary interest in·the paranormal, paired with the new scientific tools available to critical investigators, has resulted in the ghost as a commercially marketable entity. This trend indicates that interest in the paranormal and hands-on investigation following in the footsteps of TAPS is on the rise, moving from simulated and mediatized participation to active investigation as an outgrowth of *Ghost Hunters* fandom.

Through the TAPS team's use of video and audio technologies, as well as the Internet, fans also independently critique and evaluate evidence gathered and featured on *Ghost Hunters*. After each episode, critical viewers head to the show's discussion boards to analyze the investigation, mull over potentially paranormal proof that may have been missed, or even challenge the TAPS team's findings. One of the show's most controversial and debated segments to date occurred in the second season premiere when the team headed to New Orleans's Myrtle Plantation. The infrared cameras caught a lamp moving across a table in the plantation's supposed "slave shack" and "[t]he next day, online fans went into a frenzy. Upon close inspection, fans concluded, the lamp was being pulled by its own cord. ... And the so-called slave shack, Internet researchers said, was built recently and never housed slaves."[16] However, the scientific approach to this piece of video footage was spearheaded by TAPS themselves, who returned to the site and attempted to recreate the same situation and search for alternate possibilities, such as the lamp cord being pulled, tugged, or tangled around the leg of a chair, with no results comparable to those caught on video. While this contested evidence has not been definitively debunked, the technological savvy surrounding *Ghost Hunters*, which, in fact, is encouraged by the show itself, is working to create an informed and skeptical base of viewers who self-identify with the investigators they see onscreen and enjoy the feeling of simulated participation as they watch at home with a critical eye, debunking and debating along with the TAPS team.

Editing and Episode Structure

Adding to the simulated participation established by the critical, technological construction of the ghost as a figure of futurity, the structure of each *Ghost Hunters* episode also works to invite viewers to vicariously experience the investigation at hand. According to SciFi Channel senior vice president of original programming Mark Stern, the success of *Ghost Hunters* "can be attributed to their reality style, in which viewers watch a team seeking answers rather than a narrator presenting information."[17] In Stern's words, this format "gives you a great opportunity to deal with paranormal subjects with great credibility. It gives viewers a chance to feel like they're watching it happen, and they can judge whether to believe it or not, rather than being told what to believe."[18] The structure of the show echoes this participatory and process-oriented identification, taking viewers from introductory information about the case through "The Investigation," "The Analysis," "The Findings," and "The Reveal," with each of these stages signaled with an onscreen title and individual case details.

Balancing a familiar structure with the anticipation of moments of excitement or surprise from potentially paranormal activity, *Ghost Hunters* viewers have a concise idea of what they will see when they tune in to the series. Generally speaking, each episode begins with introductory information about the case, including a pitch or briefing, usually filmed at TAPS headquarters; in this expository scene, the investigative team and their viewers find out about the individual case, including where it is located and details about the claims of paranormal activity. Through this process, the members of the TAPS team remain firmly situated as the experts, a position they have achieved through trial and error, by pioneering new investigative techniques and championing paranormal investigation as a legitimate space of inquiry (a claim which remains contested in skeptical circles). Though the TAPS team's endeavors are firmly situated within a scientific discourse, there is no hard science of ghost hunting. TAPS members could be said to have earned their status as experts because they have set the contemporary standards for paranormal investigation and its legitimacy (especially in the way it maintains a tension with skepticism). However, as alluded to by Stern, much of the self-identification of fans with the TAPS team evidences a populist impulse, rather than a simple desire for hierarchical, authoritative answers.[19] After all, TAPS founders Hawes and Wilson are plumbers by day, who have nevertheless been able to turn what started as a fascinating hobby into an international sensation; they are literally Everymen who have made it big. The television program's position on the SciFi Channel echoes this combination of populism and expertise as well, with the channel's signature line-up of cult programming such as *Doctor Who* and *Battlestar Galactica* paired with personality-based reality programs like *Ghost Hunters, Scare Tactics,* and *Destination Truth*, which are marketed based on fear and varying degrees of simulated audience participation.

However, *Ghost Hunters* is unique in the level of virtual participation offered to viewers. In the exposition portion of each episode, the fan receives an abridged version of the same background information available to the onscreen investigators, with fans positioned *within* the methodology adopted by the TAPS team, allowing viewers to feel knowledgeable and prepared to watch the coming investigation with a critical eye. This expository segment is often wrapped up with a montage of representative moments showing the team preparing and packing the equipment and heading out to the evening's investigation, edited to show integral steps in the process while eliminating narratively non-compelling footage. Once the team arrives at the investigation site, the exposition section of the episode is completed, with a tour and background information provided by the homeowner or another expert on the site, such as employees in the case of a business investigation.

After another montage sequence of the team setting up, *Ghost Hunters* goes "lights out" and "The Investigation" begins. This is the section of the program in which viewers are most dramatically positioned in connection with the TAPS team, "with camera operators chasing TAPS members as they go about their ghost-hunting business."[20] In the investigative process, *Ghost Hunters* overlaps with mainstream reality television, which often uses "recording 'on the wing' … frequently with the help of lightweight video equipment, of events in the lives of individuals and groups"[21] to create an onscreen narrative for fans. As these observations demonstrate, mobility is a key component in encouraging the simulated participation *Ghost Hunters* viewers are looking for: because the camera crews are able to follow the investigators wherever their investigation takes them, with even greater intimacy achieved through the use of individual hand-held cameras showing the perspective of the investigators themselves, the sense of simulated participation can be achieved. Viewers are positioned as side by side with team members throughout each investigation – seeing what they see, hearing what they hear, and vicariously experiencing what they experience, though this last goal can of course only be achieved incompletely. Ultimately, the participation offered to viewers remains illusory because an extensive investigation is condensed, through judicial editing, into a twenty-five-minute segment.

Another montage sequence of the team packing up and briefly following up with the clients usually ushers viewers through the conclusion of the investigation and into the next stage of the program: "The Analysis." Editing is an integral part of the presentation of this stage and the review of hours of raw video and audio evidence is condensed, discussed, and revealed to Hawes and Wilson in the space of a few minutes onscreen. This is one of the key moments in the program where the illusion of simulated viewer participation breaks down. There simply is not enough time within a sixty-minute show format, usually with two cases per show, to include more than the most critical moments of footage, as decided by the editors and production company in a selection process that highlights simulation rather than participation on the part of the viewer.

The editing techniques used to distance the viewers' participatory identification in the evidence review stage serves two additional purposes: they resituate the TAPS team as unquestioned experts, no matter how much fans have felt "part of" the investigation; and they create suspense to build toward the scientific climax of *Ghost Hunters*, "The Findings." The tension leading up to the revelation of the findings is often further manipulated through editing by a quick cut to commercial break immediately before the showing of the evidence itself, with the break heightened by a shot of a team member reacting to some piece of evidence that they are exclaiming over but which goes, for the moment, unseen by viewers at home. The findings tend to comprise no more than a few seconds of video or audio footage and the scientific approach is predominant in this stage, with technology specialists and investigators debating the validity of evidence: dust or an orb? A voice or ambient noise? If a voice, what might it be saying? Consensus is rare and each piece of evidence is addressed from a variety of explanatory perspectives, re-establishing the critical approach evidenced in *Ghost Hunters* and adopted by the fan discourse surrounding the program.

Last but not least comes "The Reveal," when Hawes and Wilson return to the investigation site to share the evidence and discuss their findings with the case client. Scientifically speaking, this discussion moves beyond fans' simulated participation in the investigation itself; usually by this point in the program, viewers have seen the raw footage the team is about to show the homeowner or business associate, and have also been privy to the discussion and evaluation of the evidence. Therefore, this final stage works to underscore the ghost as a figure of futurity which promises to remain active long after the credits have rolled, with the potential for infinite future investigations, as well as to highlight the multiple discourses surrounding the paranormal in contemporary society. Whether the TAPS team has found paranormal evidence or not, the fear, anxiety, and curiosity of the client is indicative of the engagement of the spectral and the everyday, as well as the attendant tension that usually accompanies this intersection. The final section of each investigation narrative, structured through Hawes and Wilson's discussion with the client, situates the paranormal dynamically within the realm of everyday life, capable of interacting with and affecting the people and places around it. At times the team provides evidence of alternate explanations and other times they find compelling evidence of a haunting. However, Hawes and Wilson end each reveal by advising and reassuring the client, giving them pointers for addressing underlying causes (such as high electromagnetic outputs), dealing with activity where it exists, and finally, reminding clients – and viewers – that assistance is always only a phone call away. The reveal stage, therefore, ushers viewers back into the discourse of the day to day, positioning the ghost as a figure of futurity which has been explored but not exorcised, along with the reassurance that when the everyday and the paranormal overlap, there are experts up to the task of investigation. This moment also serves as a final challenge to the simulated participation of *Ghost Hunters* fans, re-establishing and validating the TAPS team as the best in their field. But the reclamation of participatory status is never further away than the next episode, as the *Ghost Hunters* and their viewers head "on to the next one."[22]

Halloween 2007: *Ghost Hunters Live From the Waverly Hills Sanatorium*

The discourse surrounding *Ghost Hunters* has invited formal viewer participation in a number of ways, including online discussion boards hosted by the show's SciFi. com site,[23] a text-message system to keep faithful fans updated,[24] public events, and an annual meeting called TAPSCON, where TAPS members meet and greet viewers, talk about their paranormal research, and even lead ghost hunts.[25] However, the *Ghost Hunters Live* Halloween special investigations from the Stanley Hotel in 2006, Waverly Hills Sanatorium in 2007, and Fort Delaware in 2008 are by far the most wide-ranging, accessible, and comprehensive examples of participatory viewing surrounding the program.

The *Ghost Hunters Live* investigation from Waverly Hills Sanatorium starts off with an introduction by Josh Gates, host of another SciFi Channel original series, *Destination Truth*. As Gates tells viewers, Waverly Hills is "one of America's signature haunts" and with *Ghost Hunters Live*, "*you* are a part of the investigation." Gates then takes viewers inside for a look at the TAPS Interactive Headquarters, where the technology of the investigation and the simulated participation of viewers are all highlighted. As Gates explains, the live investigation has several "interactive features," including "unfiltered, uncensored, and raw" video and digital photo footage, so that viewers "can see them firsthand and tell us what *you* see," an invitation which glosses over the limitations inherent in the television medium and mediation of televised and online investigation materials provided to viewers. In addition to accessing and reviewing footage online, the companion site for the investigation also featured a "Panic Button," which fans were invited to use to send their small-screen observations to the Interactive Headquarters, which then passed those tips on to the teams in the field. Gates's introduction serves to reset the parameters for the live investigation, encouraging and validating a heightened form of simulated participation.

The technological engagement continues to build a simulated participatory viewer experience throughout the investigation, with hundreds of thousands of messages coming in from all over the U.S. However, the technological interaction was most fully realized when several viewers reported the same observation: seeing a face on the ceiling of the sanatorium's body chute as Hawes and Wilson descended with the thermal imaging camera. While the majority of follow-up based on viewer suggestions did not make it on-air, in the case of the reported face, Gates's communication, and TAPS lead investigators Jason Hawes and Grant Wilson's further investigation underscored the interactive nature of the live investigation. In this case, not only did viewer observations benefit the investigation as a whole but fans were able to see the direct effect of their participation physically carried out by the lead investigators, who responded to the audience's request, focusing their attention on the area of suspected activity while simultaneously providing a discourse of skepticism and debunking. As Wilson explained as they continued their investigation of the body chute, the "spray paint on the walls will reflect stuff.... Maybe that's what they're seeing," explaining the role of visual matrixing in the attempt of eye and brain to make sense of the material before it, often creating the illusion of an image where none in fact exists.[26] While the phenomenon viewers had reported could not be conclusively explained, fans had the opportunity to participate and see their observations and requests acted upon by the TAPS team, validating the simulated participation they regularly engage in watching *Ghost Hunters* week after week.

Ghost Hunters Live also emphasizes the interactive nature of the Halloween investigation through the editing and presentation of the episode itself. Following the pattern established by regular episodes, the live special follows investigators throughout the evening, positioning viewers in a state of interactivity, allowing them to feel as though they are there with the TAPS team. However, significant departures from the traditional *Ghost Hunters* episode structure include the filming and presentation of the investigation in "real time," the alternating views between teams based on the level of immediate activity, and direct address of viewers by members of the *Ghost Hunters* team. The real-time format of the Halloween investigation creates a sense of urgency, encouraging fans to focus their attention exclusively on the investigation at hand; after all, rather than being pre-recorded, this investigation is happening now and viewer observations could change its course and help the team produce scientific proof of the paranormal.

This sense of immediacy is heightened by an editing approach which cuts between teams on a spontaneous and unpredictable schedule. With regular season episodes, the *Ghost Hunters* editing team has the opportunity to feature teams equally and to include segments that show the team before, during, and after potentially paranormal activity. In the live special, however, editing decisions to cut from one team to another within the real-time structure are necessarily guided by where notable activity may be occurring. Therefore, in cutting abruptly from one team to another in an effort to catch and broadcast the paranormal activity being experienced by the latter, viewers always join the active team *in medias res*: the activity prompting the editing cut to that team has already begun, leaving the moment that provoked the edit offscreen. This differs dynamically from the editing process for regular season episodes, which, through the stages of production and post-production, can include the contextual material surrounding paranormal activity, featuring a team experiencing activity more predominantly than a team which has an uneventful investigation. This is a luxury the editing team is not afforded by *Ghost Hunters Live*: because activity could occur to any team at any time, which team to televise becomes little more than a guessing game. The unpredictability heightens the simulated participation of viewers, bringing fans even more dramatically into the mediatized investigation to experience the real-time thrill of the TAPS team members' search for the paranormal.

The presentation of *Ghost Hunters Live* also differs significantly from regular season episodes in the direct address of viewers by members of the TAPS team. Such direct addresses in regular season episodes of *Ghost Hunters* are usually framed through the presentation of information: TAPS team members give definitions of technological equipment or paranormal theory, often against an official black and yellow TAPS logo background. Direct address is also consistently used when the team is wrapping up a case following the reveal with the client, though even then the summary is given off to one side, as though the investigators are conversing critically with one another rather than speaking to their audience members. Therefore, the direct address technique is most often used to establish expertise or present information to the viewer. The role of explanation becomes deflected in the *Ghost Hunters Live* investigation at Waverly Hills, with any background information presented through discussion with their guest investigator for the evening, wrestling superstar Elijah from *Extreme Championship Wrestling* (*ECW*); Elijah, then, stands in for the uninformed viewer, a proxy which allows technical and introductory information to be presented within the real-time format without breaking the investigation up with pre-recorded direct address material. Hawes and Wilson also wrap up the live televised portion of the investigation by directly addressing the camera and acknowledging the contributions of fans. As Hawes says, "we definitely have to say thank you to all the viewers," pointing to the camera and, by extension, the fans themselves. The dedication and contribution of fans is explicitly acknowledged and appreciated, allowing fans an ultimate moment of simulated participation.

Finally, *Ghost Hunters Live* includes contestants from the program's "Hunt for the Hunter" contest, with the three finalists being brought along for a short period during the evening's investigation. The featured contestants are all amateur ghost hunters, inviting viewer self-identification and another level of simulated participation: by seeing someone like themselves investigating with the TAPS team, fans have their feelings of interactivity and participation validated. Each of the finalists accompanies a team of investigators through a section of the sanatorium, talking about their own paranormal experiences and taking part in video and audio sessions. However, the "Hunt for the Hunter" segment is the most contested section of the live investigation in terms of simulated participation. In the end, the contestants are found promising but lacking; as tech manager Steve Gonsalves comments, "being a fan of the show and our team is just not enough." The discourse of interactivity and participation becomes complicated here, with the TAPS team established as the premier group in paranormal investigating and the unquestioned experts in their field. Significantly, this discussion occurs toward the conclusion of the televised investigation, mimicking the analysis, findings, and reveal stages in regular season episodes, through which expertise and authority are similarly re-emphasized.

Ghost Hunters Live heightens the participatory aspects of the fan discourse surrounding the program. Through the use of technology and communication between fans and the TAPS team, the simulated participation viewers enjoy informally when critically watching individual episodes of *Ghost Hunters* is validated, with fans having a chance to interact with the team and the investigation in a mediated and mediatized process. Through a combination of interactive technologies, the use of real-time formatting, spontaneous editing, and direct audience address, *Ghost Hunters* fans are interpellated as integral participants in the investigation of Waverly Hills Sanatorium. However, the equilibrium of expertise and amateurism is re-established, as it always must be, through the discourse surrounding the "Hunt for the Hunter" finalists, reminding viewers that knowledge, research, and field experience are more important than fandom and simulated participation.

Conclusion

Ghost Hunters participates in the scientific discourse of paranormal investigation pioneered over a century ago by the SPR. However, the series also redefines ghost hunting for the twenty-first century. First, the ghost is framed not as a figure of the past but as a figure of futurity, with a direct impact on the contemporary everyday world and therefore relevant and immediate; echoing Derrida's *revenant*, the ghost as addressed through the series continues to return, with the promise of ongoing paranormal activity. Second, viewers are encouraged, through the use of technology, editing, and live episodes, to act as simulated participants in *Ghost Hunters* investigations. Both the regular season episodes and the live Halloween investigation usher viewers through a process of simultaneous identification and distancing: fans are included as an integral part of investigation and invited to critically position themselves alongside TAPS team members. However, when the investigation comes to an end, through the ritual presentation of the analysis, findings, and reveal, the presenters are re-established as the only true experts. *Ghost Hunters* negotiates discourses of science, the paranormal, and fandom to provide its viewers with a unique view of haunting, one which is mediated through their critical perspectives, as well as through editing and the television format. The program combines critical scientific inquiry through video, audio, and electromagnetic field readers, with the affective engagement of the viewer as a (virtual) investigative team member. Through this signature approach, *Ghost Hunters* participates in a new type of active fandom, where the physical and online discourse of fans creates texts that haunt the televisual hauntings, making viewers always already part of the investigation.

NOTES

1   "*Ghost Hunters* Triumphs with Best Season Ever!," SciFi Channel Press Release. *The Futon Critic: The Web's Best Television Resource*, June 19, 2008, http://www.thefutoncritic. com/news.aspx?id=20080619scifi01.

2   Henry Jenkins, "Interactive Audiences? The 'Collective Intelligence' of Media Fans," in

Fans, Bloggers, and Gamers: Exploring Participatory Culture (New York: New York University Press, 2006), 136.

3   Jacques Derrida, *Specters of Marx: The State of the Debt, The Work of Mourning, and the New International*, trans. Peggy Kamuf (New York: Routledge, 1994), 11.

4   Marina Warner, *Phantasmagoria: Spirit Visions, Metaphors, and Media into the Twenty-first Century* (New York: Oxford University Press, 2006), 236.

5   Ibid., 242.

6   Jeffrey Sconce, *Haunted Media: Electronic Presence from Telegraphy to Television* (Durham: Duke University Press, 2000), 65.

7   Ibid., 75.

8   Ibid., 81–84.

9   Ibid., 85.

10   Jeffrey Andrew Weinstock, "The Spectral Turn," in *Spectral America: Phantoms and the National Imagination*, ed. Jeffrey Andrew Weinstock (Madison: University of Wisconsin Press, 2004), 5.

11   Jason Hawes and Grant Wilson, with Michael Jan Friedman, *Ghost Hunting: True Stories of Unexplained Phenomena from The Atlantic Paranormal Society* (New York: Pocket, 2007), 13.

12   James Hibberd, "In Search of Today's Ghost Stories," *Television Week* 24, August 22, 2005.

13   Hawes and Wilson, *Ghost Hunting*, 263.

14   Kirby, Carrie, "Ghost Hunters Utilize Latest in Technology: Paranormal Research Has Become a Popular Pursuit," *San Francisco Chronicle*, October 31, 2005, http://www.sfgate.com/cgi-bin/article.cgi?f=/c/a/2005/ 10/31/BUGDCFFS8Q1.DTL%20.

15   Hibberd, "In Search of Today's Ghost Stories."

16   Ibid.

17   Ibid.

18   Ibid.

19   This populist impulse is a divergence from the SPR, whose members came from "the ranks of wealth and influence in late Victorian Britain," making the group's paranormal investigation an elitist endeavor. See Warner, *Phantasmagoria*, 238.

20   James Hibberd, "Lights, Camera … Apparition!" *Television Week* 24, August 22, 2005.

21   Su Holmes and Deborah Jermyn, "Understanding Reality TV," in *Understanding Reality Television*, ed. Su Holmes and Deborah Jermyn (New York: Routledge, 2004), 2.

22   Along with Wilson's reassurance of clients that "we're here to help," the phrase "on to the next one" is ritualistically repeated at the end of each investigation by Hawes, establishing a discourse of familiar expressions as well as a set structure and approach, carrying viewers over from one investigation to the next.

23   http://www.scifi.com/ghosthunters. In addition to discussion boards, the site also offers full episodes so that viewers can rewatch and review investigations, additional footage and interviews with TAPS team members, and a "Gear Guide" so that fans can try their hand at their own paranormal investigations, with expert advice on this high-tech equipment.

24   http://www.scifi.com/mobile/.

25   http://tapscon2.com.

26   As defined by Hawes and Wilson, matrixing is "[t]he natural tendency of the human mind to add details to sensory input (perceived through the visual, auditory, olfactory, or tactile senses) so as to create a familiar or easily understood pattern. In effect, matrixing is mentally 'filling in the blanks'" (266).

Chapter 13

The Haunted Lecture Theater: Ghosts in the Academy in the BBC's *Sea of Souls*

Catherine Spooner

What does it mean for a university to be haunted? What kind of ghosts might be raised within the walls of the academy, and what might these hauntings mean for the production of knowledge or knowledges within them? The BBC's drama series *Sea of Souls* offers a forum for the exploration of these questions. The program traces, over the course of three series and a two-part special screened on BBC1 between 2004 and 2007, the investigations of a Parapsychology Research Unit based in the fictional "Clyde" University in Glasgow. The team is led by Dr. Douglas Monaghan (Bill Paterson), and supported in the first series by PhD student Megan (Archie Panjabi) and research fellow Andrew (Peter MacDonald), and from the second series onwards by PhD student Justine (Dawn Steele) and junior academic Craig (Iain Robertson). Similarly to *The X-Files*, with which the series initially drew comparison, in each episode the research team attempts to get to the bottom of an apparently supernatural mystery, usually with ambiguous results. At the same time, they struggle for research funding and juggle academic commitments with messy personal lives, just like their non-fictional counterparts.

Supernatural drama underwent a surge in the first decade of the twenty-first century, as television networks attempted to cash in on the success of American series such as *The X-Files* and *Buffy the Vampire Slayer*. *Sea of Souls* was one of the first of this new wave to be made for British television, and while the supernatural theme, "monster of the week" format, close-knit investigative team, and mixture of comedy and terror evidently derive from its American counterparts, it also clearly owes a debt to British workplace-based dramas such as *Casualty* or *The Bill*, and scenic detective serials such as *Midsomer Murders* and *Inspector Morse*. These generic parameters to a certain extent influence the representation of the supernatural in the show: well-known British character actors and location shooting in Scotland and London give the appearance of "quality" drama, while the overall tone is naturalistic, even when dealing with the supernatural. In the first two series, the paranormal is evoked by props, lighting, sound, editing, and camerawork rather than by elaborate special effects; nothing shown on screen falls outside the boundaries of possibility. In this respect the program follows the pattern of "gentlemanly restraint" laid down by the BBC's adaptation of M. R. James's ghost stories in the 1960s.[1] Outright horror is eschewed in favor of suggestion. This lineage is particularly appropriate given the academic setting of many of M. R. James's tales, with their stuffy male protagonists troubled by the ghosts and demons uncovered by their obscure research. The representational subtlety established in series like the BBC's *A Ghost Story For Christmas* plays into *Sea of Souls'* theme of academic skepticism, enabling a significant residue of doubt to surround even the most astonishing cases. The third series' increased special effects budget and adoption of computer-generated imagery heralded a self-consciously more sensationalist approach, and its move away from skepticism towards outright confirmation of the supernatural. This had profound effects on the representation not only of the supernatural, but also of the academy.

In his study of the campus novel, *Ancient Cultures of Conceit*, Ian Carter has pointed out how crises in the academy tend to coincide with clusters of televised campus dramas (for example *The History Man* and *Brideshead Revisited* in 1981 when university cuts were being fine-tuned).[2] Carter offers no definitive relationship between government policies and TV dramas, but suggests that there is more to it than simply programming values. *Sea of Souls* was the most academically "authentic" of a number of academic Gothic dramas with which it roughly coincided: ITV1's *Afterlife* (2006–2007), featuring Andrew Lincoln as a Psychology lecturer at the University of Bristol, researching Lesley Sharp's disturbed spirit medium; and BBC1's *Bonekickers* (2008), a series based around an archaeological research team at the fictional University of Wessex, whose digs always fortuitously unearth occult mysteries, if not actual supernatural visitations. The university as a locus for hauntings is a theme that has, for some reason, touched a cultural nerve. It would be over-simplistic to draw any facile conclusions about the relationship between the sudden fascination with paranormal academic dramas and the contemporary crisis in British universities surrounding under-funding, management culture, the Research Assessment Exercise, and top-up fees, but it does seem more than a coincidence. There is no *Buffy the Vampire Slayer*-like mapping of real-life horrors onto supernatural ones – what we might think of as the "High School is hell" formula. There is, however, a sense that these departments are embattled: in the first series of *Sea of Souls*, for example, Monaghan is continually required to justify the Research Unit's existence to the Dean. There are clashes about money and publicity, too, between *Bonekickers'* altruistic team and their worldly Head of Department. More typically, though, the economic threat to the academy is interiorized or displaced onto the supernatural.

The generic format of *Sea of Souls*, with a new mystery to solve every week, tends to produce an uncomfortable sense that it is the academics' role not only to pursue knowledge for its own sake, but also, by getting to the bottom of supernatural phenomena, to help those in the community who are haunted – a role more like that of a psychiatrist or a detective. Nevertheless, as academics, they repeatedly find themselves unable to intervene in the events they observe, appearing oddly redundant at the climax of each episode as the supernatural drama plays itself out. The inconclusiveness of the team's investigations, which can never "prove" the supernatural as they never sufficiently fulfill empirical criteria, seems neither to produce measurable research outcomes nor to fulfill an effective role in the wider community. Craig's complaint in the Series 2 episode "Empty Promise" that visiting academic Peter Locke (Colin Salmon) hasn't published anything for three years is symptomatic of a more extensive malaise, as research results are invalidated, trial computer programs abandoned, and books either left incomplete or languishing unread on bookshop shelves. Academia's self-reflexive questioning of its own relevance in contemporary culture is figured as a crisis in the production of knowledge itself.

Out of this crisis of confidence repeated ghostly manifestations emerge. In her book *Ghostly Matters*, Avery Gordon suggests that "the ghost imports a charged strangeness into the place or sphere it is haunting, thus unsettling the propriety and property lines that delimit a zone of activity or knowledge."[3] In *Sea of Souls*, the university is both the place that is haunted and the zone of knowledge that is unsettled. It is not always the university buildings themselves that stand in for the haunted house – although sometimes they do, for instance in the Series 3 episode "Sleeper" when an overnight sleep experiment goes wrong and the laboratory becomes infested with physical manifestations of the subject's nightmares. It is through the university, however, that the hauntings are gathered together, assembled into a body of knowledge. This is physically represented in the first series by individual chapters of Dr. Monaghan's unfinished book, *The Cultural Acceptance of PSI*. In Part 1 of "Possession"[4] we see him contemplating the manuscript: the chapters are carefully demarcated from one another by folded slips of paper printed with their individual titles. Within the academic monograph, diverse phenomena are discretely taxonomized, placed within an ordered system, and made available for intellectual scrutiny.

If the university provides a means through which a wide range of supernatural phenomena can be gathered together, then it becomes, to borrow Foucault's term, a kind of paranormal *heterotopia*, in which different orders of supernatural phenomena coexist.[5] In the first series, for example, we have psychic twins, a child who appears to remember a former life, and ritual human sacrifice; the second series investigates a poltergeist, a cursed soldier, and a psychic entertainer. If the modern university is implicitly a humanist institution, from which the supernatural is by definition excluded,[6] then the haunted lecture theaters and laboratories of *Sea of Souls* offer a kind of "counter-site" in which, as Foucault suggests, the "real site" can be "simultaneously represented, contested and inverted" (231). Monaghan's struggle to finish his book demonstrates the difficulty of placing the paranormal within conventional academic parameters: he is forced to discard the final chapter when one of the pair of psychic twins he is studying murders her sister. This body of knowledge continually exceeds the framework that the academy attempts to place around it.

It is, moreover, a very specific kind of knowledge that is made strange through the practices of haunting in *Sea of Souls*: that of scientific rationalism. Although the very first episode focuses on an art historian, whose professional preoccupation with images of twins betrays her psychic link with her unknown sister, in general the program is keen to assert its disciplinary purity, with its researchers dismissive of non-scientific approaches. At the beginning of the Series 2 episode "Omen Formation," Craig jokes at a press launch that "Philosophy is to science what pornography is to sex – a poor substitute. Although bizarrely, some people seem to prefer it." Professional skepticism is continually placed under threat, however, by narrative events. In "Empty Promise," Craig exposes a professional psychic's cold reading techniques live on radio before being left lost for words when the psychic correctly identifies the small town where he grew up. This provides, in microcosm, an illustration of the program's most characteristic strategy: although there could still be a rational explanation for how the psychic knew this specific location, the skeptical viewpoint is significantly challenged. There is always a supernatural residue that cannot be explained, and that is increasingly privileged as the series progresses.

So far, perhaps, so familiar: the use of the irrational to problematize Enlightenment values is a familiar critical assessment of Gothic fictions. Fred Botting's *Gothic*, the standard introduction to the subject, states for example that "Gothic figures have continued to shadow the progress of modernity with counter-narratives displaying the underside of enlightenment and humanist values."[7] In *Ghosts: Deconstruction, Psychoanalysis, History*, Peter Buse and Andrew Stott explain that "In recent years, cultural historians have been alert to the processes of exclusion performed by Reason on non-Enlightenment practices where ghosts found or remained in favor," and suggest that, "Instead of saying that there is an outside of reason which has been neglected, perhaps we need to inspect the inside of reason and see how it too is haunted by what it excludes."[8]

Sea of Souls does participate in this tradition, but it also does something more. The supernatural does not merely problematize the acquisition of knowledge, but it is also in itself a means of accessing, or producing, knowledge. Hauntings profoundly affect the characters, causing them to confront their own prejudices and preoccupations, and as such they offer the potential to radically reinvent what we understand by scientific research. Avery Gordon points out the self-reflexive nature of any academic study of haunting: "Of course, the tricky thing is that scholars too are subject to these same dynamics of haunting: ghosts get in our matters just as well. This means that we will have to talk to and listen to ghosts, rather than banish them, as the precondition for scientific or humanistic knowledge" (23). This statement is reinforced over and over again in the course of *Sea of Souls*. The research team must listen to ghosts, listen to what they are telling them, both about the case in hand and about themselves, before any kind of knowledge can be achieved. As Gordon continues, "Being haunted draws us affectively, sometimes against our will and always a bit magically, into the structure of feeling of a reality we come to experience, not as cold knowledge, but as a transformative recognition" (23). This "transformative recognition" is what the characters in *Sea of Souls* repeatedly undergo. In doing so, they move towards what Donna Haraway has described as "situated" or "embodied" knowledges: knowledges that evade the "god-trick" of conventional science, the act of "seeing everything from nowhere."[9]

Feminist critiques of science such as Haraway's have insisted on the embodied nature of vision: that the notion of the objective observer is a myth founded in patriarchal power structures. The "unmarked" or objective position, according to Haraway, is that of the white male: "This is the gaze that mythically inscribes all the marked bodies, that makes the unmarked category claim the power to see and not be seen, to represent while escaping representation" (188). In contrast, she advocates "partial perspective," an acknowledgement of the limitations and responsibilities of vision (190). Gordon's emphasis on haunting as a way of knowing offers an alternative way of achieving partial perspective: while ghosts may appear to be the antithesis of embodiment, opening oneself to haunting is opening oneself to knowledge of what has been excluded, othered, disappeared. The uncanny visions experienced by the characters in the first two series of *Sea of Souls* are not that of the all-seeing eye of Western science or monotheistic religion, but illegitimate, improper, and discomforting modes of "transformative recognition."

In the Series 1 episode, "Shades of Evil,"[10] Megan tells Andrew that, "To make any great discovery, people have to make a leap of faith." Andrew responds, "Religion is about faith. Science is about facts." These two opposed approaches persist in tension throughout the three series. However, as the program develops, the leap of faith is increasingly privileged over hard facts. The intuitive approach to research practised by PhD students Megan and Justine is grounded in emotion, empathy, and experience. Both Megan and Justine are shown to be rich in emotional intelligence, which they use in order to gain information unavailable to their less socially aware colleagues. Justine in particular is suggested to have psychic insight of her own, which not only conveniently enables her to discover important clues, but also problematizes the subject–object relationship within research. In a scene from the Series 2 episode "Amulet," Justine puts herself through the same test for psychic ability that the unit has been using on various subjects, with startling results. The test involves lifting identical parcels containing natural substances, and reading – or guessing – what they contain. Watching a research subject take the test, Justine begins to experience brief visual flashes that apparently reveal the environments from which the contents of the parcels derive – a forest for wood, a beach for sandstone, and so on. Subsequently, she runs the test on herself, and as she lifts the first parcel, the camera zooms towards an extreme close-up of light reflected on her iris, as if entering her eye and recording her inner sight. Impressionistic camera work recreates the dizzying rush of the vision: slow motion is juxtaposed with speeded-up film, creating a sense of temporal dislocation; fast cutting between point-of-view shots of the forest or beach, close-ups of Justine's startled gaze, and brief establishing shots of her standing within the visionary landscape create spatial disorientation. The light reflected on Justine's iris becomes the sun above her head, linking exterior and interior; moreover, the glare of the sun on the lens draws attention to the camera and thus to the act of looking. The camera encourages the viewer both to share Justine's vision, apparently entering her consciousness through her eye, and to observe her as an object within it. It remains unclear whether Justine sees her own body within the landscape as the viewer does, or merely experiences it. Part of Justine's gaze is directly shared, and part more ambiguously so.

This experiment does not take place in rigorously controlled conditions. It is not scientifically verifiable in this sense. But the camera's aligning of the viewer's gaze with both Justine's visionary one and that of an impartial observer conveys a certain narrative authority. This authority is *both* emotional and empathetic *and* that of empirical scrutiny. A partial, subjective, intuitive viewpoint collides with, and radically revises, an omniscient, objective, rational one. The camera grants magical access to "the truth" of the shared vision, which renders empirically collated evidence superfluous. For the duration of the fiction, at least, the viewer suspends disbelief.

Although it is the principal female characters in the series who are associated with empathy and intuition, the series avoids a simplistic coding of the supernatural as feminine. Likewise, Justine's psychic abilities are not merely a straightforward disruption of masculine logic with feminine intuition. This gendered binary is not played out in terms of the series, which shows both men and women visited by the paranormal or possessing supernatural powers. Rather, the trope of haunting enables the disruption of conventional epistemologies. Through the experience of the supernatural, the protagonists of *Sea of Souls* are forced to confront their own dearly held beliefs in scientific rationalism, to acknowledge that science offers just one way of knowing among many, and not always the most useful one. As the protagonists, and especially the male protagonists, become more open to the otherness represented by the ghosts and apparitions they encounter, they are forced to re-evaluate their skepticism, and admit wonder and even faith.

Methodological questions about the process of acquiring knowledge are explicitly raised in the Series 2 episode "Omen Formation." Craig is in the middle of an attempt to devise a fool-proof computer program for testing ESP, while Justine is working on a research proposal about near-death experiences. Both are on a quest for certainty, for absolute scientific proof, but both are forced to recognize that this is incommensurate with their reliance on human subjects. Craig, confronted by Dr. Monaghan's ethical concerns, responds to Justine's question, "What about our duty of care?" with the rejoinder, "Our duty is to the truth!" For Craig, the truth *is* out there, and empirical science provides the means of accessing it. Both he and Justine are disappointed, however, when they are forced to realize that their methods are inherently flawed: Craig discovers a loophole in his program, which has failed to factor out human error, while Justine realizes her interviews are invalid as she has been asking leading questions.

The knowledge provided by haunting, however, seems to offer more insight. The main focus of the narrative centers around an AWOL British soldier haunted by visions of his own death since being cursed by a civilian he killed during service in Bosnia – a condition initially diagnosed by Monaghan as an extreme form of post-traumatic stress known as "omen formation," whereby the traumatized subject imposes order on the world by reading it in terms of signs and portents, thus feeling they are able to predict future adverse events. On his death, the haunted soldier passes on the Serbo-Croatian curse to Monaghan, who immediately begins to experience a parallel set of symptoms. Most significantly, he begins to see visions, which, like the soldier's, seem to portend his own death. It is unclear whether Monaghan is himself suffering from post-traumatic stress, or whether the curse is real. Seemingly pursued by a figure in an army parka, Monaghan insists, "I don't believe in ghosts," but nevertheless relates to Justine a story of how his father appeared to him just after he had, unknown to Monaghan, died in hospital. Justine's response, "We all have our ghosts," implicitly personalizes the process of haunting, locating it within individual memory. As events appear to substantiate Monaghan's premonitions, and he is knocked off a pier in front of a passing boat, it seems the curse is confirmed. In a similar way to the portrayal of Justine's visions in "Amulet," the camera enters Monaghan's consciousness, recording a near-death experience of his own in which he encounters his dead father. In this episode, therefore, the haunting passes from the subject of study to the experience of the academic; they are not investigating or even witnessing a haunting, but are themselves haunted. While Monaghan remains skeptical after his experience, his worldview is nevertheless profoundly shaken by it. The normal channels through which scientific knowledge is acquired have all proved fallible, and his own experience remains uncontainable within those frameworks.

Sea of Souls' paranormal heterotopia therefore opens up a space for epistemological critique, moving towards a position evoking that of "situated" or "embodied" knowledges. The researchers in Sea of Souls are constantly encouraged to confront their own "partial perspective," and acknowledge the limitations of the "god-trick" of conventional science, of "seeing everything from nowhere." Knowledge, rather, comes from a variety of different sources, some of which might resemble those of conventional research, and some of which are seemingly numinous or located in personal vision. Knowledge, furthermore, is seldom constructed as an end in itself; rather, it involves an exorcizing or laying to rest or bringing to light within the wider community. Listening to ghosts has a social function; it entails interaction and responsibility.

The first two series of Sea of Souls sustain the tension between rationalism and faith, allowing its characters to hesitate between the two. The third series pushes Monaghan and his colleagues further towards a position of belief. An increased special effects budget and use of computer-generated imagery enables the unambiguous representation of the supernatural on screen, so that in the series finale "Rebound," for example, flickering electricity suffuses a woman's skin, Monaghan is thrown bodily across a room, and, finally, a demon briefly appears during a magical ceremony. This shift from the evocation of uncanny states of mind through camera work to concrete visualization has the effect of implicitly endorsing the supernatural, removing it from the subjective realm of the individual to that of shared supernatural spectacle. Although it might seem that this would further the potential for haunted epistemologies, in actual fact, by removing uncertainty, it replicates much more familiar structures of knowledge. The opposition between science and faith is questioned, but rather than a space opening up between the two, the hierarchy is simply reversed.

To a certain extent, this assessment replicates a history of presumptions regarding the representation of the supernatural on television: as Helen Wheatley demonstrates, early adaptations of ghost stories were validated by critics for their "restraint and decorum" (43), a judgment loaded with class values and presuppositions about both the purpose of television and the value of Gothic fictions. This attitude can in turn be traced back to eighteenth-century Gothic novelist Ann Radcliffe's privileging of terror, as stimulating the imagination, over the degrading literalness of horror.[11] The bold visualizations of the supernatural in *Sea of Souls'* third series are, in the context of the history of British television, a more risky venture. However, the addition of computer-generated special effects does function here to simplify other means of televisual evocation of the supernatural, and to close down some of the more sophisticated questions the earlier two series raise.

The treatment of Justine and Monaghan's developing personal beliefs in the third series illustrates this shift. Justine's own psychic powers are increasingly foregrounded, and in the Series 3 episode "Oracle" become the phenomenon under investigation. The more heavy-handed approach to the supernatural typical of this series, however, means that the sense of epistemological critique is blunted. Early in the episode Justine and Craig argue about research methods, Craig criticizing Justine's use of her subjects' dream diaries: "What happened to objective measurements and controlled laboratory conditions? … Writing down your dreams – that's completely subjective, how are you even going to quantify the results?" Justine defends her investigations as "complementary" to more rigorously controlled experiments, implicitly suggesting that there is more than one way of gathering knowledge. However, as she finds herself having precognitive visions triggered by touching material objects, she opts to relinquish the role of scientist for that of "guinea-pig." Despite Craig's insistence on finding a rational explanation (a conviction Monaghan dismisses as itself unscientific), her visions continue to exceed the parameters science places on them. In line with Series 3's more sensational aesthetic, the visions are no longer evoked through vague, fleeting images, a highly mobile camera, and fast editing, but through highly dramatic, digitally manipulated "flash-forwards" showing, for example, a sequence in which a chequered floor unfolds across the laboratory, bloody handprints appear on the wall, and a woman walks towards Justine holding out her arms as blood blooms across her white dress. Aside from some brief, low-angled, extreme close-ups on Justine's face, the camera sticks to the classical Hollywood style of shot/reverse-shot, effacing its own presence. The viewer is not implicated, but is positioned as omnipresent, "seeing everything from nowhere." On one level, the episode appears to continue to interrogate the division between scientist and experimental subject. On another, the provision of absolute visual certainty presents the outcome of the experiment as the *fait accompli* that Monaghan warns against.

Monaghan himself may keep an "open mind" after his uncanny premonitions and near-death experience in "Omen Formation," but in the final episode of Series 3, when he encounters an alchemist with occult powers, he has the equivalent of a Damascene conversion. His initial dismissal of magic as "pyrotechnics" presents a self-reflexive acknowledgement of the supernatural as televisual spectacle. Yet publishing magnate Christopher Chambers's admonishment, "Deny magic – deny centuries of learning and wisdom" positions magic as parallel to academia as a means of acquiring knowledge. In the course of the episode, the team encounter learned societies devoted to its study, a publishing industry that disseminates its texts, an emphasis on reading and interpretation, an insistence on the importance of rules (a kind of methodology) in magical practice, and a pedagogic hierarchy of students and adepts. Chambers as Rosicrucian sage is in many respects Monaghan's double: a solitary figure dedicated to the pursuit of knowledge, and prepared to sacrifice meaningful intimate relationships in order to do so. Ironically, it is Monaghan, the scientist, whose book-lined study resembles an antiquated library, while Chambers lives in a design-conscious modern apartment. His exploitation of modern technology in his magical practice parallels the Research Unit's employment of a battery of high-tech tools in their research methodologies.

Magic, however, is a mode of knowledge that exchanges empirical observation, scientific method, for ritual observances and unquestioning faith. Chambers seeks to emphasize this substitution, telling Monaghan that "sometimes the greatest test is a test of faith." After witnessing Chambers banish a demon in a magical ceremony, Monaghan admits that he has changed his position on the supernatural, informing Justine and Craig that, "Last night I set aside a lifetime of rationalism and witnessed something that has fundamentally changed the way I think. I can now unapologetically state that I fully believe in magic." The rational doubt of the first two series thus gives way to an assertion of belief. Although belief in the supernatural may on the surface seem the more radical attitude of the two, here it is paradoxically reassuring: the provision of absolute certainty by the series' main figure of intellectual authority resolves the epistemological tension of the series so far. The computer-generated visualization of the demon provides the "evidence," if any is needed, to confirm Monaghan's viewpoint. Magic merely repeats the "god-trick" of science, simply presenting an alternative means of "seeing everything from nowhere." It offers knowledge as transcendence, as completed vision, mediated through a hierarchy of powerful males, in contrast to the partial perspectives opened up by haunting.

The final episode of *Sea of Souls'* third series turns, therefore, from listening to ghosts to conjuring demons, and in doing so shifts from a struggle with redundancy and failure to new fantasies of omnipotence. As the program has more to show, it has less to say. Yet the haunting of academia figured in the earlier episodes of the series does offer an intelligent response to crises affecting the academy in the early twenty-first century, from the practical problem of how to engage with the wider community to more abstract questions concerning the construction of subjectivity and the production of knowledge. Listening to ghosts in *Sea of Souls* does prove to be transformative, in Avery Gordon's words, and as such is an ongoing process, one that continues to shape both the individuals concerned and their intellectual trajectories. Ultimately, perhaps, universities are better off haunted: ghosts, with their tendency to unsettle our comfort zones, militate against complacency, and encourage us to keep asking questions.

NOTES

1   Helen Wheatley, *Gothic Television* (Manchester: Manchester University Press, 2006), 47.
2   Ian Carter, *Ancient Cultures of Conceit: British University Fiction in the Post-War Years* (London and New York: Routledge, 1990).

3   Avery Gordon, *Ghostly Matters: Haunting and the Sociological Imagination* (Minneapolis: University of Minnesota Press, 1997), 63.

4   Episode also known as "Seeing Double."

5   Michel Foucault, "Of Other Spaces," in *The Visual Culture Reader*, ed. Nicholas Mirzoeff (London and New York: Routledge, 2002), 229–236.

6   "Humanism" is defined by the *Concise Oxford Dictionary* as "a system of thought that is based on the values, characteristics, and behaviour that are believed to be the best in human beings, rather than on any supernatural authority."

7   Fred Botting, *Gothic* (London: Routledge, 1996), 1–2.

8   Peter Buse and Andrew Stott, ed., *Ghosts: Deconstruction, Psychoanalysis, History* (Basingstoke: Macmillan, 1999), 3, 5.

9   Donna Haraway, "Situated Knowledges: The Science Question in Feminism and the Privilege of Partial Perspective," in *Simians, Cyborgs and Women* (London: Free Association Books, 1991), 189.

10   Episode also known as "Mind Over Matter."

11   Ann Radcliffe, "On the Supernatural in Poetry," in *Gothic Documents*, ed. E. J. Clery and Robert Miles (Manchester: Manchester University Press, 2000), 163–172. Originally published in *New Monthly Magazine* 16 (January 1826): 145–152.

Part 4

Other Ghostly Spheres

Chapter 14

Genius Loci: Memory, Media, and the Neo-Gothic in Georg Klein and Elfriede Jelinek

Arno Meteling

The Hall of the Dead: Gothic and Mnemonics

Gothic literature, film, or television series with ghosts as popular stock characters usually ponder the rules of communication between the living and the dead. In most cases there is an asymmetry between them, for although the ghosts admittedly inhabit the world of the living, they have no natural place in it. Moreover, ghosts, like images or characters on a photograph or in a film, are usually not able to change or develop. Like the psyche's reaction to trauma, ghosts are often forced to repeat the same thing over and over again or at least to stay in the same place forever. As a consequence, ghosts tend to establish a timeless zone of inertia in the flow of the narrative, creating a cyclical ahistoric or posthistoric state, or, as Jacques Derrida puts it, the "end of history."[1] Despite Derrida's reference to *Hamlet* as a central context for his hauntology, ghosts in literature, film, or television series are usually not responsible for time being completely out of joint. Instead, ghosts seem to be specific figures of anachronism, or more precisely, of asynchronicity, representing a static moment of the past haunting the present. As literary or filmic devices, ghosts therefore often operate as erratic monuments or hieroglyphs that signify a disturbing incident that happened in the past, a secret that has to be deciphered in order to understand the repercussions for the present.

One of the chief literary precursors of the modern ghost novel is the Gothic fiction of the eighteenth century, a literary genre that, besides dealing with ghosts, family curses, damsels in distress, and evil villains, evokes fear not only by describing horrific events, but by creating a certain mood of terror or horror derived from its setting. The Gothic novel is always about spatial arrangements, most obviously about architectural spaces like haunted houses, castles, dungeons, cemeteries, attics, or crypts. Significantly, Horace Walpole not only names the first Gothic novel, *The Castle of Otranto* (1764), after its setting but emphasizes its realism in the preface of the first edition (in the guise of an anonymous editor):

> Though the machinery is invention, and the names of the actors imaginary, I cannot but believe that the ground-work of the story is founded on truth. The scene is undoubtedly laid in some real castle. The author seems frequently, without design, to describe particular parts. *The chamber*, says he, *on the right-hand; the door on the left-hand; the distance from the chapel to Conrad's apartment*: these and other passages are strong presumptions that the author had some certain building in his eye.[2]

Considering that the novel is a fantastic one with supernatural effects that border on the comical and the grotesque (including a giant helmet that falls from the sky and kills the villain's son), the emphasis on the spatial authenticity of the castle is conspicuous and proves the importance of setting for the Gothic novel.[3] Since its reformulation in the nineteenth century, the dark and brooding atmosphere of haunted houses and castles also increasingly reflects the inner conflicts of the characters. With Edgar Allan Poe's 1839 story *The Fall of the House of Usher*, the Gothic tale establishes the notion of an almost corporeal connection between the protagonists and the buildings they are situated in. Roderick Usher's decadent and fragile mind mirrors exactly the brittle state of his house and vice versa. Most modern ghost novels adopt this Gothic correspondence between characters and building, sometimes transforming the house itself into a storehouse of repressed memories and thereby anthropomorphizing it, as most prominently in Shirley Jackson's seminal 1959 ghost novel *The Haunting of Hill House*.[4]

Gothic fiction, with its fixation on the nexus of static memory and location, also suggests a model of memorizing or "storing" things that is based on the ancient and medieval technique of "mnemonics" or *ars memoriae*. The most important feature or image of mnemonics is the "method of loci," also called "memory palace" or "theater of memory." These "theaters" organize and help to remember things by putting the images (*imagines*) of memories in certain imaginary storage rooms, thus giving mental spaces discrete addresses (*loci*). In order to retrieve the facts, the memory artist only has to walk through the imaginary palace or theater and look where the different objects, persons, or events are deposited. Ideally, everything remembered is unified in a single, complex memory building. Semiotically, these mental memory spaces can be read as "haunted spaces," inhabited by the ghosts or imaginary representations of the referential objects, persons, or events.

Mnemonics did not only involve vague remembrance or recollection of the past. Rather, it was a formal institution and discipline of the mind that not only taught how to learn something by heart but brought sense and order into the world. The art of memory therefore had an important part in the discipline of rhetoric.[5] The story of the mythical origin of mnemonics and its inventor, the Greek poet and rhetor Simonides of Ceos (c. 556–468 BC), can be found in Cicero's *De oratore* (55 BC) as well as in

Quintilian's *Institutio oratoria* (AD 95): After the roof of a banquet hall has collapsed and left all of the people in the hall dead under the rubble, Simonides, who escaped the catastrophe by chance, is the only one who is able to identify each of the dead by remembering the exact places they took at the table. Hence, one could argue that the origin of mnemonics not only shows the art of memory as a way to bridge the past and the present in the mind of the memory artist, but that it does this by connecting the temporal with the spatial. Furthermore, Simonides can be credited with revealing that the order and sense of the world are dependent on memory: when the roof collapsed, the corpses under the rubble were literally transformed into unidentifiable chaos, but by remembering their places in the hall and, respectively, their places in the world, Simonides restored the ordered and meaningful universe of signification. Finally, this mythic anecdote shows that from its inception mnemonics was bound to the notion of death.

Carpathian Castles: Neo-Gothic and the Media

While the ghosts from the eighteenth century up to popular ghost novel classics like *The Haunting of Hill House*, Richard Matheson's *Hell House* (1971), or Stephen King's *The Shining* (1977), were – like *imagines* in mnemonics – strictly confined to discrete locations, the ghosts in some later literary and filmic examples leave these spatial limits behind. While ghost novels with a traditional take on the Gothic, with its stress on dark and brooding locales, can be read as literary, albeit bizarre and warped, versions of theaters of memory, the advent of modern electronic media not only changes the cultural notion of memory in general, but also seems to have an impact on the narrative of the ghost story. Probably the most famous and globally successful example of this change is Kôji Suzuki's neo-Gothic ghost novel *Ringu* (*Ring*) (1991) with its sequels and transmedial multitude of manga, television, and film versions.[6] While it continues certain Gothic traditions, such as the background of a cryptic past that concerns a crime in the family, it frees the ghost – the vengeful spirit of a murdered girl – from all spatial confinements by displacing it to a mobile "non-place,"[7] namely a videotape. This narrative maneuver not only integrates the new media of film and video into the story – by telling a tale about the ultimate horror or literal "snuff" movie, as everyone who watches the video is destined to be literally frightened to death – but is also a comment on the memorial and distributing capabilities of modern media, since the only way to avert the ghost's curse and survive the video experience is to make a copy of the videotape and give it to someone else. Echoing Plato's fears that external "dead" media (as writing was to him) will not only render the living memory of human beings useless and obsolete, but also lead to the forgetfulness of one's soul,[8] the implementation of new media in the modern ghost story offers a new and critical angle on the relationships between memory, media, and the human soul.

It is common knowledge that the inception of modern media like photography, sound recording, or film created a new kind of uncanniness and a global movement of occultism and spiritualism in the nineteenth and early twentieth century: "Ghosts

… haunt modern media, with their common ability to spirit voice, image, and word across vast distances without death or decay."[9] Of course, by now people are used to the incorporeal voices and images of modern media. An answering machine that has memorized someone's voice is no longer scary. But hearing the voice of someone who died shortly after leaving the message might still be an uncanny experience. And even today people try to decipher messages from the dead using different media like tape recorders, radio, or television. Significantly, the logic of spiritualism – perhaps equal to the logic of hermeneutics – seems to be that the less information a medium delivers, the more information the interpreter can get from it. White noise therefore often works best for spiritualists.

The increased role of media in real-life spiritualism and the practices of photographing the dead or even ghosts in the nineteenth century also had an impact on the Gothic novel. The most famous example of a nineteenth-century take on the genre is probably Bram Stoker's vampire novel *Dracula* (1897), which can be read as the multi-media version of the eighteenth-century epistolary novel. The vampiric Transylvanian Count leaves his Carpathian Castle on the fringe of Western civilization – literally a place "beyond the woods" – for London, the then-"capital of the world," to fight not only Abraham van Helsing and his consorts but a network of new media, comprising typewriters, phonographs, telegraphs, and even telepathic messages.[10]

A lesser-known example of an adaptation of the Gothic that infuses it with new media is Jules Verne's *Le Château des Carpathes* (*Carpathian Castle*) (1892). It has all the trappings of the genre, sporting a village full of superstitious villagers, a dark forest, and a deserted castle in the Carpathian Mountains. Furthermore, the novel is about ghosts haunting all of these spaces. One protagonist, Count Franz de Telek, even goes mad when he gets to see and hear the spectral apparition of the dead opera singer Stilla, whom he wanted to marry. But the programmatic preface, the narrator's none-too-subtle ironic tone, and, of course, the inventor Orfanik's confession at the end, lead to the conclusion that *Le Château des Carpathes* is, if not a parody, at least a modern exorcism of everything that defines the Gothic genre.[11] Thus, in the vein of Verne's science fiction novels, the hauntings that terrorize the villagers as well as the visitors of the castle are revealed in the end as special effects, as technical "tricks" (272) fabricated by Orfanik using more or less futuristic devices such as a phonograph, a telephone wire connecting the castle and the village, and some form of holographic device resembling a film projector, operating with a "mirror" (271).

For the reader of *Le Château des Carpathes* it is obvious that the author is trying to debunk the trope of the haunted castle by exposing it as a product of imagination and science, and therefore as the effect of technological trickery. Verne's novel asks to be read as a modern, rationalistic, and skeptical comment on every spooky castle and scary haunting in earlier Gothic novels. What is interesting about this strategy is that by reducing the hauntings to mere special effects the novel shows that ghosts are effects of asynchronicity as well as of dislocation. Verne's novel stresses that, first, ghosts are defined in temporal as well as spatial terms, and second, that ghosts equal the definition of media. All media are able to conjure ghosts by memorizing sounds and images and reproducing them independently at another time and place. Third and consequently, Verne's novel shows that ghosts are strongly related to the ability to memorize, either by certain techniques of the mind or with the help of artificial, mediated memories. Curiously, one has to add a fourth aspect, namely that instead of demystifying everything, the rationalization of the haunting stops at mentioning the technical "tricks." Although the novel clearly makes its point that ghosts only exist in the reader's mind, stirred up by some rhetorically imaginative descriptions and a spooky writing style, self-referentially showing that Gothic novels operate with technical trickery and special effects, the events that remain unexplained, such as the death of Stilla, whose voice and life are stolen by a phonograph, are amplified. Verne, rather than providing fully satisfactory scientific explanations for these events, introduces a new kind of Gothic. This "neo-Gothic" is about the new and uncanny technologies, especially the new media, that are not only able to span time and space, but also shape a new imagination and figuration of ghosts.

Germany's Media Afterlife

A contemporary example of the way ghosts have left their old haunting grounds in the Gothic novel for the transient non-places of new media is Georg Klein's short story "Unsere lieben Toten. Ein spiritistischer Versuch" ("Our Beloved Dead: A Spiritualist Attempt"), published in his anthology *Von den Deutschen* (*On the Germans*).[12] As Klein is known for his experimental emulations of trivial literary genres,[13] one could assume that this story is Klein's take on the popular ghost story. But considering the numerous references to film and other media, it becomes clear that the story is not based on a literary genre at all, but on the latest wave of ghost movies, especially those of Japanese origin. Possible sources are Hideo Nakata's *Ringu* (*The Ring*) (1998), the film-version of Suzuki's novel, a movie that literally shows a ghost crawling out of a television set to go after its victims,[14] or Kiyoshi Kurosawa's *Kaïro* (*Pulse*) (2001), which tells of ghosts appearing on an Internet website slowly sucking all the living into an electronic limbo.[15]

Klein's story revolves around a man who has just died. In the beginning, the dead man sees his corpse lying in a hospital. His so-called "Totenblick" ("dead's vision") then notices his new "Totenkörper" ("dead body"). This appears to be an empty shell, one that is immediately referenced to the medium of film, or more precisely, compared to the representation of corpses in the black-and-white Hollywood movies of the 1940s.[16] The second-person narrator, speaking to the focalizing ghost protagonist, tells of the changes regarding perception in the "reality of the dead." Although the dead man is still capable of hearing, everything seems to him – in another film reference – like a "muffled soundtrack," the "soundtrack of being dead" (108). In order to compensate for this, he has developed a new sense, a synesthetic mixture of seeing and feeling that something is sucking at his eyes. Next, an invisible force steers him to the entertainment media and electronics department in the Karstadt department store, which seems a natural place to go for the dead man.[17]

But, strangely enough, he is no longer able to recognize the pictures and colors on the screens of the store's television sets. Instead, standing before a wall of television sets, he only sees something white pouring out of them, a kind of "electronic" "media milk." In the department store, the dead man then meets another dead man, with a black-and-white "dead body," but with a still "sharp" silhouette. This man is the famous German boxer Gustav "Bubi" Scholz (1930–2000), who proceeds to tell the protagonist all about life after death. He especially warns him about "Gertraud the cruel," a retired history teacher and hobby radio spiritualist who is trying to reach her dead brother through "slant-eyed technology," in particular a new Sony long-wave radio (an obvious reference to the role of media in Japanese ghost movies). When Scholz concludes that "Gertraud is a great medium. In radiophonic mnemonics nobody is better" (112),[18] he explicitly connects the ancient technique of mnemonics with new media, especially with broadcasting media. Therefore, from a ghost's perspective, spiritualism is equaled to memory work.

The most important aspects for the dead are the so-called "mnemotones." These are the particles forming the electronic milk that pours out of television sets and other media apparatuses and feeds the dead until they disappear into the final emptiness to become "whirls of snowflakes in the magnetic blizzard of oblivion" (117).[19] As long as people remember the dead, they have a ghostly existence, a filmic black-and-white afterlife. In contrast to most of the ghosts in the history of Gothic literature, these ghosts theoretically are free to go wherever they want, but de facto they rely on the media and have to be near newspapers, radios, telephones, or television sets to be fed with mnemotones, for they consist only of condensed memory. The last stage of being dead is logically to be transformed into white noise, the entropic lack of any recognizable information. Thus, the currency of the afterlife, in the shape of electronic mnemotones, is remembrance and attention, and the dead act more or less like junkies in the neighborhood of the media that conserve and produce this memorial energy.

What is life after death according to Klein? It is definitely and literally a media or, more precisely, a television existence, for like a television broadcast, it is a non-life totally dictated by the categories of attention and memory. When nobody can remember the dead anymore, they diffuse. But this ending in forgetfulness is regarded ambiguously by the narrator. Although the dead crave attention and remembrance exactly like the living (especially when they appear in the media), being forgotten is the only way for a merciful final ending. The narrator realizes that salvation does not lie in the nexus of media and memory, but in its opposite: in the complete forgetfulness that may be achieved by the destruction of all media. So, the narrator remarks, if there is any mercy to be found for the dead with regard to media, it is in their transitoriness. Even if celluloid should prove resistant or if memory should somehow be stored on silicon crystals in a computer, there is always the possibility that a catastrophe would destroy all media and therefore all memory of the dead. The narrator then closes the story with the statement that "nothing is cursed with eternal remembrance" (117–118)[20] and that the "moderate mnemotone-flow of our contemporary civilization," the milk of being remembered by others – or as it is formulated in the text, "being memorized" – offers the solace that "we," the focalized protagonist, and perhaps the narrator and the reader, might meet again as dead beings (118).[21]

Despite conjuring up images of a total destruction of all media and therefore of all memory and all ghosts, the narrator seems to end the story in a conciliatory tone, envisioning a possibility of "meeting again," of everyone – "we" – effortlessly communicating with each other, as on Pentecost or in the revelatory sense of the Apocalypse. Although spiritualism is exposed as, at best, disturbing to ghosts and regarded usable only as a self-serving form of memory work, conveying false images of order, sense, and justice in the world, but not as a real means of communication with the dead, in the end the narrator alludes to the possibility of actual contact. However, in contrast to ghost stories in the Gothic tradition, which are about communication between the living and the dead, in "Unsere lieben Toten" such communication is clearly reserved for ghosts, since it is only possible in death.

Austria's National Apocalypse

At a certain point, the narrator of Klein's story makes the small and very general remark that even the former history teacher and hobby radio spiritualist Gertraud has understood – "after forty years of service in school" – that there is no real exchange possible between "history and the minds of the living." There could be "no massacre so big and important" that it would establish a communication that "could do any justice to the dead" (117).[22] Although it is not expressed explicitly, this comment alludes to the Holocaust in National Socialist Germany and to the topos of its incomparability. But besides mentioning Gertraud's spiritualist attempts to contact her lost brother, who probably died being run over by a Russian tank in World War II, the story does not elaborate on this. The only function of the allusion seems to be to stress the story's point of a general impossibility to establish any real communication – with the help of electronic media or not – between the dead and the living. Trying to speak with the dead, as the story according to its subtitle performatively attempts, seems to be more of a memory practice than the initiation of a two-way communication. Even the point of view in Klein's story is occupied by a second-person narrator and not the focalizing ghost. As a result, the reader is unable to gain any real insight into the dead character. The story thus denies any chance of a "weak messianic power"[23] to redeem the loss of historical possibilities. People remembering the victims of the Holocaust only do this for themselves, not for the dead. There seems to be no possibility of a "Bewältigung der Vergangenheit," of getting over the past (117).

While in Klein's text the memory of the Holocaust is limited to a single and rather indistinct remark, it can be considered one of the main topics in Elfriede Jelinek's 1995 ghost novel *Die Kinder der Toten* (*The Children of the Dead*).[24] The novel deals specifically with Austria's repressed National Socialist past, which is continuously hinted at through allusions to masses of dead and their hair (394), tattoos with numbers (494), ovens and "burning chambers" (640), and the idea that the ground of Austria literally consists of dead people. The polyphonic language of the novel also tries to give the dead a voice, as the main protagonists, whose lives are more or less traced in the novel, are ghosts. These are Gudrun Bicherl, a former student of the humanities who slit her wrists, Edgar Gstranz, a James-Dean-like skier who was killed in a car accident, and Karin Frenzel, a widow who fell to her death in a mountain gorge. The eternal repetition that is one of the signatures of traditional Gothic ghosts has changed, since the fate of the three is to be resurrected in different identities and then to die all over again. The result of this reincarnation cycle is that the dead progressively lose the memories of their former lives. Like Sigmund Freud's model of memory, the "mystic writing-pad,"[25] all superficial memory is erased in the next phase of their ghostly existences. Only some very intense or traumatic experiences still leave traces. In the case of the three ghosts, these are the fragmented and horrific details of their deaths. Edgar, for example, is not able to remember his car accident but has a vague recollection of the smell of gas and burned flesh (43).[26]

Jelinek's unique mode of writing novels is similar at least in its basic approach to Klein's: she takes a literary genre or fragments of several genres and deforms them by using her own idiosyncratic, allusive, and always polyphonic language. This strategy is usually used to lay bare the mechanisms of violence and violent speech acts, and to show the superficiality of language in popular culture, advertising, and media in general. In the case of *Die Kinder der Toten*, however, it is not the ghost novel that is to be subverted in this way; instead, it becomes Jelinek's means. She uses the peculiar perspective of the ghost novel and numerous references to horror literature and zombie movies to deform another popular genre in Germany and Austria, namely the *Heimatroman*. This Heimat novel is a type of trivial and kitschy regional novel celebrating the beauty of nature as well as the happiness and simplicity of the people living in the Bavarian or Austrian Alps. Contrasting with the super-idyllic harmony normally conveyed by these novels is not only the horrific content of *Die Kinder der Toten* but also its language, for everything in the sentences and paragraphs is meshed together and out of joint, producing, to put it briefly, a "Gothicization" of the *Heimatroman*: an exposition of this genre's, and the homeland's, horrors.

One important aspect of the novel is the role of nature. The landscape in *Die Kinder der Toten* draws clearly upon the literary conventions of the pastoral with its "fine air, deep woods … beautiful mountains … streams, a clear river" (7–9).[27] But nature as an idyll is, as the novel conveys, always a construct of the tourism industry. It is a cultural product that has to be "compared to a guidebook" and is always in danger of not being "in the right place" in the registers of the bureaucracy (82). In answer to these requirements, nature is also a destructive force defending itself against culture's exploits, causing, for example, a massive landslide at the end of the novel. Earlier, it also manifests as a hellish landscape displaying horrific sights. One example of this is a reference to Hugo von Hofmannsthal's famous description of the failing "ability to use words" in his *The Lord Chandos Letter* (1902) with the narrator's thoughts disintegrating like "rotten mushrooms" in his mouth: "There are faces waking up under Edgar's feet, more and more faces growing out of the grass like rotten mushrooms blown up …" (198).[28] With this allusion, Jelinek self-referentially shows that the horrific diegetic landscape in her Gothic *Heimatroman* is literally the textual landscape of the Gothic language she employs, and that it is also the only proper way to describe her home country.

The fact that ghosts wander freely through the beautiful Austrian landscape and that bloody death is an integral part of nature in *Die Kinder der Toten* hints at a crucial passage in one of the paradigmatic texts of the English Romantic movement: William Wordsworth's epic *The Prelude*.[29] Verses 538 to 563 revolve around the narration of an eight-year-old boy who presumes that somebody has drowned in a calm lake because nothing can be seen except some clothes on the lake's shore. The next day people search for a swimmer with grappling irons and poles. Suddenly and "'mid that beauteous scene / Of trees and hills and water" the dead man bolts right up, disturbing the lake's surface and showing his "ghastly face, a spectre shape – / Of terror even," thereby destroying the bucolic idyll "of trees and hills and water." This scene can be considered an allegory of reading a Gothic or horror novel. It references the sudden, violent, and horrific disturbance of a text that is otherwise characterized by its smooth and calm surface.[30] Significantly, this more or less autobiographical text by Wordsworth is mentioned in Paul de Man's essay "Autobiography as De-Facement," which chiefly discusses the rhetorical trope of prosopopoeia, meaning

the fiction of an apostrophe to an absent, deceased, or voiceless entity, which posits the possibility of the latter's reply and confers upon it the power of speech. Voice assumes mouth, eye, and finally face, a chain that is manifest in the etymology of the trope's name, *prosopon poien*, to confer a mask or face (*prosopon*).[31]

Prosopopoeia is the central trope of the autobiographical genre and shows that rhetorical figurality is opposed to a literal reading of literature. According to de Man it can be regarded as "the very figure of the reader and of reading" or even "the master trope of poetic discourse."[32] Colin Davis concludes that for de Man "the speech of the dead is fiction"[33] and by "imposing a fiction of agency," the "prosopopoeia defaces the dead at the very moment it gives them face" (79). It is the reader's task to succumb to the fiction that the dead may speak.

The ghost is, of course, a very literal incarnation of prosopopoeia. In Jelinek's Gothic take on the *Heimatroman* the ghost can be read as the voice, the face, and the defacement of "Austria," exposing it as the land of the dead. Regarding the genre of the ghost novel, *Die Kinder der Toten* signifies an end to its traditional notion of memory, spawning a new kind of ghost that allegorically represents the repressed and traumatic past of a whole country or nation. Conspicuously, the pagination of *Die Kinder der Toten* goes up to 666, with the last page left unnumbered. This obviously refers to the "number of the beast" in the Book of Revelations and therefore hints at the advent of the Antichrist during the apocalypse. This apocalypse actually occurs at the end of the novel in the shape of a massive landslide ("Vermurung") that literally buries everyone in the Austrian valley under mountains of rubble, effectively killing them all.[34] But the climactic catastrophe is not to be read as an apocalypse in the biblical sense. Rather, it is a "profane apocalypse," as coined by James McFarland for the diegetic world of George Romero's 1978 zombie movie *Dawn of the Dead*.[35] There is no soteriological component to this apocalypse, no promise of salvation.

Instead, the dead already walk the earth, side by side with the living, with the ghosts in *Die Kinder der Toten* manifesting the meaninglessness of a constant present time in an Austria that has forgotten or repressed its past. Complementing this, the haunted Austria in the novel is also characterized by a non-stop flow of meaningless words and information, for example, in mass media, especially in the shape of the *Musikantenstadl*, a program for older people broadcast by the television stations ZDF and ORF, featuring trivial and kitschy music that is associated with Bavaria and Austria. Television is also compared to a "musty oven" that "swallows a few hundred people without any effort" (606),[36] which is another allusion to concentration camps and effectively equals the state of watching television with falling victim to genocide. In a way, therefore, Judgment Day is already present, but it suppresses any possibility of real salvation. There is no place for memory in an eternal apocalypse either, for there is no past. Memory work is supplanted by an eternal cycle of un-life. Finally, after the landslide-apocalypse and especially after the complete burial of the Pension Alpenrose hotel under mountain rubble, which echoes the original story of mnemonics, there is no Simonides of Ceos available to remember the places of the dead in order to identify them. Instead, there is a "Nachrichtensperre" (665), a news embargo ordered by officials.

Even in the face of an apocalyptic catastrophe, which strikingly leads back to the origin of mnemonics, any chance of memory is denied. The victims stay unrecognized, not to be reintegrated in an ordered world of signification, which hints at the fact that there was no structured cosmos of signs and referents to begin with. This, in addition to the repression of the past and the lack of any possibility for a change in the future, can be called the "end of history" or the "end of discourse," a "limited" "eschatology" as Derrida puts it in *Specters of Marx*, but without the ghost only appearing "after the end of history."[37] Here, they are present all the time. The political theological term for this state of frozen time is *posthistoire*. According to Hannes Böhringer, the *posthistoric* is related to the concept of the *katechon*, a device or state of society that hinders the arrival of the apocalypse.[38] It is interpreted by Carl Schmitt as the "historical power to restrain the appearance of the Antichrist."[39] The main feature of the *katechon* is that nothing is allowed to change or develop. Consequently, this state can be regarded as an ongoing apocalyptic catastrophe, albeit a profane one, since it offers no hope of an ending or final salvation. Ghosts are the natural inhabitants of the *posthistoire,* for they are the very incarnation of unchangeability.

Thus, the ghosts in Klein and Jelinek are not revenants in the traditional sense, coming back from the dead to haunt the living and certain places with a purpose in mind, as in *Hamlet*, *The Castle of Otranto*, or *The Haunting of Hill House*. They do not signify a personal event of the past, such as an unfulfilled quest or an undiscovered crime in their former lives. Because no place is meaningful to them, they are not confined to a specific location. Ghosts in this type of neo-Gothic literature do not keep any secrets so there is nothing to be deciphered by the living; or – to put it in a more general way – these ghosts have nothing to say to the living. Communication, in Klein's story as well as Jelinek's novel, takes place between ghosts only. These neo-Gothic narratives even change their points of view from the living to the dead or at least present ghosts as focalizing characters. Moreover, in comparison with the *method of loci* in ancient and medieval mnemonics and under the influence of new media and their uncanny technical storage capabilities, the function of the ghost as a sign for the necessity of memory has shifted. The ghost has become an extra, or ornament, in a diegetic world that already has all the trappings of the afterlife, be it hell, a black-and-white intermediate zone dependent on "mnemotones," or some kind of apocalyptic, posthistoric limbo. At best, ghosts survive as self-referential elements of an "allegory of reading," revealing the ghost novel itself as an unchangeable and dead piece of memory, a corpse that only comes alive as a ghost in the process of reading.

NOTES

1   "Inszenierung für das Ende der Geschichte." Jacques Derrida, *Marx' Gespenster: Der verschuldete Staat, die Trauerarbeit und die neue Internationale*, transl. Susanne Lüdemann (Frankfurt am Main: Fischer, 1995), 27.

2   Horace Walpole, *The Castle of Otranto*, ed. Michael Gamer (London: Penguin, 2001), 7.

3   Walpole and Beckford gave their Gothic visions a distinctly material shape by building mansions following specific Gothic designs. These are Walpole's Strawberry Hill and Beckford's Fonthill Abbey. See Norbert Miller, *Strawberry Hill: Horace Walpole und die Ästhetik der schönen Unregelmäßigkeit* (München: Hanser, 1986).

4   Shirley Jackson, *The Haunting of Hill House* (London: Penguin, 2006).

5   See Frances A. Yates, *The Art of Memory* (London: Routledge and Kegan Paul, 1966).

6   Kôji Suzuki, *Ring*, trans. R. B. Rohmer and Glynne Walley (New York: Vertical, 2004). See also Denis Meikle, *The Ring Companion* (London: Titan Books, 2005).

7   See Marc Augé, *Non-Places: Introduction to an Anthropology of Supermodernity* (London: Blackwell, 1995).

8   See Plato, *Phaidros. Sämtliche Werke 4* (Reinbek bei Hamburg: Rowohlt, 1958), 54–55. According to the international Stephanus pagination system: Plato, *Phaedrus*, Chapter 59, 274 b 9–275 c 4.

9   John Durham Peters, *Speaking Into the Air: A History of the Idea of Communication* (Chicago and London: University of Chicago Press, 2000), 75. See also Wolfgang Hagen, "Der Okkultismus der Avantgarde um 1900," in *Konfigurationen: Zwischen Kunst und Medien*, ed. Sigrid Schade and Georg Christoph Tholen (München: Wilhelm Fink, 1999), 338–357; Georges Didi-Huberman, "Superstition," in *Ordnungen der Sichtbarkeit: Fotografie in Wissenschaft, Kunst und Technologie*, ed. Peter Geimer (Frankfurt am Main: Suhrkamp, 2002), 434–440; Erhard Schüttpelz, "'We cannot manifest through the medium.' Der Geisterangriff auf Edward B. Tylor (London 1872) und der transatlantische Spiritismus," *Ästhetik und Kommunikation* 35/127 (2004), 11–22; Sabine Haupt, "Strahlenmagie. Texte des späten 19. und frühen 20. Jahrhunderts zwischen Okkultismus und Sciencefiction. Ein diskursanalytisch-komparatistischer Überblick," in *Gespenster: Erscheinungen – Medien – Theorien*, ed. Moritz Baßler, Bettina Gruber, and Martina Wagner-Egelhaaf (Würzburg: Königshausen & Neumann, 2005), 153–176.

10   See Friedrich Kittler, "Draculas Vermächtnis," in *Draculas Vermächtnis: Technische Schriften* (Leipzig: Reclam, 1993), 11–57.

11   Jules Verne, *Das Karpathenschloß* (Zürich: Diogenes, 1977).

12   Georg Klein, "Unsere lieben Toten. Ein spiritistischer Versuch," in *Von den Deutschen: Erzählungen* (Reinbek bei Hamburg: Rowohlt, 2003), 106–118.

13   Klein's novel *Libidissi* (1998) is a take on the spy novel, the novel *Barbar Rosa* (2001) has "detective story" as its subtitle, and *Die Sonne scheint uns* (2004) has all the trappings of a horror novel, with its protagonists allegorically exploring the horrors of Germany's past in an old, run-down skyscraper.

14   This movie echoes both David Cronenberg's *Videodrome* (1983) and Tobe Hooper and Steven Spielberg's *Poltergeist* (1982).

15   Other examples of the interaction of ghosts and media in film are *The Sixth Sense* (Shyamalan, 1999), *Stir of Echoes* (Koepp, 1999), *Ju-on* (*The Grudge*) (Shimizu, 2000), *The Others* (Amenábar, 2001), *White Noise* (Sax, 2005), *Nos Miran* (*They're Watching Us*) (López Amado, 2002), and *El Orfanato* (*The Orphanage*) (Bayona, 2008).

16   "In älteren Hollywood-Filmen, in Schwarzweißproduktionen aus den vierziger Jahren des vorigen Jahrhunderts, wurden die Toten so dargestellt, wie Sie jetzt aussehen: fast wie im Leben, die normale Statur, komplett bekleidet, allerdings farblos, in fein abgestuften Grautönen schimmernd, als wäre Ihre Totengestalt durch einen weichzeichnenden Filter gelaufen. Und so gilt Ihr erstes Staunen im anderen Zustand der Erkenntnis, wie gut die amerikanische Unterhaltungsindustrie damals, mitten im Zweiten Weltkrieg, die Wirklichkeit der Toten getroffen hat" (107).

17   This may be another filmic reference, in this case to George Romero's zombie film *Dawn of the Dead* (1978), which takes place in a shopping mall.

18   "Gertraud ist ein großes Medium. In der radiophonen Mnemotechnik macht ihr keiner etwas vor."

19   "Flockenwirbel im magnetischen Schneesturm des Vergessens."

20   "Nichts ist zu ewigem Gedenken verflucht."

21   Klein conspicuously uses the uncommon and stronger word "Memorieren" where the more common "Erinnern" ("remembering") would suffice: "Und was den mäßigen Mnemotonenfluß unserer gegenwärtigen Zivilisation angeht, sollte es Ihnen und mir – im Ernst! – ein gewisser Trost sein, daß wir uns in der kurzen Spanne, in der noch die Milch fremden Memorierens zu uns strömt, als Tote wiedersehen könnten."

22   "Als ehemalige Geschichtslehrerin, nach vierzig Jahren Schuldienst, hat sie verstanden, daß man sich seine Toten nicht ausleihen kann – den einzelnen nicht und keine Millionen. So groß und bedeutsam ist kein Massaker, daß zwischen den Vorstellungsvermögen der lebenden Hirne und der Historie ein Austausch zustande käme, der den Toten Gerechtigkeit widerfahren ließe."

23   See Walter Benjamin, "Über den Begriff der Geschichte," in *Walter Benjamin: Ein Lesebuch*, ed. Michael Opitz (Frankfurt am Main: Suhrkamp, 1996), 665–676.

24   Elfriede Jelinek, *Die Kinder der Toten* (Reinbek bei Hamburg: Rowohlt, 1995).

25   Sigmund Freud, "A Note upon the 'Mystic Writing-Pad' (1925)," in *The Ego and the Id and Other Works (SE Vol. XIX)*, ed. James Strachey (London: The Hogarth Press and the Institute of Psychoanalysis, 1961), 225–232.

26   On the subject of car crashes and other traffic accidents in Jelinek's novels, see Claudia Lieb, *Crash. Der Unfall der Moderne* (Bielefeld: Aisthesis, 2009).

27   "Dafür gute Luft und tiefe Wälder. Und schöne Berge, die etwa um die zweitausend Meter hoch sind … Bäche, ein klarer Fluß …"

28   "Doch da sind Gesichter, die unter Edgars Fußbreite aufwachen, immer mehr Gesichter, die aus dem Gras herauswachsen wie modrige Pilze, die sich aufgeblasen haben, schon fährt Edgar über ihre Engelssamen." This allusion was previously noted by Roland Innerhofer, "'Da tauchen Menschen auf und verschwinden wieder.' Horrorszenarien in

Elfriede Jelineks Roman *Die Kinder der Toten*," in *Horror und Ästhetik*, ed. Claudio Biedermann and Christian Stiegler (Konstanz: UVK, 2008), 86–101.

29 William Wordsworth, *The Five-Book Prelude*, ed. Duncan Wu (Cambridge: Wiley Blackwell, 1997), 127–128.

30 Cynthia Chase, "The Accidents of Disfiguration: Limits to Literal and Figurative Reading of Wordsworth's Books," in *Decomposing Figures: Rhetorical Readings in the Romantic Tradition* (Baltimore and London: Johns Hopkins University Press, 1986), 13–31.

31 Paul de Man, "Autobiography as Defacement," in *The Rhetoric of Romanticism* (New York: Columbia University Press, 1984), 75–76.

32 Paul de Man, *The Resistance to Theory* (Manchester: Manchester University Press, 1986), 45, 48.

33 Colin Davis, "Can the Dead Speak to Us? De Man, Levinas and Agamben," *Culture, Theory & Critique* 45, no. 1 (2004): 78.

34 "Die Pension Alpenrose im sogenannten Tyrol/Stmk.... wurde mitsamt allen Menschen, Tieren und Personal, die sich in der Fremdenpension aufgehalten hatten, von einer Vermurung, welche aus der Grabenenge eines verlegten Wildbachs ausgebrochen war, zuerst aufgehoben, dann ein Stück weggeschoben und schließlich verpackt und zugeschüttet" (663).

35 See James McFarland, "Profane Apokalypse. George A. Romeros Dawn of the Dead," in *Splatter Movies: Essays zum modernen Horrorfilm*, ed. Julia Köhne, Ralph Kuschke, and Arno Meteling (Berlin: Bertz & Fischer, 2006), 29–46.

36 "... sie hätten das alles vielleicht im muffeligen Ofen des Fernsehens gezeigt ... der pro Sekunde ein paar hundert Personen mühelos verschlingen kann."

37 Derrida, *Marx' Gespenster*, 27–28.

38 Hannes Böhringer, "Die Ruine in der Posthistoire," in *Begriffsfelder: Von der Philosophie zur Kunst* (Berlin: Merve, 1985), 25.

39 Carl Schmitt, *The Nomos of the Earth in the International Law of the Jus Publicum Europaeum* (New York: Telos, 2003), 59–60.

Chapter 15

Haunted Habitability: Wilderness and American Haunted House Narratives

Christine Wilson

When Shirley Jackson published *The Haunting of Hill House* in 1959, she drew on a long tradition of haunted house narratives.[1] More importantly, she introduced a variation to the traditional haunted house – the sentient, animated, malign house – that would influence the genre for the next fifty years. Poe's "The Fall of the House of Usher" is creepy, and Hawthorne's *The House of the Seven Gables* is haunted, but Jackson's Hill House is alive. Starting with Jackson, narratives in which houses constitute a major character began appearing more frequently. Ghosts occasionally materialize in these textual and filmic narratives, but the house itself is the primary source of action. Haunted house texts thus began to express explicitly spatial anxieties. Critics frequently interpret horror narratives along the same line, arguing that they expose cultural concerns and subvert dominant paradigms.[2] Dale Bailey, in *American Nightmares: The Haunted House Formula in Popular American Fiction*, writes that stories about haunted houses "present deeply subversive critiques of all that we hold to be true – about class, about race, about gender, about American history itself."[3] I want to add space to that list. Judith Richardson, in *Possessions: The History and Uses of Haunting in the Hudson Valley*, acknowledges the spatial element of haunting when she says, "Varied and ambivalent, hauntings represent problems, foregrounded in this [Hudson Valley] region, regarding possession and dispossession, rootedness and restlessness."[4] Nearly all haunted house narratives focus on how inhabitants try to make their space livable, whether that involves exorcizing demons, changing the atmosphere through Feng Shui, or documenting strange happenings. At the most basic level, haunted house stories explore the relationship between subjects and their home space.

What is more surprising is that these stories' spatial concerns dovetail with those of environmental scholars, including ecocritics and nature writers. Ecocriticism developed in the early 1990s as a distinct school of criticism that analyzes the relationship between literature and the environment. Ecocritics, like race and feminists critics before them, have explicitly political goals. They hope that the study of the environment in the field of literature will help address the environmental crisis. Post-Jackson, some haunted house texts figure the house as a wilderness space that must be made habitable. Depicting homes as wilderness spaces links haunted house narratives to the contemporary environmental schools of thought that propose that one solution to the current environmental crisis is a closer subject–space connection or, as Lawrence Buell calls it, an increased *place attachment*.[5]

I do not read haunted house narratives as a critique of the American Dream, per se. Instead, they represent a broader exploration of how the subject relates, and should relate, to space, particularly space that does not conform to the subject's desires and expectations. Richardson points out the intersections of popular texts about haunting and the preservation and conservation movements of the early twentieth century, saying that ghosts are "put ... to tangible social use" (175). In the same vein, contemporary haunted house narratives, which are almost always categorized as part of popular culture, challenge the subject–space ideals, such as a close personal connection and a positive affective relationship, that ecocritics venerate.[6] Instead, these texts suggest that an ethical subject–space relationship necessitates a much more distant approach.

It is no coincidence that the promulgation of animated haunted house stories coincides with the time that wilderness preservation efforts reached their zenith. Post-World War II, Americans visited national parks in droves, and environmentalists were increasingly effective at protecting natural space. More importantly, a fully-fledged "philosophy of the value of wilderness" had emerged.[7] Americans view(ed) wilderness space as a much-needed respite from restrictive cultural norms and acted accordingly to preserve what was viewed as an important resource. Stories in which the house itself figures as a natural space tap into this wilderness ethic, while at the same time capitalizing on the profound ambivalence toward this space that historically pervades the cultural imagination.[8]

Wilderness, of course, is a problematic term, loaded with connotations and ambiguities. In *Wilderness and the American Mind*, Roderick Nash argues that it can be considered a "state of mind" but prefers to think about the environment as a spectrum "ranging from the purely wild on the one end to the purely civilized on the other – from the primeval to the paved" (6). Though the terms of this spectrum may be fluid, it almost goes without saying that generally houses do not fall on the wilderness end. But we need not take wilderness quite so literally. The definition that I find most useful dates to 1340 and incorporates not just the space in question, but also the subject–space relationship: "Something figured as a region of a wild or desolate character, or in which one wanders or loses one's way."[9] While wilderness retains its spatial aspects, this definition adds the perspective of the subject by emphasizing that it is a space "figured" as "wild and desolate." Haunted house narratives typically do not propose that the house is a literal wilderness, but they most certainly imagine them as spaces of animation, unruliness, and often desolation. In fact, one of the reasons that Hill House and its descendents are so frightening is because they are unnaturally natural. They defy the boundaries between domestic and natural space, the wild and the domesticated, subject and object, and the animate and inanimate. They are, as Jackson so memorably says, "born," not made (70).

Mark Z. Danielewski's *House of Leaves* exemplifies the wilderness aspect of haunted houses.[10] It would be an understatement to say that *House of Leaves* is not your garden-variety haunted house story, since it is far more complex, structurally and thematically, than the other texts I discuss. Its literary complexity removes it, generally, from being classified as a popular horror novel. N. Katherine Hayles introduces the novel in her essay "Saving the Subject: Remediation in *House of Leaves*": "Camouflaged as a haunted house tale, *House of Leaves* is a metaphysical inquiry worlds away from the likes of *The Amityville Horror*."[11] I cannot disagree entirely with Hayles. Instead of following the traditional haunted house formula, this book is a frame narrative composed by Johnny Truant on Will Navidson's (fictional) documentary, *The Navidson Record*, about his "haunted" house. Truant compiles *House of Leaves* from notes and fragments written by the dead man Zampano. Complete with footnotes from real and imaginary scholars, as well as spatial malformations and fluctuations, it is safe to say that this novel defies conventional interpretation.

Camouflage or not, the haunted house aspect of the novel should not be neglected – clearly space, and its various ramifications, is an important thematic and structural element. Furthermore, Danielewski engages in many of the generic tendencies of other haunted house texts, especially within the Navidson portion. Will Navidson, Karen Green, and their two children move into a new house, hoping that it will provide a fresh beginning for them. Shortly after they begin to settle in, though, the house starts exhibiting strange spatial tendencies: a large black closet, which later morphs into a gargantuan ever-changing labyrinth, appears; the inside of the house measures larger than the outside. After the initial appearance of the closet, Navidson exposes the text's figuration of the haunted house as wilderness space when he organizes an "expedition" to explore it. The people he summons to take part in the exploration are all literal wilderness explorers. The leader of the team, Holloway Roberts, is a "professional hunter and explorer," and his two companions, Jed Leeder and Wax Hook, are mountain climbers and guides (80–81). Navidson's choice of companions reveals the true nature of the house. It is more akin to Mount McKinley than a house; thus, it should be explored by people who are accustomed to the great outdoors.

The description of the closet/hallway/labyrinth confirms the idea that the house is actually a wilderness. For example, when Hook peers down the staircase that appears in the hallway and says, "It's so deep, man, it's like it's almost dream like," the narrator continues, "The last comment is actually not uncommon, especially for individuals who find themselves confronting vast tenebrific spaces" (85). As a living wilderness space, the closet/hallway morphs and shifts throughout the novel. It is impossible for the reader (and the inhabitants for that matter) to ascertain the actual nature of the house because it is under constant interpretation by Navidson, the explorers, and the frame narrator(s). It is, in the words of the definition of "wilderness," a place "in which one wanders or loses one's way." As if to emphasize the connection between the house and wilderness, the frame narrator, Johnny Truant, fixates on Holloway Robert's statement that they got lost in the house: "What did Holloway mean by 'lost'? How could anyone be lost in a house for days anyway?" (6). The reason Holloway can get lost "in a house" is, of course, because it is not an ordinary house at all.

Stephen King's television series *Rose Red* (ABC, 2002) and Robert Marasco's novel *Burnt Offerings* link haunted houses to wilderness less explicitly.[12] Nevertheless, the connection appears via the texts' insistence that the houses are organic, growing entities. Rose Red expands through its own volition, long after it has been abandoned, as illustrated by two slides of the house in which the current photo shows a much larger version of the sprawling estate. Like the House of Leaves, Rose Red also enlarges internally in inexplicable ways. The house in *Burnt Offerings* regenerates as the inhabitants of the house commit acts of violence against one another. Because these texts consistently use the trope of the house as wilderness, the question becomes: What do these texts have to say about the problem of wilderness?

On the one hand, the hostility these texts portray toward wilderness spaces rivals that of early American pioneers, who believed that wild spaces were liable to produce immorality in its inhabitants.[13] The fear that the wildness of haunted houses will provoke people to act wildly manifests when characters eschew their emotional attachments in favor of physical violence and promiscuity. In *The Haunting of Hill House*, Eleanor's actions become increasingly erratic, ending in her violent suicide. In *House of Leaves*, various characters become crazy, but most notably Roberts shoots one his fellow explorers in a fit of paranoia. Anne River Siddons, in *The House Next Door*, uses the same trope when each of the subjects living in the "house next door" engages in extramarital, non-normative sexual relations, all supposedly under the influence of the malign house.[14] In *Rose Red*, Ellen Rimbauer's behavior becomes more and more unstable as her alignment with her house grows. Likewise, in *Burnt Offerings* Marian eschews her husband and son in favor of her burgeoning bond with the house. Not surprisingly, then, many of the inhabitants (and readers) despise and fear these wild houses. However, surprising affection for these houses balances the pioneer-like antipathy. Note in the above examples that part of what inspires violence is an affective, intuitive connection with the house in question. Eleanor's suicide is at least partially inspired by her desire to be eternally part of the house. The attachment these heroines feel for their domestic space constitutes the most important link to, and critique of, ecological scholarship's concept of place attachment.

Within this type of diegesis, inhabitants' attempts to make their houses livable are more important than discovering the source of the haunting. What these narratives are really about is how to make wilderness space into home space. It bears mentioning that inhabitants who are unsuccessful at creating a livable space for themselves fail because they try to domesticate wilderness. Karen Green, in *House of Leaves*, takes up Feng Shui shortly after the large black closet appears. Kathy Lutz, in *Amityville*

Horror, covers the shelves with contact paper and scrubs the toilets when black tar fills them. The houses interpret these attempts at homemaking as domineering and react accordingly. Instead of responding to Feng Shui as a domestic space should, and exuding harmonious energy, the House of Leaves literally eats Karen's Feng Shui objects. The Amityville House simply refuses to respond to Kathy. These seemingly mundane moving-in rituals affirm the dual nature of haunted houses, but more importantly, they call into question the ethics of creating habitability in wilderness spaces. When domestication refers to domestic space, it indicates the process of making a home, but when it involves natural space, domestication is rife with negative connotations. Scholars often associate it with imperialism, colonialism, and environmental degradation.[15] When natural space is domesticated, it undergoes drastic transformation in the name of making it safe for domesticators. While such domesticators think they are simply making a home for themselves, they do so at the expense of the natural features of the land, not to mention its human and non-human inhabitants. In the case of haunted houses, both definitions of domestication apply.

Further, the deployment of domestication in an attempt to settle unruly houses exposes the gender implications of haunted house texts. It is no coincidence that females in these texts try to use traditional housekeeping tasks to subdue the houses, while the males try to conquer the house through exploratory tactics. At first glance, haunted house narratives seem to affirm the traditional association of women with domestic spaces and men with wilderness spaces. Lorraine Anderson and Vera Norwood explain that, historically, women did not have access to wilderness spaces, and thus women's writing about natural spaces tended to center on the home.[16] Within the framework of haunted house stories, women are confronted with wilderness spaces at home, and their impulse to handle this kind of space with contact paper and interior decorating seems to confirm the stereotype that women are unsuited for wilderness spaces. Furthermore, haunted houses enact a tyranny of domesticity, insofar as they present domestic spaces that require never-ending caretaking, from women, just to maintain the barest amount of livability. The black tar in the toilet will always need cleaning, and the Feng Shui objects will always have to be replaced. The houses of these narratives will never acquiesce to becoming passive spaces. Traditionally masculine modes of domestication are no more effective, however. In *House of Leaves* Roberts tries to domesticate the house. He explains:

> We're taking pictures. We're collecting samples. We're trying to reach the bottom of the stairs. Who knows, if we do that then maybe we'll even discover something before Navidson starts all the hoopla involved with raising money and organizing large scale explorations. (94)

The house rewards Roberts's attempts by driving him mad and then eating him.

The fact that all of these characters are so intensely unsuccessful at their attempts to conquer space brings me to one of the pleasures of haunted house texts – space always wins. Space's victory over the subject's misguided or plain mean-spirited attempts to control it is a welcome antidote to the all-too-real fact that, in daily life, space almost never wins. Strip malls replace wetlands. McMansions spread with alarming speed. Forests fall. Oil drills threaten national wildlife preserves. Even older suburbs are not safe from the development of new condominiums. Natural space is increasingly paved-over and subdued. Yet haunted houses create a space, albeit imaginary, in which space can prevent the subject from large-scale domination.

Haunted house narratives reverse Western industrialized society's hierarchy of space deplored by Henri Lefebvre, who introduces the concept of the spatial triad, a blend of lived, perceived, and conceived space.[17] Lived space is the everyday space of living. It is the house, the office, the corner coffee shop. Perceived space indicates the way humans interact with space on a sensory level. Conceived space, finally, is the way we think about space. The epitome of conceived space is the blueprint – the outline and schemata of what we think lived and perceived space might look like. Lefebvre's primary concern in *The Production of Space* is that the spatial triad is currently imbalanced, so that conceived space receives most of the emphasis at the expense of lived and perceived space. When logic and theory are favored over lived experience, argues Lefebvre, it disadvantages the subjects who are attempting to live their everyday lives.

Haunted houses upend this current imbalance by presenting a lived and perceived space that deliberately and joyously defies conceived space. Navidson of *House of Leaves* spends weeks and uses countless resources trying to ascertain how the inside measurements of his house can be slightly larger than the outside ones. Conceived space simply will not coincide with lived and perceived space: Navidson sees that the room inside is slightly larger than from the outside, a conceptual impossibility. His senses cannot be denied, but they cannot be confirmed cognitively either. For people like Navidson, the haunted house poses an unsolvable problem. Either he is crazy, or his house is haunted, or both. Either way, his space is unlivable. Surprisingly, the space of the haunted house is not unlivable for everyone. Navidson's children, Chad and Daisy, do not find the inconsistent measurements a problem, nor do they look askance at the large closet that mysteriously appears. Instead, they cheerfully play in the new space, "oblivious to the deeper implications" (24). They are not scared because they do not share the adult preoccupation with conceived space. Childish innocence and lack of awareness are not the only paths to a habitable haunted house, though.

What works even better to make haunted houses habitable is to form a place attachment to the house in the vein of Lawrence Buell. Successful inhabitants of haunted houses do not try to change them at all; they identify with the wildness and use it to their own benefit. Buell, often touted as the father of ecocritism, defines place attachment in his most recent book, *The Future of Environmental Criticism*, as the bond that occurs between humans and places. He envisions place attachment spatially as a set of concentric circles, with the home place occupying the center position, and other places (such as work and second homes) lying in the outer circles. Temporally, place attachment accumulates from personal experience and a knowledge of the history of a place. Finally, Buell adds that place attachment can also be produced through the imagination, which allows one to have an attachment to foreign or unfamiliar places. Lest he be accused of thinking of place attachment too narrowly, Buell explains that, in order to be meaningful, place attachment has to be socially recognized. However, despite his claim that "it can't just be 'my' memory place, but also 'ours'" the concept remains fiercely individualistic, with the individual in question at the very center of the circle (76). Recall that place attachment is most intense at the center of the circles – the individual home.

The concept of place attachment is crucial to ecocriticism. Ecocritics invoke it in hopes of "bringing human communities back into a more responsible set of relationships with the earth."[18] Many ecocritics agree that environmental reform necessitates place attachment, and they emphasize and admire place attachment within literary works. In nature writing, place attachment is equated with security and safety, and even self-awareness. The logic is that a personal connection to a particular place will inspire love, respect, and caretaking of a place. The problem with current subject–space relationships, for ecocritics, lies within people's general disconnection from place, which leads to a laissez-faire attitude toward caring or preserving the earth. The wilderness ethic that I alluded to at the beginning of my essay builds upon a foundation of place attachment, reasoning that people will not be inspired to protect wilderness areas in the U.S. if they do not feel connected to them. The solution for environmentalists, then, is to convince and cultivate an affection for wilderness, instead of fear of or disdain for it. In the late 1970s, it finally became clear that the wilderness preservation movement, which had been active for over fifty years, was meeting with some success among the general public. But the anxiety about how to properly respond to wilderness space was far from over.

The problem with wilderness spaces, as haunted houses document, is that they are not particularly habitable. They are wild, they sometimes try to eat inhabitants, and, if nothing else, they are intimidating and potentially overwhelming. None of these things, to put it mildly, are conducive to producing place attachment. Yet, haunted houses often offer portraits of inhabitants who exhibit such a fierce attachment to their home that any ecocritic or nature writer would be envious. And they have this attachment not in spite of, but because of, their houses' wildness. Like Henry David Thoreau, John Muir, Barry Lopez, and Terry Tempest Williams, successful haunted house characters become one with the wilderness of their house. Unlike the idyllic vision ecocritics have of this particular subject–space relationship, however, haunted house narratives portray it as fraught with violence, for subjects and space alike.

Rose Red, its companion text *The Diary of Ellen Rimbauer*, and Marasco's *Burnt Offerings* demonstrate this antagonistic relationship. *Rose Red* aired on ABC as a mini-series in 2002. King purportedly wanted to create the "scariest haunted house" story ever, and while it garnered huge ratings for ABC, he tried to accomplish this goal by compiling elements from previous narratives. In the mini-series, a group of psychics, led by Joyce Reardon, a parapsychologist, spends the weekend at Rose Red, an ever-expanding haunted house. (Jackson's *Haunting of Hill House* is a clear inspiration.) The real-life Sarah Winchester mansion served as a model for the house, and the mini-series spawned a number of spin-offs, including a website for a fictional university and a novel called *The Diary of Ellen Rimbauer*.[19] I focus primarily on the latter because it is this text that depicts Ellen Rimbauer's, the original mistress of the house, uncannily close relationship with her haunted house.

Ellen reacts atypically to Rose Red's impressive string of violence (including the disappearance of eighteen women and the death of five men). Instead of objecting to the tendency of her house to eat her party guests and family members, Ellen becomes friends with the house and, in the process, harnesses some of its powers. Ellen admits that she is beginning to "understand" Rose Red and that she listens to what Rose Red is saying (155). The diary-style novel fixates on the burgeoning relationship between Ellen and her house. An identification with Rose Red is never fully realized, but the boundary between the house and Ellen becomes increasingly blurred. For example, when Ellen describes Rose Red's voice, she says: "A voice I heard utter from my own mouth" (178). In return for Ellen's friendship, Rose Red occasionally eats women who are troublesome to Ellen (e.g. the mistresses of Ellen's husband, John). Instead of running away in horror, Ellen becomes part of the house itself. She resists and resents Rose Red, but never rebels. In 1950, she disappears into the house, consummating their eternal bond to one another. This narrative subverts the hostility between haunted house and inhabitant that dominates most haunted house narratives. Ellen forms a place attachment to her home, and in some ways, experiences a certain amount of happiness as a result. Instead of trying to domesticate space, she revels in its natural qualities. But, as *Burnt Offerings* shows, this subversion of hostility comes at a high price. A less conflicted (though no less problematic) habitability emerges in *Burnt Offerings*. Marian Rolff and her family find a beautiful summer house that they can rent for a few hundred dollars for the whole summer. The house offers them a much-needed respite from their cramped apartment in New York City. The only catch is that three times a day they need to deliver meals to the door of an elderly woman who lives in the house but never leaves her room. Though they both express misgivings about this situation, Marian convinces her husband to rent the house anyway, and they, their young son, and an elderly aunt move into the house for the summer.

Marian, unlike Ellen, feels an immediate connection with the house. Upon first seeing the antique-laden mansion, she muses: "To be able to live with something so beautiful – not own, merely live with, for a month, two months. *God*" (35). While Dale Bailey makes a compelling argument that Marian's enthusiasm results from domestic greed (73), her sentiment about the house is more aptly described as awe. She does not want to own or even change the house; she just wants to appreciate and nurture it back to life. Like the ideal ecocritical spatial dweller, she values and respects its space. Quickly, the house rewards her with an intense experience of inner peace and security. Marian discovers the central room in the house, from which a mysterious hum emanates. It becomes her "sanctuary," her "grace," and her access to complete "peace and isolation" (214, 190, 150). Marian's intensely close connection to the house is clearly spiritual, if not religious. Marian finds the house habitable because, for her, the house offers all that it promises – physical, emotional, and psychological safety. She happily merges with the house. It enriches her everyday life, and she finds complete satisfaction in the daily domestic rituals of dusting, cleaning, and arranging. Through Marian, the house literally comes to life and, in turn, through the house, Marian figuratively comes to life. Before she came there, she was unhappy, uncomfortable, and dissatisfied with her life. But in the house, she is at home in every sense of the word. There, the reader is told, she manifests her "true" and "essential" self. Eventually, she so integrates with the house that she becomes part of its life force. She accomplishes this feat through a rather strange process of sitting in a special chair: "She clutched the arms of the chair and felt the force of the hum not outside herself but in her, issuing forth and driving itself into the house and grounds, all the way down to the smallest bits of crystal, the tenderest green shoot" (259). Marian's unification with the house evokes the idea that the difference between self and (natural) space has dissolved, a prominent trope in some types of nature writing. Dana Phillips, for example, claims that contemporary writing is commonly thought of as "a nonfiction prose essay describing a first-person narrator's efforts to establish an intensely felt emotional connection with the natural world."[20] He further describes (and critiques) this connection as an "epiphany" in which the self and that which is outside the self "are experienced as one thing" (202).

So far, there seems to be nothing wrong with Marian's relationship with the house, nor does it seem haunted. And this is precisely the point – from Marian's point of view, the situation is fully amenable. *Burnt Offerings* provides the strongest critique of the individualism that dominates ecocritical concepts of sense of place (remember Buell's insistence that the center of place attachment is the individual home). What is wrong with her place attachment is that it fully depends upon violence toward the other inhabitants of the home. Marian takes responsibility for the reinvigoration of the house, continually saying, "[the house] was alive, all around her it was alive, and how else had it come but through her?" (214). The actual source of life in the house, however, is much more sinister. True, the house regenerates itself. The old shingles are shed and shiny, new ones appear in their place, the sidewalk by the pool heals its cracks and fissures, and the greenhouse fills itself with elaborate blossoms. The source of these seemingly miraculous repairs, the reader knows, is the misfortune, pain, and even death of the other inhabitants of the house. For example, the walkways around the pool are refurbished only after Marian's husband, Ben, inexplicably almost drowns their son David in the pool during a session of roughhousing gone awry. The greenhouse explodes into blooms after Elizabeth, the elderly but healthy aunt, dies of unknown causes. In other words, just like the other haunted houses, this one feeds off the pain and misery of the inhabitants. Marian's awareness of this parasitism, coupled with her denial of the implications, perverts Buell's place attachment by presenting an intensely solipsistic version of it.

For the female characters in *Rose Red*, *The Diary of Ellen Rimbauer*, and *Burnt Offerings*, haunted houses act as a wilderness space that is much more akin to the relationship between women and space that Stacy Alaimo describes. She explains that women writers often appealed to nature "as a space apart from the domestic" that can function as a "model for female insurgency."[21] Within natural space, then, women can find freedom from cultural constraints, particularly domestic ones.

While that is true, to a degree, for both Ellen and Marian, this freedom comes at a much too high ethical price.

Clearly, ecocritics oppose violence and would decry a place attachment that pitted individuals against one another or allowed one group to so thoroughly dominate another. Or would they? One of the things that haunted house narratives do is bring out (through exaggeration) the real problems with the subject–space relationship. The key issue that underlies the haunted-ness of haunted houses, and that also implicitly undergirds place attachment, is possession. Haunted house narratives show that possession is always troubled by what, or who, came before. This preoccupation with history and rightful possession forecloses the possibility of ever truly possessing the space in the present.

Characters in haunted house narratives show an obsession with possession. Anne River Siddons unintentionally illustrates this preoccupation when she explains why haunted houses resonate particularly with women:

> The haunted house has always spoken specially and directly to me as the emblem of particular horror. Maybe it's because, to a woman, her house is so much more than that: it is kingdom, responsibility, comfort, total world to her … to most of us, anyway, whether or not we are aware of it. It is an extension of ourselves; it tolls in answer to one of the most basic chords mankind will ever hear. My shelter. My earth. My second skin. Mine.[22]

The repetition of the word "my" along with the staccato "mine" emphasizes that haunted houses produce horror because they thwart ownership and control. The ability to own, and therefore control, a house, a space, is essential for well-being, according to Siddons. She conflates "house" with "shelter," "earth," and finally the body ("second skin") to emphasize the "rightful" ownership of the house.

The trope of possession/ownership also emerges strongly with haunted house texts' reliance on the proverbial "house on an Indian burial ground." Each of these narratives, at some point, hypothesizes that what is really wrong with the house is that it was built on top of an Indian burial ground. This clichéd theme highlights the long-lasting White guilt regarding land-use in America. It hearkens back most clearly to Hawthorne's *The House of the Seven Gables,* which is concerned with nothing if not the inappropriate ownership of land.[23] Haunted houses play with the idea that wrong deeds, especially when it comes to stealing land, will not go unpunished.

On a more explicit level, the word "possess" is chronically repeated in haunted house narratives. A series of passages illustrates this point. Near the end of Jackson's *The Haunting of Hill House,* shortly before her suicide, Eleanor rants: "They can't turn me out or shut me out or laugh at me or hide from me; I won't go, and Hill House belongs to *me*" (245). Before Siddons's "house next door" is constructed, the narrator, Colquitt Kennedy, evinces an unreasonable and hostile attachment to the site of the house: "Aren't you the lugubrious one, though, Mrs. Colquitt Hastings Kennedy, sizzling martinis and weeping over a piece of ground that doesn't even belong to you, I told myself. But it does, I said back. It's more mine than it will ever be theirs, these dreadful, faceless Buddy and Pie people and their awful faceless baby."[24] Marian, of *Burnt Offerings*, muses: "It delayed itself until she was alone again, with the sitting room door closed; and at first the realization jolted her like a shock wave: the house was insinuating itself into the deepest part of her being; it was taking possession of her" (189). Not surprisingly, Danielewski gets to the crux of the matter when one of the fictional critics writes: "Perhaps Rosenbaum's conclusion is even the best: 'lord knows why but no one ever seems comfortable staying there,' as if to imply in a larger way that there are some places in this world which no one will ever possess or inhabit" (414). This is exactly the problem – that the subject feels it cannot inhabit a place without possessing it first. Note, too, that the term "possess" in these instances does not indicate a literal property ownership but rather an emotional connection.

In other words, haunted house narratives suggest that to truly be at home in a place is to form a place attachment. And to form a place attachment, one has to own the space in question. At the same time, haunted houses show that ownership is impossible, or at the very least, incomplete. The problem with this for ecocritics is that owning space, natural or otherwise, is complicit with dominating space. Whether we consider Carolyn Merchant's argument in *The Death of Nature* that "nature" started dying with the rise of property ownership, or Buell's criticism of "owning" and thus controlling nature, possession of land is not a popular idea among ecocritics and other environmental scholars.[25] Furthermore, these texts suggest that the concept of place attachment may obscure relevant history, including a history of imperialism and violence; therefore, it may also be complicit with that imperialism. In the light of haunted house narratives, therefore, place attachment shifts from a benign idea to a concept fraught with ethical complications. When we look at haunted house narratives' portrayal of place attachment, we are forced to ask of narratives that claim a place attachment to a more "natural" space: Whose land is it that we are becoming attached to? And what does that attachment mean? What are its personal and social implications? Until ecocriticism thoroughly addresses these questions, its staple concept of place attachment will remain haunted.

NOTES

1   Shirley Jackson, *The Haunting of Hill House* (New York: Penguin Books, 1959).

2   Carol Clover, in *Men, Women, and Chainsaws: Gender in the Modern Horror Film* (Princeton: Princeton University Press, 1992), for example, interrogates how horror films critique and expose cultural expectations and assumptions about gender. Joan Hawkins's *Cutting Edge: Art-Horror and the Horrific Avant-garde* (Minneapolis: University of Minnesota Press, 2000) analyzes how horror and other "trashy" films expose assumptions about taste, and hence about class. As part of an (arguably) Gothic tradition, it makes sense that horror texts would be read this way, since Gothic texts are usually interpreted as either subversive or symptomatic. See Fred Botting, *Gothic* (New York: Routledge, 1996), 7, 19. If treated as subversive, critics claim that they critique conventional social structures and dominant literary paradigms. If treated as symptomatic, they are read with an eye toward the anxieties they manifest.

3   Dale Bailey, *American Nightmares: The Haunted House Formula in Popular American Fiction* (Bowling Green: Bowling Green State University Popular Press, 1999), 6. Bailey

is one of the few scholars who address haunted house narratives extensively. Individual articles examining this genre favor texts that incorporate ghosts, such as Toni Morrison's *Beloved* or Henry James's *The Turn of the Screw*. Derridean "hauntology" tangentially relates to my discussion of haunted houses, but the current discussions of the term focus more on questions of history and metaphorical haunting, whereas my own analysis concentrates on animated, as opposed to haunted, space. See Jacques Derrida, *Specters of Marx: The State of Debt, the Work of Mourning, & the New International*, trans. Peggy Kamuf (New York: Routledge, 1994). Along with Derrida, Freud is also tangentially linked to haunted houses. See Sigmund Freud, *The Uncanny*, ed. David McLintock (New York: Penguin Classics, 2003). Freud's concept of the uncanny is nearly a perfect match for haunted houses. Freud himself says that "As we have seen, some languages in use to-day can only render the German expression 'an *unheimlich* house' by 'a *haunted* house.' We might indeed have begun our investigation with this example, perhaps the most striking of all, of something uncanny, but we refrained from doing so because the uncanny in it is too much intermixed with what is purely gruesome and is in part overlaid by it" (222). For a specific analysis of the uncanny in architecture (including haunted houses), see Anthony Vidler, *The Architectural Uncanny* (Cambridge, MA: MIT Press, 1992) and Nele Bemong, "Exploration #6: The Uncanny in Mark Z. Danielewski's *House of Leaves*," *Image & Narrative* 5 (2003), http://www.imageandnarrative.be/uncanny/nelebemong.htm.

4   Judith Richardson, *Possessions: The History and Uses of Haunting in the Hudson Valley* (Cambridge, MA: Harvard University Press, 2003), 6.

5   Lawrence Buell, *The Future of Environmental Criticism: Environmental Crisis and Literary Imagination* (Malden: Blackwell, 2005), 62.

6   *The Ecocriticism Reader*, ed. Cheryll Glotfelty and Harold Fromm (Athens: University of Georgia Press, 1996), for example, features articles by Scott Russell Sanders, Leslie Marmon Silko, and Vera Norwood that argue (broadly speaking) that a close connection between humans and space and a keen attention to natural space are essential for environmental health. Buell's *The Environmental Imagination* (Cambridge, MA: Belknap Press of Harvard University Press, 1995) tries to remedy the way American literary history has emphasized the "representation of the natural environment as a major theme while marginalizing the literature devoted most specifically to it" by reviving interest in "environmentally oriented work" (9). Implicit in his argument is that an attention to place and natural space matters, and that it is better to pay attention to these issues than to ignore them. In creative works, figures like Gary Snyder, John Muir, Wendell Berry, and Terry Tempest Williams are well known for their claims about the importance of subject–space relationships.

7   Roderick Nash, *Wilderness and the American Mind*, 4th edn (New Haven: Yale University Press, 2001), 317.

8   Ibid., 55.

9   "Wilderness," *The Oxford English Dictionary*, 2nd edn, CD-Rom (Oxford: Oxford University Press, 2004).

10 Mark Z. Danielewski, *House of Leaves* (New York: Pantheon Books, 2000).

11 N. Katherine Hayles, "Saving the Subject: Remediation in *House of Leaves*," *American Literature* 74, no. 4 (2002): 779.

12 Robert Marasco, *Burnt Offerings* (New York: Delacorte Press, 1973).

13 Nash, *Wilderness and the American Mind*, 24.

14 Anne River Siddons, *The House Next Door* (New York: Harper Paperbacks, 1978).

15 See Frieda Knobloch, *The Culture of Wilderness* (Chapel Hill: University of North Carolina Press, 1996) and Donald Worster, *Nature's Economy: A History of Ecological Ideas* (Cambridge, UK: Cambridge University Press, 1977).

16   Lorraine Anderson, *At Home on This Earth: Two Centuries of U.S. Women's Nature Writing* (Hanover: University Press of New England, 2002), 5. Vera Norwood, *Made From This Earth: American Women and Nature* (Chapel Hill: University of North Carolina Press, 1993), xviii.

17   Henri Lefebvre, *The Production of Space*, trans. Donald Nicholson-Smith (Malden: Blackwell Publishing, 1984).

18   Christopher Preston, *Grounding Knowledge: Environmental Philosophy, Epistemology, and Place* (Athens: University of Georgia Press, 2003), xiv.

19   Joyce Reardon, ed., *The Diary of Ellen Rimbauer: My Life at Rose Red* (New York: Hyperion, 2001). Reardon is a character in the mini-series *Rose Red*; the actual authorship of the text is contentious.

20   Dana Phillips, *The Truth of Ecology: Nature, Culture, and Literature in America* (New York: Oxford University Press, 2003), 185.

21   Stacy Alaimo, *Undomesticated Ground: Recasting Nature as Feminist Space* (Ithaca, NY: Cornell University Press, 2000), 16.

22   Siddons quoted in Stephen King, *Danse Macabre* (London: Warner Books, 1981), 305.

23   Nathaniel Hawthorne, *The House of the Seven Gables*, ed. Milton R. Stern (New York: Penguin Books, 1981).

24   Siddons, *The House Next Door*, 16.

25   Carolyn Merchant, *The Death of Nature: Women, Ecology, and the Scientific Revolution* (San Francisco: HarperOne, 1990).

Chapter 16

Gothic Affects: Digitally Haunted Houses and the Production of Affect-Value

Bruno Lessard

> For Gothic was the name we gave to that great phenomenon irreconcilably opposed to the classical, a phenomenon not bound to any single period of style, but revealing itself continuously through all the centuries in ever new disguises.[1]

In his landmark study of postmodernism, Fredric Jameson observes that the present age would be characterized by "the waning of affect."[2] Of course, as Jameson points out, it would be foolish to argue that at some point affect completely disappeared. For Jameson, affect stands out as a key notion to make sense of late capitalism's appropriation of intensity. Indeed, his remark raises several questions that in fact point to the commodification of affect in media cultures. Updating a Marxist concept, we could speak of affect-value to describe how contemporary media and franchises have tapped into and have thoroughly commodified affect to the point of surfeiting. The problem does not seem to be that affect has waned, as Jameson argues, but that its current form has become less visible, even though one could claim that it has never been more present. How can we explain this apparent paradox?

The problem may be that affect has not so much waned as it has functioned as a haunting presence that has to be reassessed in light of the transformation contemporary media have generated. In order to do so, one must avoid describing affect with terms borrowed from psychology (e.g., self, ego, etc.) or psychoanalysis (e.g., desire, lack, etc.) and falling back on concepts unfit for describing the role of affect today. Affect also has to be distinguished from its cousin, emotion, because they belong to close but fundamentally different planes of human experience. Affect functions at the level of pre-individuality and generates pre-narrative forms of experience such as intensity. Arguably a useful type of experience for cultural and media studies, an affect such as intensity can be described as a "nonconscious" and non-narrative modality of experience that differs from emotional states that are subjective, personal, and meaningful, and can often be described by individuals as they experience them. The non-linguistic and non-narrative nature of affect stands out as one of its foremost modalities of emergence. Mostly manifested in the skin and on the surface of bodies, affects such as intensity and anxiety vary and serve as embodied interfaces between bodies, images, and objects.

In the following pages, Gothic affects will serve as the guiding thread to explore the critically unsuccessful film adaptation of Shirley Jackson's 1959 novel *The Haunting of Hill House*,[3] Jan de Bont's 1999 *The Haunting*, which strives to go beyond Robert Wise's own 1963 adaptation also titled *The Haunting*.[4] De Bont's film tells the story of a group of four insomniacs who are invited to stay at Hill House, a reputedly haunted mansion built by the long deceased landlord Hugh Crain, in order to participate in a study on insomnia. Eleanor (Nell), the main character, is woken up one night by dead children's voices that beg her to be saved from Crain's afterlife stronghold on their souls. The four characters will have to fight Crain's spirit, which haunts the house and wants to kill whoever stands in its way. The film culminates in a computer-generated (CG) confrontation between the lead character, Nell, and Crain's spirit. Nell's sacrificial death eventually allows countless murdered children's souls to be set free. Basing his adaptation on the latest technological wizardry, de Bont capitalizes on special effects in order to scare his audience. Having been attacked for its uninspired rendering of the original, de Bont's film was meant to update the 1963 film for contemporary audiences using the latest digital effects to make visible what Wise deliberately chose to leave in the dark, that is, the phantomlike presence that haunts Hill House.

At the outset, two initial problems must be addressed to contextualize the 1999 film's critical failure: the supposedly inescapable influence of Wise's *The Haunting* on both critics and de Bont's film itself, and the ensuing comparisons between the films that have been proposed to analyze the functioning of the digital haunted house. Indeed, it is quite puzzling that most commentators keep discussing de Bont's film as though it were a *remake* of Wise's 1963 adaptation when in fact it is not; the films simply function as different adaptations of the same Jackson novel.[5] As a matter of fact, executive producer Steven Spielberg has remarked that he and de Bont chose to "travel the road not taken by Wise" and that their main intention was to adapt the novel in order to "deliver the goods for modern audiences."[6] Notwithstanding Spielberg's self-assurance as to what "modern audiences" need, de Bont's film has to be judged on its own terms without recourse to comparisons with Wise's film, however attractive such comparisons may be.[7] The tension may be that critics have not been able to find the proper critical tools to examine a film such as de Bont's.

I am, consequently, less interested in offering another interpretation of the cinematic narratives than in providing an epistemological account of the conditions of intelligibility of de Bont's film and its critical assessment: the reasons that supposedly explain its failure (as though they were inherent in the film itself) and the justifications that configure this "failure" in film criticism. First, I will clarify my use of "affect" – not by turning to its use in film theory,[8] but by aligning it with its blatant promotion in our neoliberal and biopolitical societies. Second, the use of affect in contemporary Gothic films will be shown to possess its own historical antecedents as trans- and inter-media haunting. The sparse critical literature on de Bont's film attests to the lack of historical depth that has characterized its reception so far. I maintain that a proper historical contextualization of the film within the context of Gothic art and its affective genealogy will demonstrate that the film's haunted spaces simply do no more than push to its logical conclusions the spectacular and embodied aesthetics that has characterized Gothic art ever since the late Middle Ages – that is, an ever growing concern for the reproduction of life as affect, affect as life. As my main intention is to shed light on the conditions of intelligibility of the reception of the 1999 film, I will briefly retrace the journey of affect as life and movement in a number of art forms and media in order to properly foreground the discussion of the film. Finally, I examine the doubling of life as affective movement in de Bont's work by turning to the film's discourse on dead children's afterlives and its CG reanimation of visual arts and media. The production's dual emphasis demonstrates that its affect-value is accompanied by a retrograde concept of life as pathos in the form of the main female character's ethical sacrifice. The rehabilitation of de Bont's *The Haunting* in critical circles is not my main objective; rather, I wish to highlight the manner in which the critical vocabulary that has been used to make sense of such a film fails to reveal the commodification of affect in Hollywood productions, which dovetails with the pervading management of affect in control societies. This essay therefore functions as an initial foray into what could be called the biopolitical economy of Hollywood productions.

Affect-Value: Producing and Commodifying Intensity in the Biopolitical Age

The concept of affect-value could bridge the gap between the political economy of contemporary Hollywood films, the pervading presence of digital effects in these productions, and their reception within film and cultural studies.[9] Indeed, the way in which 1990s films and more recent productions have created environments in which affect is tightly linked to CGI (computer-generated imaging) deserves more attention, and the critical fate of de Bont's film can help us better understand how the production of affect functions today. The sterile discussions that have accompanied its reception in terms of storyline, flat characters, overreliance on CG effects, and showing/not showing the monster, point to the need for another type of assessment.

The subtle change of emphasis in terms of "affect markers" contributes to differentiate the two films, singling out the 1999 production and its biopolitical context. Indeed, the scientists' object of study discloses the true nature of the films. In Wise's film, anthropologist Dr. Markway studies the supernatural, extrasensory perception, and paranormal phenomena, whereas the scientist in de Bont's film, Dr. Marrow, studies fear and performance anxiety but not insomnia, as the subjects of the experiment are led to believe under false pretenses. Their invitation to Hill House, a reputedly haunted house, is a pretext to generate the affects, emotions, and feelings that both men want to investigate. The difference is that de Bont's film reflects our biopolitical age in which affects, feelings, and emotions have to be investigated, managed, and controlled, and, in the case of the entertainment industry, reproduced as commodified intensity.[10]

I concur with Matt Hills when he claims that too much is lost in current theorizations of affect in terms of differentiating between emotion and affect, and that it may become quite difficult for critics to describe the affects of subjects who willingly engage in practices that provoke a weird amalgam of emotion and affect.[11] In order to avoid this pitfall, I prefer to turn to the production of affect, or affect generation, and forgo individual experiences in order to focus on the conditions of intelligibility of affect today and its promotion in CG productions such as de Bont's film. Affect is not only pre-individual and pre-linguistic; the possibility of its discussion in the last two decades or so results from the neoliberal promotion of techniques of the self that favor individual choice, personal growth, and self-development. A well-rounded theory of affect would have to explain how it evades the very vocabulary that has been used to promote personal experiences under late capitalism and its cooptation in various forms of discourses and commodities. Therein lies the difference between perceiving affect as world-making or analyzing the world as becoming-affect.

Michael Hardt and Antonio Negri approach the notion of affect from a perspective different from that adopted in cultural studies and theory. Departing from the tradition of political economic writings that blindly bypass affect, they argue that today's post-Fordist world, in the form of what they call "Empire," is imbued with affect, but in a way that is fundamentally related to a new type of "work" that demands from employees that they cultivate *affective* skills. In Hardt and Negri's account, affect is assimilated to the production of emotion in terms of immaterial labor; that is, "labor that creates immaterial products, such as knowledge, information, communication, a relationship, or an emotional response."[12] Building on the opposition between industrial (i.e., material or Fordist) labor and immaterial (i.e., affective) labor, the authors argue that the latter characterizes the control societies and the age of surveillance in which we live.

Hardt and Negri's notion of affect could be adopted to write a different account of both CGI and the reception of de Bont's work. They align affect with affective social networks and workplaces that, in the case of a film post-production crew, display the knowledge and expertise necessary to animate CG worlds. Cinematic post-production requires, as countless making-of featurettes demonstrate, hundreds of work hours from young staff members who work with new media tools late into the night in precarious jobs. The blurring of the boundary between life and work testifies to the change in workplaces themselves: designers play video games in their spare time; they can eat while they work, and are encouraged to work as many hours as they can to the point that they are always working, one way or another.[13] What I find most compelling for our purposes is Hardt and Negri's insight that immaterial labor as affect is "labor that produces or manipulates affects such as feeling of ease, well-being, satisfaction, excitement, or passion" (108). It is precisely these conditions of intelligibility on which Gothic has always relied and which digital effects have come to exacerbate in order to manipulate audiences' reactions. Given their theorization of affect-value and its socio-cultural contextualization, Hardt and Negri's work can be rerouted to merge the political economy of media and cultural studies. It is therefore the reconstruction of the conditions of intelligibility of cinematic Gothic within the regime of biopolitical production that would help explain the failure of a film such as de Bont's.

The Haunting of Affect: Gothic Architecture, Literature, and Cinema

The rise of Gothic architecture and the survival of its guiding principles in today's visual media such as cinema, television, and video games testify to the manner in which a visual production such as de Bont's film commands a critical treatment that will accentuate both its indebtedness to the past and its reflection of the age in which it emerged. What is particularly interesting in the case of the 1999 film is that it recycles numerous characteristics associated with Gothic through the ages: it builds on Gothic architecture via what critics have called the "Gothic line"; it taps into the spectacle, the heightened emotions, and the proto-visual spectacle of literary Gothic; and it expands on 1940s neo-Gothic cinema to finally offer a Gothic production for the biopolitical age, in which the concept of "life" has become key to making sense of the way in which our socio-political experiences should be understood. Finally, the film's apotheosis, featuring an underdeveloped confrontation between Nell and Crain, opens the door to a fourth transition in the genealogy of Gothic. Indeed, the CG production of Crain, and, most importantly, its function within the screen space, brings to mind the "boss fight" that the video game player often has to face at the end of a level. CG Crain thus bridges the gap between Gothic cinema, CG Gothic, and video games in the long genealogy of forms and media that has characterized the haunting of Gothic through the ages.[14]

In the case of CG Gothic, as in the case of 1940s neo-Gothic film and Gothic literature before it, we can note the haunting of certain motifs and forms that reveal how much emotion and affect have been the object of a gradual intensification and even blatant reproduction through the ages. Art historian Wilhelm Worringer's comments on Gothic architecture establish a number of parameters that would be taken up in the neo-Gothic revival in literature, modern cinema, CG productions, and video games. A number of Worringer's notions clearly stand out as parameters for our inquiry: expressivity, non-organic life, and the dual notion of emotion/affect.

Of particular importance to the art historian is the Gothic line and, for us in these pages, so is the emphasis Worringer places on life and the recurring use of life imagery to describe Northern or Gothic art. Here I am less interested in the accuracy of Worringer's claims – after all, the absence of case studies makes it difficult to assess the arguments put forward – than in retracing the development of Gothic as an artistic problem related to life itself. Indeed, when Worringer speaks of the Northern ornament as a "super-organic mode of expression" (41) and when he discusses the "pathos of movement which lies in this vitalized geometry" as a line that "appears to have an expression of its own, which is stronger than our life" (42), these descriptions are as much about ornament as they are about the description of artistic practices that merge with a life-inflected art historical vocabulary.[15] The fact that the Gothic line is "full of expression, full of vitality" (70) tells us little about Gothic lines themselves, but it discloses Worringer's desire to merge art form and life in critical discourse.

The association between Gothic, life, and art form is given another inflection when Worringer claims Gothic expresses the "exalted pathos of youth" (82). Here the art historian touches on a notion that will be at the heart of literary Gothic and its cinematic heirs, namely, emotion and affect as ideals that are to be generated. More importantly, this "pathos," characterized by "an unnatural convulsive tension" and a "powerful frenzy of sensation" (114), paves the way for a novel understanding of space. Indeed, Gothic space differs from ancient Greek space, again according to Worringer, on the basis of the former's wresting from space "a vitality of expression" (158) that facilitates the coming to life of the sensuous pathos of Gothic that is to be desired in the first place. As Worringer describes it, Gothic architectural space relies on a visual spectacle and embodied impact that force us to reconsider the legacy of Gothic through the ages in order to investigate the transformations it has incurred in other artistic phenomena and media environments. When Worringer mentions that, upon entering a Gothic cathedral, one "encounters an intoxication of the senses … a mystical intoxication of the senses which is not of this world" (159), we can rest assured that affect, sensation, and emotion have become as primordial in the construction of the cathedral as they are in art historical discourse. The sensuous and affective dimensions of Gothic can only take form in the context of a critical practice that will be attuned to these aesthetic and corporeal dimensions, which equally rely on their hypostasized presence in the work. The overwhelming nature and often violent enrapture of Gothic space, as "sensuous-super-sensuousness" (176) or "*Sinnlich-Übersinnlich*"[16] and affect-value, would undergo a crucial transformation in what is known in literary studies as the "Gothic revival."

A primordial characteristic of Gothic, as noted by a number of scholars, is its reliance on visuality and spectacle. Insofar as this can be relayed through the written word, Gothic writers' descriptions of emotional states often went beyond their medium of expression in a way that sought to question the boundaries of expressive forms: "Though [Gothic writers] always insist on the powers of feeling and imagination, they tend to concentrate on external details of emotional display while leaving readers to deduce for themselves complex inner psychological movements."[17] The rise of Gothic cannot be separated from a dual emphasis: the heightened display of emotion and the visual characterization of emotion to the detriment of inner motivation and psychology. The creation of Gothic emotion has to be linked to exterior stimulation, a point that has led to the critique of Gothic as a mode that relies too heavily on sensation, melodrama, and theatrical display.[18] Therefore, the intermedial ambiguities at the heart of Gothic seem as disturbing as the plots of the novels themselves, and the fact that these novels provoke pictorial effects, or *ekphrasis*, appears equally problematic in terms of defining what Gothic affect is. For, as we can imagine, the depiction of emotional states in visual media mobilizes a different economy of expression from the one found in print culture. Yet it is precisely here, at the intersection of print and visual culture, that Gothic manifests its most singular characteristic. Cinematic Gothic reveals that affect has survived to this day, but its shape-shifting presence demands that we pause and attend to its transformative nature in visual cues, sensationalism, and polarized emotional states.

Literary Gothic therefore tells of the fate of affect as a haunting presence across media. Gothic's alleged reliance on affect allows us to better understand the reception of de Bont's cinematic Gothic in the context of a trans- and inter-media phenomenon that culminates in affect-value. It may not be that important that "the culture of the spectacle ... produces close parallels to the sensationalism of the Gothic."[19] What matters is how these tentative parallels take shape and what they tell us about the creation of emotion and affect in the biopolitical age. A sustained critique of affect generators should focus on the resurgence of Gothic in contemporary cultural artifacts such as de Bont's *The Haunting* and go beyond the emphasis on pastiche as a quintessential postmodern trait. The way in which Gothic re-emerges today, as a haunting force, merits a closer look at how emotion, sensation, affect, and technology are made to work together in Hollywood productions.

The problem with regard to visual Gothic's invisible yet haunting presence in contemporary films such as *The Sixth Sense* (Shyamalan, 1999), *The Others* (Amenábar, 2001), and *The Haunting* is to find a way to describe the shift from literary Gothic to cinematic Gothic without essentializing the differences between the two, insofar as Gothic has been a divided and intermedial notion ever since it emerged. For example, commentators on Gothic and horror film have noted a first difference that would lie in the production of emotion and affect. On the one hand, literary Gothic would rely on an invisible presence that incites a plurality of interpretations; meaning thus becomes overdetermined in the field of suggestion. On the other hand, cinematic Gothic would tend to show the threatening agent, thereby reducing the number of possibilities. Therefore, the production of affect and emotion would always be accompanied by the production of subjectivities in a dichotomous scheme that leaves little room for the contradiction and hybridity that has always fueled Gothic.

A film such as Wise's *The Haunting* already problematizes the aforementioned distinction between literary and cinematic Gothic. The problem may arise when, as in Wise's film, Gothic does away with the immediate visible presence of the threatening agent; the house replaces the monster. Instead of a physical presence haunting space, we have physical space h(a)unting the characters. Characters and spectators hear pounding and thumping noises and see doors bend. It is therefore appropriate to speak, as Misha Kavka does, of the cinematic Gothic's use of the "plasticity of *space*" to convey emotion and affect, thereby disclosing "an underlying link between fear and the manipulation of space around a human body."[20]

While I agree with Kavka's description of the cinematic Gothic's use of space to transform the feelings and affects found in literary Gothic, I nevertheless wish to argue that there is more at stake in the case of contemporary Gothic films such as de Bont's *The Haunting*. First, a tension lies in Kavka's clear-cut distinction between the Gothic film's and the horror film's modalities of disclosure. Kavka argues that in Gothic "something ... remains shadowed or off-screen," while the horror film would present "something terrifying placed before our very eyes but from which we want to avert our gaze" (227). Kavka goes on to refine the dialectic between seeing and not seeing by adding that in the horror film there is something to see that we try *not to see*. In the case of Gothic, she maintains, the dialectic is different in the sense that it is "part of the structure of visualization itself" (227). Indeed, she suggests that it is not that we do not want to see, but that we cannot see: "Rather than the horror film's challenge to the audience to open their eyes and see, the feared object of Gothic cinema is both held out and withheld through its codes of visual representation" (227). But what are we to make of de Bont's film? According to Kavka's distinctions, the film would be a horror film. However, given the fact that most commentators have discussed it as a remake of a Gothic film based on a Gothic novel, the 1999 production would also qualify as a Gothic film due to its lineage and, most importantly, its flaunting of computer-generated effects that returns us to the architectural Gothic's emphasis on life imagery and literary Gothic's emphasis on proto-visual and emotional spectacle. The film's association of CGI with the history of visual arts and media deserves closer scrutiny. In de Bont's film, the role of CGI is to double the life-giving essence of cinematic movement by animating the art historical objects found in the film and by reanimating visual media such as cinema.

The Monster's Two Bodies: On the Use and Abuse of CGI for (Non-Organic) Life

De Bont's film's arguable failures would stem from a disjointed ensemble of competing regimes of vision, forms of life, and spaces. On the one hand, the numerous carvings and engravings that are the object of close-ups and weird angles throughout the film indicate that de Bont is after a certain connection between viewer and materiality that evokes haptic vision and its tactile viewpoint.[21] On the other hand, the film's Gothic revival, using CGI to generate a visual spectacle supposedly worthy of contemporary audiences, conflates the non-organic potential of technology and the organic forces of actors. The type of affect that is generated using haptic vision and nonorganic life forms via CGI culminates in the mobile engravings that the spectator contemplates on a few occasions. Moreover, the film promotes two types of Gothic space: the architectural Gothic and the Gothic affect as embodied space. The tension that stems from these two sets of terms leads to a type of hybrid cinematic construction that partly explains the general confusion surrounding the film's effects on spectators. However, as the above reconstruction of the film's architectural, literary, and cinematic antecedents demonstrates, de Bont's *The Haunting* creates "Gothicity" in the age of biopolitics and digital technologies, and relies on the production of affect-value. The film presents the spectator with a double concern for life as movement: Nell frees the souls of children caught in Crain's purgatory, thereby foregrounding the film's concern with the afterlife, and CGI animates the art historical past via various forms of movement.

Of course, what differentiates de Bont's Gothic from Worringer's is the actual movement generated by the cinematic apparatus. We are no longer speaking of cathedrals or churches. In de Bont's film, the use of CGI is haunted not only by the spectacular aesthetics that has characterized Gothic over the ages, but also by the need to recreate life's movement itself. Indeed, usually inanimate objects such as carvings, engravings, paintings, and sculptures are endowed with life and movement. It is therefore the animation of visual arts that this cinematic endeavor is intent on foregrounding as the gift of artificial life. This nonorganic life goes hand in hand with the nonorganic lines of which Worringer speaks in his path-breaking remarks on Gothic. With the rise of CGI, Gothic films such as de Bont's can push the boundaries of nonorganic life well beyond what earlier Gothic films achieved. Critics' recourse to traditional categories such as round and flat characters, showing or not showing the monster, does not tap into Gothic's long history as visual and emotional spectacle and fails to do justice to transformations in contemporary cinema and its production of affect-value.

If there were an anomaly, it would be a Gothic film that would not raise the production of affect and spectacle to the rank of virtue. The "exalted pathos of youth," as Worringer says of Gothic, could not be more appropriate to describe the use of CGI in the botched confrontation between Nell and Crain with which the film culminates. The combination of digital technologies and ethical sacrifice is deeply unmoving, and the fact that it is meant to be horrific and redemptive all at once demonstrates that it is the combination of pathos, affect, and technological prowess that is the true Gothic monstrosity, even more than digital Crain himself. One could argue that the film itself is the monstrous construction that fails to fruitfully join together Gothic's foremost principles: visual spectacle, the now commodified production of affect and emotion, and the concern for life itself. Recognizing these three principles leads us far away from the incomplete accounts that have accompanied the reception of the 1999 film so far.

Finally, the use of CGI in the film has to be divided into two different uses that equally strive to depict the generation of affect and emotion via life movement. On the one hand, various CG effects are quite unsophisticated in their rendering of movement and life. For example, Crain's eyes that watch the group; the statue that grabs Dr. Marrow and almost drowns him before he decides to put an end to his "experiment"; and the "cage" that traps Nell on her bed. These moments must have indeed incited laughter in the audience, as some critics have noted. On the other hand, a particular use of CGI, when linked to the tradition of Gothic's representation of nonorganic life, is quite impressive. For example, the carvings and engravings showing numerous faces of children are given life as the film unfolds. Similarly, the use of digital drapery throughout the film, from the early confrontation between Nell and her sister to the movement of children in drapes and sheets, and Crain's own menacing face in the drapes, testifies to the ingenuous use of CGI at several points in the film and accentuates the art historical and Gothic genealogy to which such a film belongs. Even in the case of apparently non-CG moments, the reproduction of cinematic movement that stems from the flipping of still photographs of Carolyn,

Crain's second wife, turns the photo album into a cinematic flipbook that further marks the transition from visual arts to media *qua* the discovery of the illusion of life as artificial movement.

Furthermore, what should we make of the film's foregrounding of Rodin's *Gates of Hell*, an art historical reference that has gone completely unmentioned in the harsh comments on the film? The French sculptor's magnum opus is passed over in the critical literature, even though the film could be said to be framed by two representations of the gates: the one near the beginning when Theo, another female guest at Hill House, and Nell tour the house while getting to know each other, and the more dramatic role the same "gates of hell" play in digitally coming to life at the end of the film when Nell confronts Crain. In the first instance, the gates are used to showcase Nell's insights into purgatory's *raison d'être* (as opposed to that of hell) and provide a window onto Nell's past as a frustrated woman yet caretaking daughter. On the second occasion of its foregrounding, Rodin's sculpture, now in the form of a CG gate of hell, takes Crain into the underworld. Once again, this time by turning to Rodin's work, de Bont's *The Haunting* uses the art historical past to play with the themes that have occupied the film since the beginning: the notions of human life as commodified affect and CG movements as illusions to be unmasked. In this film the history of Gothic thus unfolds the production of life as affect and emotion. When Hollywood appropriates this history and combines it with digital technologies, the quest for the production of lifelike movement, associated with affect and emotion, often gives rise to unforeseen monsters that defy critical descriptions, as the case of de Bont's film has shown.

The foregoing arguments have taken issue with the reception of CGI using de Bont's *The Haunting*, and they have implicitly claimed that such reception is symptomatic of a larger malaise in societies in which technology and life have become so intertwined that they demand a reconsideration of CGI's function that will go beyond hasty value judgments. Hardt and Negri's proposition to rework the premises of political economy in order to offer a reshaped understanding of labor in the twenty-first century has helped us make sense of the role of affect today. They posit that new commodities and new forms of labor demand a new theory of both value and subjectivity that takes into account language, media, knowledge, and affect. The integration of these precepts, derived from a novel way of understanding the potential contribution of biopolitical economy within film studies, must go hand in hand with a historical account of art forms that will be attuned to the way in which haunted houses and Gothic have a long prehistory that in turn haunts contemporary cinema, television, and video games. The critical reception of de Bont's film shows that it is not CGI per se that is the problem, but the haunting legacy of Gothic that may have come to its logical dead end in being intent on generating affect at all costs prior to rethinking its various assemblages of media affects. In true anachronistic fashion, perhaps it is Worringer who stated it best about haunting, life, and the use of CGI in contemporary Gothic films when he said that "[b]ehind the visible appearance of a thing lurks its caricature, behind the lifelessness of a thing an uncanny, ghostly life, and so all actual things become grotesque" (82).

NOTES

1   Wilhelm Worringer, *Form in Gothic*, trans. Herbert Read (New York: Schocken, 1957), 180.
2   Fredric Jameson, *Postmodernism, or, The Cultural Logic of Late Capitalism* (Durham: Duke University Press, 1991), 10.
3   Shirley Jackson, *The Haunting of Hill House* (London: Penguin, 1984).
4   The critical literature on Wise's *The Haunting* is almost unanimous as to the film's unprecedented impact on spectators and thorough mastery of the production of Gothic affects. See Jeremy Dyson, *Bright Darkness: The Lost Art of the Supernatural Horror Film* (London: Cassell, 1997), 228–243; Matt Hills, "An Event-Based Definition of Art-Horror," in *Dark Thoughts: Philosophic Reflections on Cinematic Horror*, ed. Steven Jay Schneider and Daniel Shaw (Lanham, MD: Scarecrow Press, 2003), 138–157; Richard C. Keenan, *The Films of Robert Wise* (Lanham, MD: Scarecrow Press, 2007), 120–127; Pam Keesey, "The Haunting and the Power of Suggestion: Why Robert Wise's Film Continues to 'Deliver the Goods' to Modern Audiences," in *The Horror Film Reader*, ed. Alain Silver and James Ursini (New York: Limelight Editions, 2000), 305–315; Anna Powell, *Deleuze and Horror Film* (Edinburgh: Edinburgh University Press, 2005), 166–174; Steven Jay Schneider, "Thrice-Told Tales: *The Haunting*, from Novel to Film … to Film," *Journal of Popular Film & Television* 30, no. 3 (2002): 167–176; Bruce R. Smith, "*The Haunting*: Jan De Bont Reinterprets a Robert Wise Classic," *Popular Culture Review* 12, no. 1 (2001): 127–133; and Aaron Smuts, "Haunting the House from Within: Disbelief Mitigation and Spatial Experience," in *Dark Thoughts: Philosophic Reflections on Cinematic Horror*, ed. Steven Jay Schneider and Daniel Shaw (Lanham, MD: Scarecrow Press, 2003), 158–173. It is noteworthy that most comparisons between Wise and de Bont, at least to my knowledge, have favored the former. Only Éric Dufour, *Le Cinéma d'horreur et ses figures* (Paris: Presses Universitaires de France, 2006), 98–99, has tried to bridge the gap between Wise and de Bont, albeit too briefly.
5   For example, Steven Jay Schneider mentions that "Jan De Bont's [is a] poorly-realized (to put it mildly) Hollywood remake of *The Haunting*." "Barbara, Julia, Carol, Myra, and Nell: Diagnosing Female Madness in British Horror Cinema," in *British Horror Cinema*, ed. Steve Chibnall and Julian Petley (New York: Routledge, 2002), 129. He also argues that "despite winding up as a film that betrays the spirit (pun intended) of its literary and cinematic precursors, the 1999 *Haunting* still bears traces of both its adapted and remade status" ("Thrice-Told Tales," 168). Smuts touches on the representation of the ghost and derides "Jan De Bont's criminally bad remake of *The Haunting* (1999) … with its goofy computer generated monsters" (167). More pertinent is Cavallaro's comparison, which historically foregrounds the nature of her claim: "De Bont's film, arguably less scary, prioritizes the association between self and environment by recourse to a quintessentially Gothic theatricality of stunning special effects." Dani Cavallaro, *The Gothic Vision: Three Centuries of Horror, Terror and Fear* (New York: Continuum, 2002), 90.
6   Quoted in Keesey, "The Haunting," 305.
7   Comparisons have taken several forms, but they always privilege Wise's film's subtlety with regard to hiding various elements from spectators, whether it be the threatening presence or the real motive behind Eleanor's death. See, for example, Schneider, "Diagnosing Female Madness," 130; Keesey, "The Haunting," 315; and Hills, "An Event-Based Definition," 154.

8   See Steven Shaviro, *The Cinematic Body* (Minneapolis: University of Minnesota Press, 1993), and Barbara Kennedy, *Deleuze and Cinema: The Aesthetics of Sensation* (Edinburgh: Edinburgh University Press, 2002). As Hills remarks on the different accounts of emotions and affects in cultural studies, there seems to be something equally lost in film theory with the use of affect, namely, a more profound engagement with social and political individuation grounded in historical accounts of media development, migration, and adoption. See Matt Hills, *The Pleasures of Horror* (New York: Continuum, 2005), 24.

9   My concept of affect-value takes inspiration from Antonio Negri's concept of "value-affect," which he uses to describe the type of value that traditional political economy has failed to grasp within its perennial categories: "when we look at things from the point of view of political economy – in other words, 'from above' – the theme of 'value-affect' is so integrated into the macroeconomic process that it is virtually invisible." Antonio Negri, "Value and Affect," *boundary 2* 26, no. 2 (1999): 79.

10   Even though I am cognizant of the physiological differences between affect and emotion, I consider that Hollywood does not really make the difference when it is time to reproduce and commodify intensity and feelings. The merging of affect and emotion is in fact an ingenious strategy on the part of Hollywood.

11   See Hills, *Pleasures of Horror*, 24–32. For two influential, albeit diverging, accounts of affect, see Lawrence Grossberg, *We Gotta Get Out of This Place: Popular Conservatism and Postmodern Culture* (New York: Routledge, 1992), 79–87, and Brian Massumi, *Parables for the Virtual: Movement, Affect, Sensation* (Durham: Duke University Press, 2002), 23–45.

12   Michael Hardt and Antonio Negri, *Multitude: War and Democracy in the Age of Empire* (New York: Penguin, 2004), 108.

13   To illustrate this point, Hardt and Negri give the example of Microsoft workers: "Think how at the high end of the labor market companies like Microsoft try to make the office more like home, offering free meals and exercise programs to keep employees in the office as many of their working hours as possible" (145).

14   The Gothic revival in video games has been the object of few publications. For a book-length analysis of the Gothic and horror elements in the video game franchise *Silent Hill*, see Bernard Perron, *Silent Hill. Il motore del terrore* (Milan: Costa & Nolan, 2006).

15   Consider the following claim: "The contrast between Classical building organism and Gothic building system becomes the contrast between a living, breathing body and a skeleton" (107). Worringer clearly establishes a dichotomous view of Gothic that relies on organic imagery to the point that art history merges with a vitalist politics of art.

16   Wilhelm Worringer, *Formprobleme der Gotik* (Munich: R. Piper & Co., 1912), 122.

17   Coral Ann Howells, *Love, Mystery, and Misery: Feeling in Gothic Fiction* (London: Athlone Press, 1978), 15.

18   As Howells notes: "Gothic techniques are essentially visual in their emphasis on dramatic gesture and action and in their pictorial effects, giving the reader an experience comparable to that of the spectator at the theatre" (16).

19   Allan Lloyd Smith, "Postmodernism / Gothicism," in *Modern Gothic: A Reader*, ed.Victor Sage and Allan Lloyd Smith (Manchester: Manchester University Press, 1996), 15.

20   Misha Kavka, "The Gothic on Screen," in *The Cambridge Companion to Gothic Fiction*, ed. Jerrold E. Hogle (Cambridge, UK: Cambridge University Press, 2002), 210, emphasis in original.

21   I derive these concepts from Ronald Bogue, who discusses Deleuze's reading of and indebtedness to Worringer's theories of the Gothic line for the formulation of his concepts of haptic and optic vision. See Ronald Bogue, *Deleuze on Music, Painting, and the Arts* (New York: Routledge, 2003), 136–155.

Chapter 17

Ghosts in the Machine: The Body in Digital Animation

Alla Gadassik

An Animated Debate

From its very beginning, cinema has been haunted by animation. After all, some of the earliest examples of moving pictures were created from strips of drawings, and resembled cartoons much more than the live-action recordings we have come to associate with traditional film. By the time the first moving pictures were astonishing modern audiences with visions of celluloid crowds and trains, pioneer animators were already playing with cinematic reality through editing, stop-motion photography, and other techniques that exploited the magical qualities of cinema. Perhaps the growing discipline of film studies was helped to maturity by proclaiming a separation from its magical roots, for despite its spectacular beginnings, animation has largely been marginalized (albeit with some nostalgia) by traditional media theory. This is the sentiment of Tom Gunning's essay on the occasion of cinema's centenary, in which he describes animation as film history's forgotten and unfulfilled potential.[1] Alan Cholodenko goes so far as to argue that all cinema is a subset of animation, since both live-action film and animation are suspended between the stillness of individual frames and the artificial movement of the projector – between realism and fantasy, between life and death.[2]

As digital video manipulation becomes the norm in film production, former boundaries between live-action and animation no longer seem relevant in the contemporary landscape of hybrid moving images. Most digital films combine elements of the filmed with elements of the hand-made, and demand a re-examination of how reality is re-presented on the screen. Animation is becoming increasingly pervasive on the Internet, in public spaces, and on traditional screens of cinema and television. However, even though animation has supposedly triumphed in the digital age, it is also undergoing a crisis. We might characterize this as a crisis of identity, for at its heart lies a question of definition: *what* is animation? Realizing the difficulty of placing contemporary films into different categories, animator Keith Lango wistfully writes: "Let's just call it all animation and be done with it."[3] When live-action, animation, and special effects are all fused into seamless CGI photorealism, it becomes difficult to distinguish the contributions of the different components. In the entangled web of computer effects and "motion capture" technologies, the traditional role of the animator has also become uncertain. The new landscape of virtual simulation threatens to marginalize the figure of the animator, or at least replace the hand of the artist or actor with computer rendering software.[4]

Instead of waving farewell to traditional models of animation, I wish to examine this internal conflict in digital cinema. In this essay, I investigate how the animator's presence, which was so central to early cinema, has been brought into question by the technological developments of digital media. In keeping with the theme of this collection, it is important to note that the term *presence*, which refers to embodied proximity, can also be used as a synonym for a ghost or apparition. In this sense, my discussion of a material and corporeal foundation for animated realms already evokes the haunting interplay of reality and illusion, or embodiment and simulation, which characterizes cinema and digital media.

A major claim of this essay is that dominant accounts of animation neglect the significance of the animator's presence in the frame of cinema history.[5] These accounts divorce the process of animation from the physical figure of the animator, and place the emphasis on the technological marvels of the cinematic apparatus. The development of digital media in the past few decades has led to a tendency of privileging technology, language, and information over corporeal presence and embodied creative imagination. In line with this tendency, scholars like Lev Manovich, Mark Langer, and Dave Clark, among others, focus on digital technology's ability to simulate photo-indexical reality, transform life and motion into malleable data, and offer animators an unprecedented amount of mediated control. Within these dominant frameworks, the artist's actual body is seen as a fleeting and accidental curiosity in animation, irrelevant in the grander scheme of moving image technology. This disregard for the body returns to haunt the figure of the animator in digital cinema, as digital technology struggles to erase or replace all traces of the artist. By downplaying the role of the body in animation history, digital cinema theorists dismiss an important site of creative expression and corporeal resistance to technological control.

I argue that embodied performance is a central, albeit overlooked, feature of traditional animation. By incorporating their own bodies and the bodies of human actors into early hybrid films, pioneer animators drew attention to their physical connection to the motion on the screen. This connection has remained vital to a diverse range of animation artists throughout the twentieth century.[6] In considering the effacement of the animator's presence in animation history, I hope to illuminate the source of contemporary anxieties surrounding the disembodying visions of digital cinema.

Digital Cinema as Animation

Although animation has been widely neglected by twentieth-century film studies, the development of digital technology has significantly changed this attitude. As computer-generated special effects, immersive 3D games, and animated web banners become commonplace, the inseparable links between cinema and animation are difficult to ignore. Techniques traditionally associated with animation (frame-by-frame construction of movement, character modeling, color and shape manipulation, etc.) are now deeply entrenched in most mainstream moving image production. Even the latest thematic trend in Hollywood cinema – blockbuster films based on fantasy novels or comic book heroes – borrows from marginalized narrative genres that have traditionally been associated with animated production.

Reflecting on the blurring lines between animation and live-action, numerous scholars have pointed out the futility of separating animation from other modes of film production and of establishing hierarchies between them. Mark Langer has gone so far as to call digital cinema the "end of animation history."[7] Langer does not claim that animation techniques will cease to exist; however, he argues that since the discipline was primarily defined by comparisons with live-action film, its chief defining element, for all intents and purposes, has become obsolete. For Langer, this historical development presents an opportunity to recognize all moving images as hybrid constructions, to be subjected to common methods of analysis. Although Langer proclaims the end of animation history, I suggest he actually means to argue for the end of cinema history, since his vision of the digital hybrid belongs neither to the realm of animation, nor to that of live-action. Instead, digital films can appeal to the realism of live-action, while employing the construction techniques of animation. Thus, for Langer, the internal contradictions of cinema history have been resolved in the labyrinth of special effects, 3D modeling algorithms, and other ways of constructing reality.

Lev Manovich comes to a similar conclusion, when he defines digital cinema as the ultimate triumph of the "super-genre" of animation.[8] Like Langer, Manovich looks at historical connections between live-action and animation. By defining "animation" as the manual construction of moving images, he argues that cinema began as animation. Early pre-cinematic experiments, such as the zoetrope or the praxinoscope, were composed entirely of painted sequences and some of the earliest films included frame-by-frame slicing and matting techniques. These manual constructions of the moving image were later hidden during the twentieth century's reliance on live-action realism. With the exception of a few artists, most pre-digital filmmakers treated the camera as an objective observer, which offered glimpses of reality. The indexical properties of cinema established traditional live-action film as somehow more "honest" than the visibly constructed animated film.

In digital film, almost every project relies on significant post-production construction. Digital technology translates images into uniform data (pixels), which are easily open to manipulation. Even traditional film projects undergo digital post-production, and it is common to significantly alter the images. The high degree of construction, which is applied to all footage, aligns digital cinema with traditional animation techniques. This has led Manovich to his often-quoted assertion that "digital cinema is a particular case of animation that uses live-action footage as one of its many elements ... born from animation, cinema pushes animation to its periphery, only in the end to become one particular case of animation" (302). Live-action becomes merely one option among a diverse range of effects, along with various algorithms, filters, and image generators. Eschewing the "bluntness, sterility, and banality" of recorded footage, Manovich privileges the hyper-realism or collage compositions of 3D computer animation (294).

Both Langer and Manovich believe that digital cinema has brought to light what has been historically understated in film studies – that all moving images are constructed, that all film presents an illusion of life, and that digital technology fulfills cinema's destiny to create a fully malleable, infinitely transformable visual landscape. Both theorists see this destiny as incompatible with traditional models of film and continuous with the historical development of animation. If cinema has, as Cholodenko claims, always been haunted by animation, then recent work in animation theory marks the return and potential triumph of the specter.[9]

Powers and Marvels

While cinema theory has often overlooked animation, traditional animation theory has strived to compensate for the neglect by extolling the art form. In earlier writings on live-action and animation distinctions, animators are often seen as magicians or gods – introducing viewers to the marvels of film technology, or bringing forth new worlds with the help of the cinema apparatus. Such metaphors for animation are often traced back to early animated films, which repeatedly featured the figure of the animator in a self-reflexive act of producing a magical trick or imbuing objects with life.[10] These early self-reflexive cartoons, which shared a common iconography of "the hand of the artist," showed the animators as they encountered the new moving drawings and often engaged in a battle with the created characters. The animated and the live-action ("real") worlds would often collide, and the animator would become entangled in the wondrous show.

Most often, theorists analyze these self-reflexive cartoons through the lens of technological exploration. For example, Thelma Schenkel writes that early animators seemed like magicians playing with "the new toy they were helping invent, and the more elaborate the games they could devise, the more appealing they would be to the audience."[11] Within such a framework, the early hybrid films present a step in the innovation process, as the artist introduces viewers to the technology of the cinema. Donald Crafton also argues that the artist's corporeal presence is not a significant part of early animation.[12] Crafton writes that spectators were less interested in the figure of the magician than in the attractions and curiosities of cinema. In his analysis of Emile Cohl's animated films, he notes that "the viewer's attention was being diverted from the magician toward the mechanism of the trick" (88). This framework of animation as magic and spectacle establishes it as a process of technical discovery. It also ties animation to special effects, under the common banner of "trick film."[13] Prolonging the magic in all these cases requires continuous innovation, and the animator-as-magician becomes invested in the ownership of the trick. Some animation histories thus set up entire timelines of technical progress, charting filmmakers' competition for new technological illusions.[14] At the heart of this illusion, the animator was featured as a uniquely self-reflexive and powerful master, who could create life, put together broken characters, or bring the action to an end.[15] Examining the presence of the animator in early films, Crafton argues that "[p]art of the animation game consisted of developing mythologies that gave the animator some sort of special status. Usually these were very flattering, for he was pictured (or implied to be) a demigod, a purveyor of life itself."[16]

Dominant contemporary perspectives of digital cinema clearly align animation with such interpretive models of technological artifice and draw on the mythologies of magic and creation that surround the early self-reflexive cartoons. By celebrating digital animation's perfected illusion and malleability, established theorists like Langer and Manovich define animation history as a journey toward the artificial re-creation of life. Both thinkers are more concerned with the range of available techniques and the visual veracity of the digitally animated image than with any changes in the process of animation. Their analyses of digital cinema have the underlying assumption that animation's chief "struggle" throughout the twentieth century was its inability to faithfully imitate reality. Once this hurdle was surmounted by computer technology, the animated realm could fulfill the narrative of the early self-reflexive cartoon and jump out of the frame to launch its assault on the real world.

As such, animation's apparent triumph in the digital age is not tied to any particular aesthetic traditions, but rather to techno-centric destinies, which many theorists attribute to cinema history. Manovich champions animation theory almost entirely through a framework of technological emancipation. He admires animation's hand-crafted tradition, and yet his vision of digital cinema does not foreground the constructed character of the early animated image. Although he stresses that digital cinema allows artists to manipulate every frame of footage "by hand" (300), his models of digital production are more concerned with computer algorithms and image-capturing technology. In this network of digital techniques, the hand of the animator is seen as an antiquated curiosity, which has been rendered obsolete by faster, more powerful machines.

Animator Dave Clark adds that computer technology has made the hand (and, by extension, the presence) of the artist outdated and unnecessary.[17] First, digital technology assimilates the animator's presence into its own design, by including an interface that can be triggered by any user: "The viewer is brought into the animation process as the creator of the objects, but it is the virtual world – the frame around the object – that animates them" (146). Eventually, the hand of the user is also removed in generative animation (animation created entirely through programmed algorithms). Digital software becomes an animator in itself, entirely independent of the human artist.

At first glance, this model of digital cinema offers exciting self-fulfillment for the magicians and creators of animation. Virtual simulations open up a horizon for new techniques and skills. Sophisticated image-capturing technology, as well as a growing range of software tricks, are allowing for more cost-effective and visually impressive projects. Moreover, the technology is accessible to a wide range of aspiring illusionists. It is thus unsurprising that numerous transformative (one might say magical) properties have been ascribed to digital cinema: limitless interactivity, instant accessibility, and transcendence of time and place.

For aspiring creators, this realm seems to provide an unprecedented amount of power. A recent article by Manovich, which praises emerging technology, includes a description of digital animators as deities: "Every time you want to make a still image or an animation of some object or scene, the story of creation from the Bible is being replayed."[18] Manovich continues the analogy by imagining God creating a new universe with the help of a computer. Speaking about the digital animator's ability to not only create from scratch, but also to sample reality in "infinite" ways, he goes so far as to write that "we are in a somewhat better position than God was."[19] By converting all input into pure information – a binary code of ones and zeroes – digital networks can replicate and alter the material world through this interchangeable data. This process might take longer than filming live-action footage, but, according to Pixar Animation director Andrew Stanton, "the winning side of [computer] animation is that you have a godlike control of everything. You can basically tweak till the last second."[20]

Seductive visions of digital immortality are common in discussions of new media. The most radical support for digital creation comes from artificial intelligence proponents like self-proclaimed "futurist" Ray Kurzweil, who projects that the human brain could be mapped and "downloaded" onto a computer within the next fifty years.[21] Kurzweil has already created a sophisticated digital alter ego, and often attends functions through this digital interface. In mainstream cinema, another notable advocate of digital simulation is *Star Wars* creator George Lucas, who has repeatedly stated his wish to dispense with real sets and actors in favor of creating films entirely with CGI. While few other directors have expressed as much fervor for digital technologies as Lucas, a growing range of filmmakers are looking to motion capture technology and computer animation software to "bring life" to their visions.

Enthusiastic discussions of the liberating powers of digital technology take for granted that the animator's or actor's corporeal presence is irrelevant (or entirely absent) in contemporary cinema. The animator becomes featured as a shape-shifting, ghostly character that dissolves her body into infinite configurations. The figure of the animator is no longer a stable presence that refers to a material realm behind the cinematic apparatus. Instead, the digital filmmaker is an absent "posthuman" animator – a controlling force without a traceable source.

The Posthuman Animator

The figure of the animator has always been intertwined with the technology of the cinema. Individual artists may have manipulated successive images or planned out the movements, but the projector brought those images to life. Nevertheless, in the early films, the animator's hand was always involved in the production. In the early self-reflexive cartoon, the image of the hand insistently testified to a corporeal presence beyond the frame. Within the digital circuit, however, it "is no longer possible to distinguish meaningfully between the biological organism, and the informational circuits in which the organism is enmeshed."[22] N. Katherine Hayles writes that digital networks replace concepts of presence and absence with a series of patterns and noise. In the depth of the animation studio, the animator selects among a diverse range of possible codes and filters, and creates recognizable patterns for the audience. Animators become disembodied – "the very code they punch" (45).

It is no wonder, then, that contemporary CGI animation elicits mixed reactions among animators. Beyond the loss of control that animators may feel in the face of powerful new technology, there is also the anxiety that the magic trick has gotten out of hand, has wreaked havoc on the "real," and has played its last joke by turning the animator into a puppet of the apparatus. To a certain extent, these anxieties are related to economic concerns (worries about job status) or old work habits. However, it would be a mistake to characterize the uneasy reactions to computer animation as a passing phase or growing pains. These reactions point to an important concern over contemporary technological challenges to embodied presence – challenges that have been noted by scholars from a growing range of disciplines.[23]

The digital vision of re-creating the material world through virtual reanimation exemplifies the Cartesian tradition of separating consciousness from corporeal presence. The dualism of mind and body has become especially evident in discussions of new media, which treat virtual reality as a realm where human subjectivity can leave behind its burdensome body. What links this discourse to traditional animation theory is the belief that technology will transform the mundane everyday world into a marvellous realm, in which the creator (user) can refashion reality at will. For instance, users can enter the animated online world of *Second Life* and become the animators of their own virtual destinies.

Kevin Robins argues that these models of digital media, which propound utopian virtual realities, ignore the material realities on which they depend.[24] By turning attention away from real bodies, new media enthusiasts overlook existing social, political, and environmental influences. As Hayles reminds us, the virtual is always inseparable from the material infrastructure that it supposedly erases. In fact, "[t]his illusion of erasure should be the subject of inquiry, not a presupposition that inquiry takes for granted" (28). The disappearance of the body from digital cinema is itself an illusion that needs to be explored. Behind the virtual interface of animated bodies, the actual material bodies are left to be reanimated according to a variety of networks of control.

The rhetoric of empowerment and liberation surrounding digital technology neglects the networks of power within which that technology is embedded. As several theorists, including Manovich, acknowledge, the development of animation has long ago left the animator's workshop, and entered the complex web of military-industrial interests.[25] Many current video game engines, 3D texture algorithms, and motion capture techniques are developed by companies that have ties to military initiatives.

The technology behind many current special effects – especially CGI animation – is also used to improve military surveillance and training programs. In recent years, partnerships between the government and the entertainment industry have also been forged.[26] In this light, computer modeling software is inseparable from war simulations and the military mapping of bodies and territories.

Of course, it would be unfair and premature to accuse the filmmaking industry of active participation in current political tactics. It would also be a mistake to evoke sentimental memories of the "golden" days of cinema or animation. Many opponents of CGI technology are prone to exaggerate the contrast between the "pure" days of traditional film and the dark days of digital technology. For instance, Jean-Pierre Geuens's bitter critiques of digital media are full of nostalgia for the preciousness of celluloid,[27] and contempt for the "nihilistic tendencies" of digital film.[28] Negative responses such as his ignore the continuities between various modes of filmmaking and neglect to consider the expressive potential of various media. Still, such anxieties about the attitudes that underlie current applications of digital technology should not be dismissed entirely. The drive for creative power and virtual immortality that fuels contemporary discussions of digital animation is not too dissimilar from the ethos of control in contemporary global politics. In their celebration of digital technology, many CGI enthusiasts mirror the same attitude that characterizes modern science, medicine, and warfare. In all these spheres, human life and its material reality are increasingly treated as "standing reserve," a term coined by Martin Heidegger in his discussion of the totalizing impulse of modern technology.[29] To view something as "standing reserve" is to treat it as raw and undifferentiated energy, made available for exploitation. For example, the modern term "human resources" reflects contemporary models of work that treat human labor as a stream of manageable and interchangeable energy.

One can find similar models of human labor in current digital cinema techniques. Digital animation converts the work of the animator into code, information, and statistical data. The latest development in animation, motion capture technology, is invested in seizing (capturing) the energy of human life (movement). Motion capture grabs the gestures of a moving body, strips the information of any unwanted fleshly "material," and stores the data for reconfiguration. Movements can then be tweaked, replaced, and modified at will. For example, in the recent adaptation of *Beowulf* (Zemeckis, 2007), Angelina Jolie's pregnant body was captured for the film, stripped of clothes and the visible signs of her pregnancy, and then combined with an entire catalogue of digital body parts. The infringement of the star's unwanted real body (her pregnancy) was resolved through a kind of digital abortion, until only the desired traits and details were left in the frame. The final composite in the film is a hybrid of Jolie's body and digital modifications, although the alterations are invisible to the audience.

In addition to capturing and storing human motion, CGI developers are also working on reproducing the movements and imperfections that are produced by an artist's hand. Even the hand-drawn approach to animation, which in the past referred to a human presence, can soon just as easily be designed by a rendering program.

The gestures of an artist, like the motions of an actor, can be mapped and stored for computer simulation. For example, a recent study investigates hand drawings of thirty artists and proposes algorithms that will be able to calculate how an "average" artist will draw the outline of any object.[30] This information will allow computer programmers to simulate hand-drawn effects by running algorithms that try to imitate the gestures of a human animator.

These non-photorealistic filters are being added to the growing bag of digital tricks. Formerly, the central mark of animation was the trace of artistic construction (doodles, erasures, clay fingerprints, etc.). Currently, these traces can either be removed as unnecessary by-products, or added through computer code. With the disappearance of these traces, the presence of the animator also disappears from the frame of the project. Digital animation thus both fulfills and destroys the myth of the animator as "god" or creator.

An Animated Defense

Although the mass-production of animation is not new to the digital age, the loss of any traces of an animator is something that could only be facilitated by the computer image. Digital cinema throws the animator's presence into question and challenges conventional myths about the importance of the artist in animation. In the entertainment industry, a number of new models have attempted to defend these myths against the onslaught of sophisticated CGI technology. I will outline the two most common models that are prevalent in animation discussions, seminars, and training manuals. In both models, animators defend their position in digital cinema by appealing to the same tropes of magic and creation that have characterized traditional discourses on animation.

The first model can be described as the "labor defence." Animators point to the painstaking labor that digital animation demands. For instance, frame-by-frame touch-ups are required even in the case of motion capture. Also, the combination of various elements onto a single layer (known as compositing) is a difficult process that requires a skilled eye and an ability to produce a seamless final project. Mainstream animation productions employ entire teams of animators, some of whom specialize in particular areas like hair, plants, or character joints. Animators are needed to direct actors in motion-capture production, as well as to configure the appropriate computer codes. Without the practiced touch of the human, argue industry analysts, the final project would lack any life or soul. While this argument keeps professional animators temporarily secure in their jobs, it reduces animation to a skilled trade that happens to be commercially viable for the entertainment industry. For now, teams of animators are needed in order to maintain the illusions. In the future, their presence will depend on industry changes and technological developments.

The second defence, which I will call the "story defence," is more concerned with long-term prospects for animators. According to this defence, even the most sophisticated technology cannot produce a compelling and engaging story for the audience. The success of animation depends on the believability of the characters, their ability to suggest human personalities and evoke emotional responses in viewers. According to such a model, animators are defined as storytellers and animation is defined as the range of techniques that are used to deliver the plot. The affinity between this story model and the myth of the "absolute creator" is clear. It is as though animators have relinquished control over the process of animation and transferred it to narrative control. The goal of creation is thus disconnected from any essential qualities of animation and is linked to the creation of narrative. This defence poses another challenge for supporters of animation. Undoubtedly, animation can be used to convey narratives; however, the same is true for film, theater, literature, stand-up comedy, etc. What would motivate a storyteller to choose animation as her medium? What makes some techniques preferable to others? The discussion will inevitably have to come back to myths of control and the powers of technology.

Both defences are inadequate in recuperating the presence of the animator in digital simulation. The first defence casts the animator as a technician, because it emphasizes the cinematic apparatus over the presence of the artist. The animator is featured as a technician or laborer – an operator of the machine. The second model appears to bestow onto the animator a unique creative power. However, it ties that creative power to technological progress. As such, it too succumbs to visions of simulated reality. Traditional accounts of animation emphasize the magical properties of moving image technology, or construct a narrative about the animator's super-human abilities. As I have argued in this essay, these models of animation are reflective of broader contemporary discourses on technological supremacy and material re-creation. Within the framework of digital cinema, these models become prophetic, as the apparatus threatens to displace, replace, or radically modify the presence of the animator. The "posthuman" digital animator thus becomes ever more reliant on technology and its attached political strings.

It is not my intention to make foreboding prognoses about animation or digital technology. Rather, this essay notes the challenge that the cybernetics of information poses for the self-defined magicians and creators of animated cinema. Within this ambiguous and often problematic context, animation, perhaps more than traditional film, presents a chance to explore more corporeally grounded relationships with the moving image. After all, the bodies of the animators are inscribed in the very origins of cinema. This is why in spite of numerous predictions of the triumph of simulation – predictions that can be traced for well over a century – the body continues to haunt the virtual networks of digital animation. Early animated films are haunted by the figure of the animator (or the figure of the actor), whose movement serves as the mold or model for the animated character. The presence of the artist in the frame of the film, or behind the frame of the traced animated image, continues to add what Joanna Bouldin called a kind of ontological *thickness* to the image.[31] Animation continues to require the movements of the animator and the actor not only for economic reasons, but also for the body's unruly complex motion (and, by extension, its claims to life). Despite attempts to foreground the sophisticated and developing marvels of digital technology, contemporary animation maintains an uneasy alliance with the bodies that inhabit its virtual networks. The space of digital media, from *Second Life* and video games to CGI blockbusters and scientific animated models, therefore, remains haunted by the material body.

An exemplary citizen of this haunted space is *Emily*, a virtual character produced and heavily promoted by digital animation company Image Metrics. *Emily* is a demo of the company's sophisticated animation capabilities; it (or "she") is often compared with earlier CGI failures, and featured as a more successful and realistic version.[32] The promotion trailer for *Emily* begins with the caption: "Emily is not real." Viewers are then introduced to an animated female actor, who proceeds to joke and muse about the company's ability to generate lifelike characters. The goal of the demo is to amaze potential users and clients with *Emily*'s believable realism. However, *Emily*, as well as all other demos released by the company, is based entirely on sophisticated data captured from real actors and applied by animators. In *Emily*'s case, the face and gestures of the virtual heroine are near exact doubles of actress Emily O'Brien. For the initial demo, O'Brien's hair was even left untouched, in live-action form, and only the face was remodelled in the computer. So what do Image Metrics creators mean when they claim that *Emily* is "not real"? After all, everything about the animated character that amazes viewers depends entirely on a "real" actor, whose body supports the virtual mesh. What is most peculiar is that behind-the-scenes footage of the process reveals the real O'Brien watching herself in animated form, and exclaiming with wonder that she was fooled into believed that the image "is me." It is as though O'Brien herself forgets that her body was scanned and digitized in order to create the final project. Instead, the digital *Emily* begins to take on a life of her own, with the real Emily O'Brien left behind as a shadow or specter. *Emily*'s case is only of many examples of the way enthusiastic and critical analyses of CGI photorealism neglect the ongoing presence of an embodied participant in the development, production, and engagement with animated worlds and characters.

The title of this essay is a reference to the popular philosophical concept of the "ghost in the machine." Traditionally, the "ghost in the machine" refers to an elusive guiding spirit (i.e. the mind or soul) of an organism. In philosophy, this question of human spirit has haunted the Cartesian split of mind and body. Similarly, pop culture seems fascinated with mind/body separations (humanoid robots, lifeless automatons, to name a few). To a certain extent, animation reflects this tradition, since it offers visions of inanimate objects that come alive and seem to have a mind of their own. However, instead of the original image of a body haunted by a mind or spirit, digital animation offers a virtual reality (a "mind" of information) that is haunted by the missing bodies of actors and animators. Recent media scholarship has offered important critical analyses of new media production and cinematic spectatorship, in the hope of establishing embodied relationships with the rapidly developing technology. My intent here is to supplement these explorations by foregrounding the ways in which animation can participate in discussions of embodied cinema. In Gunning's essay on the animated "ghost in the machine," the author argues that animation can expose and reveal the magical artifice and the creative potential of the technological apparatus. I argue that animation also has a long tradition of revealing living, breathing bodies, whose invisible presence moves between the frames of the cinematic mechanism. Instead of focusing solely on technological development, animation scholars should also acknowledge the complex relationship between digital worlds and their supporting material realms.

NOTES

1   Tom Gunning, "The Ghost in the Machine: Animated Pictures at the Haunted Hotel of Early Cinema," *Living Pictures: The Journal of Popular and Projected Image Before 1914* 1, no. 1 (2001): 3–17.

2   Alan Cholodenko, "Introduction," in *The Illusion of Life: Essays on Animation*, ed. Alan Cholodenko (Sydney: Powers, 1991), 1–45.

3   Keith Lango, "And the award for best rendered film goes to...:," blog entry, February 2007; http://www.keithlango.com/wordpress/?p=478. Lango wrote these lines in response to the 2007 Academy Award nominations in the Animation category. All but one of the nominated films relied heavily on motion capture technology in order to model characters after human actors. Many animators consider the use of motion capture to be a betrayal of traditional animation methods.

4   Moreover, industry excitement with computer-generated acting performances similarly leaves the traditional actor in a precarious position.

5   In recognition that animated landscapes and characters are often collaborations between animators and actors (whose movements contribute to the performance), many of the arguments may be extended to a discussion of actors in animation.

6   A broader discussion of animation as embodied filmmaking – the focus of my current research – remains outside the scope of this essay.

7   Mark Langer, "The End of Animation History," *Society for Animation Studies Newsletter* (2002), http://gertie.animationstudies.org/index.php. Langer borrows here from Francis Fukuyama's model of history, which, in turn, relies on a Hegelian model of historical progress.

8   Lev Manovich, *The Language of New Media* (Cambridge, MA: MIT Press, 2001).

9   Cholodenko, "Introduction."

10 Examples include the works of Stuart Blackton, Emile Cohl, the Fleischer brothers, and Walt Disney's *Alice Comedies* series.

11 Thelma Schenkel, "Exploring the Cinema of Figurative Animation," PhD diss., New York University, 1997, 74.

12 Donald Crafton, *Before Mickey: The Animated Film 1898–1928* (Cambridge, MA: MIT Press, 1987).

13 It remains a point of debate whether special effects strive to erase awareness of the trick, or whether effects are always wrapped up in elements of exhibition and informed astonishment. Did the haunted objects in early trick films alarm viewers' impressionable sensibilities, or was there always an understanding that the invisible ghost was in fact the filmmaker?

14 See, for example, Michael Frierson, "Clay Animation Comes Out of the Inkwell: The Fleischer Brothers and Clay Animation," in *A Reader in Animation Studies*, ed. Jane Pilling (Sydney: John Libbey, 1997), 82–92.

15 See Donald Crafton, "Animation Iconography: The 'Hand of the Artist,'" *Quarterly Review of Film Studies* 4 (1979): 409–427; Donald Crafton, *Emile Cohl, Caricature and Film* (Princeton: Princeton University Press, 1990); Alan Cholodenko, "(The)

Death (of) the Animator, or: the Felicity of Felix, Part II: A Difficulty in the Path of Animation Studies," *Animation Studies* 2 (2007): 9–16; Cholodenko, "Introduction"; Langer, "The End of Animation History."

16   Crafton, *Before Mickey*, 11.

17   Dave Clark, "The Discrete Charm of the Digital Image: Animation and New Media," in *The Sharpest Point: Animation at the End of Cinema*, ed. C. Gehman and S. Reinke (Toronto: YYZ, 2005), 138–151.

18   Lev Manovich, "Image Future," *Animation: An Interdisciplinary Journal* 1, no. 1 (2006): 30.

19   Ibid. Manovich's analogy echoes some of the enthusiasm that surrounded early film. For example, avant-garde filmmaker Dziga Vertov, whose writings influenced Manovich's work, proposed that cinema technology could help construct a new society (and a new human being). In some ways, Manovich's analogy makes a stronger case for digital media, since he argues that the digital creator can generate limitless permutations and simulations of reality, without necessarily having to sample anything.

20   Rick McGinnis, "Wall-E: A Five Year Labour of Love," *Metro Toronto*, June 20, 2008, http://www.metronews.ca/toronto/Entertainment/article/722178.

21   http://www.kurzweilai.net/index.html?flash=1.

22   N. Katherine Hayles, *How We Became Posthuman: Virtual Bodies in Cybernetics, Literature, and Informatics* (Chicago: University of Chicago Press, 1999), 35.

23   See Vivian Sobchack, *Carnal Thoughts: Embodiment and Moving Image Culture* (Berkeley: University of California Press, 2004); Mark Hansen, *New Philosophy for New Media* (Cambridge, MA: MIT Press, 2004); Anna Munster, *Materializing New Media: Embodiment and Information Aesthetics* (Lebanon, NH: University Press of New England, 2006); Lisa Bode, "From Shadow Citizens to Teflon Stars: Reception of the Transfiguring Effects of New Moving Image Technologies," *Animation: An Interdisciplinary Journal* 1, no. 2 (Spring 2006): 173–189. Jeffrey Sconce, *Haunted Media: Electronic Presence from Telegraphy to Television* (Durham: Duke University Press, 2000) also offers a fascinating, detailed analysis of the historical and cultural ambivalence surrounding virtual disembodiment.

24   Kevin Robins, *Into the Image: Culture and Politics in the Field of Vision* (London: Routledge, 1996).

25   See Lev Manovich, "Reality Effects in Computer Animation," in *A Reader in Animation Studies*, ed. Jane Pilling (Sydney: John Libbey, 1997), 5–15; W. Carlson, "A Critical History of Computer Graphics and Animation," 2003, http://design.osu.edu/carlson/history/lessons.html; Paul Crogan, "Logistical Space: Flight Simulation and Virtual Reality," in *The Illusion of Life II: More Essays on Animation*, ed. Alan Cholodenko (Sydney: Power, 2007), 368–399.

26   Sharon Ghamari-Tabrizi, "The Convergence of the Pentagon and Hollywood: The Next Generation of Military Training Simulations," in *Memory Bytes: History, Technology, and Digital Culture*, ed. Lauren Rabonovitz and Abraham Geil (Durham: Duke University Press, 2004), 150–173.

27   Jean-Pierre Geuens, "Visuality and Power: The Work of the Steadicam," *Film Quarterly* 47, no. 2 (1993): 8–17.

28   Jean-Pierre Geuens, "The Digital World Picture," *Film Quarterly* 55, no. 4 (2002): 16.

29   Martin Heidegger, "The Question Concerning Technology," in *The Question Concerning Technology and Other Essays*, trans. William Lovitt (New York: Harper Perennial, 1982), 3–35.

30   Forrester Cole et al., "Where Do People Draw Lines?," *SIGGRAPH* Article 88, 2008, http://portal.acm.org/citation.cfm?id=1360687.

31   Joanna Bouldin, "Cadaver of the Real: Animation, Rotoscoping, and the Politics of the Body," *Animation Journal* 12 (2004): 7–31.

32   See http://technology.timesonline.co.uk/tol/news/tech_and_web/article4557935.ece; http://compscigail.blogspot.com/2008/09/emily-and-uncanny-valley.html; http://www.image-metrics.com/.

Chapter 18

The Ghost Worlds of Modern Adolescence

Pamela Thurschwell

Inner absorption and reverie is one marked characteristic of this age of transition. Who has not had spells of mental involution and absent-mindedness, when thoughts went "wool-gathering" and the soul was haunted by automatic presentations that take the reins from the will and lead us far away in a rapt state, now reminiscent, now anticipatory, into a world of dreams or ghosts?[1]

G. Stanley Hall, whose massive two-volume 1904 work *Adolescence* has been seen by many as the founding text of our modern *Sturm und Drang* sense of adolescence, here suggests that this "age of transition" has a natural affinity with ghosts and prophetic dreams. Adolescence, it seems, is caught between the past of childhood and the future of adulthood, a strange and uncanny temporal state that partakes of both backward-looking haunting and forward-looking desire. Hall's rhetoric universalizes this adolescent inwardness. The question "who has not had spells of mental involution …?" reminds us that all adults have experienced adolescence, and that we all might have found ourselves, at some point, immersed in that in-between, "rapt state, now reminiscent, now anticipatory" that defines adolescent time for Hall. As the title of Joyce Carol Oates's famous short story about the dangers of being a teenage girl in the early 1960s – "Where are you going, where have you been?" – suggests, the ur-questions addressed to the adolescent are both temporal and spatial.[2]

As Hall's work begins to indicate, the modern adolescent is, in a sense, created by holding together two opposing temporal schemes. On the one hand, there is adolescence as a passing phase, a few brief moments in time on the trajectory from childhood to adulthood. On the other hand, at the end of the nineteenth century and the beginning of the twentieth, the "adolescent" is also being redefined as a "case," as a specific locus for concerns about the potential criminality, waywardness, or deviance that accompanies the insecure cultural space between childhood and adulthood (before taking that apparently logical next step into economic productivity and sexual reproduction). As the twentieth century progresses that space will be filled by definite indicators of shared identity (sub-cultural styles, music, clothing, etc.), which mark someone out as a member of a group called the "young," although in the beginning of the twentieth century it might be easier to chart that particular identity as it is assigned by others.[3] But the tension between adolescence as phase, and adolescence as identity, and via identity, as emerging social problem, remains. To put it another way, adolescence as a time of life may eventually be left behind by everybody, but in the meantime what do we do about all those boys hanging out on street corners?[4] Or all those girls menstruating earlier than they used to?[5] What if they, for economic or other reasons, never move "forward," never take their place in an adult labor economy or procreative reproduction (within the expected-to-be stabilizing bonds of heterosexual marriage)? Whither then the adolescent?

In this essay I want to suggest that Hall's wonderfully evocative quotation about the adolescent "world of dreams and ghosts" may be a good place to begin to analyze some popular representations of late twentieth/early twenty-first-century adolescents, who similarly occupy haunted spaces and unsettling temporalities. However, I want to ask whether contemporary adolescence is marked not only by an anticipatory relation to the future and a haunted relationship to the past, but also by something even less assimilable to teleological notions of time and progress. What if the ghosts of adolescence are not simply about the continued presence of those future and past times, haunting those caught in the age of transition, but also about the fear or desire that those (past and future) times will never come, or have never been?

I explore the ramifications of these questions by looking at three representations of contemporary adolescence: Daniel Clowes's graphic novel *Ghost World* (1998),[6] the 2001 film that was made of the book directed by Terry Zwigoff, and, briefly, another angst-ridden, ambiguously supernatural teenage movie released in 2001, Richard Kelly's *Donnie Darko*. In these works it is not entirely clear whether the adolescents involved are meant to have the attributes of ghosts (inhuman, insubstantial, or deathly; moving between different times; apparently unanchored by place), or whether it might be conventional society itself that is spectral and unreal – a ghost world of adulthood.[7] Ghosts resemble adolescents in that they are defined by their liminality, caught between timeframes. If ghosts exist uneasily between the worlds of the living and the dead, then adolescents exist uneasily between childhood and maturity. For both adolescents and ghosts, one might argue, "time is out of joint." Growing up, of course, always means growing up towards death.

However, it is not only time that is layered and complicated for ghosts and adolescents. Space is also awkwardly arranged, for where do ghosts and adolescents "properly" belong? In contemporary ghost films such as *Ghost* (Zucker, 1990), *Truly, Madly, Deeply* (Minghella, 1991), *The Sixth Sense* (Shyamalan, 1999), and *The Others* (Amenábar, 2001), ghosts encroach upon and crowd the live people who perceive them; kicked out of the world of the living, they refuse to settle into a grave or afterlife, and instead occupy space where they should not properly be.[8] Adolescents also uncomfortably unsettle location, dismantling the difference between public and private space. They "hang out" or "hang around"; propelled out of the family, they are not yet a full part of an adult labor economy in the "outside" world. From Hall onwards, adolescents have been represented as out of place in the house, but dangerous out on the street.[9]

These loose connections between the liminal status of ghosts and adolescents in terms of their "out of joint" temporalities and locations might be made clearer by turning to *Ghost World* and the ways in which its teenage girls uneasily occupy their late twentieth-century milieu. To consider the fractured time and space of the adolescent, I will first look at some ways in which the book and film of *Ghost World* imagine adolescence as haunting and haunted. The wasted modern landscape of *Ghost World* suggests why both the adolescent and the ghost might have no particular place to go. I will then turn to how these ghostly, adolescent dislocations of time and space might help us reflect on Fredric Jameson's influential discussion of time and space in postmodernism. Is the eerie urban/suburban twilight landscape of *Ghost World* completely subsumable to Jameson's and Baudrillard's understanding of the simulacrum? If so, is there then no way out, no way of imagining a livable future, for the adolescents of *Ghost World*? I will finally turn briefly to a central affective connection between adolescents and the elderly we find in *Ghost World* and in *Donnie Darko*, to consider whether this might help us think further about where adolescents are going, and where they have been.

Daniel Clowes's *Ghost World* is a brilliantly bleak portrayal of the long dark suburbia of the soul of two teenage girls, Enid and Rebecca, recently graduated from high school and staring into the abyss. Facing a future which seems to contain nothing but dead-end service jobs and deteriorating eyesight, Enid and Rebecca hang out in one diner after another, observing and collecting society's outcasts. Terry Zwigoff's film of the book, written with Clowes, inserts a stronger narrative and romantic arc than the episodic comic.[10] The graphic novel focuses on the gradually unraveling relationship between the two girls, while the film lessens the fusional, homoerotic intensity of that friendship by giving Enid a competing friendship/romance with oddball Seymour, played by Steve Buscemi. Both film and book represent the post-high school world of the late adolescent as a space that may be impossible to occupy, except as a kind of ghost.

Early in the film we see Enid and Becky's high school graduation dance, a scene predicated on similar scenes in countless American high school movies. The camera focuses initially on the backs of Enid and Becky in retro 1960s dresses, swaying in time to the music, looking very much like little girls. The dresses refer backwards in two directions, both to their own childhoods and to an earlier era. At the dance it is established that Enid and Becky are not going to college. When Todd, who has a crush on Becky, asks them about their future plans, he voices the dilemma of the movie, "I knew you two would do something different." But what are they going to do? All the possible narrative trajectories that the world of *Ghost World* offers to Becky and Enid, from majoring in business to working at a faceless coffee chain to becoming an artist (when the representative artist, Roberta, Enid's summer school art teacher, is pretentious and unsympathetic), are untenable, rejected, or rejecting. When Enid asks "so, Todd, what are you going to be when you grow up?," there is obviously a sour irony in simply asking the question; Enid's tone suggests any ambition to do anything, in the world they live in, will be limiting, dull, and vacuous, and that time moving onwards is itself the problem.

This sense of "No Future," which resonates palpably through the film, grounds Enid's melancholic, but not straightforwardly nostalgic relationship to the personal and historical past.[11] When Seymour, the nerdy record-collector, shows Enid his collection of 78 records and obscure old junk, she is fascinated, saying, "This is my dream room – I would kill to have stuff like this." It is the stuff, the consumer goods of the past, that can inspire emotion in Enid. Things become the focus of Enid's historical nostalgia; it is not that she believes the past would have been a better place for her that might have saved her from the desolate present. When Seymour shows her the 1920s racist advertising sign of the fried chicken fast food chain he works for (originally called Coon's Chicken, before it changed its name to Cook's), it becomes clear that the past was no better than the present. In fact, as Seymour points out, it was probably in many ways worse, if less hypocritical.

The representation of time and space in the book and film alternates between an arguably postmodern, ironic distancing – an awareness that everything, including the stuff of memory and self, can be bought or sold – and a painful recognition of loss, transmitted through objects. Although flâneur-like (and sometimes cruelly detached) in her collecting of people, places, and objects, Enid also manifests an intense investment in a personal and historical nostalgia that is at odds with her image. Enid's relationship with Becky disintegrates because Becky wants to move forward, even if it is only into their own apartment and a crappy job at a fake Starbucks, whereas Enid constantly refuses any kind of future whatsoever. In the film, when Becky tells her that in order to look like good tenants for an apartment they will have to dress nicely and act like yuppies, Enid immediately dyes her hair green in retro-punk defiance. Similarly, when she needs money Enid decides to hold a garage sale; she would rather sell her past than agree to enter a work economy geared towards the future.

In the "Garage Sale" chapter of the book it becomes clear that Enid's sale will not actually produce any exchanges: we immediately see her refusing to sell an odd doll from her childhood, "Goofie Gus," to a passing customer, "some jerk with a trendy haircut," as she calls him.[12] For Enid, selling her past looks like one way to avoid the other, more obvious option of becoming economically independent, which Becky adopts by entering the workforce. When, in the film, Enid repeatedly puts off moving into a shared apartment with Becky, a rejected Becky angrily retorts, "Have fun living with your dad for the rest of your life." If for Becky their own place signifies at least a limited independence, for Enid it is a capitulation that can only lead to a continued ghostly existence, a surrender to the bleak 1990s postmodern McWorld of adulthood – the sprawling wasteland of coffee chains, malls, fake 50s diners, and computer stores, and the soul-destroying service jobs which define them. Instead of entering this world, through the garage sale, Enid makes a half-hearted attempt to further "ghost" herself by liquidating her past, selling off what is uniquely hers (even if those unique signifiers of her past are inevitably also commodities). In the corresponding scene in the film, Becky is surprised to find that Enid has put up for sale the dress she lost her virginity in (how much more symbolic of a unique identity or singular occurrence can you get than that?). It becomes clear that Enid cannot enter an exchange economy this way, because when someone actually wants to buy something, like the dress or the doll, she cannot bring herself to part with it. In the comic, Enid and Becky abandon the yard sale for other public spaces, a diner and then a supermarket, Enid only remembering that she has left all her stuff sitting out unprotected later that evening, when watching TV at Becky's house. When Becky asks her, "How much did you make at your garage sale?" (20), Enid runs off into the night, back to her yard, to find her table ransacked, but the frowning Goofie Gus doll still there. The final frame of that chapter sees a tiny Enid cradling Goofie Gus under moonlight, whispering "Thank God!" (20).

Enid's desire to divest herself of the past and its detritus contrasts with her nostalgic yearning for an imagined-to-be uncomplicated, pre-lapsarian childhood. This is represented most potently by her wish to recover an old record, "A Smile and A Ribbon," recorded by a child singing act of the early 1950s, Patience and Prudence. In the comic, Enid's father finds the single for her, and in the penultimate chapter, she listens to it repeatedly while sobbing in her bedroom (62). This comes after Enid has had a fight with Becky and a failed sexual encounter with their friend Josh; the 45, the (very personal) commodity connecting Enid to her past, seems to function as a substitute for the connections she is failing to make with others in the present. The crackling sound of the old single, which goes "FTT-FTT-FTT" throughout the scene (a noise replicated in the movie), ties the poignancy of the moment into a specific anxiety about modern, or postmodern, archiving and obsolescence. What would become of Enid's past and sense of self if the ability to play that record disappeared, if for instance, as is quite likely at that moment in the 1990s, she no longer had a record player capable of playing singles? Enid, in fact, cannot listen to Seymour's records since she cannot play 78s. Are records still records if what they record is unsalvageable? In *Ghost World*, the ghosts of childhood and of history are precariously lodged in these haunting, nearly obsolete recording technologies, the 45 and the 78. In the film, Seymour collects original 78s of obscure blues recordings. The 78 comes to represent a (racialized) version of lost authenticity as unrecoverable and as out of place in the modern urban landscape as the delta blues itself. One scene in the film has a distraught Seymour in a bar watching an aging delta-blues musician perform, virtually ignored by the audience, as the opening act for an all-white frat boy band called Blues Hammer, which goes on to massacre Seymour's beloved blues. *Ghost World* relies on a shared scathing aesthetic and critical sensibility, the belief that Enid (or Seymour) can sort out the wheat from the chaff, the authentic reproduction (the crackling 45 or 78) from the inauthentic reproduction (the terrible blues covers band). For Enid, the emotional "real" of the personal past, and for Seymour, the "real" of America's cultural past, are lodged on records that display their authenticity via their imperfect sound quality and their nearly obsolete technological media. If, in some sense, Enid and Seymour both resemble ghosts it may be partly because they are like their record players, "out of time," preferring earlier historical moments, with all their scratches, to the empty homogenous present.

Enid is represented as desiring other times and places from the opening of the film. The film's credit sequence cuts between shots of a raucous dance scene from a little-known 1965 Bollywood film (Raja Nawathe's *Gumnaam*) and a *Rear Window*-like pan through a depressing array of apparently enervated lives glimpsed through the back windows of their apartment buildings. Jason Sperb points out that when the camera finally settles on Enid dancing wildly around her bedroom while the dance number from *Gumnaam* plays on her TV, it seems as if she draws life and energy from the television, whereas the others watching television in the framed-like-TV apartment scenes appear dead or deadened.[13] Sperb argues that "as a teenager in America simulation constitutes [Enid's] only point of reference for history or authenticity; however she simultaneously acknowledges the possibility of some true reality, somewhere, something not commodified ..." (210). She thrives off, but also repudiates the simulated, pop-culture-soaked landscape she is born into. This beginning further identifies her with the coolness of obscurity, the past, and the foreign (it also invites masks and disguises, as the dancers in the scene all begin the dance in masks as if at a masked ball, and on the front of the book Enid appears in a sex shop bondage mask which makes her look a little like Batman).

As Sperb argues, *Ghost World*'s representation of time and space appears to support Jameson's contention that late capitalism suffers from a crisis in historicity and an excess of the simulacrum:

> [t]he new spatial logic of the simulacrum can now be expected to have a momentous effect on what used to be historical time. The past is thereby itself modified: what once was ... the organic genealogy of the bourgeois collective project ... has meanwhile itself become a vast collection of images, a multitudinous photographic simulacrum.[14]

Jameson suggests that under postmodernism, history and culture are uncoupled from a sense of the past; where once we might have lived through history, we now go somewhere – to the store, or cinema, or online – and purchase a simulacrum of it. The surreal semi-urban streets that Enid and Becky traverse conform neatly to Jameson's ideas in many ways. They feed a sense of the postmodern uncanny, replicating the same chain stores on every street corner in every town. (The ending of the film sees Enid walking past a procession of chain store signs: Mario's, Radio Shack, All State. This version of California – if it is California – clearly could be all states.) But the girls' reaction to the profusion of duplicates and conglomerate capital, the postmodern ghost world the adults have built, is not simply the detachment of the flâneur. Enid and Becky both revel in and disdain the inauthenticity of Hubba Hubba, "the Original 50s Diner" (in the film it is Wowsville: The Original 50s Café, located in a mini-mall and sporting a waiter with a bad late 1980s/early 90s hairstyle.[15]) The diner is so terrible as a copy, such a failure as a pastiche, it almost becomes an original again.[16] When Josh says, "aren't there hundreds of places like this?," Enid replies, "Not hardly. This is the Mona Lisa of the bad fake diners" (in the film it is the "Taj Mahal of fake Fifties' diners"). What would it mean to have an auratic "original" – a Mona Lisa or Taj Mahal – of bad fake diners? Can there be an affective content, other than the pleasures of cynicism or irony or feeling superior to one's surroundings, attached to this kind of space? Why might the adolescent in particular haunt these kinds of postmodern spaces? If this kind of description fits Jameson's assessment of a postmodern culture affected by a "well-nigh libidinal historicism" (18) – a reduction of history to commodity, which allows one to create, sell, and buy the past as ordered, rather than as time passages experienced and understood – then perhaps the adolescent, whose youth prevents him or her from having much access to even recent history, is the perfect knowing customer for this relation to the past. "Libidinal historicism" could well describe Enid's reaction to the ghost world she's been given; her desire to incorporate the stuff of the past seems to indicate a desire for another, more authentic way of being, some endpoint other than the eviscerated ones adulthood appears to offer. Or perhaps it indicates some other way history might have gone so as not to lead to the contemporary landscape. Inevitably, Enid's desire for a more authentic, meaningful past is one that takes place at the level of style, commodities, and images. Modern adolescence may be inseparable from the movement summed up neatly by the title of George Melly's memoir, *Revolt into Style*: the argument that embracing a philosophy or an attitude such as punk's "No Future" may begin as revolt, but leads inevitably to the buying of t-shirts.[17]

Ghosts, of course, are anachronistic by definition; they are always out of time, and Enid is ghostlike in her pursuit of anachronism. One way of reading a common choice by adolescents who display a deliberately anachronistic style, is that it is a rebellion against current historical conditions and choices (or lack of choices). A mod revival might suggest a longing for an earlier historical moment when different kinds of adolescent resistance were imagined as possible, involving different kinds of identifications across class, gender, or sexuality. When Enid dyes her hair green and dresses up as a punk she is distressed when no one "gets" her statement. As she tells Becky, "It's not like I was 'going punk' or something ... Anybody with half a fucking brain could see that I wasn't dressed like some modern hardcore asshole ... It was like an old 1977 punk look ..." (25). Enid is anxious to maintain a clear identification with an impossibly past moment. To be perceived as adopting contemporary styles – "going punk" – is repellent to her, whereas an immersion in the retro, even if it is only a knowing representation of the ghost of punk, is good. Is this a clear choice between a sincere submersion and a knowing, ironized, adoption of a style? I do not think so. In *Ghost World* the choice for Enid is not simply to ape the styles of the past (either as parody or pastiche). Rather, she would like to reject the present by immersing herself in the past, even if she also perceives that the context of the present (Jameson's "libidinal historicism") makes that total immersion impossible. Enid says to Becky after the punk rock conversation,

> I wish I could just come up with one perfect look and stick with it ... Like what if I bought some entire matching 1930's wardrobe and wore that every day ... The trouble with that is you look really stupid and pretentious if you go to a mall or a Taco Bell or something ... and you have to act a certain way and drive an old car and everything and it's a real pain in the ass! (25)

Making oneself into a ghost of a past style, as a kind of protest, will inevitably emerge as ironized, because of the contrast between a 1930s outfit (or even, perhaps, a Johnny

Rotten look) and a Taco Bell. The context of multinational capitalism renders every style possible, but simultaneously flattens it into just another consumer choice. Is there any way an adolescent, disgusted by the present, which seems to offer no exits but unsatisfactory ones, can partake of some past set of social circumstances without immediately falling into pastiche?

In her article "Packing History, Count(er)ing Generations," Elizabeth Freeman argues that not every contemporary adoption of past style can be subsumed into the postmodern marketplace, that there may be "crossing[s] of time" that are not "postmodern pastiche," but rather "stubborn identification[s] with a set of social coordinates" that exceed the historical moment of the identifier.[18] She calls these stubborn identifications "temporal drag," "with all the associations that the word 'drag' has with retrogression, delay and the pull of the past upon the present."[19] For Freeman, temporal drag contrasts with and supplements Judith Butler's influential use of drag in *Gender Trouble* as a performative copy that deconstructs the possibility of the original.[20] Freeman's temporal drag is always anchored in past ideas, styles, and politics, which may come to seem embarrassing, essentialist, backwards looking (as Freeman says, a drag, or as Enid might put it, a pain in the ass), but which highlight "the interesting threat the genuine pastness of the past sometimes makes to the political present" (728). Temporal drag may be another way to read *Ghost World*'s anachronisms, in that it could bracket the question of postmodern irony or cynicism, and recognize the genuine need of the adolescent for a different relation (even if only through a kind of fantasized temporal disjunction) to an unsatisfactory present that he or she had no part in building. There may be nothing quite as ghostly as the temporal dragster, stubbornly anchoring him or herself in an outmoded style and time.

But can anachronism signify a politics, or is this desire for an impossibly different world, one which is past, simply a capitulation to the impossibility of a politics? Henry Giroux has argued that *Ghost World* seems evacuated of a political analysis that could create an escape route for Enid or other adolescents. It is missing different possibilities, configurations of community and political action that are not totally foreclosed by the postmodern wasteland. As refreshing as the film is (given the treatment youth have received in a host of popular representations over the last twenty years), it resonates too intimately with a major aim of neoliberalism, which is to "make politics disappear by, in part, producing cynicism in the population." Cynicism does more than confirm irony as the last resort of the defeated: it also substitutes resignation and angst for any viable notion of resistance, politics, and social transformation. It is precisely on these terms that *Ghost World* both indicts and reflects the very society it attempts to portray through the eyes of alienated teenage girls.[21] In a sense it is this question of viability –"viable notions of resistance" – that haunts *Ghost World* and makes haunting one of its central questions. Who are the dead – the adolescents who wander the streets, between times, between homes, or the others who uphold the viable, but eviscerated world?

Towards the end of the *Ghost World* graphic novel, Enid is studying for an entrance exam that would allow her to move away to the east coast and attend college there. She buys a second-hand hearse to drive east in, and in one scene, she and Becky use it to return to a deserted amusement park (Cavetown USA) that they had visited as children.

As they drive, Enid says, "We're hurtling back in time to a savage era where dinosaurs rule the earth" (72). The deserted Cavetown (in which all the dinosaurs look smaller than they remembered) and the hearse seem to bookend the adolescent dilemma, caught between a desire for a deep, almost evolutionary regression to childhood and the fear that the only way of hurtling out of their particular ghost world is in a hearse. As the book draws towards a close, after Enid has discovered she did not pass the college entrance exam, there are fewer and fewer words in each panel. Enid, who has spent most of the book talking over the quieter Becky, seems to be almost literally fading out, into a ghostly silence. In a series of panels we see the hearse for sale in front of her house, Enid sitting on a beach yelling "you little fucker" for no apparent reason at a child (77), and her chasing a figure she catches scrawling the recurring graffiti "Ghost World" on a wall. (When looking at old photographs with Becky earlier, Enid discovers a picture that she took when she was eight of the same graffiti on her garage door (63).) Enid's cursing of the child seems like both warning and mourning – the adolescent's rage at the continued existence of childhood. In the final scene in both book and film, Enid boards a bus on a route that had previously been out of service. Earlier we had seen an old man, Norman, waiting for that bus, apparently futilely. It is clear that the elderly Norman cannot function as a way of assuaging Enid's anxieties about what aging means. He wants out too. When, seeing Norman sitting on the bus stop bench, Enid says to him, "I know you'll always be here," he replies aggressively, "That's what you think. I'm leaving town." Enid finally watches him board a bus that will take him away, out of the film altogether. Is the bus another version of the hearse – an exit that only leads to death? Or is there an elsewhere to the postmodern nowhere and everywhere of *Ghost World* which perhaps only the very old, or the very stubborn, can access? What are the politics involved in reactivating a bus line that appears to be out of service?

I want to end with just the briefest of explorations of the ways in which this question of the politics (or lack of politics) of postmodernism might be taken up obliquely by the vaguely supernatural endings of *Ghost World* and another film that enacts in an almost literal way Freeman's temporal drag: *Donnie Darko*. Richard Kelly's *Donnie Darko* is also a ghostly time-travel narrative, one in which a troubled, apparently psychotic adolescent, is really at the center of a complicated time-travel mistake. Time, it seems, has gone off on a tragic, tangential trajectory and it becomes the mission of Donnie Darko to redeem it, by turning back time and sacrificing himself (to a mysterious death from a falling piece of plane that he narrowly avoids in the first scene of the film) so that his girlfriend and other members of his family might live. Mirroring in some ways Enid's connection to the elderly Norman, Donnie is drawn to an old lady, Roberta Sparrow, also known as Grandma Death, who has written a book called *The Philosophy of Time Travel*. (She is also constantly checking for a letter in her mailbox, a letter that Donnie eventually sends, completing one of the many paradoxical time circuits in the film.) *Donnie Darko* can be seen almost literally to enact a version of temporal drag, in which the function of the adolescent is to stop time, and turn it around.[22] Both works fit into a sub-genre of teen time-travel films for which I would like to suggest the label of "magical teen realism," in which the adolescent is imagined as holding not some youthful potential that might redeem a corrupt culture headed towards disaster, but rather an ambiguous ability to derail time, to stop it, or drag it back. *Ghost World* and *Donnie Darko* also both suggest an attraction or a match between the adolescent and the aged, who mirror each other in their uncomfortable relationship to the time and space they occupy, both appearing anachronistic and out of time. The movements of these works through time and space never allow the audience to know for sure which is in reality the most ghost-like, liminal, and awkward feature of their narratives: the adolescent protagonists, or the insufficient postmodern terrains they appear doomed to haunt but from which they finally find spectacular and spectral ways (discontinued bus, plane crash, or time travel) to exit.

NOTES

1   G. Stanley Hall, *Adolescence: Its Psychology and its Relations to Physiology, Anthropology, Sociology, Sex, Crime, Religion and Education, Vol. 1* (New York: D. Appleton, 1925), 311–312. I would like to thank Dave Tolchinsky and Dana Luciano for early discussions that helped me to think through many (now, glaringly obvious) connections between ghosts and adolescents.

2   Joyce Carol Oates, *"Where Are You Going, Where Have You Been?,"* ed. Elaine Showalter (New Brunswick: Rutgers University Press, 1994).

3   See for instance, Dick Hebdige, *Subculture: The Meaning of Style* (London: Methuen, 1979) or Jon Savage, *Teenage: The Creation of Youth, 1875–1945* (London: Chatto and Windus, 2007).

4   See Geoff Gilbert's chapter "Boys: Manufacturing Inefficiency" in *Before Modernism Was* (Houndmills: Palgrave MacMillan, 2004) for a fascinating argument about the creation of the juvenile delinquent at the turn of the century, the boy on the street corner, and his resonance with Modernism.

5   These are two of Hall's pressing concerns.

6   Daniel Clowes, *Ghost World* (Seattle: Fantagraphic Books, 1998).

7   For a fascinating discussion that insists that "Ghost World" refers to the inauthentic, postmodern, duplicated world of the film, and not in any way to Enid, see the Internet Movie Data Base discussion, particularly the analysis of onethreemc (December 8, 2008) found at www.imdb.com/title/tt0162346.

8   For a related argument see my article, "Refusing to Give Up the Ghost: Some Thoughts on the Afterlife from Spirit Photography to Phantom Films," in *The Disembodied Spirit*, ed. Alison Ferris (Brunswick, Maine: Bowdoin College Museum of Art Catalogue, 2003), 20–31.

9   If the fears for boys revolve around their appearance in the public sphere – loitering, occupying space without motive or intent – perhaps one problem for adolescent girls from the late nineteenth century onwards may be their inability to comfortably occupy homes. I am thinking of examples ranging from Henry James's *The Awkward Age* (1899), in which Nanda Brookenham seems superfluous in her mother's house because her advanced age gives away her mother's, to the awkwardly situated adolescents of Elizabeth Bowen's novels, such as the orphaned ward Portia Quayne of *The Death of the Heart* (1938), whose presence in the house is disastrous for herself and the other occupiers.

10 Clowes and Zwigoff worked together on the film and there is a sense of a true, happy partnership throughout. See Dan Clowes and Terry Zwigoff, "Q & A with Dan Clowes

and Terry Zwigoff," *Image TexT: Interdisciplinary Comics Studies* 1, no. 1 (2004); http://www.english.ufl.edu/imagetext/archives/v1_1/zcqa/.

11   My arguments about adolescence relate to Lee Edelman's arguments about queer temporality in his *No Future: Queer Theory and the Death Drive* (Durham: Duke University Press, 2004) in various ways that I do not have the space to expand on here.

12   Clowes, *Ghost World*, 15.

13   Jason Sperb, "*Ghost* without a Machine: Enid's Anxiety of Depth(lessness) in Terry Zwigoff's *Ghost World*," *Quarterly Review of Film and Video* 21, no. 3 (2004): 210.

14   Fredric Jameson, *Postmodernism or, the Cultural Logic of Late Capitalism* (London: Verso, 1991), 18.

15   Clowes, *Ghost World*, 43. Sperb also comments on this incident in the film (211).

16   This campy flip-flopping of bad and good is one of the defining traits of postmodern irony. Earlier at the graduation dance, Becky says "this is so bad it's good," to which Enid replies, "This is so bad it's gone past good and back to bad again."

17   George Melly, *Revolt into Style: The Pop Arts* (Oxford: Oxford University Press, 1989).

18   Elizabeth Freeman, "Packing History, Count(er)ing Generations," *New Literary History* 31 (2000): 728.

19   Ibid.

20   Judith Butler, *Gender Trouble: Feminism and the Subversion of Identity* (New York: Routledge, 2006).

21   Henry A. Giroux, "Teen Girls' Resistance and the Disappearing Social in *Ghost World*," *Review of Education/Pedagogy/Cultural Studies* 24, no. 4 (2002): 300–301. (Quote from Lawrence Grossberg, "Why Does Neo-Liberalism Hate Kids? The War on Youth and the Culture of Politics," *The Review of Education/Pedagogy/Cultural Studies* 23, no. 2 (2001): 133.)

22   The film itself is set consciously in 1988 during the Bush/Dukakis presidential campaign and plays with time in many other ways as well. See Garrett Stewart, *Framed Time: Towards a Postfilmic Cinema* (Chicago: University of Chicago Press, 2007) for an interesting argument about how *Donnie Darko* uses the context of non-cinematic media such as video games to frame its imagination of time travel.

Part 5

Ambient Ghosts: Spectral Images, Sounds, and Bodies

Chapter 19

The Haunting of the Everyday in the Thoughtographs of Ted Serios

María del Pilar Blanco

A basic premise of this collection is that haunting has gained prominence in all areas of culture in recent years. In this essay, I will be looking at the figure of "thoughtographer" Ted Serios as a way of analyzing this resurgence in interest in haunting and the paranormal. As detailed below, the Serios case emerged initially in the 1960s in *Fate*, a magazine devoted to the paranormal, and has resurfaced at different points in other media such as television shows, and more recently in museum exhibitions. I want to explore the ways in which everyday spaces and experiences are evidenced in the Serios thoughtographs, alongside an analysis of this history of popular and critical curiosity about the supernatural. How the Ted Serios case has evolved from its origin tells a revealing story about how we theorize the everyday, and how in turn this narrative of the everyday has developed its own cycles of re-enchantment.

One of the most iconic short stories dealing with the way in which photographs manage to make the everyday strange is Julio Cortázar's "Blow-Up" from 1959, which later served as inspiration for Michelangelo Antonioni's 1966 film. The narrator in the story, a translator and aficionado of this younger art, notes that, "one of the best ways of battling boredom and nothingness is to take photographs, an activity that should be taught from an early age, as it demands discipline, aesthetic education, a good eye and sure fingers."[1] Michel, the narrator, takes a snapshot of a possible scene of a scandal, and by the end of the story the promise of photography's documentary vision fades into the pixels of the image, leaving a constantly moving reality that allows for no stable interpretation. The expectation of producing lucid images yields bad ones instead, as Cortázar's beautiful nightmare points to photography's capacity to replace reality with uncertainty, and to even scar the realm of the real – what Susan Sontag describes as "the trace," "something directly stenciled off the real."[2]

Photographs have the propensity to take on a life of their own, and the image-maker (the photographer) is violently made dead by the medium at which he feels so skillful. To add to the difficulties of misinterpretation, the ubiquity of photographs and their capacity for dispersion makes for a complicated construction of events *after the fact*.

The self-assurance that, with enough skill, photography and photographer can render a realistic version of life, does not speak for the multiple directions that this medium has followed throughout its history. The idea of skill and professionalism as requirements for photography began to turn especially problematic in the late 1940s with the advent of the "Land" Polaroid camera. The Polaroid, which at first was an expensive upper middle-class commodity (the first Model 95 camera, which came out in 1948, was worth the equivalent of US$760 today), increasingly democratized the event of picture-taking.[3] While at first a rather tricky technology that required help from instruction manuals, as Peter Buse has detailed in a recent article, with the arrival of the SX-70 in 1972, Polaroid pictures became user-friendly.[4] Whether it was policemen taking instant pictures of crime scenes, or a family enjoying their scenic vacation, Polaroid cameras increasingly allowed for that quick and easy rendition of public and private memories. In a recent eulogy that followed the Polaroid Company's announcement on February 8, 2008 that they would cease to produce this technology by 2009,[5] Michael Kimmelman wrote that

> mystery clung to each impending image as it took shape, the camera conjuring up pictures of what was right before one's eyes … The miracle of photography, which Polaroids instantly exposed, never lost its primitive magic. And what resulted, as so many sentimentalists today lament, was a memory coming into focus on a small rectangle of film.[6]

This rhetoric, which recalls the "magic" and "primitivism" of photography (culminating with the thrill of awaiting the captured Polaroid image), opens a conceptualization of everyday life as constantly inviting occasions of enchantment. With the Polaroid, the "miracle" of photography occurred in the easy movement of images from inside to outside the camera box, and one by one the memories of everyday lives came gently into view.

However, enchantment in the photographed events of the everyday can be revealed in more surreptitious, not to mention dramatic, ways. In recent years, there has been a rebirth of critical and popular interest in the tricks of ghost photography in the nineteenth and twentieth centuries,[7] all of which transpired in the privacy of the photographer's darkroom. Grand-scale museum exhibitions have been organized in recent years, such as Le troisième oeil: photographie et l'occulte at the Maison Européene de la Photographie in Paris (November 2004 to February 2005), and its North American version, called The Perfect Medium: Photography and the Occult, which was housed in New York's Metropolitan Museum of Art from September to December 2005.[8] As Tom Gunning has explained, ghost photography went hand in hand with the rise of the Spiritualist movement, as the desire to communicate with the dead was actually fueled by the development of new technologies, such as photography and telegraphy:

Since Spiritualists saw their revelation as fundamentally modern, casting out the outmoded Calvinist beliefs in original sin and hellfire damnation, they welcomed evidence that their new revelation of the afterlife could be established "scientifically." For Spiritualists spirit photography was more than an amusement and could expand their new forms of spiritual manifestation.[9]

From its birth, therefore, ghost photography fed the need to prove the afterlife, as well as the continuing possibility of conversation between living and dead. Deeply experimental, ghost photographs can range from double exposures of posers and their dead relatives (in certain instances the ghostly subjects were dead presidents, as in the case of the William Mumler photograph of Mary Todd Lincoln with an image of her late husband, Abraham Lincoln, hovering above her), to images of spirit mediums shedding ectoplasmic emissions from various bodily orifices, to spiritual "effluvia" surrounding "electrified" body parts, as in the case of the beautiful experiments carried out by Jacob von Narkiewicz-Jodko in 1896. The pictures at the Metropolitan Museum exhibit (which I visited) construct a history of curiosity in the diverse manifestations of ghost photography, an interest that, according to *New York Times* critic Randy Kennedy "peaked by World War II," although it never really went away.[10] Heralded by critics as a "hilarious," "charming," "spooky," and "beautiful" exhibition, it welcomed a total of 163,987 visitors,[11] a fact that tells us that, even within the supposedly highbrow space of a museum, sensationalism and curiosity over the paranormal – not to mention the strange history that surrounds the quest for the afterlife using the technologies of the everyday – have been able to retain a sizeable audience.

The interest in the paranormal would not survive without some necessary aporia, that edge of uncertainty that surrounds a history full of flukes and fraudulent accounts of haunting. In both reviews of The Perfect Medium for *The New York Times*, this indispensable morsel of inexplicability lies in the figure of Ted Serios (1920?–2006). In his article, "Ghost in the Lens, Tricks in the Darkroom," Michael Kimmelman dwells on "the gap between technology and art," whereby past wonders might appear to a present audience as "ludicrous." He then moves to conclude his article with this:

... Which leaves the odd case like Ted Serios. An elevator operator in Chicago who found that under hypnosis and with a few drinks under his belt, he could project images from his mind straight onto Polaroid film, in the 1960's, in cahoots with a Denver psychiatrist and psychic researcher, Jule Eisenbud, he produced thousands of "thought photographs." These are creepy, blurry, off-kilter Blair Witch-like pictures of automobiles and hotels and shadowy men in uniform, which have yet to be fully explained away.

In hindsight they may come to look like Margery's ectoplasms, quaint relics of our own undying enchantment with the unseeable. Then again, who knows? Life, like art, can defy logic, too.[12]

Kimmelman's speculation that Serios's Polaroids might or might not one day achieve the ludicrous status of other ghost photographs says something about the not-yet-complete obsolescence of the Polaroid. The strange case of Ted Serios is so off-putting in part because of the immediacy in which the strangeness was produced (the minute, or minute and a half, in which the thoughts slowly appeared within the white frame of the Polaroid), an immediacy that has resonance with the current "digital" public. Without a darkroom in which to produce the trick or hoax, the phenomenon of the supernatural has here an origin and genealogy in an as-yet inexplicable elsewhere. In other words, there is something that is excruciatingly mundane, democratic, and openly quotidian about the Serios phenomenon. Is it even possible to compare his pictures with those other entrances of the haunted and paranormal into the experience of the "everyday"? What can we make of this morsel of strangeness that continues to reappear alongside already explainable fabrications of the paranormal?

The career of the Chicago "thoughtographer" combines this and a number of other anxieties surrounding the photographic medium as an index of the everyday, which we should consider alongside the many discourses on the photographic image and the representation of the everyday that were emerging in the 1960s as well as in our contemporary theorizations of visual media. In particular, I want to ask how the Serios case challenges our established ways of looking at and reading images, and how it might pose a challenge to the methods we have used to explore the mysteries of the affective experience of the everyday. My subsequent discussion will thus consist of two levels: I will describe the context in which the case of Serios's thoughtography was and has been disseminated, and move on to consider the implications of Serios's iconicity (or lack thereof) for our current theorizations of vision, visualization, and the everyday.

In 1962, the readers of *Fate* magazine – a popular publication devoted to reporting on the veracity of flying saucers, "phantom panthers in suburbia" (May 1985), and more recently the "afterlives of Jim Morrison" (in the July–August 2008 issue) – were introduced to an ex-bellhop named Ted Serios who could allegedly produce "thoughtographs": as explained in the Kimmelman article above, he could point a Polaroid camera at himself and come out with mysterious pictures of places he had never visited, and people he had never met. The author of the article was Pauline Oehler, and after much persuasion from the *Fate* editorial board, Dr. Jule Eisenbud, a psychiatrist and professor at the University of Colorado who had an interest in parapsychology, arrived in the picture to study the Serios case. His 1967 book *The World of Ted Serios: "Thoughtographic" Studies of an Extraordinary Mind* recounts the story of his experiments with Serios, performed in laboratory as well as private home settings (often in the company of different doctors' whole families). A character study as much as a testament to the difficulties in using science to prove or disprove the paranormal, Eisenbud's book is fascinating in its creation of a portrait of Serios as a remarkable, yet erratic man of little education and a penchant for heavy drinking, who, while often failing to produce anything extraordinary in his pictures (in fact, he failed more than he ever produced clear images), could cause witnesses to marvel at his creation of distorted landscapes on the surface of instant film. When Eisenbud finally met with the elusive Serios at the Palmer House Hotel in Chicago on April 3, 1964, the first trial pictures were dark (what the psychiatrist would eventually call "blackies"):

> Print number 1, the first try, came out perfectly black on development. "A black cat on a dark night," quipped Ted, not the least bothered by his failure. More chatter, mostly about what he could do when "hot." A couple of cigarettes more.[13]

It was not until the tenth and eleventh shots that Ted became, by all accounts, "hot," as evidenced in the following passage:

> ... Ted claimed he was hot again and insisted on shooting one right after another. He *was* hot. Picture number 10, shot at 11:30, Ted's heart pounding away like a trip-hammer, was again a partial blackie, but this time there was an area of light fogging in the center of the circular black shadow and nothing else. And picture number 11, shot right afterward, was again a bull's-eye, as became apparent the moment we stripped the developed print away from its backing. Glowing in the center of a murky but nonetheless quite distinguishable "photograph" were the letters STEVENS on an illuminated sign over the marquee of the old, no-longer-standing Chicago Hotel (it had burned down some years before ...). (32–33)

Many critics of Eisenbud and Serios have since tried to call the whole series of experiments a hoax, including the famous illusionist by the stage name of "the Amazing Randi," who attempted to reproduce the Serios phenomenon to reveal the trick, but according to all accounts, he failed to render the same results.[14] I should mention that Serios did have an incredibly suspicious item with him at the time of thoughtographic production – a round cardboard tube with cellophane taped on both ends, which he liked to call a "gismo," and which Ted said allowed him to "concentrate." Eisenbud goes to great lengths in the 1967 book to dispel any qualms about this object, as he recounts that professional witnesses (doctors, psychologists, and magicians) scrutinized it and found no fugitive images on either end of the gismo. Moreover, suspicions about the gismo necessarily fizzle when the (perhaps too gullible) reader of the Eisenbud book discovers that many of the successful images in his experiments were produced with two doctors holding the camera twenty-plus feet away from Serios, and in controlled laboratory conditions where, for example, Ted was placed inside an electrically charged metallic-mesh box called a Faraday cage.

As a way of leading readers into "glimpses of a kind of truth" about the Serios case (300), Eisenbud often moves into a rather dense psychoanalytical rhetoric. In the chapter "The Importance of Being Serios" (the witty choice for the title is representative of the psychiatrist's attempt at a range of registers throughout the book), Eisenbud addresses Serios's genetic and hormonal normality, as well as his emotional instability. "According to his Rorschach and other psychological-test responses," he writes, "his world, and what uncertain human relationships it provides, is deteriorating, decaying, crumbling, and falling apart" (297). As a means of solving the puzzle that is Serios, Eisenbud links the thoughtographer's "abandoned child complex" to the latter's witnessing of the *"primal scene"* during a childhood spent sleeping in his parents' bedroom, a situation that brought on a lifetime of nightmares about "earthquakes, and of struggle with and sometimes pursuit by powerful male figures" (299).

Eisenbud echoes and directly references William James's own frustrations at his failed attempts to convince his peers that the paranormal can and should be taken seriously by the scientific profession, as in his 1909 article "Confidences of a 'Psychical Researcher'" (*American Magazine*, October 1909).[15] Despite the remarkable advancements of science throughout the twentieth century, there is a poignant continuity between James and a doctor like Eisenbud: the scientific method and paranormal events remain suspended in an uneasy relationship of disapproval, and the latter continues to be relegated to the dark corners of the eccentric and the improbable – an example of what Michael Leja describes as the increasing propensity and desire to doubt visual phenomena, to "look askance," beginning in the American nineteenth century with figures like William Mumler (d. 1884), the most infamous creator of spirit photographs.

Again, my interest in Serios's case is more cultural than parapsychological. Rather than enter into a discussion of the possible routes into dispelling the myth of thoughtography, I want to look at the pictures themselves – the *noumena* rather than the *phenomena*, so to speak – to see what they have to say: the material reality of the images emerging from Polaroid film, and the way they represent visions of random untraveled landscapes, displaying distorted impressions of a world that is nevertheless in existence somewhere. And I want to ask *where* we can place the Serios case in our understanding of everyday life, both within this context of 1960s American culture, as well as our own contemporary moment. While the scientific strand of sense-making all but rejects the "world" that Eisenbud represented in his 1967 book, a contemporary discourse on visual culture, which often pays attention to the *strangeness* of everyday space and everyday life, might welcome the inexplicability of the Serios thoughtographs. Where everyday life theory focuses on the ways in which quotidian objects can be scrutinized to the point of becoming strange apparitions within our known landscapes, and (conversely) where it deals with the way the new and strange becomes familiarized into culture, here we have something mundane – a photo produced via Polaroid (which Buse facetiously describes as "the imaginary for imbeciles" (34)) – that is impossibly strange *as it is*, and continues a strange existence to this day. The thoughtographs are strangeness made *literal*: their presence elucidates the twists and turns of perception of what we take to be real and *there*. But, rather than presenting us with the possibility to possess a photographic subject through the production of its image, these thoughtographs come to represent the discontinuity or lack of connection between and within images – the dispersion of those immediate apprehensions of any given scene, and ultimately the inability to possess a scene.

One of the most poignant examples of this is a set of photographs taken in the home of Dr. and Mrs. Gerome Gersten, displaying two people overlooking what appears to be an urban landscape below (Fig. 1).

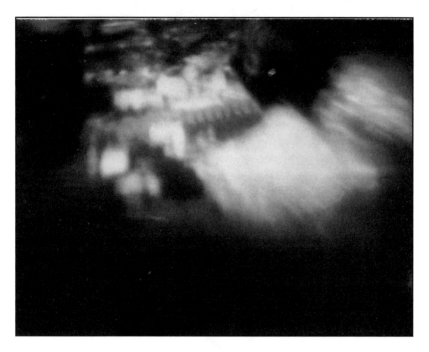

Figure 1: Ted Serios thoughtograph (1965). Courtesy of the Jule Eisenbud collection on Ted Serios and thoughtographic photography, University of Maryland, Baltimore County.

The Polaroid almost records the motion of leaning forward that results in the "streamer" effect of the lights in the print, and a second picture (not displayed here), according to Dr. Eisenbud, shows one of the figures with the head "bent ... forward and downward" (116). What strikes us about this set of pictures is the lost quality of the photograph – its unlocatability, but also the way these people are not facing us, and yet we uncannily participate in their actions and their motions, as they look upon an unfamiliar "somewhere." In terms of Roland Barthes's useful idea of the *punctum*, the "accident which pricks" us in a photograph,[16] this pair of Serios thoughtographs is open to opposite interpretations. The photograph's reluctance to show us what it is representing can lead us to conclude that there is no apparent contingency, no "co-nature" between image and referent, because the latter is always and already lost to us. In this respect, the lack of specificity anywhere in the picture eliminates the possibility of an affective "prick." On the other hand, however, the whole photograph itself might function as *punctum*, because it represents what appears to be an accident of perception, which moves us, makes us curious. The mystery of the woman and man's faces, as well as the swirling, incandescent landscape below, point to Barthes's "subtle *beyond*" (59), the not seen, yet irreversibly represented thing.

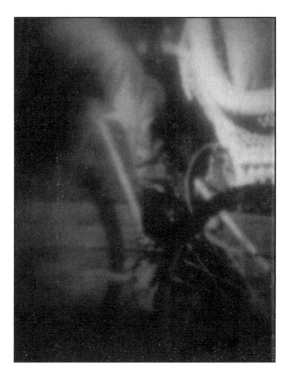

Figure 2: Ted Serios thoughtograph (1965). Courtesy of the Jule Eisenbud collection on Ted Serios and thoughtographic photography, University of Maryland, Baltimore County.

The Serios geography features immediate snapshots of the mundane: a spokes-eye view of a bicycle (Fig. 2), a glimpse of cars driving on a road. But it can also elevate itself to "cosmic" levels, as with the examples of the thoughtographs of the Soviet Vostok rockets that were first launched into space in 1960, and the picture of the Mariner rocket during an experiment where he had been allegedly more interested in the news about space travel than in the "target" image of the Maintenon Castle in France (Fig. 3). There is a sense that the environment presented in Serios's thoughtographs denotes a species of distraction that in a way responds to a collective/cultural psychic reality, something that stands in rather stark contrast to what Pierre Bourdieu theorized in 1965 in *Photography: A Middle-Brow Art* as this medium's "nominalism," its lack of "abandon[ment] to the anarchy of individual intentions."[17] Bourdieu's prescriptive argument would undoubtedly fail to account for the dispossessed and disorienting landscapes that immediately emerge

Figure 3: Ted Serios thoughtograph (1965). Courtesy of the Jule Eisenbud collection on Ted Serios and thoughtographic photography, University of Maryland, Baltimore County.

in the Polaroid thoughtographs, where the category of "individual intention" is doubly removed from the viewer. In our everyday existence, there are matters that preoccupy us at ground level, and there are others that steal our attention on the level of imagination (as in, for example, space events, which captivated audiences in the 1960s, but which had not been entirely assimilated to what we would consider everyday experience). I want to suggest that the Polaroid photograph, whose material reality is iconic of the everydayness of life, is here able to gather the disorienting processes of *how we think* during the everyday, and how the mind travels through the many dissociated "events" of the quotidian.

The Serios experiments tackled the idea of what Eisenbud calls "traveling clairvoyance" quite literally. Many of the "target" pictures (experiments in which a photograph was kept hidden from Serios to see if he would be able to psychically discern what it was and produce a Polaroid thoughtograph of it) were representative of that middle-class tourism that Sontag refers to as the banal "way of certifying experience" (9). The Serios brand of tourism (which transpired in an inebriated state in a Colorado upper-middle-class living room) is again quite unique. Here, Serios's response to this particular challenge is a ghostly portrait of Westminster Abbey taken from a canted perspective, where the luminosity of the building is replaced with what appear to be shadows and fog. It should be noted that Eisenbud and the others present noticed that the thoughtograph produced a portrait of the Abbey taken from a different angle, and with a different set of shadows from the original target (59). On a purely material level, we can look at this Polaroid and call it "bad" photography, an ephemeral wasted print in a pre-digital age when such snapshots meant money down the proverbial drain. On a conceptual level, however, and if we follow Eisenbud's train of thought, pictures such as these are representative of what is happening in Serios's "mind's eye," so that "his senses ... depend on what he knows, what he has gotten information about in some other way entirely" (241). I want to argue that what we have here is the literalization of an *impression* in its simplest form, what Georg Simmel referred to as the continuously shifting "snapshots" of everyday life which are representative of a particular subjective perception.[18] Put differently, the knowledge acquired from what appears to be a basic (albeit allegedly mysterious) perception of an image or scene is inexorably entangled with a set of sensations, as well as a particular strand of sense-making, so that the easily consumable picture of the iconic London church is made strange forever.

Possibly the most remarkable representation of the impressions of Serios's "mind's eye" is the thoughtograph pictured on the cover of this book, which emerged on a night when he was trying to get an image of the Chicago Hilton where he used to work, and instead got the Denver Hilton – a blurry color shot taken from an angle that, according to Eisenbud, would only have been possible "with a different lens" and "only with some special contrivance for getting the cameraman well into the air" (235). This is one of the better-known examples of what Eisenbud called "distortions," images which comply with his hypothesis that the "real" location of the "mind" is not necessarily *in* the body simply because it exists within it – the mind actually commands how we experience space in the first place (237). "Our sensory apparatuses," he writes, "are constantly in states of variable excitation from the world around us, which is never still ... yet behaves" with apparent constancy of meaning yielded by the agreement of the senses with one another (239). In a thoughtograph like the one of the Denver Hilton, we come across a singular brand of *dérive* (without the Situationist International political project), where a sensual, affective perception of space displays irreducibly particular ways of seeing – and what is more, they are *equivocal* ways of perceiving reality, where the mind's eye takes the rein.

Yet another example of Serios's equivocal perceptions is a picture of Williams's Stable in Central City, Colorado. In this particular Polaroid, the windows of the building appear to be narrower than they were in reality, according to a picture taken later by Eisenbud. In addition, the masonry on the building was different from the one on the actual building. As Eisenbud explains, while the "actual livery stable is old pressed brick," Serios's picture displays "a kind of imbedded rock," a masonry that had also emerged in previous thoughtographs (168). In the world of Ted Serios, the imagery of everyday life becomes open to seemingly endless visualizations, to immediate apprehensions (thanks to the instant gratification of the Polaroid camera), all of which display a defiance of the ways in which human existence is spatially and temporally organized and experienced *normally*.

Is it too singular, too particular for us to take notice of the world of Ted Serios in this day and age? Is a conjugation of this world that opened up in the American Midwest in the 1960s with a theorization of everyday life even worth pondering? Let me go back to the beginning of the essay. If, according to the narrator in "Blow-up," photography is a skill that demands an eye for the "aesthetic," what methods do we have in contemporary critical discourse to address the Benjaminian "unconscious optics" that emerge in Serios's thoughtographs, which are not only produced so unorthodoxically but, arguably, *badly*? Can they inhabit the realm of the aesthetic? We need to ask ourselves where we can possibly locate this subjectivity that wanders throughout an external, yet strange world.

Throughout the late 1970s and early 80s, Ted Serios seems to have gone back to where he started, relegated as he was to that area of popular culture occupied by publications like *Fate*: his story appeared in the 1977 documentary *Amazing World of Psychic Phenomena* (hosted by Raymond Burr of *Perry Mason* and *Rear Window* fame) and the weekly TV series *In Search of ...* (hosted by Leonard Nimoy from *Star Trek*).[19] He resurfaced in the summer of 1991 as part of a photographic exhibition in Woodstock, NY, curated by Robert Mahoney, called "Inherent Vice." The term "inherent vice" refers to the propensity for material to deteriorate because of the combination of its components, and Mahoney's concept for the exhibition was a play on this idea: he chose photographers (Kathy Grove, Dennis Farber, Elaine Reichek, Bill Albertini, Melissa Wolf, and Serios) who use old photos whose meanings have changed over time. In her review of "Inherent Vice," *New York Times* critic Vicki Goldberg describes how an artist like Reichek, for example, hand-paints over documentary war photography, thus giving the image "an aura of art" that was not intended in the first place.[20] Goldberg has this to say about the series of photographs created by Serios, who incidentally is the last photographer mentioned in the article:

"Inherent Vice" also includes ... photographs by Ted Serios, "a 76-year-old nonartist." Emanations from Mr. Serios's head when he thinks about hidden photographs are said to take or develop photographs on emulsified paper. The results are not of great esthetic interest, but the method surely beats investing in a Nikon.

It seems at first an odd choice to include the Serios phenomenon – which had during the history of its documentation been attributed to paranormal brain activity and not to any nuanced appreciation of history and the politics of the image – among the conscientious works of these artists. If anything, the inclusion of the thoughtographs appears to be a weird entrance of the unconscious, rather than conscious, interpretation of images into this exhibit. However, in an essay included in the exhibition catalogue, Mahoney focuses on the *aged* quality of the Serios photographs, on what appears to be their instant manufacturing of always and already historical snapshots:

The curious thing about the physical process in real-time presence involved in Serios's events is that they result in photographs that look like they were taken 150 years ago; that is, they have a built-in retrogression. This may serve to minimize the psychic event or be taken to provide a key to the psychology of old photo misreading.[21]

What Mahoney is drawn to is the way Serios's thoughtographs literalize the inevitable historicity of images; in other words, they warn us about the "nostalgia bomb ticking inside all of us" (12) when we look at old photos. Mahoney's move to negate the psychic import of the Polaroids (he does not even mention this twentieth-century medium, which would make it impossible to date the thoughtographs to a time before 1940, and opts instead for "emulsified paper" as a descriptor) signals how the previous need to understand Ted Serios has been displaced here in favor of an appreciation of the referentiality of the photographic medium.[22] The "nostalgia bomb" that Mahoney rejects represents an epistemological difference from our current ways of seeing, which are not only inclined toward material nostalgia (think of Kimmelman's homage to the defunct, yellowing Polaroid), but which ask us to remark on the haunted atmosphere of the Serios photographs. And then there is Goldberg's tongue-in-cheek response to Serios's "supposed" powers, which invites us to read the whole thing as amusing, if not ridiculous. Her dismissal of the supernatural argument in favor of her take on aesthetics stands in stark contrast with the motivation behind exhibiting Serios's thoughtographs in the contemporary art/curatorial scene, as we have seen.

This difference of approach elucidates the residual fashion of what we could call Serios's "everyday paranormal," the interaction of sensual perception and everyday life in the photographs, within the larger discourses on the aesthetic at the time. It is as though there was no place for it, and yet there it was, exhibited alongside artists who strive for aesthetic as well as political value. The discrepancy between approaches to Serios in this fourteen-year span says a lot about how we approach the importance of the everyday as a theoretical category. Goldberg's idea of the aesthetic in 1991, which appears to rely on a high-cultural value system, can be countered with what Ben Highmore has more recently brought to the fore in his *Everyday Life and Cultural Theory*: that the aesthetic, since its inception, was to be a science of the senses.[23] Goldberg's treatment of Serios's unaesthetic versions of photography should indeed be read alongside Terry Eagleton's contemporaneous remarks in 1990 regarding rationalist philosophy's approach to everyday sensory experiences: he writes that "it is as though philosophy suddenly wakes up to find that there is a dense, swarming territory beyond its own mental enclave which threatens to fall utterly outside its sway."[24] This slippery, "swarming" territory of the senses is the very material of everyday life, Highmore reminds us. Our present theoretical climate has been calling for ways to address and represent the disordered mass of everyday events.

The renewal of haunting as an open theoretical category might begin to open avenues into the study of the everyday where different disciplines and phenomenologies might not push one another into recession and out of currency. Instead, it might allow us to think of productive ways of addressing the problematic distinction between the paranormal and aesthetic creation. The immediacy and idiosyncrasy of the Serios phenomenon, aided by the ordinariness of the Polaroid image, resists any attempt at monumentalization, and what we are left with is a series of perceptions of ordinary life. For this reason, there are no handy critical abstractions to which Serios's work lends itself. The thoughtographic imagination of Ted Serios is so strange in itself – so resistant to easy or convincing allegorization – that it can be said to haunt our motivation to overconceptualize the everyday, skirting past it and offering new versions of seeing the world otherwise. If there is any kind of parable to be had from the Serios phenomenon, it takes the form of a question posed to our current lexicon for dealing with the everyday, for he makes us wonder whether we have to make the everyday into something strange in order to find it interesting.

NOTES

1   Julio Cortázar, "Las babas del diablo," in *Las armas secretas* (Buenos Aires: Editorial Sudamericana, 1966), 81. My translation.

2   Susan Sontag, *On Photography* (London, New York: Penguin, 2002), 154.

3   Quoting Richard Chalfen in his essay "Photography Degree Zero: A Cultural History of the Polaroid Image," Peter Buse notes that by 1983, "46.3 percent of American households contained a self-developing camera." Buse, "Photography Degree Zero," *New Formations* 62 (Autumn 2007): 33.

4   Buse writes about a number of Polaroid users' manuals that emerged in the 1950s and 60s, among them one by photographer Ansel Adams (in 1963) and one by scientist John Dickson in 1964 (40).

5   In recent years, the Polaroid company has reformulated its product by producing a digital version of the camera. As claimed in their website, they are "reinventing instant photography for the digital age." See http://www.polaroid.com/pogo.

6   Michael Kimmelman, "The Polaroid: Imperfect, Yet Magical," *The New York Times*, December 27, 2008, http://www.nytimes.com/2008/12/28/weekinreview/28kimmelman. html?scp=4&sq=polaroid%20&st=cse.

7   See, for example, Tom Gunning's work on ghost photography's predecessor, the phantasmagoria, in "Phantasmagoria and the Manufacturing of Illusions and Wonder: Towards a Cultural Optics of the Cinematic Apparatus," in *The Cinema, A New Technology for the 20th Century*, ed. André Gaudreault, Catherine Russell and Pierre Veronneau (Lausanne: Editions Payot, 2004), 31–44. See also Michael Leja, *Looking Askance: Skepticism and American Art from Eakins to Duchamp* (Berkeley: University of California Press, 2004).

8   Another recent exhibition featuring ghost photography was *Brought to Light: Photography and the Invisible, 1840–1900* at the San Francisco Museum of Modern Art, which ran from October 2008 to January 2009. It was curated by Corey Keller, Jennifer Tucker, Tom Gunning, and Maren Gröning.

9   Tom Gunning, "Phantom Images and Modern Manifestations: Spirit Photography, Magic Theater, Trick Films, and Photography's Uncanny," in *Fugitive Images: From Photography to Video*, ed. Patrice Petro (Bloomington and Indianapolis: Indiana University Press, 1995), 48.

10   Randy Kennedy, "The Ghost in the Darkroom," *The New York Times*, September 4, 2005.

11   Information supplied via email by Metropolitan Museum of Art Press Department, April 3, 2009. This figure, however, is considerably lower than the number of attendants to the Diane Arbus exhibition (221,918), which was housed in the Metropolitan Museum from March 8 to May 30, 2005.

12   Michael Kimmelman, "Ghost in the Lens, Tricks in the Darkroom," *The New York Times*, September 30, 2005. I should correct Kimmelman by saying that Serios did not depend on hypnosis to produce the thoughtographs. For his part, *New York Times* critic Randy Newman writes about the inclusion of Serios in the *Perfect Medium* exhibit: "[The 120 pictures in the exhibition] are ... by and large, the visual records of decades of fraud, cons, flimflams and gullibility – though there are also some pictures, like those produced by an eccentric Chicago bellhop, Ted Serios, said to be purely from his thoughts in the 1960's, that have never been adequately explained." Randy Newman, "The Ghost in the Darkroom," *The New York Times*, September 4, 2005.

13   Jule Eisenbud, *The World of Ted Serios: "Thoughtographic" Studies of an Extraordinary Mind* (New York: William Morrow & Company, 1967), 24. The phenomenon of "thoughtography" has its origins in a series of experiments conducted by Tomokishi Fukurai between 1910 and 1913 at the Imperial University in Tokyo, Japan. The doctor would ask known mediums to concentrate on a range of forms, from simple geometrical shapes to calligraphic symbols, which the mediums then supposedly imprinted on covered metallic plates that were located up to three hundred miles away (249–251).

14   According to Stephen Raude in the *Perfect Medium* exhibition book, Martin Gardner claimed in a 1982 article in *Nature* magazine that Randi was able to produce the thoughtography phenomenon, "and with more skill" than Serios. Raude says these are "unsubstantiated claims" as "Randi has never even attempted to duplicate the Serios phenomena under conditions resembling those that prevailed during Serios's tests" and he failed to produce even vaguely similar results when he was a guest on the morning television show *Today* on October 4, 1967. Raude, "The Thoughtographs of Ted Serios," in *The Perfect Medium: Photography and the Occult*, ed. Clément Chéroux, Andreas Fischer et al. (New Haven and London: Yale University Press, 2005), 157, n2.

15   In the chapter titled "The Anatomy of Resistance," Eisenbud describes the affinity between his situation and James's: "In 1901, William James described his difficulty in getting his Harvard colleagues to sit in on a session or two with one of the most remarkable mediums of the day, the paranormality of whose trance 'knowings' he, as well as numerous others who were to study her intensively over a period of twenty-five years, felt was absolutely beyond question ... I am sorry to report that several generations later the type of irrational behavior that James described, and the temper which permits it, is far from impossible" (310–311).

16   Roland Barthes, *Camera Lucida: Reflections on Photography*, trans. Richard Howard (London: Vintage, 2000), 27. I should note that Barthes depends on referential photography, mostly portraits, to elucidate his theories of the *studium* and *punctum*, and the contingency of which he speaks in *Camera Lucida* does not address the lack of specificity encountered in the Serios thoughtographs. See note 21 for further discussion of the applicability of Barthes to the Serios phenomenon.

17   Pierre Bourdieu, *Photography: A Middle-Brow Art* (Cambridge, UK: Polity Press, 1996), 19.

18   See David Frisby, *Fragments of Modernity: Theories of Modernity in the Work of Simmel, Kracauer and Benjamin* (Cambridge, UK: Polity Press, 1985), 71.

19   The episode "In Search of Ghosts in Photography" was part of the sixth season of the show, and aired in September 1981.

20   Goldberg, "Photography View; Context is All–Or Nothing," *The New York Times*, July 7, 1991, http://www.nytimes.com/1991/07/07/arts/photography-view-context-is-all-or-nothing.html?pagewanted=1.

21   Robert Mahoney, "Inherent Vice: Old Photos," *Center Quarterly* 12, no. 3 (1991):
      12. Mahoney offers a different reading of the applicability of Barthes to the Serios
      phenomenon, one which highlights the themes of realism and emanation from *Camera
      Lucida*. Mahoney posits that "Ted Serios literalizes Barthes's realism with regard to
      photography. In *Camera Lucida* Barthes writes, 'The photograph is literally an emanation
      of the referent. From a real body, which was there, proceed radiations which ultimately
      touch me, who am here.' ... I can take or leave the paranormal explanations; what
      interests me is that this reputed physical emanation is the most reductivist and literal
      rhetorical trope of Barthes's realism: It transforms realism, by means of the literalization
      of retrogression, into hyperrealism" (12). Mahoney approaches Serios's photographs via
      a questioning of authenticity and the sentimentalism that is attached to old images. His
      interpretation of the thoughtographs as "hyperreal" is problematic, given that they do
      not necessarily point to a referent (one reality and one realism), and it is precisely the
      unrecognizability of most of the images on the Polaroids that makes them so strange.
      Finally, there is another level of "authenticity" in the Serios case, which relates to the
      controversy surrounding the veracity of the phenomenon, and the intentions that lie
      behind the production of such a phenomenon.

22   Other questions that arise, when reading Mahoney and Goldberg in conjunction, are:
      if a camera is potentially unnecessary, what does this say about the practice of taking
      pictures? Is the Nikon itself the inherent vice of photography, instead of the image, which
      is likely to fade?

23   Ben Highmore, *Everyday Life and Cultural Theory* (London and New York: Routledge,
      2002), 19–20.

24   Quoted in Highmore, *Everyday Life*, 20.

Chapter 20

"Following the Ghost": The Psychogeography of Alternative Country

Anthony Hutchison

From Ethnomusicology to Geomusicology

Country music is a genre defined by a sense of place. From its inception, however, the ethnomusicology and academic treatment of "roots" music was more informed by temporal than spatial ideas. The seminal work of John and Alan Lomax in archiving a vast agglomeration of field recordings, for example, was motivated primarily by a conservation ethic – a desire to preserve the integrity of American folklore traditions in the face of an ever-burgeoning mass musical culture. Alan Lomax, in particular, was prone to view folk songs as vehicles of oral history. His work was instrumental in the formulation of the "grassroots" designation that, by the 1950s, enabled discrimination between recuperative or "popularizing" folk that, in Lomax's words, "shows us what we want to see," and a purportedly more authentic version that "shows the way it was, or is, in America for [the folk singer] and his people."[1] The stress here on tradition and the idea of roots music as an outlet for oral history has had a powerful afterlife in cultural studies of American folk, country, and blues music. As a consequence, our understanding of the communities and cultures from which these genres have typically emerged has undoubtedly been greatly enriched.

There were, nonetheless, a number of tentative spatial dimensions to Lomax's analyses and theorizations that ran alongside the more historically oriented elements. In "America Sings the Saga of America," a 1947 piece for the *New York Times Magazine*, for instance, Lomax details what he describes as a number of "dangerous potentialities" that folklore movements must reckon with. Among these are the processes of industrialization and urbanization that have radically altered much of the spatial context for American folk music:

Rural folklore can be, falsely, opposed to city folklore, thus creating or widening the split between city and country populations. We are coming to find, however, that oral literature exists in the factories and slums, as another aspect of the rural folklore.[2]

As well as noting the significance of the city as a site of American folklore, Lomax is also alert here to heterogeneous spatial elements at a national level that might account for regional patterns in the origins and geographical spread of various forms of roots music. This extends to questions of taste and preference as well as others of genre and style as ways in which the relationship between musical forms and specific cities, states, or regions might be determined. These were issues that were undoubtedly pressing given the new technologies of recording reproduction and dissemination that drove the "nationalization" of roots music in the postwar period. The fact that such forms had once been largely confined, in terms of both their production and reception, to relatively circumscribed geographical zones of origin undoubtedly gave this music much of what was regarded as its cultural integrity; it also nonetheless ensured an immense degree of variation across regions. This variation, however, could only be widely recognized once the technologies became available to bring it to wider attention. As Lomax notes in his introduction to *Folk Songs of North America*, "the map" sings.[3]

While, however, Lomax occasionally may have recognized the spatial or geographic factors that bore upon his project, he was never especially attentive to their broader intellectual or socio-cultural implications. The musical folklorists of the Lomax era were representatives of an approach that would later be defined in terms of "cultural anthropology" and, as such, remained relatively unconcerned with questions related to the impact of space, place, and locale on the folk cultures they studied. By the 1970s nonetheless a more sustained and comprehensive effort to engage with these questions had begun. The new approach was to emerge from a renegade element within the ranks of cultural geography. The differences in approach were most obviously methodological and discursive in character. Tables, charts, and maps were painstakingly assembled and conclusions relayed in the language of social science. It was time, according to the cultural geographers, for American folk music to be subjected to "a locational analysis [that seeks] to understand why various phenomena are where they are."[4]

The first edition of *The Sounds of People and Places*, a landmark work in this field edited by George O. Carney, appeared in 1978, and was the culmination of an enormously fruitful first wave of scholarship. Despite a subsequent slowdown, by 1993 a network of more than fifty of those interested in the sub-discipline had been established and, in 2003, *Sounds* itself moved into a fourth edition. In recounting the various experiences he acquired in a career given over to this topic, Carney has also usefully tabulated a number of "conceptual subdivisions" that have helped him to organize *Sounds*, such as "spatial variation" and "culture hearth" (which denote musical taste preferences and origins as they relate to region or locale). Yet just as Lomax identified possible concerns that would later be taken up by more spatially oriented musicologists and folklorists, so too has Carney pinpointed potential areas of study for those who might wish to permeate the boundaries of his own geomusicological research. It is the subdivision of "psychological and symbolic elements" more commonly negotiated by cultural critics that perhaps offers the most potential among the possible new fields identified by Carney. Such psychological and symbolic factors inherent within musical forms, Carney believes, can effectively reconstruct the spatial environment out of which they emerge; that is, they can enrich or perhaps even reconceptualize what we take to be the actual "character of a place." The example he invokes for illustrative purposes is that of "surfin' rock" as a crucial cultural component in shaping perceptions of Southern California (16).

It is clear, then, that a theoretical approach to understanding American music that embraces such "psychogeographical" interpretive strategies might be entertained in this instance. Such strategies, it will be posited here, allow us to understand the extent to which the "character of a place" is deeply informed by specific forms of the spectral metaphor. The most commonplace of these is usually that connected with the idea of a place as "haunted" by the past but, as I hope to show, this is far from the only way of configuring the relationship between history and geography in this context. Psychogeography, however, as both a critical and artistic hermeneutic, has found relatively little expression in American culture so it is perhaps worth pausing momentarily to reflect upon this before commencing such a task.

American Psychogeography

The term "psychogeography" first appears in Guy Debord's 1955 essay "Introduction to a Critique of Urban Geography" where it is defined as "the study of the precise laws and specific effects of the geographical environment, consciously organized or not, on the emotions and behavior of individuals."[5] For Debord, the need for a form of critical inquiry premised on the relationship between geography and human consciousness arises out of the novel conditions of postwar urban existence. Crucial to this postwar transformation of urban life is the rise of the automobile and the refashioning of cities such as Paris in response to what Debord describes as the demand for "the smooth circulation of [automobiles'] rapidly increasing quantity" (5).

In this context Debord rejects what he describes as an urbanism of utilitarian "convenience," which ultimately endorses such developments in favor of one commensurate with the modernism of Walter Benjamin. Benjamin's *flâneur* (from the verb *flâner*, "to stroll"), it is argued, offers us the basis for a new urbanism that values contingency, novelty, and happenstance. The motiveless pedestrianism of the *flâneur*, according to Debord, offers liberation via "the path of least resistance which is automatically followed in aimless strolls (and which has no relation to the physical contour of the ground)" (6). These remarks are the first effort towards what Debord would, three years later, having helped establish the Situationist International, theorize more rigorously in terms of *dérive* (or "drifting"). The concept of *dérive* deliberately conveys a more nuanced sense of the act of "drifting" as something that incorporates a form of "playful-constructive behaviour and awareness of psychogeographical effects." In this way it can be "completely distinguish[ed] ... from the classical notions of the journey and the stroll."[6]

Given the situationists' hostility to the automobile for its inhibition of *dérive*, it is perhaps understandable that psychogeography as a conceptual tool has never attained much purchase within U.S. intellectual life. Indeed, Debord supports his critique of the car as the "sovereign good of an alienated life" by noting how the success of the slogan "two cars per family," by the end of the 1950s, is itself being viewed as an index to American *well-being* as well as economic prosperity. Urban growth in the U.S. by this time of course was driven by many relatively new cities, particularly in the West, designed and further developed in response to rapidly expanding rates of private automobile ownership. This resulted in many new U.S. cities strangely de-centered to European eyes, characterized by "sprawl," obtrusive highways, stretched-out suburbs situated for access to strip malls and business parks – nothing, in any case, remotely resembling the glass arcades and intimate pavement life celebrated by Benjamin. Yet Debord in "Theory of the Dérive" also cites the early twentieth-century work of Ernest Burgess and the Chicago School of Sociology as an influence. In particular, he claims, "Burgess's theory of Chicago's social activities as being distributed in distinct concentric zones, will undoubtedly, prove useful in developing *dérives*" (50–51).

The other notion cultivated by the Chicago School that overlaps with the psychogeographical project is the Darwinist-cum-modernist idea of the city as an evolving organism. It is in this way that the city's sites or zones are inextricably connected to the past, a past characterized, according to Debord's fellow situationist Ivan Chtcheglov, by "ghosts bearing all the prestige of their legends."[7] The figurative nature of the language here, which includes both non-corporeal and spectral alongside evolutionary and biological tropes, underpins Chtcheglov's claim in "Formulary for a New Urbanism," that "all cities are geological." Psychogeography might thus be viewed as a depth model of interpretation that draws on, but is not reducible to, Marxist and Freudian methods insofar as its design is to reveal hidden forces. The means by which this is achieved is via a type of historically informed cognitive cartography. As Debord claims:

With the aid of old maps, aerial photographs and experimental dérives, one can draw up hitherto lacking maps of influences, maps whose inevitable imprecision at this early stage is no worse than that of the first navigational charts; the only difference is that it is a matter no longer of precisely delineating stable continents, but of changing architecture and urbanism.[8]

"Maps of influences," of course, recalls the combination of cultural studies and cartography that Carney's geomusicological project consisted of. It is, however, the psychogeographers' insistence on the *symbolic* attributes of space in this context that is most suggestive. In particular, their emphasis on urban space as marked by specters, and "geological" or multi-layered in its historicity, might provide us with the tools to extend Carney's project into the "psychological and symbolic."

The Old, Weird America

The notion of American roots music as a form haunted by the nation's multi-layered past is now a commonplace one. Indeed, for a nation often glibly characterized as harboring and wilfully cultivating an "ahistorical" consciousness, the U.S. has produced popular indigenous musical forms almost obsessively preoccupied with the ghosts of the past.[9] Nowhere is this more evident perhaps than in the work of Bob Dylan, arguably the most important and influential American musician and composer of the past half-century. If we put to one side the flurry of albums released in 1965–1966, which placed Dylan squarely at the center of that period's efforts to reinvent rock and roll as an "art" form, we find that much of his earlier and subsequent work has been more concerned with renovation than it has with innovation. From the early Woody Guthrie-influenced folk records to the "old-time" worship of *The Basement Tapes* (1975) and *John Wesley Harding* (1967) to the neo-spirituals of his late 1970s "'Christian'" phase and late "'minstrel'" records such as *Good As I Been To You* (1992), *World Gone Wrong* (1993), and *Love and Theft* (2001), Dylan has been striving to keep alive a number of overlapping American "roots" idioms.

These records suggest that perhaps the music forms with the biggest impact on Dylan's repertoire over the years are those strands of country blues, old-time, bluegrass, and minstrelsy brought together in Harry Smith's *Anthology of American Folk Music* (1952). This collection of songs recorded between 1927 and 1932 by obscure jug bands, family groups, and assorted folk musicians, both black and white, gave considerable cultural momentum to the mid-century folk revival. Much of this revival was, of course, *urban*-based and it was out of the lively Greenwich Village scene that Dylan himself emerged in the early 1960s.

This axis running from songs first performed and composed in the nineteenth century, recorded for the first time in the 1920s and 30s, and "recovered" during the mid-century folk revival is brilliantly traced in Greil Marcus's *Invisible Republic: Bob Dylan's Basement Tapes*.[10] In this work Marcus uses Dylan's 1967 recordings with The Band as a way of exploring the ways in which traditional balladry and song convey a sense of the strangeness and otherworldly quality of the American past. Importantly, he notes a crucial difference between the motivations of those at the forefront of the folk revival (the young Dylan included) and the Dylan who stepped out of one counter-culture in 1967 in order to immerse himself more deeply in some of the roots traditions he had ostensibly stepped back from around 1964.

These roots traditions underpinned the music on *The Basement Tapes*. The difference this time was that Dylan would come closer to seeing this music in its own idiosyncratic terms. Whereas the folk revival still stood in the cultural shadow of the Old Left, much of the time privileging material thought to support progressive political ends, the Dylan of the late 1960s saw in the music of the American past something altogether more complex and unnerving. This was, in Marcus's words, the "old, weird America"[11] of the central and southern Appalachians so conspicuous in the record collection of the proto-beatnik Harry Smith. It was a world that, in many ways, only finally came "down from the mountain" when recording technology became portable and the commercial potential of this music was recognized in the 1920s and 1930s. The most well-known process of this sort, the 1927 Bristol, Tennessee sessions, in which producer Ralph Peer taped music by the likes of Jimmie Rodgers and Harry Smith favorites The Carter Family, has been described as country music's "big bang."[12] As Marcus claims, this music now seemed to strike Dylan with a new force. *The Basement Tapes*, in this way, was a response to Dylan's altered understanding of this tradition: "it was as if he saw traditional music as being made less by history or circumstance than by particular people, for particular, unknowable reasons – reasons that find their analogues in haunts and ghosts" (29).

The ethic and spirit of *The Basement Tapes* was undoubtedly an animating impulse behind the emergence of "alternative country" in the 1990s. What Marcus describes as the record's "palavers with a community of ghosts" (86) was also in evidence in a good deal of the work produced by artists associated with this movement. Uncle Tupelo, the "first band" of alt. country, encapsulate the "down home" feel of "old time" music in their very name, which combines a family designation (recalling *Anthology* artists such as Mother Maybelle Carter and Uncle Eck Dunford, the Williamson Brothers, and so on) and the obscure Mississippi birthplace of Elvis Presley. Their first album, *No Depression* (1990), was named after the Carter Family classic "No Depression in Heaven."

If Uncle Tupelo often filtered their pre-World War II country influences through more recent sounds emanating from post-punk and 1980s hardcore, Gillian Welch's first album *Revival* (1996) indulged in a more faithful return. Songs like "Orphan Girl" and "Miner's Refrain" were clearly cut from old-time cloth, but Welch's material could also offer intriguing twists on a number of the genre's familiar themes. "Caleb Meyer," for instance, from her second album *Hell Among The Yearlings* (1998), might best be described as a post-feminist murder ballad. Murder ballads were most commonly framed in terms of *amour fou* or sexual jealousy; they could be told from a male point of view ("Knoxville Girl," "Banks of the Ohio," "Omie Wise") or a female one ("Henry Lee," "Frankie and Johnny"). Here, however, Welch reframes the form to go beyond these conventions and, in the process, conveys a more profound sense of the violence and alienation that informed the psychic life of those inhabiting isolated mountain communities. The song is sung from the perspective of Nellie Kane, whose husband has gone on business "off down the mountainside" to Bowling Green, presumably the relatively populous south-central Kentuckian town which serves as a county seat. On learning of this, her neighbour, Caleb Meyer, a drunken moonshiner, drops his bottle and sexually assaults her. The song goes on to detail Nellie's resistance:

I cried My God, I am your child
send your angels down
Then feelin' with my fingertips,
the bottle neck I found

I drew that glass across his neck
as fine as any blade,
and I felt his blood pour fast and hot
around me where I laid.

The invocation of angels and children, and the crisp description of the woman's composure and presence of mind, convey a sense of stillness amid the chaos of rape. This sense is compounded by the quiet, understated single-syllable diction of the subsequent verse ("as fine as any blade," "fast and hot"). All these elements ultimately foreshadow the haunting Nellie feels must await her:

Caleb Meyer, your ghost is gonna
wear them rattlin' chains.
But when I go to sleep at night,
Don't you call my name.

Caleb Meyer's voice promises to join those countless others present among the "hollerin pines" in which he "lived alone." This is a closed, unforgiving world in which the supernatural looms large in the lives of the innocent as well as the guilty. Indeed, the distinction is complicated in "Caleb Meyer," who is murdered with his own weapon, a "victim" of alcoholism, loneliness, and what passes for masculinity in such sealed worlds. The mountainside here is clearly articulated as a haunted space both before and after the attack. The psychic life of both protagonists is a troubled one marked by dead time, poverty, and the religious-existential dread captured so neatly in the colloquial notion of the "God-forsaken" place. Ghosts are unavoidable as everyone carries the pain of earlier generations eking out existences on remote scrubs of land. These are people who bear the scars of frontier hubris, trapped between the desperate need for God amid a landscape that seems to provide overwhelming evidence of his absence.

Uncle Tupelo and Gillian Welch represent one strand of the "ghosting" element so close to the surface in alternative country. Their approach, a self-conscious invocation of the specters of the "invisible republic," is more or less in line with that cultivated by Bob Dylan and The Band back in the late 1960s. Nonetheless, there was another strand that emerged in the 1990s that placed such "palavers with a community of ghosts" within some strikingly novel spatial contexts.

The New, Weird America

Undoubtedly the most significant broad factor shaping country music in the last quarter of the twentieth century has been the destabilization of its traditional non-urban context. The transition to a post-industrial corporate service economy and the consolidation of large-scale agribusiness both served to rapidly increase levels of urbanization and suburbanization. The country music culture industry itself also underwent an intense process of corporatization in the 1980s and 1990s. One repercussion of this was the concentration of more and more artists, songwriting, studio work, and radio stations in Nashville, Tennessee by the end of the century. The dominance of the mass-marketed corporate "arena" sound that evolved from this was one context for the emergence of "alternative country" in the 1990s. As already noted, this music was much more directly rooted in rural white evangelical culture and folklore, its sound anchored in frequently distinct rural and non-urban locales. As such, spectral tropes drawn from the cultural landscape of traditional pre-modern communities and transferred generationally through oral cultures were much more common.

One of the most distinctive elements within alternative country, alongside what is, after all, a fairly uncomplicated desire to return to the sound and ethic of a pre-corporate age, is the extent to which themes and motifs have been quite self-consciously repositioned in postmodern environments. Such environments, in the first instance, are spatial, but the result – a frequently jarring effect that carries a strong scent of what Sigmund Freud described in terms of the uncanny[13] – is ultimately *psychogeographical.*

The turn to ghosts, by contrast, in the wake of Jacques Derrida's *Specters of Marx* seems more difficult to explain.[14] However, somewhat counter-intuitively perhaps and despite Derrida's dependence on Shakespeare's *Hamlet,* it seems to emanate from late nineteenth-century notions of the relationship between science and society. As Avery Gordon claims, it might be said to have its roots in the emergence of both psychoanalysis and Marxism as "scientific … paradigms[s] for understanding the impact of unseen forces."[15] As Derrida and Gordon note, Marx's work is replete with spectral metaphor and Freud's notion of "repression" applied as much to society and Western civilization as it did to individuals.

In his well-known 1919 essay Freud foregrounds two central factors in his own understanding of the uncanny. Firstly, he draws attention to the way in which the idea refers to the de-familiarization of the familiar. The process is, for Freud, a menacing and frequently frightening one captured better by the closest German translation of the *unheimlich* (rendered back into the English as the "unhomely"). This meaning effectively neutralizes the more benign undertones of the uncanny. Instead we feel a greater sense of the "conflict of judgement" (156) imposed upon us as the *heimlich,* the "homely" or "familiar" in an especially sharp form, is reconstituted as the "unhomely." In other words, something we recognize intimately is *both there and no longer there.* The second element underpinning the idea of the uncanny is its atavistic appeal to what Freud describes as "the old *animistic* view of the universe, a view characterized by the idea that the world was peopled with human spirits … this phase did not pass without leaving behind in us residual traces that can still make themselves felt" (147). Freud, then, not only maps out the uncanny with reference to the spectral ("human spirits") but also draws attention to its temporal and spatial moorings in, respectively, an "animistic" phase of the collective past and the trope of the "home." Elsewhere in the essay he illustrates the concept by drawing on ghost stories and Gothic horror narratives. Again, if we take the nation-state (or a part thereof) as a home(land) we can transplant this analysis back onto Marcus's work in which an "invisible republic" underwritten by ghostly presences is revealed in Smith's *Anthology* and Dylan's *Basement Tapes*. The old, uncanny America of the *Anthology*, Marcus claims, was always at bottom "a mystery, an assurance that against every assurance to the contrary, America itself was a mystery" (96).

The specters, unsurprisingly, remain in the twenty-first century. Alternative country artists such as Uncle Tupelo, Gillian Welch, Grant Willard Conspiracy, Wilco, Jim White, and others have ensured that, if anything, such preoccupations have intensified. In a 2002 essay Marcus develops the idea that Smith's project was essentially directed at re-imagining the nation in terms of his own eccentric "outsider" status (the beatnik archivist who often lived as a tramp) as well as that of the *Anthology* artists.[16] Marcus claims that, in this way, Smith promoted a mode of "modernist" folk music, defined as such by its "dramatization of subjectivity" and by the fact that whereas before "the song sung the singer," with Smith's collection "the singer sings the song." The key here, for Marcus, lies in the music's "singularity" – and, we might add, the uncanny, haunted quality it harbors – that "leave[s] the listener with a sense of jeopardy, uncertainty, a morbid sense of past and future" (311).

Towards the end of the piece Marcus takes the opportunity to praise the Albuquerque-based contemporary alt. country husband-and-wife duo The Handsome Family as the group who have "taken up Smith's offering more fully" than any other. The "everyday surrealism" of Rennie Sparks's lyrics and the vocals and music of Brett Sparks, which "mine the deep veins of fatalism in the Appalachian voice" (312) combine to give expression to the haunted spaces of the postmodern world. Their work presents a psychogeography of contemporary America, underwritten by Harry Smith sensibilities.

The urban context is a defining feature in the character of alt. country as a genre. Many of the artists' origins in urban punk scenes has led them to compose "country" music not only characterized by lyrics focused on urban life, but also accompanied by more diverse and often more technologically advanced sources of instrumentation. The Handsome Family's tuba-punctuated "The Woman Downstairs" from *Through The Trees* (1998), for instance, begins with an invocation of Chicago as "where / the woman downstairs / starved herself to death last summer" and ends thus: "The cops wandered through / her dusty rooms / one of them stole her TV." Like many of their songs it foregrounds the alienation of the socially excluded by paying close attention to the grotesque texture of the closed environments they inhabit: the laundromats, the corner bars, the abandoned street dogs. The "disappearance" of the socially excluded leaves a trace in songs such as this, which can be viewed as efforts to follow their ghosts. As Gordon notes:

Following the ghost is about making a contact that changes you and refashions the social relations in which you are located. It is about putting life back in where only a vague memory or a bare trace was visible to those who bothered to look. It is sometimes about writing ghost stories, stories that not only repair representational mistakes, but also strive to understand the conditions under which a memory was produced in the first place, toward a countermemory, for the future. (22)

Through The Trees concludes with a more literal invocation of the spectral in which a third-person narrative describes a "ghostly" self who "runs up credit card bills / and clogs up the toilet with bottles of pills." "My Ghost" is a contemporary fable of modern madness where "bi-polarity" is underwritten by the forces of a corporate pharma-psychiatry industry and an infantilizing culture of reward: "Here in the bipolar ward / if you shower / you get a gold star." The song ends on a note of defiance evident in the description of a space haunted by the suggestively prophetic sound of the patient's ghostly alter ego: "days pass slow in slippers and robe / but my ghost still bangs on the roof / like John the Baptist in the rain."

"My Ghost" features horns and jaunty autoharp strums, contrapuntal elements which frequently, as elsewhere in the music of the Handsome Family, serve up an uncanny fusion of the grotesque and the tenderly affective. *Through The Trees* and later albums also feature the melodica, a wind instrument with a keyboard attached to the pipe. Invented by the German company Hohner in the 1950s, the melodica often affords a ghostly backdrop for the band's music. Brett Sparks has also increasingly come to make use of technological advances in musical production – particularly those connected with digital recording equipment. Indeed this formal element also has increasingly come to find *thematic* expression in Rennie Sparks's lyrics. Such concerns are best understood with reference to spectral tropes as well as those Jeffrey Sconce, in a remarkable critical study, has described in terms of "electronic presence."[17]

Last Days of Wonder

In *Haunted Media: Electronic Presence from Telegraphy to Television*, Sconce details the way innovations in electronic media technologies have given rise to anxieties and preoccupations normally associated with the spiritual domain. In particular, nineteenth-century developments in electrical science, telegraphy, and wireless communications, as a result of their capacity to compress space and time, were seen to present a model of subjectivity "reconstituted through technology as an entity at once interstitial and uncanny" (28). In this respect we can say that the music of the Harry Smith *Anthology*, itself preserved as a result of new developments in electrical recording equipment, embraces this model. Indeed, we might go on to say that it is this music's uncanny registration as "electronic presence," combined with the cultural interstitiality Marcus highlights, that leaves listeners with a nagging, inchoate sense of its "modernism."

One of Sconce's central aims is to note the shifting ways in which what Freud describes as the "residual traces" of our "animistic" spiritual inheritance continue to transmute with each "miraculous" electronic invention of late modernity. In his analyses of the underlying metaphysics of nineteenth-century ideas of electricity as a "life force" (7), telegraphic "presence" (14), and 1920s experiments in "ghost broadcasting" (75), Sconce convincingly charts the evolving uncanny of electronic media. The haunted space here, of course, is disembodied, immaterial space, from the "ether" of radio waves to the cyberspace of the postmodern imaginary.

In *Last Days of Wonder* (2006), The Handsome Family engage in a fascinating musical exploration of a number of these ideas. Automation, notions of the "life energy" of electricity and electrical consumer products, as well as, more generally, the psychic impact of contemporary U.S. consumer society, have long been themes in their work. *Last Days of Wonder*, nonetheless, seeks to extend the spatial boundaries within which such explorations usually occur. Formally, there is an even greater amount of experimentation, particularly with reference to new digital home recording technologies (the album was recorded in the garage of the Sparks' Albuquerque home). The computer, for example, was central to the recording procedures. Thousands of samples were collected on the band's hard drive – an old Mellotron loop, for instance, inspiring "These Golden Jewels."[18] More fundamentally, the band fused digital recording techniques with vintage instrumentation. Pedal steel guitar and musical saw performances were emailed in from Chicago and London respectively and drums were recorded programmatically, that is, in the way in which one would operate a drum machine – one piece of kit at a time. The recordings would then be spliced together on a Mac PC.[19]

The uncanny soundscapes that emerge from the process underpin the content of Rennie Sparks's lyrics. The record, in this respect, demonstrates an extraordinary degree of formal and thematic integration best illustrated, perhaps, by the song that can be regarded as the album's centerpiece. "Tesla's Hotel Room" presents a condensed poetic summary of the last days of Serbian-American inventor and engineer Nicola Tesla, who was responsible for the development of alternating current at the end of the nineteenth century. For a number of years the direct current system of his wealthier and more ruthless rival Thomas Edison was favored over AC, but Tesla's polyphase system, being more reliable, efficient, and safe, eventually won out. Despite being a pioneer in wireless communications as well as electrical engineering, however, Tesla was an inhibited and inhibiting "outsider" figure who would live out the final decade of his life impoverished and alone in a New York City hotel.

It is these final years that the song alights on, describing the particulars of the room itself, a space rendered uncannily vivid by the supplementary references to Tesla's own haunted dreams of future scientific invention. These include "a camera to photograph thoughts, vacuum tube lights, wireless phones." The potency of this lyric lies in the juxtaposition of a seemingly "miraculous" innovation alongside others from the late nineteenth and twentieth century, now woven into the fabric of our everyday lives. The broader context here, of course, is provided by the album's title, which seemingly alludes to Max Weber's secularization thesis. In "Science as a Vocation," Weber describes modernity as a process fundamentally characterized by "disenchantment," as increasingly entrenched and widely disseminated processes of rationalization replace religious ideas as central sources of cultural, social, and political authority.[20]

Yet as Sconce points out, overly tidy separations of the secular and the sacred, the scientific and the spiritual, invariably disregard a "shadow history of telecommunications that continues to this day" (83). Telecommunications technology, in particular, is resonant as a consequence of the wonder and unease innovation in the field perpetually generates. In its defiance of "corporeal common sense" such innovation reproduces "nervous ambivalence ... a simultaneous desire and dread of actually making such extraordinary forms of contact" (83). The continual interest of great scientists such as Marconi and Einstein, as well as Edison and Tesla, in technological projects designed with occult, paranormal, and extraterrestrial forms of "contact" in mind testifies to this link.[21]

Perhaps even more so than the group's earlier releases, *Last Days of Wonder* seems motivated by a desire to combat the process of disenchantment announced by Weber, to retrieve the "counter-memory" of figures such as Tesla – that is, figures drawn from both the "old" and the "new, weird America." Such figures can also be positioned within an indigenous, visionary Romantic tradition that, since Emerson, has sought salvation via immersion in deep experience and "wonderment" – particularly as it is directed at the nation's geography. The album is replete with a sense of wonder at the continuing possibility of profound human connection even in the most ostensibly de-humanizing environments: before the security cameras overlooking a graveyard ("White Lights"), amid the cigarette machines and "fallen pins set right up again" ("Bowling Alley Bar"), and on a golf course at night ("Flapping Your Broken Wings").

Last Days of Wonder also contains a singular take on the type of "supermodern" environment Marc Augé delineates in his work *Non-Places*.[22] "All The Time In Airports" inhabits the consciousness of an airline passenger who speaks of seeing a mysterious entity during the dead time before or between transit. The spectrality of the vision – which could be the spooked singer's self-reflection – underlines Augé's idea of the airport as a *non-place*. An image is glimpsed "in the windows of the shuttle trains" or "in the lines of people / waiting at the frozen yoghurt stand." The entity is seen "flipping through the pages / of books by millionaires," "sleeping in a chair," and "sitting on your suitcase." Post 9/11 anxieties, too, are clearly addressed: "And, as I pull my shoes off / put my coins in the plastic tray / I see you past the X-ray machine / Just a hundred feet away." This verse might be seen to touch upon the fear and dread that attend twenty-first-century constructions of the terrorist as specter (consider the videotapes of pre-recorded messages and CCTV images of suicide bombers' prior movements). Whatever the case, the song gives a remarkable degree of expression to Augé's notion of the non-place as

A world ... where transit points and temporary abodes are proliferating under luxurious or inhuman conditions ... where the habitué of supermarkets, slot machines and credit cards communicates wordlessly, through gestures, with an abstract, unmediated commerce; a world thus surrendered to solitary individuality ... (78)

The musical momentum of the track is sustained by an uneasy mix of conventional folk baritone and a submerged but continuous moog-synth which provides a metronomic, rhythmic counterpoint.[23] This "folktronica" generic hybrid structure adds to the disorienting effect of the song. What it underlines here, even more emphatically than is the case in the band's earlier output, is a preoccupation with the psychogeography of American space (and, we might add, in this particular instance, non-space). The Handsome Family's musical project is thus ultimately one of a recuperation that involves the reconstruction of the present as much as the past. They understand that the only way we can leave our mark on the world, the only way to invest the future with hope, is by forging the counter-memories of tomorrow. This necessarily involves the steadfast pursuit of those specters that refuse to be exorcised from our *new* as well as our old spatial environments. The focus on the contemporary as it bears upon ideas about past, present, and future is crucial insofar as it points to a prospective, political dimension to *Last Days of Wonder*. In developing these more diverse and expansive approaches to following ghosts, then, alt. country artists may well be enabling generations to come to more readily follow our own.

NOTES

1   Alan Lomax, "Getting To Know Folk Music" (1960), reprinted in Lomax, *Selected Writings 1934–1997* (New York: Routledge, 2003), 204.

2   Alan Lomax, "America Sings the Saga of America" (1947), reprinted in Lomax, *Selected Writings*, 90, emphasis in original.

3   Alan Lomax, *Folk Songs of North America* (Garden City, New York: Doubleday, 1960), xv.

4   George Carney, *The Sounds of People and Places: A Geography of American Folk and Popular Music* (London: Rowman and Littlefield, 1997), 2.

5   Guy Debord, "Introduction to a Critique of Urban Geography" reprinted in Ken Knabb, ed., *Situationist International Anthology* (Berkeley: Bureau of Public Secrets, 1981), 5.

6   Guy Debord, "Theory of the Dérive" (1956), reprinted in Knabb, *Situationist International Anthology*, 51.

7   Ivan Chtcheglov, "Formulary for a New Urbanism" (1953), reprinted in Knabb, *Situationist Anthology International*, 1.

8   Debord, "Theory of the Dérive," 53.

9   For a collection of essays that stresses the importance of "spectrality" in a broader national cultural context see Jeffrey Weinstock, ed., *Spectral America: Phantoms and the National Imagination* (Madison: Popular Press, 2004).

10   Greil Marcus, *Invisible Republic: Bob Dylan's Basement Tapes* (London: Picador, 1997).

11   This is the title Marcus published the book under in the U.S.

12   See Charles K. Wolfe and Ted Olsen, eds., *The Bristol Sessions: Writings About the Big Bang of Country Music* (Jefferson: Mcfarland Publishers, 2005).

13   Sigmund Freud, *The Uncanny*, trans. David Mclintock (London: Penguin, 2003).

14   Jacques Derrida, *Specters of Marx: The State of the Debt, the Work of Mourning, & the New International*, trans. Peggy Kamuf (London: Routledge, 1994).

15   Avery Gordon, *Ghostly Matters: Haunting and the Sociological Imagination* (Minneapolis: University of Minnesota Press, 1997), 196.

16   Greil Marcus, "American Folk," *Granta* 76 (2002): 301–315.

17   Jeffrey Sconce, *Haunted Media: Electronic Presence From Telegraphy to Television* (Durham: Duke University Press, 2000).

18   Sampling is itself now understood as a key "ghosting" phenomenon by a number of contemporary musicians, music critics, and scholars alike. Indeed a group of artists

who foreground this element in their own projects have been associated with a "sonic hauntology" movement.

19 These details are described on the press release for *Last Days of Wonder*. See http://loosemusic.com/handsomefamily/index.html.

20 Max Weber, *From Max Weber: Essays in Sociology*, trans. and ed. H. H. Gerth and C. Wright Mills (New York: Oxford University Press, 1946), 129–156.

21 For discussions of these figures in this context see Sconce, *Haunted Media*, 76, 81–83, 96–97.

22 Marc Augé, *Non-Places: Introduction to an Anthropology of Supermodernity* (London: Verso, 1995).

23 "Moog" was the generic name given to a number of the early analog synthesizers developed in the 1960s by Robert Moog. Moog's work developed from his interest in the theremin – an electronic instrument described as "similar to that of a ghostly, wailing human voice." Trevor Pinch and Frank Trocco, *Analog Days: The Invention and Impact of the Moog Synthesizer* (Cambridge, MA: Harvard University Press, 2004), 14. The distinctive, high-pitched sound of Moog's early models, interestingly, can evoke a similar sensation and has thus given the moog something of a haunting, "retro" vibe to twenty-first-century listeners.

Chapter 21

Haunted by a Melody: Ghosts, Transgression, and Music in *Twin Peaks*

Isabella van Elferen[1]

> This is clearly a place that inspires dreaming about darkness and light. And who knows what dreams are real?[2]

David Lynch and Mark Frost's television series *Twin Peaks* (ABC, 1990–1991) is set in a quiet, small American town. From the first camera shots observing the discovery of Laura Palmer's murdered body, however, the tranquil countryside atmosphere is shot through with ambiguity. The nostalgic home is by no means idyllic, but reveals itself as a borderland where life and death, ghosts and humans, and good and evil, dwell side by side. The disturbing soundtrack that Angelo Badalamenti composed for the series has often been described as the most eerie film music ever. It accompanies the ghostly dimension of the series and conjures up ghosts, making them discernible even when the eye does not see them. The *Twin Peaks* specters haunt the viewer even more than they do the characters, because Badalamenti's music gives them a ghostly voice that is often only heard by TV audiences.

This essay explores the spectral dimensions of *Twin Peaks*, both on the level of plot developments and on the level of their cinematic and musical mediation. Combining Bataillean ideas regarding transgression with theories of spectrality and haunting, I argue that medial agents such as film, phones, turntables, and soundtrack not only summon the ghosts of Twin Peaks, but are also operative factors in taking both televisual characters and audiences into a transgressive space where dichotomies collide. Media in *Twin Peaks* are spectral voices expressing the suspicion that there is no meaning behind mediation, no referentiality behind presentation. Andrew Smith describes ghosts as "historical beings because they are messengers about the preoccupations of a particular age.... Ghosts are never just ghosts; they provide us with an insight into what haunts our culture."[3] What do Laura Palmer, Bob, and the

Red Room people tell us about televisual mediation, and which role does the series' soundtrack play in bringing about their spectral messages?[4]

Ghosts and Transgressions

Twin Peaks starts out as a detective story: a girl has been killed, there are some resemblances to another murder (that of Teresa Banks, whose story appears in the *Twin Peaks*-prequel *Fire Walk With Me*), and FBI agent Dale Cooper is called in to solve the mystery. This plot set-up initially leads the viewer to think that this story is about facts, and will evolve in a linear and teleological way, like any whodunit. Nothing could be more deceptive, though, as a simultaneous blueprint for the series is that of a soap opera, in which the viewer witnesses the lives and loves of a group of characters. The plot line is not linear but chaotic, and never-ending rather than teleological.

The confusing combination of plot designs becomes seriously disturbing, however, when the ghosts of *Twin Peaks* make themselves known. There are five of them, and they are cast as characters that are not quite as ephemeral as the ghosts in traditional ghost stories or horror films. The central ghost character is Laura Palmer, the dead girl who is always present *in absentiae*. Her ghostly antagonist is Bob, a spirit who lives inside his human hosts, and makes them do evil things – like kill Laura Palmer. Bob used to have a partner in crime, Mike, who is also a "parasite" feeding on other beings. Besides Bob and Mike, who are explicitly associated with evil, another duo of ghostly characters appears to Cooper. In an unsettling dream he sees himself twenty-five years in the future in a red room, an almost empty space lined with red curtains and featuring a geometrical pattern in black and white on the floor. Here he meets the "Man from Another Place" (MFAP), a strange, small dancing man dressed in red who gives him enigmatic messages in backwards speech loops. Related to MFAP as his opposite outside of the Red Room is the Giant, whom Cooper meets in visions when he is awake. These two ghostly beings are not related to either good or evil; they seem to dwell somewhere in between that dichotomy, and establish the link between both. They are ghosts of liminality.

Whereas "traditional" ghosts in stories or films often appear according to conventionalized representational models, the ghosts in *Twin Peaks* seem to elude such models, which makes it hard to grasp what they are, what they do, and how to understand them metaphorically. The *Twin Peaks* ghosts do not dress in white sheets and are not transparent or bloody; they appear to be much more like "normal people" than fits the comfort zone. Correspondingly, if ghosts are usually dead people returning from their ghostly realm to haunt the living in the "real" world, it is unclear in this case whether these ghosts are dead, alive, or neither, and whether ghostly and human spaces are so evidently separated. The cinematography of *Twin Peaks* underlines the physical and psychological closeness of these two spaces. Ghosts, moreover, are traditionally filmed in short shots and jump cuts, so as to establish a clear cinematic distance between the ghostly and the human. In *Twin Peaks*, these techniques are only employed when someone is "damned" (which happens only twice); in all other cases the characters have fairly relaxed conversations with them. The series' soundtrack also works differently than that of other ghost films. Only Bob's first appearance in the series is traditionally scored with a violin and brass crescendo building up and suddenly erupting in three loud, fully orchestrated, dissonant explosions set in by gong beats. Such scoring clearly demarcates the distance between haunted reality and visiting ghost; but the scored music for all other ghost scenes is uncannily unexciting, consisting of long-sustained low notes and a vague suggestion of wind (Bob, Mike, Giant), or a jazzy sax tune (MFAP).

The ghosts in *Twin Peaks*, then, are not as Other as traditional ghosts, and neither is the space that they inhabit clearly separated from the non-ghostly world. If ghost stories traditionally stress that the world of humans and the world of ghosts are ultimately non-unifiably separated from one another, this separation is at most unclear in *Twin Peaks* – there is possibly some ghostliness everywhere. The only traditional ghost here is Laura Palmer, the dead girl who haunts the town of Twin Peaks and the series. She appears to be the ghost of innocence, a figure who strikes a clear contrast with the evident evil of her killer. Is the ghost of Laura Palmer that unambivalently innocent, though? Does she fit that conveniently into the binary mold of the traditional ghost story?

In addition to the confusing ontology and function of the spectral *Twin Peaks* characters, the TV viewer gradually discovers that the woods around the town hide the dark secrets of the White and Black Lodge. These mythological places represent the garden of Eden, where people are innocent and life is good, and the garden of Evil, where no one is innocent and perversion constitutes both norm and deviation. The Black Lodge is the home of Bob and Mike. In between the Black and White Lodge is the Red Room, the "waiting room," as MFAP calls it, which is visited by Cooper in his dream. The Red Room can be seen as Purgatory, a twilight zone inhabited by the liminal ghosts MFAP and Giant. These three worlds emanate from the woods, but their energies stretch out to the town of Twin Peaks. The White and the Black Lodge, moreover, are not separated from one another by the firm lines of law, morality, or even reality. They seem to exist simultaneously, one reality being the shadow side of the other. The soap opera characters each have their other, often dark, sides: Laura Palmer's father Leland is a caring dad and uncle, but kills his daughter and niece, and Laura is unmasked to have led various double lives, involving several lovers, prostitution, cocaine abuse, and an ill-fated death-wish. Characters and plot developments can flip from one to the other side *with a snap of the fingers*, unnoticeable from either the diegetic characters' or viewers' standpoints.

Leland Palmer's behavior, for instance, is extremely unpredictable and puzzling. In Episode 2 he stands next to the record-player and frantically snaps his fingers with a very frustrated expression on his face. He puts on an old jazz record, takes Laura's photo, and "dances" with it, spinning around his own axis while weeping and yelping at an increasing volume, ignoring the ringing phone. When his wife Sarah comes in and tries to stop him, they struggle, the photo frame breaks, and in a Macbeth-like move, Leland smears his blood on the photo. The TV viewer can only sympathize with Sarah's desperate cry – "What is going on in this house?" Is Leland simply grieving excessively, or is he switching sides from Bob-inhabited killer to bereft father? If so, where are the borders between the two? These questions are not answered onscreen; on the contrary, ambivalence and confusion continue to be built up, coming to their enigmatic climax in the last episode of the series.

The town of Twin Peaks is thus haunted by pervasive ambiguity, which is also reflected in the series' narrative strategies. While Cooper tries to solve the murder case he discovers no real clues except those in his dream, but instead becomes enveloped in all the mysteries in the town and the woods around it. Already in Episode 1 the teleology of the detective story is nowhere to be found, and it only decreases as the series develops. As such, *Twin Peaks* radically dismantles various televisual conventions. On a plot level, the borders between ghostly and human spaces as well as those between good and evil are continuously transgressed. This motif is met by the anti-linear, dreamlike narrative of the series, which endorses a further and even more destabilizing transgression: that of the boundaries between the real and the imaginary, the mediated and the unmediated.

Fred Botting and Scott Wilson have argued that because of the constant plot transgressions *Twin Peaks* operationalizes Baudrillard's notion that "the principle of evil is synonymous with the principle of reversal," a notion they link to Georges Bataille's ideas regarding transgression.[5] Their Baudrillardian reading of Bataille is framed dialectically between the affirmation and negation of good and evil. Bataille, however, takes a decidedly *non*-dialectical viewpoint. He asserts that indulging excessively in the affirmation of a limit through, for instance, sexual experience in eroticism offers a way to eventually suspend the dialectic.[6] Affirming the limit into ecstatic, transgressive rapture simultaneously exposes the limitlessness of the limit and, thereby, enduringly negates originary signification: "Transgression … constitutes a permanent short-circuit of referentiality."[7] By ultimately, if temporarily, transgressing the boundaries between dialectical opposites (two beings, flesh and spirit, norm and taboo, etc.), eroticism endorses what Bataille envisions as the sovereignty of the non-dialectic.[8] In his "Preface to Transgression" Foucault elaborates on the non-dialectical nature of Bataillean transgression:

> Transgression does not seek to oppose one thing to another, nor does it achieve its purpose through mockery or by upsetting the solidity of foundations; it does not transform the other side of the mirror, beyond an invisible and uncrossable line, into a glittering expanse…. Its role is to measure the excessive distance that it opens at the heart of the limit and to trace the flashing line that causes the limit to arise. Transgression contains nothing negative, but affirms limited being – affirms the limitlessness into which it leaps as it opens this zone to existence for the first time.[9]

Both Bataille and Foucault also refer to mysticism as a form of eroticism, of the suspension of dialectics.[10] The mystical experience is engendered by religious ecstasy (*raptus mysticus*), in which the borders between the human and the divine, the sensual and the sacred, cease to exist in a limitless abyss of non-referentiality.

This annihilating rapture, Bataille contends, leads to the sovereignty that is the goal of transgression.

It is this type of transgression that *Twin Peaks* interrogates. The series narrates the omnipresent possibility of transgressing into postdialectic limitlessness: Bob's obsessive evil-doing, Laura Palmer's hungry eroticism, Leland Palmer's frantic dancing and singing, and Cooper's transcendent endeavors are all excessive affirmations of varying limits, leading eventually to their annihilation. As a result, events in *Twin Peaks* lose referential grasp and their narration escapes signification.[11] Ghost world and everyday world are not separated in the plot, and Lynch makes no attempt to push the story back into pre-transgressive normativity:

> It's the doppelgänger thing – the idea of two sides to everyone. … People were really upset that it ended with an evil Cooper who'd been taken over by Bob. But that's *not* the ending. That's the ending people were stuck with. That's just the ending of the second season. If it had continued …[12]

Twin Peaks's ghosts are "abstractions in human form"[13] that cannot be framed in terms of the binaries of life and death, good and evil: they personify the permanence of the "two sides to everyone" and as such they ceaselessly dwell on the limitless limit. This explains why these ghosts could not be traditional ghosts, haunting dead that are phenomenologically determined by dialectic binaries. Nor could the series be a traditional, teleological detective story; Lynch and Frost did not want to have the murder mystery solved until much later (or never) but were forced by ABC to come up with a killer. *Twin Peaks* addresses the eternal cycles of transgression in human life, not hermeneutic questions of who did what, when, and how.[14]

The constant transgressions in the *Twin Peaks* plot are represented onscreen almost unnoticeably. Almost. For although the appearance of ghosts, ghostly spaces, and the darker sides of Twin Peaks are presented without the distancing methods of jump cuts and orchestral crescendos, the TV audience immediately senses that something strange is going on. Cinematography and soundtrack endorse a visceral uncanniness: why do the ghosts of Laura Palmer, Bob, and MFAP so persistently haunt both series and audience if they appear only *once* in Season 1? And why is the melody that accompanied the discovery of Laura Palmer's body, and that keeps reappearing in each episode, so strangely *unheimlich*? How does the insistent transgressive motion of the series seem to extend to the audience?

Hauntographical Media

The transgressive aspects of *Twin Peaks*'s cinematography have sometimes been explained through the fact that the plot relies heavily on dreams as a structuring device. Lynch often bases his work on his own dreams, and Kelly Bulkeley contends that dreams have two main functions in his works: that of a Freudian understanding of the power of the unconscious on the one hand, and that of a blurring of the Lacanian Real and Imaginary on the other.[15] These dream elements, of course, underline *Twin*

Peaks's fascination with transgression. But the supernatural and spectral aspects that are so decisive for *Twin Peaks*'s atmosphere are not only connected to dreams. The series is also a televisual manifestation of the Gothic, a genre that concerns itself with crossing borders and the uncanny, which it presents as the ghosts of repressed anxieties and desires. The Gothic genre foregrounds the fragmented and hidden dimensions of the Self and of the Real. It unveils the absent presence of the past, of the Other, of the unconscious – of Laura Palmer and Bob – within the here and now. Through a continuous affirmation, transgression, and annihilation of dialectic opposites of meaning and non-meaning, signification and non-signification, on both narrative and medial levels, the Gothic seeks to open and inhabit a Bataillean zone of absolute decontextualization. The Gothic is located in a perpetually ambivalent in-between – between the Black and White Lodge, in this case – that is haunted by the ghosts of the repressed: sexual violence, fear, possessive love.

Twin Peaks's spectral dimensions operate through the uncanny agency of mediation. The uncanny is an indispensable part of narration; the creation of text is the creation of ghosts, "images without origin" that roam spaces without origin.[16] Besides the spectrality of narrative, language itself is far from a stable signifier. It constitutes a virtual space that may reflect upon events and concepts in the culture surrounding it, but does so in a temporally disjointed, ultimately self-referential way that distances it from ontological provenance.[17] Jacques Derrida has taken this thought to its radical consequence in the concept of *hauntology*, the idea that originary signification is an ontological impossibility because all meaning is informed, overshadowed, and haunted by the ghosts of other meanings.[18] Narration and mediation thus represent no more (and no less) than the explicit rupture of meaning from signification.

I want to argue that the uncanny and hauntological dimensions of mediation are among the paramount characteristics of the Gothic genre. Fred Botting has argued that Gothic literature "demystifies" the dark space of the unconscious, of Otherness, of transgression, by rendering it visible through narration. Moreover, Gothic narration explicitly puts itself in the foreground *as* narration, as artificiality, as a virtual space that lacks phenomenal signification: "[T]he labyrinth of fiction offers no other ground, no ultimate reality, no depth and no origin."[19] The uncanny in Gothic narration is the unrepresentable lurking behind presentation, the unreferential saliently present in reference. It is the putting onto the *limen* of language the limits of dialectic and the possibility of their transgression: narration is affirmation of the hauntological void behind language, a space of absolute decontextualization, and the Gothic's excessive over-narration opens the limitless space of transgression. This space is the territory of long-forgotten fears and forbidden desires that take the narrative shape of ghosts. The uncanny agency of narration thus operates on two intertwined levels: first, the narrative level of conjuring up the non-originary; and second, the medial level of opening the transgressive space of non-referentiality.

This not only holds true for text: every act of narration, be it textual, visual, or auditory, can evoke overlaps of (non-)meanings and (non-)realities. The camera may observe reality but distorts it in the editing process, the phone may transmit vocal communications, but turns them into disembodied voices without origin. The media through which the narrative is voiced thereby become *hauntographical agents*, revealing nothing but the hauntological void behind the symbolic, thus opening a space that is a liminal, postdialectic abyss. Lynch seems intuitively aware of the hauntological void installed at the very instance of mediation. In his works mise-en-scène, shooting technique, editing, non-diegetic inserts, flash edits, and temporal disruptions foreground film as a hauntographical medium that unsettles cinematic continuity and signification. In this sense Lynch goes a step further than the Gothic authors Botting discusses: rather than "just" confirming the virtual space of narration he consistently disrupts narrative contingencies so that the symbolic order of (cinematographic) language is laid bare to its hauntological bone. *Twin Peaks* thus shows that the Gothic instrument of narrative or medial excess can be employed in various degrees of hauntographical agency. If the Gothic signifies a "writing of excess," as Botting contends,[20] then this excess must be defined as the expenditure of signification which opens up the empty space of the non-originary. And in that sense the Gothic may be redefined as a writing of *access*, too, as it enables entrance into this empty space.

In *Twin Peaks*, the uncanny agency of mediation is operative on both described levels. It firstly shows its workings in the spectral narrative of the series. Narration creates ghosts, media conjure up specters; in a very direct way *Twin Peaks* is haunted by the ghosts of other films, books and music (L. Frank Baum's *The Wizard of Oz* and Lewis Carroll's *Alice in Wonderland/Through the Looking Glass* are important presences), which are invited by that insistent spectral presence in language, intertextuality. Media also quite literally summon up ghosts in *Twin Peaks*. Electricity acts as the transmitter of otherworldly forces, as each ghostly appearance is accompanied by a shrill electronic sound, and often by flickering or stroboscopic lights. Jeffrey Sconce has shown that the historical reception of electronic media has always ascribed a certain uncanny power to the electricity that enables their working.[21] Since electricity (*la fée électrique*) is the power behind all these forms of telepresence, it does not surprise that it functions as the transmitter of ghostly presence in *Twin Peaks*.[22]

Media not only create ghosts in *Twin Peaks*; a second result of their autonomous agency is that they actively destabilize the borders between human and ghost worlds. This level of medial hauntography is the opening of the liminal space beyond referentiality, the transgressive space that endorses the Freudian repressed to manifest itself in ghostly shape.[23] In *Twin Peaks* this space is established by a spectral appropriation of medial communication. Whereas electricity transports the supernatural, other media blur the boundaries between here and beyond, people and specters, by communicating spectral messages and thereby placing the ghostly within human reality. It is remarkable that most of these media are auditory: phones, microphones, turntables, live music, and major Briggs's radio wave transmitter (which receives messages from outer space) often carry communications that are related to the ghostly dimension of *Twin Peaks*. As Sconce has examined, the role of auditory media corresponds with their ability to allow "voices from the void" to be heard.[24]

The most remarkable boundary-blurring auditory media in the series appear in the dream scene in Episode 2. Dale Cooper is welcomed in the Red Room by MFAP and meets Laura Palmer, who whispers the name of her killer in his ear. The speech of both ghosts sounds odd, an effect established by recording the actors' texts while spoken backwards and then playing it in reverse and overlaying it with a slight reverb. While these are clearly disembodied spectral voices, their over-editing points the listener's attention to the void they originate from. Recording technology separates a sound from its origin, thereby problematizing issues of presence and distance;[25] the Red Room's seemingly non-significant text lines sounding out in echoing backward loops strengthen this effect to its extreme, thereby exposing the gaping hauntological emptiness behind language and mediation. Red Room speech shows that there is a third space between narrator and perceiver: the uncanny space of mediation that belongs neither here nor there.[26] The utter non-referentiality of this medial space endorses a transgression of the dichotomy of ghostly and human realms, so that the dialectical questions evoked by the Red Room scene (Is it ghostly? Is it real?) are swept off the table by the annihilating gesture of mediation.

To complicate things further, *Twin Peaks*'s hauntographical media not only blur *on*-screen boundaries. Helen Wheatley has argued in her discussion of *Twin Peaks* that the television – a little box containing disembodied ghosts visiting and returning in repetitive episodes – is especially apt to evoke the uncanny as its consumption is situated within the domestic sphere: TV can literally make the home unhomely as it blurs the distinctions between perceiver and perceived.[27] When the One-Armed-Man is inhabited by Mike in Episode 13, his voice is pitched down to an eerie low tone and overlaid with heavy reverb. Thus medially exposed as a ghost, he looks directly into the camera and explains that Bob's true face can only be perceived by "the gifted and the damned." Is he addressing Cooper and Sheriff Truman, the television audience, or both? The in-plot soap opera *Invitation to Love* ironically comments on this effect of TV: when Sheriff Truman walks into his office and asks his secretary Lucy "What's going on?," she gives him a run-down of the latest developments in the soap, whereupon Truman confusedly replies "No … I meant what's going on *here* …" Mediation renders dichotomous notions regarding the real, the imaginary, or the ghostly irrelevant.

The autonomous agency of media is underlined by the almost obsessive foregrounding of medial apparatuses throughout the series. Here, too, auditory media prevail: telephones, microphones, tape recorders, turntables, and cassettes are not only very often filmed in still-life shots, they also often do not or only half-work, or convey (human or ghostly) messages that are puzzling at the very least. These media destabilize the indexical objectivity that we like to attribute to recording media:[28] whereas one would like to think that media simply record and reproduce reality as it is, the media in *Twin Peaks* show that that "reality" is all but simple and unambivalent, and not at all easy to reproduce. Media's disruption of indexicality is a direct result of their hauntological non-origin: when referentiality is dismantled, signification becomes hauntography and points only to the liminal space of transgression. Phone calls are explicitly related to the realm of the non-factual in Episode 1, when Lucy receives a phone call for Dale Cooper and tells him that it "sounds like long-distance. It has that open air sound, you know, where it sounds like wind blowing … like wind blowing through trees." The comparison of phone lines to trees rustling in the wind, which appear frequently in short non-diegetic inserts clearly related to the mysteries in the woods around *Twin Peaks*, is a telling indication that phone communication does not have to be taken at face value. Lynch's own appearance as FBI officer Gordon Cole is emblematic of the way auditory media function as indexicality disrupters. Cole's hearing is gone, and he carries a large and conspicuous hearing aid that looks like phone lines plugged into his ears. Whereas conversations with Cole normally have to be conducted at screaming volume, which at times leads to a species of slapstick-comedy confusion, he *does* make phone calls, and he *can* hear Shelly Johnson's soft voice. This raises the questions of whether hearing and listening are subjective, variable abilities, and whether mediated sound reflects "reality" or something quite different. In fact, the only medium in the series that simply seems to record messages as straightforward indexical reflections of spoken messages is Dale Cooper's tape recorder. And this tape recorder, via which Cooper addresses someone called Diane, is so exceptional in its dry factuality – "Diane, it's Agent Cooper here. A believer in facts" (March 1, 5 pm) – that it has raised a great amount of speculation among *Twin Peaks* fans.

Through his framing of the themes of transgression and ambiguity in emphatically untrustworthy medial representation, Lynch creates a convergence of over- and under-determination leading to a televisual *sfumato* (reminiscent of film noir) that reaches right into the core of Gothic liminality. Misha Kavka has argued that "Gothic film should not be thought of as a medium of representation, but as a medium through which things are allowed to pass, from the past into the present, from death into life, from the beyond to here and back again."[29] *Twin Peaks* demonstrates the various ways – conjuring up ghosts, opening a liminal space of non-referentiality, disrupting indexicality – in which visual media can function as such a Gothic gateway. The ghosts of *Twin Peaks* are not only in the machine, they also use it to transmit their messages, and pop out of it when they deem appropriate. It is as if the hauntography of mediation is constantly rubbed in our face: media are important factors in the series' continuous transgressions – indeed, the medial apparatus seems to be the very locus of transgression here. The medium itself becomes the ghost, the *doppelgänger* of the plot ghosts, with its own Kittlerean spectral voice. The medium is the emptied-out message, the transgressive massage.

"Let's Rock": *Twin Peaks*'s Sonic Spectralities

Most of the transgressive media in *Twin Peaks* are auditory, and of those auditory media music is doubtlessly the most powerful in its uncanny workings. Music plays an especially large role in the blurring of boundaries between ghostly and human spaces in the series. There are roughly three (overlapping) types of music in *Twin Peaks*: besides diegetic and non-diegetic music (traditional score music and soundscape music), there is the semi-diegetic music and sound in the Red Room. All of them play active roles in the ghostly, psychological, and physical transgressions in the plot as well as in the viewer's perception. The soundtrack to *Twin Peaks*, moreover, is one of the operative forces for the appearance of ghosts, which manifest both diegetically (narrative) and extra-diegetically (mediation).

Televisual and film music's spectrality begins with the very notion of non-diegetic music – this is music that is not part of the plot, is not heard by the characters, but only perceivable by the TV or film audience. In the listener's mind the sounds evoke personal and cultural memories, emotions and experiences that attach themselves to the ones presented onscreen. The spectral dimension of non-diegetic film music has been described by Kevin Donnelly:

> [T]he soundscape itself might be conceived as an analogy to the virtual space of mental processes, as a repository of half-memories, primal emotions and the seemingly illogical. "Ghosts" inhabiting a film are often little more than shapes, momentary musical configurations or half-remembered sounds. Music can suggest, or even can lead directly to, an elsewhere, like a footnote.[30]

Donnelly argues that because of its slippery way of acquiring meaning through such unconscious mental processes, music provides an uncanny subtext to film or television. For this reason, music can function as an apt representation of supernatural presences or events: it conjures up ghosts by nature. This type of intertextuality is more direct and, through its personal and affective components, more effective than linguistic or visual intertextuality. In *Twin Peaks*, ghosts of other times and places are evoked by references to old jazz tunes (Leland Palmer, Audrey Horne) and hints of rock guitars (James Hurley).

Like the other media in the series, music also literally summons up ghosts – but it does so in superlative. The Laura Palmer leitmotif is the paramount example. The theme sets in as the pilot episode starts and accompanies the discovery of the girl's body. The simple but *unheimlich* melody, a slow repetitive drone circling in palindrome fashion around a minor third, attaches itself easily to the memory. Nothing happens, really; in perfect accordance with the plot narrative, the drones flow, repeating themselves in a non-linear way without the relief of a cadence, almost stopping time. The lack of a bass line or indeed of harmonic progression gives the tune a floating, non-belonging character; when the bass finally sounds, its single deep on-beat confirmation feels like a death bell chiming and tuning in to the "lonesome foghorn" that Pete Martell brings into the conscious experience of this soundscape. The theme keeps returning throughout the series, always reviving the unspoken uncanniness of that first scene – sometimes when Laura Palmer is talked of, but more often when she is absent for plot characters. This makes her an almost constant absent presence for TV audiences. The repetitive leitmotif here *is* Laura Palmer's ghost. It haunts onscreen and offscreen spaces at the same time, thereby loosening the boundary between the two and creating a liminal medial space of its own: the compositional minimalism of the slow tempo, melodic repetition, and static harmony adds to the stillness and claustrophobic feel of this musical space. Gothic television does indeed invade the domestic space here, and the TV viewer might ask herself with Sarah Palmer, "What's going on in this house?"

The diegetic music in *Twin Peaks* remarkably often accompanies moments of transgression in the plot. Other than the auditory media described above it does not communicate messages directly, but its presence often indicates a transition from here to beyond: from human to ghostly spaces, from White to Black Lodge. Leland Palmer's character change while listening to an LP in Episode 2 has been described above; music makes him transgress the boundaries of the two sides of himself, and his singing and dancing seem to come from a no man's land in between – this is neither Leland nor Bob, but some liminal, utterly context-less person. The scene in which he kills Maddy in Episode 14 also starts with a record player, and ends with him dancing with the half-dead girl while crying out his daughter's name. Randolph Jordan contends that Lynch's explicit shots of the circular motion of turntables suggests the flowing over of one world into another (one wonders whether Laura and Leland Palmer's initials are coincidental).[31] Both Leland's turntable scenes and other scenes with diegetic music, moreover, involve dancing, and often dancing in circular motion. It is as if by dancing characters physically partake in the transgressions set in by the music, being moved away from the here and now by its specters from the beyond. Music, more than any other medium in this series, destabilizes boundaries and creates a transgressive medial space of its own.

The music in the Red Room has a similar but even more "messy" function. MFAP announces that "where we're from, there is always music in the air" and starts dancing to the tune of a walking bass line that repetitively runs up and down the scale of C minor, and a jazzy sax melody moving in triplets. This "semi-diegetic" music has no discernible source: it is unclear where it comes from, or even who hears it. In Episode 29 this disturbing effect is heightened by the sudden appearance of a jazz singer in the Red Room who evidently *mimics* the fully orchestrated song "Under the Sycamore Trees."[32] Like the other auditory media in the series, these hauntographical performances destabilize medial indexicality and mirror nothing but their non-origin. Their explicit non-referentiality invites transgression of any kind, but while it is clear that MFAP's dancing is an affirmation of the limitless limit, the viewer can only guess which type of transgression is set in motion here. When Cooper wakes up after his Red Room dream, the Laura Palmer theme sounds, but as he smiles somewhat sardonically he snaps his fingers and MFAP's dance tune returns in the soundtrack. Is this a transgression of plot or viewer's reality? Of spectrality? The only "reality" at hand seems to be the liminal space of the music in the air.

The music in *Twin Peaks*, then, has a particularly strong agency on both levels of uncanny narration: the hauntological level of conjuring up the non-originary and the hauntographical level of opening the transgressive space of non-referentiality. With regard to the first level, it is interesting that much of the music in the *Twin Peaks* soundtrack is written for synthesizer, which has been described by Richard Middleton as a creator of musical doubles and non-sounds.[33] The synthesizer works according to the principle of schizophonia,[34] the separation of a sound from its origin that leads to the sounding of phantom voices; the synthesizer compositions thereby symbolize the theme of absent presence in the series' plot. In a similar way the *Twin Peaks* soundtrack, like its speech and visuals, employs recording technology to disrupt indexicality, as the music is played at a slower pace than at which it was recorded. Musical narration in the series is thus as explicitly spectral as its cinematography.

Music's transgressive potencies have been described by Gilles Deleuze and Félix Guattari, who argue that music is "on the side of the nomadic" because, when activated, it challenges spatial and temporal constellations.[35] Through its strong mnemonic and affective workings, sounding music creates lines of flight towards liminal spaces of time, space, and emotion that the listener cannot but embark upon: musical experience is continual becoming.[36] Deleuze and Guattari's nomadic evaluation of music explains how it can be instrumental for transgressive processes. Whereas Bataille envisions that post-dialectical sovereignty can be brought about by affirmation and expenditure of either good or evil, music can escape even these dialectical starting points. Music *itself* is a form of "absolute decontextualization"; existing only in sonic waves, it occupies time but defies any form of meaning or signification. All meaning attributed to music is inscribed, acquired through momentaneous appropriations and reappropriations that will, however, be perennially subverted. Deleuze and Guattari's desire to territorialize the refrain[37] is a telling (but not very successful) attempt to locate signification in a medium that, despite containing referentially informed details, always escapes time, space, and signification. Even when music is repeated, "repetition is a repetition of difference, so memory grasps it only by crossing that difference, covering it with a singular sonic quality," and so all that remains of musical signification is the void of contingency.[38] These qualities render music vectral as well as spectral: music activates vectors into the realm of memory, emotion, and imagination, and in this capacity it is an excellent vehicle for the transgression that is the theme of *Twin Peaks*. Its hauntographical resistance of referentiality helps suspend dialectics and thereby provides the gateway to the Gothic borderland of post-dialectics.

This aspect of music becomes especially tangible on the dance floor. Dancing is as physical as it is mnemonic and affective: sometimes harmony, rhythm, or timbre makes us move our bodies almost involuntarily. In a situation like this, dancing can function as a physical participation in music's vectral qualities: we can literally dance the night away, towards the unknown land beyond, from White to Black Lodge.[39] The music in *Twin Peaks* thus functions as a liturgy to the transgressions within and without the series' plot, consistent with Adam Evens's assertion that "sound is where time and space collide."[40] Music's vectors make both plot characters and TV audiences jump back and forth between the timespaces of the human and the ghostly, past and present, reality, imaginary, and unconscious. They activate the mysterious mantra that summons Bob, and that was tattooed on Mike's severed arm. Music's vectors open up the transgressive space "between two worlds" – good and evil, ghostly and human, on- and offscreen spaces – when one chants these lines, the first of which was found on a note at the place where Laura Palmer was murdered:

Through the darkness of future past,
The magician longs to see
One chants out between two worlds:
Fire, walk with me

Of all the hauntographical media in *Twin Peaks*, music has the strongest and uncanniest agency. Music is a ghost and invokes other ghosts; it is explicitly present as a medium, and explicitly non-referential; it opens up spectral spaces and allows a transgression of the spectral. The haunting melodies of *Twin Peaks* are the spirits of popular TV. Without warning, judgement, or even mercy they take characters and TV viewers into the transgressive borderland of Gothic liminality, the hauntological non-referentiality of medial space.

NOTES

1   I could not have written this article without my sister Marjolein van den Heuvel – my ghost writer and the lighter side of me.
2   Dale Cooper's message to Diane, 28 February, at Black Lake Cemetery.
3   Andrew Smith, "Hauntings," in *The Routledge Companion to Gothic*, ed. Catherine Spooner and Emma McEvoy (London: Routledge, 2007), 153.
4   I will focus mainly on the episodes that were directed by Lynch, as the aspects of *Twin Peaks* discussed here are typical for his cinematography.
5   Jean Baudrillard, "Death in Bataille," in *Symbolic Exchange and Death* (London: Sage, 1993), 154–158. Quoted in Fred Botting and Scott Wilson, *Bataille* (Houndmills, Basingstoke: Palgrave, 2001), 149ff.
6   See Nidesh Lawtoo, "Bataille and the Suspension of Being," in *Lingua Romana* 4, no. 1 (2005), http://linguaromana.byu.edu/Lawtoo4.html.
7   Joost de Bloois, "A Postscript to Transgression: The Gothic in Georges Bataille's Dissident Avant-Gardism," in *Nostalgia or Perversion? Gothic Rewriting from the Eighteenth Century until the Present Day*, ed. Isabella van Elferen (Newcastle: Cambridge Scholars Press, 2007), 53.
8   Georges Bataille, *Eroticism* (London and New York: Marion Boyars, 2006), 12–13.
9   Michel Foucault, "A Preface to Transgression," in *Michel Foucault: Aesthetics, Method, and Epistemology*, ed. James Faubion (London: Penguin, 1994), 74.
10 See Bataille, *Eroticism*, chapter II.5; Foucault, "A Preface to Transgression," 69f.
11 The Red Room scenes epitomize this non-referentiality. Lynch explains that he wanted to create a "free zone, completely unpredictable and therefore pretty exciting but also scary." Quoted in *Lynch on Lynch: Revised Edition*, ed. Chris Rodley (London: Faber & Faber, 2005), 19.
12 Ibid., 182.
13 Ibid., 178.
14 Ibid., 180. See Eric G. Wilson, *The Strange World of David Lynch: Transcendental Irony from Eraserhead to Mulholland Dr.* (New York and London: Continuum, 2007), viii.
15 Kelly Bulkeley, "Dreaming and the Cinema of David Lynch," *Dreaming* 13, no. 1 (2003): 56.
16 Julian Wolfreys, *Victorian Hauntings: Spectrality, Gothic, the Uncanny and Literature* (London: Palgrave Macmillan, 2001), 2–3.
17 See Fred Botting, "The Gothic Production of the Unconscious," in *Spectral Readings: Towards a Gothic Geography*, ed. Glennis Byron and David Punter (London: Macmillan, 1999).
18 Jacques Derrida, *Specters of Marx: The State of the Debt, the Work of Mourning, & the New International* (London and New York: Routledge, 2006). See also Wolfreys, *Victorian Hauntings*, 21.

19   Botting, "The Gothic Production of the Unconscious," 29–32.

20   Fred Botting, *Gothic* (London: Routledge, 1996), 1.

21   Jeffrey Sconce, *Haunted Media: Electronic Presence from Telegraphy to Television* (Durham: Duke University Press, 2005).

22   "Lynch re-mystifies electricity," writes Mark Allyn Stewart in *David Lynch Decoded* (Bloomington: AuthorHouse, 2007), 108.

23   See Smith, "Hauntings," 148.

24   Early experiments with both telephone communication and auditory recording technology evoked the hopes and fears of being able to hear the dead. See Sconce, *Haunted Media*, 60; Jonathan Sterne, *The Audible Past: Cultural Origins of Sound Reproduction* (Durham: Duke University Press, 2006), chapter 6.

25   See Jacob Smith, *Vocal Tracks: Performance and Sound Media* (Berkeley: University of California Press, 2008), 45, 51.

26   See Sconce, *Haunted Media*, 201ff. Sconce argues, like Botting does with regard to text, that this third space is a simulacrum, a virtual space; hauntography, however, gives this space its own transgressive agency.

27   Helen Wheatley, *Gothic Television* (Manchester: Manchester University Press, 2006), 7, 17ff. See also Sconce, *Haunted Media*, chapter 4.

28   See Mary Ann Doane, *The Emergence of Cinematic Time: Modernity, Contingency, the Archive* (Cambridge MA: Harvard University Press, 2002), 25, 208, 219f.

29   Misha Kavka, "The Gothic on Screen," in Jerrold E. Hogle, *The Cambridge Companion to Gothic Fiction* (Cambridge, UK: Cambridge University Press, 2002), 227–228.

30   Kevin J. Donnelly, *The Spectre of Sound: Music in Film and Television* (London: BFI, 2005), 172.

31   Randolph Jordan, "Starting from Scratch: Turntables, Auditory Representation, and the Structure of the Known Universe in the Films of David Lynch" (master's thesis, Concordia University, Montréal, 2003), http://www.soppybagrecords.net/randolph-jordan/David-Lynch-Thesis.htm.

32   This scene is revived and intensified in the Club Silencio (*nomen est omen*) scene in Lynch's 2001 film *Mulholland Drive.*

33   Richard Middleton, "Last Night a DJ Saved My Life: Avians, Cyborgs and Siren Bodies in the Era of Phonographic Technology," *Radical Musicology* 1 (2006), http://www.radical-musicology.org.uk/2006/Middleton.htm.

34   R. Murray Schafer, *The Tuning of the World: Toward a Theory of Soundscape Design* (New York: Random House, 1977), 273.

35   Gilles Deleuze and Félix Guattari, *Nomadology: The War Machine* (New York: Semiotext(e), 1986), 88.

36   Gilles Deleuze and Félix Guattari, *A Thousand Plateaus: Capitalism and Schizophrenia* (Minneapolis: University of Minnesota Press, 1987), 299–309.

37   Ibid., 310–330.

38   Aden Evens, *Sound Ideas: Music, Machines, and Experience* (Minneapolis: University of Minnesota Press, 2005), 50–51.

39   See Timothy D. Taylor, *Strange Sounds: Music, Technology and Culture* (New York: Routledge, 2001), 184ff.

40   Evens, *Sound Ideas*, 53.

Chapter 22

Occultic Inscriptions: The Modern Ghost-Tattoo in Japan, from Kyôsai to Horiyoshi III

Sean Somers

The episode "Stranger in a Strange Land," from the television series *Lost* (ABC, 2004–present), interpolates a subplot of Thai tattoo practices to set up a main character's back-story.[1] Forlorn, lonely, and wandering the beaches of Phuket, an American doctor, Jack, befriends an arcane Thai woman, Achara, played by Bái Líng.[2] Initially, he is suspicious of Achara's furtive behavior – she accepts envelopes of cash, taking young men into dark wardens, suggesting some sinister occupation. But to Jack's surprise, her career has nothing to do with the usual *femme fatale* stereotypes of drugs or prostitution. Jack trails Achara into a backroom atelier equipped with ink, needles, calligraphy scrolls, ritual candles, and many dictionaries on Chinese characters and their historical origins as the classical seal script (*zhuànwén*). Achara, it turns out, earns her money and notoriety as a highly sought-after tattoo artist. Jack then exclaims, smug with having solved the enigma, "This is a tattoo parlor. That's your big secret? The envelopes, the gifts?" Achara, however, denies that she is a *tattoo artist*, if by that Jack means a superficial sketcher, a trendy practitioner of skin-deep ornamentation. With her hands clasped in a *wai*, the Thai gesture of greeting and respect, Achara elaborates, "I am able to see who people are. My work is not decoration. It is definition. And this … this is my gift."

By *seeing*, Achara identifies her occultic capacity to gaze into a soul's interior canvass: she practices a psychometry through touch, ink, and needle to find the ghosts in each person. Her ability to *see* is linked to her ability to *mark*: in bringing forth paratemporal energies from the invisible world, she clairvoyantly composes a vision of the person's ghostly self, its history and previous incarnations. She transmutes this soul-message into Chinese ideograms, ones etched on the client's flesh as a talismanic inscription.

296

Such an exotic scenario comes across as rather Orientalistic, the allure of ghost-tattoo as seen *ad orientem*: in this case, an accented shamaness enables the male hero to receive archetypal wisdom of Self during his enigmatic journey through a foreign land. That said, however, the basis for *Lost*'s depiction of Achara is not entirely bereft of authentic cultural references, with regard to practices that are understood as localized knowledge in South and East Asia. In 1925, W. D. Hambly's lengthy study of the subject of tattoos noted the ritualistic overtones that artists used during the ink-binding processes, comparing their actions to the carving of images in stone or on oracle bones. Many cultural, literary, and social precedents in different cultures support the belief that tattoos can be imbued with tutelary properties. For example, Cambodian text or Chinese logograms, as a drawn line, can also be instilled with immaterial power or apparitional presences. Through an alchemical process, the corporeal body can become becharmed by sacred design: the skin provides organic parchment for receiving the spiritually instilled potency of the inspirited ink. In Southeast Asia, therefore, the custom of *yantra tattoo* (*sak yant*), which uses geometric patterns rather than letters, is said to instill a protective ward on someone through a synergy of magical needle meeting flesh. And, as this essay will examine, Japanese tattoo practices, often associated with the occult or the outcaste, in particular have presented complex customs and associations of magic, ghostly identities, and the enjoyment of the body.

For Western audiences, Japanese presentations and depictions of the spectral enjoy, for the moment, the most popularity as representative of Asian ghostlore. Film adaptations of Suzuki Kôji's novel *Ringu*, first by a Japanese director (Nakata, 1998) and then adapted by an American (Verbinski, 2002), promoted a sensibility of the spectral that was bound up with, or was indicative of, Japanese cultural contexts. Several popular *anime*, most notably *InuYasha*, also focus on demons, parapsychology, and exorcism, further enhancing the ambience of a *ghostly Japan* within the present *zeitgeist*, which Lafcadio Hearn had first popularized in his collections and commentaries on Japanese folktales.[3] *Ringu*, although hearkening to a spiritualistic past of folk beliefs, operates through a narrative device of the circulated videocassette, through which the discarnate works in tandem with technological advancement. Sony-esque themes such as duplication, redistribution, and exposure have thus invited considerable attention from critics, uniting depictions of Japan as the land of superstition and the land of gadgets in the form of a techno-ghost.

Within the multiple personages of Japanese ghostlore, this essay approaches an under-examined subject with regard to the performance of the paranormal in Japanese pop culture: the ghost tattoo. As practiced notably by exponents such as the contemporary artist Horiyoshi III (San-dai-me Horiyoshi, 1946–), the ink-flesh merger of spirit and skin invokes classical belief systems toward the phantasmal, while strategically eschewing the modern motorized tools of the tattoo arts. Horiyoshi's designs are anachronistic in nature, but his tattoos, through their counter-cultural visibility, trouble the current cultural superego of the mainstream. The ghost, as transtemporal subject, reunites with the physical in a mode of artistic uncanniness. Tattooing, as inscribing a communication from that invisible world of spirit, entails a kind of somatic interaction with ghosts: the body itself acts as the scrying surface upon which the supernatural dimension becomes channeled and inscribed. Horiyoshi III implements into the visual dynamic of urban spaces a range of numinous imagery derived from his predecessors in Japanese art, notably Kawanabe Kyôsai (1831–1889) and literary figures such as Tanizaki Jun'ichirô (1886–1965). Horiyoshi, through what he considers to be his clairvoyant needle, negotiates the ghost into a space of current corporeality. Multiple paradoxes become enshrined with this interstice of phantasmalized ink, etched onto contemporarily socialized bodies: Horiyoshi III, forthright about his beliefs in the supernatural, invokes ancestral presences through religious iconography, using the sacred in a kind of personal adornment that is still to a large but declining extent taboo, stigmatic, and counter-normative. In this way, through the alchemical ink put onto the body through a séanced tattoo, the ghosts of the past return, revenant-ized, to integrate with the bodies of the here and now. The skin, functioning as a chronotopic host, weaves hereditary spirits into the collective psychologies of postmodernity through an illustrative narrative.

Kawanabe Kyôsai: Conferring with Ghosts in Modernist Domains

To better comprehend Horiyoshi's ghostly tattoos, as acting in a performative manner for contemporary audiences, it is useful to begin by considering those formative artistic contexts that he continually draws upon. In particular, Horiyoshi's conceptualization of the ghost's mannerisms (*shigusa*), in terms of its forms, appearances, and articulations, owes much to the illustrative precedents of Kyôsai.

Horiyoshi refers frequently to Kyôsai, whose cluttered canvasses of specters often feature a sequence of miniature vignettes, organized in a linear fashion according to spatial serialization, as a crucial influence on his spectral images. For this quality, as well as his satirical and fantastic imagery, Kyôsai may very well be considered a forerunner to *manga*, as well as developing an apparitional stylistic that inspires tattoo artists today. Kyôsai, of course, was not the first to paint phantoms. A sense of paranormal aesthetics had been, in many ways, influential on Japanese literature in most time periods, from the *ikiryô* (vengeful spirit) of *Genji monogatari* to the many shadow warriors found in *nô*. In fact, because of stylistic repetition, the rules for painting the figure of a ghost could be quite prescriptive, as legendary associations required certain canonical attributes. Fidelity to master narratives, such as the Buddhist iconography of the otherworld, dictated the kinds of visual features by which a ghost becomes readily perceived as a ghost. The ragged *kimono*, disheveled hair, glowing triangle on the forehead, and dissolving lower torso are all attributes of this kind.[4]

Artists have been, however, free to experiment with the received templates. Particularly with the advent of modernism, the pictorial tensions between canonical codes of depiction and the adaptation of new mediums and contexts expanded the dimensions of the visual framework for illustrating the phantasmal. Kawanabe Kyôsai – as well as Utagawa Kuniyoshi (1797–1861), who often worked in woodblock prints (*ukiyo-e*) – notably situated aspects of the traditionally ghostly as having a presence for modernizing Japanese society.[5] According to Steven Addiss's assessment, Kyôsai, along with Tsukioka Yoshitoshi (1839–1892), belonged to a modernist movement that "went far beyond the paradigms of Edo-period taste in their paintings and prints, expressing the unsettled nature of the late nineteenth century in Japan."[6] In terms of Kyôsai's career, no one particular timeframe can be defined as his *wraith* period. Throughout his life, Kyôsai returned to depictions of paranormal images, derived from classical ghost stories (*kaidan*), custodial images of souls damned to hell derived from didactic texts, or iconographic portraits (*zuzô*) of Buddhist saints and bodhisattvas. Noteworthy examples of this latter trend include the colorful *Kannon-sama* (c. 1895), which depicts this bodhisattva of mercy perched near a waterfall and swathed in gold gossamer scarves. In the lower left corner, a lone figure, dwarfed by Kannon-sama's perspective, prays in supplication.

Kyôsai produced several works based on the theme of *hyakki yagyô*, the night procession of the hundred demons, producing his most renowned version, now kept in the Fukutomi Tarô Collection, sometime in the 1870s or 80s.[7] This work draws upon Kyôsai's career-long experiments in illustrating the contorted anatomy of otherworldly beings. The demons dance in twisted postures, their bodies performing an almost impossible kind of yoga. Kyôsai frequently characterizes the phantasmal pseudo-body as one in pain, retaining a resemblance of its mortal shell but one rendered in a grotesque parody of physiology. For example, one of Kyôsai's portraits of Enma, the overlord of hell, shows the brutal ruler undergoing a demonic beauty treatment through the efforts of a beautiful courtesan. The procedure, however, seems torturous: the lovely attendant plucks the scalp of the withered Enma, who clutches a set of ineffectual prayer beads (*juzu*) in a passive manner. On a similar theme, Kyôsai's sketches of skeletons are reminiscent of Ikkyû's instructional sequence *Gaikotsu* (*Skeletons*, 1457), a visual/textual meditation on the ephemeral nature of the body. Kyôsai draws upon Ikkyû's focus on the decaying body as an image of chtonic reducement, from flesh, to necrosis, into hungry ghosts. Kyôsai paints a sequence of shrunken skulls, dissolving skin, and withered limbs suggesting the transmutation of corporeality into immateriality. The *rakugo* performer Enshûrô Enshi, upon viewing Kyôsai's paintings, stated that they looked like corpses, not ghosts.[8]

Kyôsai's most famous ghosts are a series of studies he composed around 1883 entitled *Yûrei-zu*, which emphasize the spectral as a lingering trace, flickering as symptomatic of a shift in the cultural order. These apparitions, while mostly phantasmal in terms of appearance, maintain a residual form of their former bodies to haunt and challenge the new modes of culture. In these works, Kyôsai includes background features suggesting typical instances of domesticity: paper-paneled lamps, *tatami* flooring, and scenes of butterflies caught in spider's webs. This observation is quite apt, for it draws our attention to the manner in which Kyôsai troubles the relationship between spirit and body, in the sense that one can never be fully disconnected from the other through the operations of memory and reminiscence. And, so, Kyôsai's paintings may be viewed as spectral depictions of a masochistic body, through which the paranormal enhances the degree of pain, positioned as it were in routine spaces of social relations.

Positioning his ghosts as a commentary on Japanese modernity, Kyôsai's tortured spirits are suggestive of Freud's notions of moral masochism. The ghost emblematizes the marginalized citizens of the past, who are now in a process of vanishing but who were also once members of the collective Japanese national polity (*kokutai*), which literally means *national body*. Modernization, in some ways a period of death-drive toward the old in favor of the new, becomes diagnostically represented by the anguished ghost-corpse. Its sufferings result from the troubled collective corpus of the *kokutai* being dismembered during a period of fragmentation and regeneration. Kyôsai reveals the condition of the ghost as one whose corpse has become, through decay, the national body's antithesis: the ghost retains a vestigial body, but as one who can no longer return to be.

Kyôsai thus investigates a realm of ghostly Japanese culturalism, a vantage point from which the phantasm can take a kind of supervisory inventory as to the presumed state of national collectivity. This sense of the fantastic as socially participatory relates to the fundamental argument of Gerald Figal's *Civilization and Monsters*, a study of *fushigi* (the mysterious) in Japanese modernity. In Figal's view, the *fushigi* did not function as a peripheral interest, dabbled in for hobbyist or specialist considerations. Rather than acting on the margins, *fushigi* operated contributively to the formation and perpetuation of the modernist condition, both subversively and supportively, in multiple areas.[9] For example, Figal examines Inoue Enryô's (1858–1919) scientific examination of *yôkaigaku* (monsterology). Inoue, although his reputation was built on his studies of ghosts and the like, pursued an ardent rationalism, opposing what he saw as superstitious, anti-scientific, and psychologically aberrational. But, at the same time, a diverse group of scholars and authors considered the characterization of the *fushigi* with such seriousness that Figal argues "objects of fantasy and folk belief … played fundamental roles in the constitution of modernity in Meiji Japan" (6), operating as a parapsychical dimension directly within ideological modes of a society undergoing a process of modernization.

Although his study offers much breadth in detail, Figal does not extend his attention very far to visual arts and artists, a gap which is surprising, considering his book's cover features Kyôsai's *Hyakki yagyô sugata utsushi-e* (*Shadow Picture of the Forms of the Hundred Night Demons*, 1867?). Nonetheless, Figal's central thesis – that depictions of the fantastic, linked to invocations of premodern lore, played a central role in defining and critiquing the formulation of Japan and *Japaneseness* – applies very much to Kyôsai. Kyôsai's many ghosts, as illustrative purveyors of *fushigi* and residual traces of the ancestral, do not become configured as a trope of nostalgia, a hangover from a displaced Japanese past. On the contrary, his ghosts, as producers of *fushigi*, operate directly within the modernist dynamic, as a mode that unsettles rational assumptions explicitly shaping the discourses of Japanese modernization. Kyôsai had formidable skills as a satirist, and parody allows his ghosts to provide periphery critiques of social change in Japanese modernity. For example, in one of Kyôsai's portraits of Enma, this overlord of hell puts on a Western style business suit, and receives a European style haircut. Such a picture has an obviously allegorical dimension: the figurations of a presumably premodern Japanese mythology will give way, in style if not content, to the designs and tastes of cosmopolitanism. Hirasawa notes that Kyôsai generally renders images adopted from the iconography of hell in a classical manner, but the artist recontextualizes them according to modern social habits, mediums, and concerns.[10]

For Horiyoshi and contemporary tattoo art, Kyôsai represented a commitment to Japanese mythological tropes in a state of flux: his capacity to work with classical stylistics could also eccentrically incorporate and refashion them into the aesthetic milieu of modernity. Kyôsai, of course, was not a tattooist. However, many books on Kyôsai can be found on the shelves of tattoo artists' salons across Japan and beyond. Kyôsai, the unorthodox *demon of painters* or painter of demons, has been received and reformulated, from inked canvasses to inked skin. By giving ghosts a formative canvas through which to return to the senses of the living, Kyôsai creates a portal through which *fushigi* enters to hauntingly inhabit the host, which is the national body.

From Woodblock Prints to Tattooed Inscription: Tanizaki Jun'ichirô and Ink as Shapeshifter

Kyôsai's presentation of the ghost within Japanese visual culture coincided with a general fascination for seeking out the paranormal in Japan. Rather like their Theosophical counterparts in London, late Meiji-era Tokyo abounded with parlor-room societies of mediums and esotericists. Their activities included séance-oriented games such as *kokkuri*, as well as more indigenous methods for contacting the dead. Indeed, something of a celebrity circuit of famous mediums came into public prominence, garnering the attention of the curious as well as the skeptical. Noteworthy examples of seers include Moritake Tetsuko, Takahashi Sadako, and most notably Mifune Chizuko, the historical model upon whom Yamamura Shizuko, from *Ringu*, is based.[11]

Within this general fascination for the bizarre and paranormal, novelists such as Tanizaki Jun'ichirô penned tales that combined elements of the eldritch with the erotic. A particularly noteworthy example of such occultic, almost tantric aesthetics is *Shisei (The Tattoo*, 1910), set in an unspecified time within the Edo-period (1603–1868).[12] Such a timeframe allows Tanizaki to depict the bordello chic ambience (*iki*) that provides atmospheric resonances to a modern audience. In his story, tattoos, their artists, and aficionados, are closely associated with the gay pleasure quarters; the counter-normative narratives of these districts challenge the dominant modes that intertwined beauty and power. They pursued their own kind of ultimatum for beauty, vying so far for it as to carve tattoos upon their bodies: "*hitobito wa kozotte utsukishisa o kisoiau, karada ni shisei o horu yô ni natta sô desu*" (8) (Beauty was their primary ideal; and, in pursuit of it, people would go so far as having their bodies tattooed). Artists cherish tattoos as they enhance attractiveness as well as sensuality, stimulating the pleasure centers of the skin while also fascinating the eye. The inked designs entice a performance of exhibitionism and intimacy between artist and client, who mutually admire through sight and communicate by touch, stroking the marks as a display of admiration and, quite likely, of foreplay (9).

Seikichi, a painter who has turned to tattooing, is in pursuit of the perfectly drawn form, seeking out in the backstreets a perfect lover to be model and easel, as tattooing allows for both. Indeed, he delights obsessively in the physiological responses of pain and pleasure in pursuit of the dream to inscribe the *pure nature* of the true soul into perfect flesh. Seikichi comes into contact with a young *maiko* (trainee *geisha*), who immediately stimulates his coinciding sexual, spiritual, and aesthetic appetites. In a kind of Rorschach test to probe her psychical suitability as an organic canvas, Seikichi shows her two rather disturbing paintings. The second, entitled *Hiryô* (*Fertilizer*), foregrounds a nationally quintessential cherry tree with a young maiden reclining against it, surrounded by men's corpses whose blood and deteriorating skin feed the *sakura*'s soiled roots. The tattoo parlor utilizes art to perform a psychosexual drama of pain and pleasure, of body and spirit. The narrator, aware of the spiritual implications, compares the moment of tattooing to Egyptian funerary rites (14).

The *maiko*'s transformation into spiritual and sexual dominance is enacted through the predatorial beauty of the tattoo's image. She absorbs, through the inked stencil of a tattooed spider, a transmogrifying force of ethereal energy: "*sore he onore no tamashii o horikomu koto de atta*" (10) (Right there, the infusion of my spirit is made complete). However, the spirit made present is that of the totemic spider-ghost; the *maiko* has become reborn through a sublimely diabolical configuration of ghost and body, inscribed by the tattoo. Now, in a ghost/mortal hybrid position of power, she exclaims to Seikichi, paraphrasing the aforementioned painting's title, "You are my manure" (17) (*koyashi*, another word for fertilizer). As the cherry-tree picture suggested, the tattoo has graphically embodied beauty through a correlated process of decay: the flesh undergoes a kind of mild putrefaction, including bloodletting, so that the colored stencil can take permanent root in the skin. The Spider's ghostly spirit, through chtonic inscription, has become marked on soul and skin, and takes its nourishment from blood and spirit.

Throughout *Shisei*, Tanizaki explores a kind of moral masochism that occurs on the fringes of Japanese art and social politics.[13] The proportions of the cultural superego, seemingly unassailable in terms of control over the subject, can in fact be overwritten through a conversion of pain and suffering into beauty and pleasure. The tattooed body releases psychical energy through its wounds, producing both kenotic purgation – the *maiko* becomes emptied of fear – and demonic possession – the *maiko* receives the soul (*tamashii*) of the Spider. Through the stigma of tattooing, Tanizaki puts forward a general critique with regard to the *kokutai* as prescriptive appearance. The tattoo, as kernel of the Real, suggests that what is done to a body can be done to the national body, and that the cultural superego is defaced through individual scarification.

Marking the Margins: Stigmatic Ink and the Cultural Fringe

The Japanese words for tattoo-arts include a number of related, but distinct, terms: *irezumi, horimono,* and *bunshin.* The literary record on such matters, going as far back as the *Kojiki* (*The Record of Ancient Matters*, 680 CE), documents the sullied reputation of tattoos as societal stigma. For example, the *Kojiki* describes the practice of tattooing criminals on the forehead. Basil Hall Chamberlain, in his translation of this text, also notes that the verb *saku* (to slit) relates to a more acceptable practice of branding with ink so as to enhance physical features.[14] For the most part, however, classical texts, including the *Nihon shoki* (720 CE), associate tattooing with punitive justice: those associated with crimes, from thievery to treason, could be permanently scarred as a form of public shaming. Such disciplinary practices, as Groemer relates, continued into the Edo era (1603–1868): the enforcement of outcaste status on criminals through tattooing evolved into a detail system of marks and brands, including coded markings placed on specific body parts so as to record the nature of the crime. Public exhibition of the marked convicts was sometimes part of the judicial sentence.[15]

As Tamabayashi Haruo has documented, the bordello culture of the Edo period appropriated tattoos for their own subcultural pleasure.[16] Prostitutes used tattooing as a way of enhancing attractiveness or status. Also, small networks that relied upon a close group dynamic that emphasized physical prowess, such as firemen, made use of markings as a form of social bonding. Tamabayashi repeatedly points out that the most skilled tattooists were also *ukiyo-e* carvers, who etched with needles using the same technique as with their carving blades.

With the advent of the Meiji-era (1868), the Japanese government banned tattoos outright for its own nationals, although this statute did not apply to visiting sailors or other foreign residents. However, in a point that McCallum examines, Japanese modernity invited a broad range of new discourses – scientific, social, and political – that allowed for a diversification of the representative meanings of tattooing, in both select groups as well as society on a broader scale.[17] Predictably, the ban helped to romanticize *irezumi*: by so forcefully pushing its practice to the margins, policy makers in fact reinforced its allure as something dodgy, dangerous, and against the direction of the forward-thinking, conventional status quo, therefore making it appealing to the disenchanted mainstream.

Perhaps because of its combined implications as forbidden and mysterious, as well as its connections to *ukiyo-e* images of the phantasmal, tattooing gradually developed its own kind of ghostly mystique. Tsuruya Namboku IV (1755–1829), a forerunner to Tanizaki, explored the theme of the inspirited tattoo in one of his major *kabuki* plays, *Sakura hime azuma bunshô* (*The Cherry Blossom Princess of Edo*, 1817). This drama visually situates the tattoo as the polytemporal insignia that enables two homosexual lovers to identify each other across different lifetimes. Since each partner selects a different gender upon a new incarnation, only through their mutually shared tattoos, which do not change with each new form, can they continually confirm the identity of the other, regardless of how their bodily appearances alter through transmigration. The tattoo, as inscription of their spiritual love, remains the constant symbolic signifier upon which the order of erotic encounters finds meaningful resolution. While the anatomical circumstances of the sexual act change, and therefore so does the imaginative redefinition of their lovemaking, the stability of their partnership, the ethereal aspect of their pleasure, is infused into the apparitional tattoo. Perhaps, then, as a kind of *objet petit a*, their psycho-sexual tattoo points to the irrecoverable origins of their first encounter; the consistency of the ghost tattoo acts as a kind of cosmological constant throughout the psycho-sexual changes of reincarnated bodies.

Horiyoshi III: Contemporary Tattoo as Psycho-Cultural Necromancy

For the contemporary Japanese imagination, tattoos are frequently associated with the criminal substrata of the *yakuza*. Mainstream assumptions have so readily correlated tattooed bodies with troublemakers that many *onsen* (bath-houses) and *ryokan* (guest inns) outright forbid entrance to those who are heavily inked. In some of the more dubious neighborhoods of Tokyo, such as the nightlife district on the west side of Ueno, graphic posters warn of *yakuza* presences. Such advisory cartoons of muscular bad boys, wrapped only in a *fundoshi* (loincloth), symbolize the dangers of organized criminals who operate in the district, an increasing concern throughout Japanese society considering the number of high-profile deaths from gangland activity recently, including the mayor of Nagasaki (2007).

Mainstream acceptance of tattoos in Japan is currently growing, but the tattoo artist retains a kind of mystique. As a kind of medium for the twenty-first century, Horiyoshi III communicates with otherworlds through the alchemy of ink. An outspoken spiritist, his tattoo designs – based on sketches refined through aesthetic oneiromancy, or dream communication with the dead – attract attention both for their technical prowess and for their occultic commitment to ghosts as incorporeal intelligences that inform our own reality. As collections of his work reveal, his art is adamantly based on a belief in the forms of subjectivity that inhabit the ethereal.[18] These include ancestral spirits, Buddhist saints, local hauntings (*jibakurei*), and other forms of spectral phenomenon. In an interview with Judit Kawaguchi, for the English-language *Japan Times*, Horiyoshi describes how his exposure to the discarnate informs his designs:

> Ghosts are real. I was painting one day in my Yokohama studio, when I saw a figure walk in. I turned to say hello and it disappeared into black powder. I told this to a psychic and he said that in the Meiji Era there was an execution ground where I live, so there were lots of ghosts wandering around my neighborhood.[19]

These sentiments may seem to reflect only a modern-day penchant for the paranormal, but Horiyoshi grounds his belief and practices through folkloric references, working with classical notions that the drawn line can be imbued with transformative energy.

Through his religiosity, Horiyoshi strikes a curious balance between an old-fashioned spiritual viewpoint and a countercultural artform. In his case, the aesthetic and emotional tones of esoteric knowledge (*mikkyô*) unite with the visual variety of the tattoo medium. As a visit to Horiyoshi's studio reveals, the figurations of piety deeply inform his tattoo practice, both conceptually and technically. A small home Shintô shrine (*kamidana*) occupies a space of honor; the Gods of ink preside over all occasions. Alongside his non-electrical equipment, Horiyoshi keeps a set of Buddhist prayer beads (*juzu*), which he uses in a purifying manner before commencing a tattoo. Likewise, in formal writing, Horiyoshi generally concludes his essays with the set phrase *gasshô hyappai* ("one hundred bows"), a salutation derived from monastic nomenclature.

Horiyoshi thus makes for a rather paradoxical combination of devout religiosity, including doctrines derived from orthodox Buddhism, and a career in what is often thought of as an unsavory profession. Part of how he negotiates this apparent incongruity is to recall the esoteric trends in religious thought that link skilled calligraphy with spiritual development, even to the point of thaumaturgy. For example, Kôbô-daishi (774–835 CE), the founder of the *Shingon* sect of esoteric Buddhism, is famous for his calligraphy, as one skillful in technique but also, more importantly, capable of filling technique with divine inspiration. In one hagiographical account, Kôbô-daishi engaged in a calligraphy contest with a visiting spirit, each writing the character for *dragon* (*ryû*) on rice paper, yet brushed with psychical transferences so that brushed words (semiotic characters) turned into animate beings through the alchemy of the ink (*sumi*).

Broadly speaking, appreciation of East Asian calligraphy assumes that, to a large extent, brushed ink expressively contains the personality of the calligrapher. Horiyoshi, who is highly talented with both needle and brush, extends this transtemporal sensibility in art by asserting that the inked image clairvoyantly transmutes a metaphysical encounter – with, for example, a ghost or guardian spirit – into an artistic transcription, a tattoo, that resonates with and through the formatively spectral encounter. When commenting on his work, Horiyoshi frequently speaks of tattooing ghosts as a kind of ontological recovery of the symbolic order, through which the flesh acts as a scrying space for negotiating both negative and positive attributes in a Buddhist worldview. The tattooed ghost informs, through its uncanniness, the mortal of the interrelated conditions between body and memory in the broader context of life and afterlife.[20]

The body thus allows for a kind of permanent mediumship, in which the ghostly dimensions become animate upon the living skin, testifying to the Buddha's teachings on desire, death, and *karma*. As Horiyoshi explains in the introduction to his stencil series *Thirty-Six Ghosts* (*Yûrei-kito san-jû-roku kinzu*), the ghost tattoo makes visible, through an illustrated narrative inserted into the public domain, the phantasm as metaphysically didactic, demonstrating concepts such as fate and fortune (*innen-inga*) or the delusion of grudges (*onnen-môsô*).[21]

These sincere gestures of a religious mindset emphasize that, for Horiyoshi, the ghost tattoo functions in a way beyond its illustrative design. Through the phantoms derived from Japanese folklore and Buddhist cosmology, Horiyoshi integrates a seemingly anachronistic worldview, a dualistic sense of spirit and matter, with a counter-normative art form that appeals to the digital mindset of contemporary youth culture. Horiyoshi's apparitional art is intended to be illustrative and visible in the public domain, confounding contemporary imaginations with traditional imagery that is nostalgic, pious, and hauntingly ghoulish. The tattoo leaves the parlor room séance and enters the visual field of the daytime streets. Horiyoshi thus enacts a concept that

Tanizaki had explored in his writing: the ghost tattoo enables an etheric projection that becomes inscribed upon the living subjective body in conflictive dialogue with the generalized national body. The multiple worlds – of the living or the dead, of hell or paradise – become transgressed in that the lingering spirits become inscribed in ink upon the human skin.

Horiyoshi recodes the appearance of the discarnate as a contemporary utterance operating through the spatio-temporal domain of the tattoo. Conceptually, the ghost tattoo exemplifies a sense of what Gilles Deleuze and Félix Guattari termed the *body without organs*: "The body without organs is not a dead body but a living body all the more alive and teeming once it has blown apart the organism and its organization."[22] The ghost tattoo, according to its ethereal nature, exemplifies the multiplicity of virtual possibilities and dimensions. By whatever selection its *host*, or tattooee, chooses, the ghost tattoo becomes affixed to skin, which is the plane of immanence and possibility. Through the alchemy of ink, the ghost carries its rupturous message of alterity, etched as enchanted figuration onto a *full body*. The array of potential psychical variables, not easily represented by this corporeal body, can be made visible through the body that is *with* organs, the mortal frame. The ink releases the revenant's thanotic energy as a release back into the world through the materialization of the ghostly image, on a host body. For Horiyoshi, then, his inscriptions must be faithful to traditional models and localized folklore in order to retain a relation to the symbolic order. What else can articulate the subject matter of vanishing particulars? Horiyoshi's work, therefore, positions and seals the ghost, as a troubling interlocutor who represents the dimension of temporal flexibility, within the contexts of the everyday and cosmopolitan.

Horiyoshi's work contains numerous examples of this procedure. Perhaps the piece that most fully articulates his sense of how ghostly ink makes a liturgy of the body is his depiction of the classical Japanese folktale "Earless Hô'ichi" (*Mimi-nashi Hô'ichi*),[23] a tale made famous in the West through Hearn's rendition of 1904. To depict the protective dimension of a spiritualized tattoo, Horiyoshi's stencil emphasizes the interplay between the scriptural text, which floats in the background because of its etheric power, with the talismanic inscription of the *sutra* upon Hôichi's body as subscribed sets of handwritten characters in the *siddham* script (*bonji*). This syllabary has longstanding associations with *Shingon* meditation, as Kôbô-daishi is said to have introduced *siddham* into Japan. Ensconced in ink, Hôichi encounters the uncanny, this wrathful apparition who is the restless undead harassing the living. In the context of a tattoo, this illustration emphasizes that, through the ghost-ink, one can offset or even subjectivize the death drive and its attendant dread. But the tattooed body acts as an *o-mamori*, a symptom of the Real, as well as a talisman of protection etched in the tissues of the body.

The paranormal correlation between holy text, as a handwritten product, and the uncanny as a negotiation between spirit and matter, appears frequently in Horiyoshi's art. In one example, *Tenma hajun* (*The Demon Overlord*) an *akuma* (demon) gnashes on a holy scroll, neither able to digest nor erase the power of the scriptural ink.[24] Perhaps Horiyoshi's favorite icon for depicting the negotiation of positive and negative attributes of the uncanny is the guardian bodhisattva Fudô Myô-ô, a figure frequently associated with *Shingon*, a sect that generally can be thought of as more esoterically inclined than other forms of Japanese Buddhism. Kyôsai's depictions of this deity maintain all of the elements of the iconography associated with his nature: an aura of flames, the demon-quelling sword, and the righteous combatant grimacing in pain. Horiyoshi heightens the confrontational theme of Fudô Myô-ô by taking him out of the precincts of the temple and inserting him within the visual fields of popular trends in contemporary Japanese culture, such as *anime*.[25]

Horiyoshi thus follows the formative example of Kyôsai, in combining aesthetic tradition with an unorthodox medium.[26] Along with Kyôsai, Horiyoshi credits artists such as Maruyama Ôkyo for developing not only the stylistic effects for depicting ghosts, but the spiritual acumen to sense their etheric bodies as well. Maruyama's most famous piece, *The Ghost of Oyuki*, depicts the classical representation of a female *yûrei*: white *kimono*, disheveled hair, hands held limply in front, a lower body dissipating into smudged grays at the bottom of the frame.[27] Horiyoshi's series *Yûrei-zu* experiments with Maruyama's model. Horiyoshi can intensify the necromantic dimensions of his work, in both sketches and actual tattoos, by employing a method for diluting an intense form of ink (*nôzumi*) into a seeping mixture which displays very subtle gradations of grey. This strategy of ink-mixing has become a hallmark of Horiyoshi III's style, having refined the technique from previous attempts by Horiyoshi I (*Ichi-daime Horiyoshi*).

Watery, amorphous, and in-between form and spirit, Horiyoshi's ghosts exhibit a kind of vitality within the blurred outlines of verisimilitude. Derived from iconographic heritage, Horiyoshi's ghosts perform as national-cultural specters that confront the current symbolic order in contemporary Japan, enhancing the *fushigi* (mysterious) developed during the modern period. As scholars such as Figal have noted, folklorism (*minzokugaku*), which owed much of its conceptual methodology to modernist concerns and prejudices, reinterpreted the lore of the fantastic bestiary according to the possibilities of new associations. Yanagita Kunio (1875–1962), in this fashion, gradually replaced the word *tengu*, a kind of heavenly dog creature, for *senzô* (ancestor) in his writings. Seemingly, he believed that ancestral spirits become interrelated with phantasmal beings of myth through the collective development of cultural memory.

Horiyoshi's discourse with the discarnate, working with the visual alterity of Kyôsai and the countercultural affect of Tanizaki's entity-tattoo, reinvents a sense of the ghostly space, one redistributed within the cultural geography of postmodern Japan. The corporeal body undergoes a kind of shapeshifting through the tattoo of ghostly ink. Horiyoshi asserts that his own mythic typologies are not a quaint leftover from a superstitious past. They are, in fact, recontextualized codes for apprehending an invisible world always on the verge of the Real. Ghosts, through ink, unite to a body *with* organs, rediscovering the full body's negotiation of death, afterlife, and the possibility of return. Perhaps this is why, on account of the necromantic potential in his art, Horiyoshi signs his work with the pen-name *yume-ten*: a dream of the heavens.

NOTES

1 "Stranger in a Strange Land" was first broadcast in February 2007 (Season 3, Episode 9).
2 *Achara* closely resembles the Sanskrit word *ācāra*, which means good conduct. According to Hinduism, generally, having *ācāra* evidences an attunement with *dharma*, or righteousness.
3 Lafcadio Hearn, *In Ghostly Japan* (New York: Little, Brown, and Co, 1903).
4 Shunkôsai Hokushû's (1808–1832) *The Ghost of Oiwa* (1826), based on the *Yotsuya kaidan*, is a noteworthy example.
5 Katsushika Hokusai (1760–1849), internationally known for his iconic *The Great Wave off Kanagawa* (*Kanagawa oki nami ura*, 1832), had also sketched apparitions and macabre subject matter for his woodblock prints.
6 Stephen Addiss, "Yamanaka Shinten'ô: The Albatross of Japanese Painting," *Monumenta Nipponica* 48, no. 2 (Autumn 1993): 336.
7 Timothy Clark, *The Demon of Painting* (London: British Museum Press, 1993), 67.
8 Ibid., 69.
9 Gerald Figal, *Civilization and Monsters* (Durham: Duke University Press, 1999), 12.
10 Caroline Hirasawa, "The Inflatable, Collapsable Kingdom," *Monumenta Nipponica* 63, no. 1 (Spring 2008): 38.
11 See *Nihon rei'nôsha retsuden* (Tokyo: Bessatsu Takarajima henshûbu, 2008) for a general overview of major personages in the psychic community in early twentieth-century Japan.
12 Tanizaki Jun'ichirô, *Shisei – Himitsu* (Tokyo: Shinchô-sha, 1994).
13 Psychoanalytic readings of masochism, aesthetics, and the body in pain as symptomatic of cultural instability can be applied to much of Tanizaki's fiction, such as *Chijin no ai* (*Naomi*, 1924).
14 Basil Hall Chamberlain, trans. *The Kojiki* (Tokyo: Tuttle, 1986), 179.
15 Gerald Groemer, "The Creation of the Edo Outcast Order," *The Journal of Japanese Studies* 27, no. 2 (Summer 2001): 285–288.
16 Tamabayashi Haruo, *Bunshin hyaku-sugata* (Tokyo: Nihon shisei kenkyû-sho, 1987).
17 See Donald McCallum, "Historical and Cultural Dimensions of the Tattoo in Japan," in *Marks of Civilization*, ed. Arnold Rubin (Los Angeles: UCLA Museum of Cultural History, 1988), 109–134.
18 For examples of Horiyoshi III's work, see his homepage: http://www.ne.jp/asahi/tattoo/horiyoshi3 and http://www.myspace.com/horiyoshi3. See also: http://hi.baidu.com/%B1%AD%C3%E6%C3%A8/blog/item/65d724de132dd85195ee374b.html and http://www.irezumi.us/eg/toukou.html.
19 Judit Kawaguchi, "Words to Live By," *Japan Times*, June 12, 2007, http://search.japantimes.co.jp/cgi-bin/fl20070612jk.html.
20 Jill Horiyuki Mandelbaum, *Studying Horiyoshi III* (Pennsylvania: Schiffer Books, 2008), 37.
21 Horiyoshi III, *Yûrei-kito san-jû-roku kinzu* (Nihon shuppan-sha, 2007), 7.
22 Gilles Deleuze and Félix Guattari, *A Thousand Plateaus*, trans. Brian Massumi (Minneapolis: University of Minneapolis Press, 1987), 30.
23 Horiyoshi III, *Yûrei-kito san-jû-roku kinzu*, 70–72.
24 Horiyoshi III, *Hyakkizu* (Tokyo: Nihon shuppan-sha, 1998), 62–63.
25 There are a number of interesting case studies in Japanese history in which the visual designs of tattoos intertwine with fads in popular culture. For example, Japanese

translations of the Chinese classic *Shuǐhǔ zhuàn* (*The Water Margin*, Jp. *Suikoden*) enjoyed a wide readership, creating something of a tattoo fad, based on popular prints. Kuniyoshi designed a series of woodblock illustrations, based on the heroic personages in the tale, entitled *108 Heroes of the Suikoden* (*Tsuzoku suikoden goketsu hyaku-hachi-nin no hitori*, 1827–1830). Horiyoshi III, in an act of homage as well as innovation, designed his own set of sketches based on the same theme. Likewise, contemporary anthologies in Japanese such as *Kyôsai yôkai hyakkei* (*The Hundred Apparitions of Kyôsai*) make clear the direct legacy of Kyôsai as ongoing influential to the Japanese tattoo community.

26   For another comparison between Horiyoshi and Kyôsai, contrast Horiyoshi's *Jigoku-zu—Enma dai-ô* (*Hell Painting: The Lord Enma*), in Horiyoshi III, *Hyakkizu*, 55, with Kyôsai's *Jigoku hensô-zu* (*Aspects of Hell*), in Timothy Clark, *The Demon of Painting*, 57.

27   Yamamura Sadako, the vindictive wraith in the film *Ringu*, resembles this painting to a very deliberate degree.

Select Bibliography

This select bibliography tentatively attempts to be representative of a body of scholarship on the ghostly and the everyday, as used by the contributors in this volume. Far from exhaustive, it is meant to offer interesting pathways into further intellectual considerations of issues revolving around ghosts, haunting, and their relation to popular culture. It both reflects the fact that spectrality is nothing new for the academy, while also pointing to the variety of interventions and reassessments of the way we use ghosts in literary, filmic, and cultural studies.

Abraham, Nicholas, and Maria Torok. *The Shell and the Kernel: Renewals of Psychoanalysis (Volume I)*. Chicago and London: University of Chicago Press, 1994.

Adorno, Theodor W. *Minima Moralia*. Translated by E. F. N. Jephcott. London: New Left Books, 1974.

Appadurai, Arjun. "Spectral Housing and Urban Cleansing: Notes on Millennial Mumbai." *Public Culture* 12, no. 3 (2000): 627–651.

Appelbaum, David. *Jacques Derrida's Ghost: A Conjuration*. Albany: SUNY Press, 2009.

Appiah, K. Anthony. "Spiritual Realism." *The Nation*, August 3–10, 1992, 146–148.

Ariès, Philippe. *L'homme devant la mort*. Paris: Seuil, 1977.

Augé, Marc. *Non-Places: Introduction to an Anthropology of Supermodernity*. London: Blackwell, 1995.

Bailey, Dale. *American Nightmares: The Haunted House Formula in American Popular Fiction*. Bowling Green: Bowling Green State University Popular Press, 1999.

Bal, Mieke. *Travelling Concepts in the Humanities: A Rough Guide*. Toronto: University of Toronto Press, 2002.

Barber, X. Theodore. "Phantasmagorical Wonders: The Magic Lantern Ghost Show in Nineteenth Century America." *Film History* 3, no. 2 (1989): 73–86.

Barthes, Roland. *Camera Lucida: Reflections on Photography*. Translated by Richard Howard. New York: Hill and Wang, 1981.

Baßler, Moritz, Bettina Gruber, and Martina Wagner-Egelhaaf, eds. *Gespenster: Erscheinungen – Medien – Theorien*. Würzburg: Königshausen & Neumann, 2005.

Batchen, Geoffrey. "Spectres of Cyberspace." In *The Visual Culture Reader: Second Edition*, edited by Nicholas Mirzoeff. London and New York: Routledge, 2005, 237–242.

Baudrillard, Jean. *Symbolic Exchange and Death*. London: Sage, 1993.

Bergland, Renée. *The National Uncanny: Indian Ghosts and American Subjects*. Lebanon, NH: Dartmouth Press, 2000.

Bernasconi, Robert. "Skepticism in the Face of Philosophy." In *Re-Reading Levinas*, edited by Robert Bernasconi and Simon Critchley. Bloomington: Indiana University Press, 1991, 149–161.

Biedermann, Claudio, and Christian Stiegler, eds. *Horror und Ästhetik*. Konstanz: UVK, 2008.

Borges, Jorge Luis, Adolfo Bioy Casares, and Silvina Ocampo, eds. *Antología de la literatura fantástica*. Buenos Aires: Editorial Sudamericana, 1998.

Botting, Fred. *Gothic*. London: Routledge, 1996.

Bouldin, Joana. "Cadaver of the Real: Animation, Rotoscoping, and the Politics of the Body." *Animation Journal* 12 (2004): 7–31.

Bruce, Susan. "Sympathy for the Dead: (G)hosts, Hostilities and Mediums in Alejandro Amenábar's *The Others* and Postmortem Photography." *Discourse* 27, no. 2–3 (2005): 21–40.

Burton, John W. "Ghosts, Ancestors and Individuals Among the Atuot of the Southern Sudan." *Man* 13, no. 4 (1978): 600–617.

Buse, Peter, and Andrew Stott, eds. *Ghosts: Deconstruction, Psychoanalysis, History*. Basingstoke: Macmillan, 1999.

Byron, Glennis, and David Punter, eds. *Spectral Readings: Towards a Gothic Geography*. London: Macmillan, 1990.

Carlson, Marvin. *The Haunted Stage: The Theatre as Memory Machine*. Ann Arbor: University of Michigan Press, 2001.

Castle, Terry. *The Female Thermometer: Eighteenth-Century Culture and the Invention of the Uncanny*. Oxford: Oxford University Press, 1995.

Castricano, Jodey. *Cryptomimesis: The Gothic and Jacques Derrida's Ghost Writing*. Montreal: McGill-Queen's University Press, 2003.

Cavallaro, Dani. *The Gothic Vision: Three Centuries of Horror, Terror and Fear*. New York: Continuum, 2002.

Cavell, Stanley. *The Claim of Reason: Wittgenstein, Skepticism, Morality, and Tragedy*. Oxford: Oxford University Press, 1979.

———. *The World Viewed: Reflections on the Ontology of Film, Enlarged Edition*. Cambridge, MA and London: Harvard University Press, 1979.

Cheah, Pheng. "Spectral Nationality: The Living On [*sur-vie*] of the Postcolonial Nation in Neocolonial Globalization." *boundary 2* 26, no. 3 (1999): 225–252.

Chéroux, Clément, Andreas Fischer et al. *The Perfect Medium: Photography and the Occult*. New Haven and London: Yale University Press, 2005.

Chibnall, Steve, and Julian Petley, eds. *British Horror Cinema*. New York: Routledge, 2002.

Clark, Lynn Schofield. *From Angels to Aliens: Teenagers, the Media, and the Supernatural*. New York: Oxford University Press, 2003.

Clery, E. J., and Robert Miles, eds. *Gothic Documents*. Manchester: Manchester University Press, 2000.

Clover, Carol. *Men, Women, and Chainsaws: Gender in the Modern Horror Film*. Princeton: Princeton University Press, 1992.

Comaroff, Jean, and John Comaroff. "Alien-Nation: Zombies, Immigrants, and Millenial Capitalism." *South Atlantic Quarterly* 10, no. 4 (2002): 779–805.

Costello, Diarmuid, and Dominic Willsdon, eds. *The Life and Death of Images: Ethics and Aesthetics*. Ithaca: Cornell University Press, 2008.

Crapanzano, Vincent, and Vivian Garrison. "Introduction." In *Case Studies in Spirit Possession*. London: John Wiley, 1977, 1–40.

Danius, Sara. *The Senses of Modernism: Technology, Perception, and Aesthetics*. Ithaca: Cornell University Press, 2002.

Davis, Colin. *Haunted Subjects: Deconstruction, Psychoanalysis and the Return of the Dead*. London: Palgrave, 2007.

———. "Can the Dead Speak to Us? De Man, Levinas and Agamben." *Culture, Theory & Critique* 45, no. 1 (2004): 77–89.

———. "*État Présent*: Hauntology, Spectres and Phantoms." *French Studies* 59, no. 3 (2005): 373–379.

De Certeau, Michel. *The Practice of Everyday Life*. Translated by S. Rendall. Berkeley: University of California Press, 1988.

De Certeau, Michel, Luce Giard, and Pierre Mayol. *The Practice of Everyday Life. Volume 2: Living & Cooking*. Translated by Timothy J. Tomasik. Minneapolis: University of Minnesota Press, 1998.

Delamotte, Eugenia C. *Perils of the Night: A Feminist Study of Nineteenth-Century Gothic*. Oxford: Oxford University Press, 1990.

Derrida, Jacques. *Archive Fever: A Freudian Impression*. Translated by Eric Prenowitz. Chicago: University of Chicago Press, 1996.

———. *Memoires for Paul de Man*. New York: Columbia University Press, 1989.

———. *Of Spirit: Heidegger and the Question*. Chicago: University of Chicago Press, 1991.

———. *Specters of Marx: The State of the Debt, The Work of Mourning, & the New International*. Translated by Peggy Kamuf. New York: Routledge, 1994.

Derrida, Jacques, and Bernard Stiegler. *Echographies of Television*. Translated by Jennifer Bajorek. Cambridge, UK: Polity Press, 2006.

Didi-Huberman, Georges. "Superstition." In *Ordnungen der Sichtbarkeit: Fotografie in Wissenschaft, Kunst und Technologie*, edited by Peter Geimer. Frankfurt am Main: Suhrkamp, 2002, 434–440.

Doane, Mary Ann. *The Emergence of Cinematic Time: Modernity, Contingency, the Archive*. Cambridge, MA: Harvard University Press, 2002.

Donaldson-Mchugh, Shannon, and Don Moore. "Film Adaptation, Co-Authorship, and Hauntology: Gus van Sant's *Psycho* (1998)." *The Journal of Popular Culture* 39, no. 2 (2006): 225–233.

Donnelly, Kevin J. *The Spectre of Sound: Music in Film and Television*. London: BFI, 2005.

Dufour, Éric. *Le Cinéma d'horreur et ses figures*. Paris: Presses Universitaires de France, 2006.

Dyson, Jeremy. *Bright Darkness: The Lost Art of the Supernatural Horror Film*. London: Cassell, 1997.

Edelman, Lee. *No Future: Queer Theory and the Death Drive*. Durham: Duke University Press, 2004.

Elferen, Isabella van, ed. *Nostalgia or Perversion? Gothic Rewriting from the Eighteenth Century to the Present Day*. Newcastle: Cambridge Scholars, 2007.

Ellis, John. *Seeing Things: Television in the Age of Uncertainty*. London: I. B. Tauris, 2000.

Elsaesser, Thomas. "Was wäre, wenn du schon tot bist. Vom 'postmodernen' zum 'post-mortem'-Kino am Beispiel von Christopher Nolans Memento." In *Zeitsprünge. Wie Filme Geschichte(n) erzählen*, edited by Christine Rüffert et al. Berlin: Bertz, 2004, 115–125.

Figal, Gerald. *Civilization and Monsters*. Durham: Duke University Press, 1999.

Fowkes, Katherine A. *Giving Up the Ghost: Spirits, Ghosts, and Angels in Mainstream Comedy Films*. Detroit: Wayne State University Press, 1998.

Freer, Ada Goodrich. *Essays in Psychical Research*. London: George Redway, 1899.

Freud, Sigmund. "The Uncanny." In *Writings on Art and Literature*. Stanford: Stanford University Press, 1997, 193–233.

Ghosh, Bishnupriya. "On Grafting the Vernacular: The Consequences of Postcolonial Spectrology." *boundary 2* 31, no. 2 (2004): 197–218.

Gitelman, Lisa. *Always Already New: Media, History, and the Data of Culture*. Cambridge, MA: MIT Press, 2006.

Glendinning, Victoria. "Phantasms and Frauds." *The Times Literary Supplement*, July 8, 1980.

Gordon, Avery F. *Ghostly Matters: Haunting and Sociological Imagination*. Minneapolis: University of Minnesota Press, 1998.

Grayling, A. C. *Skepticism and the Possibility of Knowledge*. London and New York: Continuum, 2008.

Gunning, Tom. "The Ghost in the Machine: Animated Pictures at the Haunted Hotel of Early Cinema." *Living Pictures: The Journal of Popular and Projected Image Before 1914* 1, no. 1 (2001): 3–17.

———. "To Scan a Ghost: The Ontology of Mediated Vision." *Grey Room* 26 (Winter 2007): 94–127.

———. "Phantom Images and Modern Manifestations: Spirit Photography, Magic Theater, Trick Films, and Photography's Uncanny." In *Fugitive Images: From Photography to Video*, edited by Patrice Petro. Bloomington: Indiana University Press, 1995, 42–71.

Gurney, Edmund, F. W. H. Myers, and Frank Podmore. *Phantasms of the Living.* London: Trubner, 1886.

Hagen, Wolfgang. "Der Okkultismus der Avantgarde um 1900." In *Konfigurationen: Zwischen Kunst und Medien,* edited by Sigrid Schade and Georg Christoph Tholen. München: Wilhelm Fink, 1999, 338–357.

———. *Radio Schreber: Der 'moderne Spiritismus' und die Sprache der Medien.* Weimar: Vdg-Verlag, 2001.

Hall, Trevor. *The Strange Story of Ada Goodrich Freer.* London: Duckworth, 1980.

Hansen, Mark. *New Philosophy for New Media.* Cambridge, MA: MIT Press, 2004.

Haraway, Donna. "Manifesto for Cyborgs: Science, Technology and Socialist Feminism in the 1980s." *Socialist Review* 80 (1985): 65–108.

Harries, Martin. *Scare Quotes from Shakespeare: Marx, Keynes, and the Language of Reenchantment.* Stanford: Stanford University Press, 2000.

Hawkins, Joan. *Cutting Edge: Art-Horror and the Horrific Avant-garde.* Minneapolis: University of Minnesota Press, 2000.

Hayles, N. Katherine. *How We Became Posthuman: Virtual Bodies in Cybernetics, Literature, and Informatics.* Chicago: University of Chicago Press, 1999.

Heidegger, Martin. *Being and Time.* 1927. Translated by John Macquarrie and Edward Robinson. New York: Harper & Row, 1962.

———. "The Question Concerning Technology." In *The Question Concerning Technology and Other Essays.* Translated by William Lovitt. New York: Harper Perennial, 1982, 3–35.

Highmore, Ben. *Everyday Life and Cultural Theory.* London and New York: Routledge, 2002.

Highmore, Ben, ed. *The Everyday Life Reader.* London and New York: Routledge, 2002.

Hills, Matt. *The Pleasures of Horror.* New York: Continuum, 2005.

Hitchcock, Peter. *Oscillate Wildly: Space, Body and Spirit of Millennial Materialism.* Minneapolis: University of Minnesota Press, 1999.

Hogle, Jerrold E. *The Cambridge Companion to Gothic Fiction.* Cambridge, UK: Cambridge University Press, 2002.

Howells, Coral Ann. *Love, Mystery, and Misery: Feeling in Gothic Fiction.* London: Athlone Press, 1978.

Jameson, Fredric. *Archaeologies of the Future: The Desire Called Utopia and Other Science Fictions.* New York: Verso, 2007.

———. *Postmodernism or, the Cultural Logic of Late Capitalism.* London: Verso, 1991.

Jenkins, Henry. *Fans, Bloggers, and Gamers: Exploring Participatory Culture.* New York: New York University Press, 2006.

Joseph-Vilain, Mélanie, and Judith Mishrahi-Barak, eds. *Postcolonial Ghosts.* Montpellier: Presses Universitares de la Méditerranée, forthcoming 2009.

Kittler, Friedrich. *Gramophone, Film, Typewriter.* Translated by Geoffrey Winthrop-Young and Michael Wutz. Stanford: Stanford University Press, 1999.

Köhne, Julia, Ralph Kuschke, and Arno Meteling, eds. *Splatter Movies: Essays zum modernen Horrorfilm.* Berlin: Bertz & Fischer, 2006.

Kucich, John, and Diane F. Sadoff, eds. *Victorian Afterlife*. Minneapolis: University of Minnesota Press, 2000.

Lacan, Jacques. "Desire and the Interpretation of Desire in Hamlet." *Yale French Studies* 55/56 (1977): 11–52.

Ladd, Brian. *The Ghosts of Berlin: Confronting German History in the Urban Landscape*. Chicago and London: University of Chicago Press, 1998.

Latour, Bruno. *Aramis, Or the Love of Technology*. Translated by Catherine Porter. Cambridge: Harvard University Press, 1996.

Lawler, Leonard. *Derrida and Husserl: The Basic Problem of Phenomenology*. Bloomington: Indiana University Press, 2002.

Lefebvre, Henri. *The Production of Space*. Translated by Donald Nicholson-Smith. Malden: Blackwell Publishing, 1984.

Le Goff, Jacques. *La naissance du purgatoire*. Paris: Gallimard, 1981.

Leja, Michael. *Looking Askance: Skepticism and American Art from Eakins to Duchamp*. Berkeley: University of California Press, 2004.

Levinas, Emmanuel. *Autrement qu'être ou au-delà de l'essence*. The Hague: Martinus Nijhoff, 1974; Livre de Poche edition.

Lodge, Oliver. "Experience of Unusual Phenomena Occurring in the Presence of an Entranced Person (Eusapia Palladino): Report to the President and Council of the S.P.R." *Journal of the Society for Psychical Research* 6 (November 1894): 306–360.

———. "Introduction to the Earl of Dunraven's Record of Experiences with D. D. Home." *Proceedings of the Society for Psychical Research* 35 (1925): 1–285.

Luckhurst, Roger. "The Contemporary London Gothic and the Limits of the 'Spectral Turn.'" *Textual Practice* 16, no. 3 (2002): 527–546.

———. *The Invention of Telepathy, 1870–1901*. Oxford: Oxford University Press, 2002.

Mageo, Jeannette Marie, and Alan Howard, eds. *Spirits in Culture, History, and Mind*. New York and London: Routledge, 1996.

Manovich, Lev. *The Language of New Media*. Cambridge, MA: MIT Press, 2001.

Massumi, Brian. *Parables for the Virtual: Movement, Affect, Sensation*. Durham: Duke University Press, 2002.

Marx, Karl. *Capital: Volume One*. Translated by Ben Fowkes. New York: Penguin, 1976.

Mbembe, Achille. "Life, Sovereignty, and Terror in the Fiction of Amos Tutuola." *Research in African Literatures* 34, no. 4 (2003): 1–26.

———. *On the Postcolony*. Berkeley: University of California Press, 2001.

———. "On the Power of the False." *Public Culture* 14, no. 3 (2002): 629–641.

McLuhan, Marshall. *Understanding Media: The Extensions of Man*. Cambridge, MA: MIT Press, 1994.

Merleau-Ponty, Maurice. *The World of Perception*. Translated by Oliver Davis. London: Routledge, 2008.

Moran, Joe. *Reading the Everyday*. London and New York: Routledge, 2005.

Morin, Edgar. *L'homme et la mort*. Paris: Seuil, 2002.

Munster, Anna. *Materializing New Media: Embodiment in Information Aesthetics*. Lebanon, NH: University Press of New England, 2006.

Murphy, Laura. "Into the Bush of Ghosts: Specters of the Slave Trade in West African Fiction." *Research in African Literatures* 38, no. 4 (2007): 141–152.

Noakes, Richard. "'Instruments to Lay Hold of Spirits': Technologizing the Bodies of Victorian Spiritualism." In *Bodies/Machines*, edited by Iwan Rhys Morus. Oxford: Berg, 2002, 125–63.

———. "Cromwell Varley FRS, Electrical Discharge and Victorian Spiritualism." *Notes and Records of the Royal Society* 61 (2007): 5–21.

———. "Telegraphy is an Occult Art: Cromwell Fleetwood Varley and the Diffusion of Electricity to the Other World." *The British Journal for the History of Science* 32 (December 1999): 421–459.

Oppenheim, Janet. *The Other World: Spiritualism and Psychical Research in England, 1850–1914*. Cambridge, UK: Cambridge University Press, 1985.

Owen, Alex. *The Darkened Room: Women, Power and Spiritualism in Late Victorian England*. London: Virago, 1989.

Perez, Gilberto. *The Material Ghost: Films and Their Medium*. Baltimore: Johns Hopkins University Press, 1998.

Peters, John Durham. *Speaking into the Air: A History of the Idea of Communication*. Chicago and London: University of Chicago Press, 2000.

Phillips, Dana. *The Truth of Ecology: Nature, Culture, and Literature in America*. New York: Oxford University Press, 2003.

Powell, Anna. *Deleuze and Horror Film*. Edinburgh: Edinburgh University Press, 2005.

Preston, Christopher. *Grounding Knowledge: Environmental Philosophy, Epistemology, and Place*. Athens: University of Georgia Press, 2003.

Rayner, Alice. *Ghosts: Death's Double and the Phenomena of Theatre*. Minneapolis: University of Minnesota Press, 2006.

Richardson, Judith. *Possessions: The History and Uses of Haunting in the Hudson Valley*. Cambridge, MA: Harvard University Press, 2003.

Robins, Kevin. *Into The Image: Culture and Politics in the Field of Vision*. London: Routledge, 1996.

Royle, Nicholas. *The Uncanny: An Introduction*. Manchester: Manchester University Press, 2002.

Sage, Victor, and Allan Lloyd Smith, eds. *Modern Gothic: A Reader*. Manchester: Manchester University Press, 1996.

Saler, Benson. "Supernatural as a Western Category." *Ethos* 5, no. 1 (1977): 31–53.

Schneider, Steven Jay, and Daniel Shaw, eds. *Dark Thoughts: Philosophic Reflections on Cinematic Horror*. Lanham, MD: Scarecrow Press, 2003.

Sconce, Jeffrey. *Haunted Media: Electronic Presence from Telegraphy to Television*. Durham: Duke University Press, 2000.

Sedgwick, Eve Kosofsky. *The Coherence of Gothic Conventions*. London and New York: Routledge, 1986.

Silver, Alain, and James Ursini, eds. *The Horror Film Reader*. New York: Limelight Editions, 2000.

Sobchack, Vivian. *Carnal Thoughts: Embodiment and Moving Image Culture*. Berkeley: University of California Press, 2004.

Sontag, Susan. *On Photography*. London, New York: Penguin, 2002.

Spivak, Gayatri Chakravorty, "Ghostwriting," *Diacritics* 25, no. 2 (1995): 64–84.

Spooner, Catherine. *Contemporary Gothic*. London: Reaktion Books, 2006.

Spooner, Catherine, and Emma McEvoy, eds. *The Routledge Companion to Gothic*. London: Routledge, 2007.

Sprinker, Michael, ed. *Ghostly Demarcations*. New York: Verso, 1999.

Stead, W. T. "How We Intend to Study the Borderland." *Borderland* 1 (July 1893): 3–6.

Sterne, Jonathan. *The Audible Past: Cultural Origins of Sound Reproduction*. Durham: Duke University Press, 2006.

Stoichita, Victor Ieronim. *A Short History of the Shadow*. Translated by Anne-Marie Glasheen. London: Reaktion Books, 1997.

Storey, John, ed. *Cultural Theory and Popular Culture: A Reader*. London: Prentice Hall, 1998.

Taylor, Timothy D. *Strange Sounds: Music, Technology and Culture*. New York: Routledge, 2001.

Thomas, Keith. *Religion and the Decline of Magic: Studies in Popular Beliefs in Sixteenth- and Seventeenth-Century England*. London: Weidenfeld & Nicolson, 1971.

Thurschwell, Pamela. *Literature, Technology and Magical Thinking, 1880–1920*. Cambridge, UK: Cambridge University Press, 2001.

———. "Refusing to Give Up the Ghost: Some Thoughts on the Afterlife from Spirit Photography to Phantom Films." In *The Disembodied Spirit*, edited by Alison Ferris. Brunswick, Maine: Bowdoin College Museum of Art Catalogue, 2003, 20–31.

Todorov, Tzvetan. *The Fantastic: A Structural Approach to a Literary Genre*. Ithaca: Cornell University Press, 1975.

Verschuur, Gerrit L. *Hidden Attraction: The History and Mystery of Magnetism*. Oxford: Oxford University Press, 1993.

Vidler, Anthony. *The Architectural Uncanny: Essays in the Modern Unhomely*. Cambridge, MA: MIT Press, 1992.

Warner, Marina. *Phantasmagoria: Spirit Visions, Metaphors, and Media into the Twenty-first Century*. Oxford: Oxford University Press, 2006.

Weber, Max. *From Max Weber: Essays in Sociology*. Translated and edited by H. H. Gerth and C. Wright Mills. New York: Oxford University Press, 1946.

Weinstock, Jeffrey Andrew, ed. *Spectral America: Phantoms and the National Imagination*. Madison: University of Wisconsin Press, 2004.

Weiss, Allen S. *Phantasmic Radio*. Durham, NC: Duke University Press, 1995.

Wheatley, Helen. *Gothic Television*. Manchester: Manchester University Press, 2006.

Winter, Alison. *Mesmerized: Powers of Mind in Victorian Britain*. Chicago: University of Chicago Press, 1998.

Wittgenstein, Ludwig. *On Certainty*. Translated by Denis Paul and G. E. M. Anscombe. Oxford: Blackwell, 1969.

Wolfreys, Julian. *Victorian Hauntings: Spectrality, Gothic, the Uncanny and Literature*. London: Palgrave Macmillan, 2001.

———. *Writing London: The Trace of the Urban Text from Blake to Dickens*. Basingstoke: Palgrave, 1998.

Woolf, Virginia. "Henry James's Ghost Stories." *The Essays of Virginia Woolf: 1919– 1924 (Vol. 3)*. Edited by Andrew McNeillie. New York: Harcourt Brace Jovanovich, 1988, 319–326.

Worringer, Wilhelm. *Form in Gothic*. Translated by Herbert Read. New York: Schocken, 1957.

Yates, Frances A. *The Art of Memory*. London: Routledge and Kegan Paul, 1966.

Žižek, Slavoj. *The Parallax View*. Boston: MIT Press, 2006.

———. "Repeating Lenin," http://www.lacan.com/replenin.htm.

———. *Revolution at the Gates*. New York: Verso, 2004.

Contributors

Georgiana Banita teaches in the American Studies department at the University of Constance, Germany, where she completed her dissertation entitled *Literature and Ethical Spectatorship after 9/11*. Her essays on political and literary theory in an international context, literature and visual media, as well as American poetry of the twentieth century have appeared in the *M/MLA Journal*, *Parallax*, and *Peace Review: A Journal of Social Justice*, as well as in several edited collections. She is currently at work on a book provisionally entitled *Post-American Fictions: Contemporary Narratives of Planetarity*.

María del Pilar Blanco is Lecturer in Latin American Literature and Culture at University College London. Her published scholarship includes essays on landscape, the relationship between space and haunting in hemispheric American narratives, cosmopolitanism and imagined histories, and Spanish-American modernism and technology.

Alissa Burger is a recent PhD graduate of the American Culture Studies program at Bowling Green State University. Her scholarship focuses on film, literature, gender studies, and the supernatural. Specifically, she is interested in critical film theory; representations of gender, power, and magic; and the paranormal in popular culture. Alissa is also a field investigator with Paraex, a TAPS Family paranormal investigation team.

Michael Cuntz is a researcher and lecturer at the IKKM – Internationales Kolleg für Kulturtechnik und Medienforschung – at the Bauhaus-Universität Weimar. His current fields of research are: Romance prose literature (mainly nineteenth to twenty-first century), visual narratives, French theories of culture and technology, agency and its distribution, relations between humans and things, and (hyper)normalism. Recently he co-edited (with Ilka Becker and Astrid Kusser) *Unmenge – Wie verteilt sich Handlungsmacht?* (Fink, 2008) and published "'Tell me what you don't like about yourself': Hypernormalisierung und Destabilisierung der Normalität in der US-

Fernsehserie *nip/tuck*," in *KultuRRevolution. Zeitschrift für angewandte Diskurstheorie* (2008), and "Paris au pluriel: Depictions of the French Capital in Jacques Tardi's Comic Book Writing," in *Comics and the City: Urban Space in Print, Picture, and Sequence*, edited by Jörn Ahrens and Arno Meteling (Continuum, 2009).

Colin Davis is Professor of French at Royal Holloway, University of London. His research falls principally in the area of postwar French fiction and thought, with a particular interest in the connections between philosophy, literature, and film. His principal publications are *Michel Tournier: Philosophy and Fiction* (1988), *Elie Wiesel's Secretive Texts* (1994), *Levinas: An Introduction* (1996), *Ethical Issues in Twentieth-Century French Fiction: Killing the Other* (2000), *French Fiction in the Mitterrand Years: Memory, Narrative, Desire* (co-authored with Elizabeth Fallaize, 2000), *After Poststructuralism: Reading, Stories and Theory* (2004), *Haunted Subjects: Deconstruction, Psychoanalysis and the Return of the Dead* (2007) and *Scenes of Love and Murder: Renoir, Film and Philosophy* (2009).

Benjamin D'Harlingue is a Doctoral Candidate in Cultural Studies at the University of California, Davis, where he has taught courses in Women and Gender Studies and American Studies. His dissertation is on haunting tourisms of the U.S.

Isabella van Elferen is assistant professor of Music and New Media at the Department of Media and Cultural Studies of Utrecht University. She is the author of *Mystical Love in the German Baroque: Theology – Poetry – Music* (Scarecrow Press, 2008) and the editor of *Nostalgia or Perversion? Gothic Rewriting from the Eighteenth Century until the Present Day* (Cambridge Scholars Publishers, 2007). She has published on music, literature, and the cultural history of the German Baroque, as well as on mobile phone ringtones and Gothic theory and subcultures. Her current research focuses on musical transgressions, the uncanny, and hauntology in the Gothic.

Alla Gadassik is pursuing her PhD in Screen Cultures at Northwestern University. She conducts research on the intersections of bodies and technologies in cinema and new media. She is particularly interested in animation as a form of film-making that suggests distinctive transformative possibilities within digital cinema. Alla holds an MA in Communication and Culture (York/Ryerson Universities, Toronto) and has taught digital media in the Radio and Television program at Ryerson University (Toronto). In addition to pursuing an academic career, Alla also makes digital animation projects.

Martin Harries is Professor of English at New York University, where he teaches courses on theater, modernism, and theory. He is the author of two books: *Forgetting Lot's Wife: On Destructive Spectatorship* (Fordham University Press, 2007) and *Scare Quotes from Shakespeare: Marx, Keynes, and the Language of Reenchantment* (Stanford University Press, 2000). His essays and reviews have appeared in *New German Critique*, *The Yale Journal of Criticism*, *Modern Drama*, *Theater Journal*, *TDR*, *The Hunter On-Line Theater Review*, and elsewhere.

Caroline Herbert is Senior Lecturer in Postcolonial Literature at Leeds Metropolitan University. She recently held a Canadian Commonwealth Postdoctoral Research Fellowship at Concordia University, Montreal, and a Postdoctoral Fellowship at *Figura: Centre de Recherche sur le Texte et L'Imaginaire*, also at Concordia. She is working on a monograph examining cosmopolitan narratives of Bombay/Mumbai. She has published on Salman Rushdie and Rohinton Mistry, in the *Journal of Postcolonial Writing* and the *Journal of Commonwealth Literature*, an interview with Nayantara Sahgal in *Moving Worlds: A Journal of Transcultural Writings*, and has been a subject editor for the *Year's Work in English Studies*.

Peter Hitchcock is a Professor of Literary and Cultural Studies at the City University of New York. His books include *Dialogics of the Oppressed, Oscillate Wildly, Imaginary States*, and *The Long Space*.

Anthony Hutchison is a lecturer in U.S. Intellectual and Cultural Studies in the School of American and Canadian Studies, University of Nottingham. He is the author of *Writing the Republic: Liberalism and Morality in American Political Fiction* (Columbia University Press, 2007).

Bruno Lessard is Assistant Professor of film and new media at Ryerson University in Toronto. He has published articles and book chapters in various venues such as, most recently, *Convergence: The International Journal of Research into New Media Technologies* (2009), *In the Dark Room: Marguerite Duras and Cinema* (Peter Lang, 2009), and *Sound and Music in Film and Visual Media: A Critical Overview* (Continuum, 2009). He is completing a book-length study of CD-ROM art and technology.

Arno Meteling is lecturer in German Literature and Media Studies in Cologne. His research areas include literature, film, comics, cultural and media studies. He is author of *Monster: Zu Körperlichkeit und Medialität im modernen Horrorfilm* (2006), co-author of *Die Unsichtbarkeit des Politischen: Theorie und Geschichte medialer Latenz* (2009), and co-editor of *Splatter Movies: Essays zum modernen Horrorfilm* (2006), *Comics and the City: Urban Space in Print, Picture, and Sequence* (2009), and *The Parallax View: Zur Mediologie der Verschwörung* (2009).

Esther Peeren is Assistant Professor in Literary Studies at the University of Amsterdam and researcher at the Amsterdam School for Cultural Analysis (ASCA). She is the author of *Intersubjectivities and Popular Culture: Bakhtin and Beyond* (Stanford University Press, 2008), co-editor of *The Shock of the Other: Situating Alterities* (Rodopi, 2007), and has published articles on Mikhail Bakhtin, queer television, the ghost as a gendered chronotope, and versioning.

Justin Sausman teaches modernist literature at Birkbeck College, University of London. His research focuses on the networks linking Victorian and Modernist literature with science, spiritualism, and occultism. He is the co-editor, with Roger Luckhurst, of *Marginal and Occult Sciences*, part of Chatto and Pickering's Victorian Literature and Science series. He is currently writing a book on modernism, vitalism, and occultism, exploring the links between ritual magic, evolutionary biology, electromagnetic physics, and the writings of Henri Bergson, D. H. Lawrence, and Virginia Woolf.

Sean Somers teaches in the English Department at the University of British Columbia. He has published several articles on translation theory and the intercultural connections between Japan and Europe in the twentieth century. His monograph *Ancestral Recall: The Celtic Revival and Japanese Modernism* is currently under review.

Catherine Spooner is Senior Lecturer in English Literature at Lancaster University. She is the author of *Fashioning Gothic Bodies* (2004), *Contemporary Gothic* (2006), and, with Emma McEvoy, the co-editor of *The Routledge Companion to Gothic* (2007).

Pamela Thurschwell is a senior lecturer in English at the University of Sussex and the author of *Literature, Technology and Magical Thinking, 1880–1920* (2001) and *Sigmund Freud* (2000). She is the co-editor of *The Victorian Supernatural* (with Nicola Bown and Carolyn Burdett) and *Literary Secretaries/Secretarial Culture* (with Leah Price). She is currently working on a book on the temporalities of twentieth- and twenty-first-century adolescence, titled *Out of Time*.

Karen Williams teaches film, television, and media studies at Fordham University in New York City. She is a Doctoral Candidate in the Cinema Studies Department of New York University, and is presently completing her dissertation on the American Gothic in classical Hollywood cinema, from classic horror to film noir.

Christine Wilson is currently an Instructor at Wright State University-Lake Campus in the U.S., where she teaches English. She graduated with her PhD in English from Michigan State University. Some of her other work has appeared in the journals *Legacy* and *Red Cedar Review*.

Julian Wolfreys is Professor of Modern Literature and Culture at Loughborough University. Author and editor of more than 40 books, his most recent publications include *Thomas Hardy* (Palgrave Macmillan) and *Literature, in Theory: Tropes, Subjectivities, Responses, Responsibilities* (Continuum).

Index